URBAN PLANNING METHODS: RESEARCH AND POLICY ANALYSIS

☐ URBAN PLANNING METHODS: RESEARCH AND POLICY ANALYSIS

IAN BRACKEN

METHUEN
LONDON AND NEW YORK

First published in 1981 by
Methuen & Co. Ltd
11 New Fetter Lane, London EC4P 4EE

Published in the USA by
Methuen & Co.
in association with Methuen, Inc.
733 Third Avenue, New York, NY 10017

Printed in Great Britain by
Thomson Litho Ltd, East Kilbride, Scotland

British Library Cataloguing in Publication Data

Bracken, Ian
Urban planning methods.
1. City planning
I. Title
711'.4   HT166

Library of Congress Cataloging in Publication Data

Bracken, Ian.
Urban planning methods.

Bibliography: p.
Includes index.
1. City planning—Methodology.   2. Municipal
research.   3. Urban policy—Methodology.   I. Title.
HT166.B7   307.7'6'072   81-13013
AACR

ISBN 0-416-74860-0
ISBN 0-416-74870-8 Pbk

There is a proverb that 'nothing is certain but the unforeseen', and in fact few things turn out as we expect them.

Froude (1886), *Oceana vii*

□ CONTENTS

☐ LIST OF FIGURES

☐ ACKNOWLEDGEMENTS

Permission to reproduce copyright material is gratefully acknowledged as follows:

The editor, *Architectural Design* for figure 2.6; Edward Arnold (Publishers) Ltd for figures 4.1 and 5.2 and material in Chapters 4 & 5 from D. Harvey, *Explanations in Geography*; figure 7.5 is reproduced from T. J. Lowi, 'Four systems of policy, politics and choice', *Public Administration Review* (1972), ©, by permission of the American Society for Public Administration and T. J. Lowi, all rights reserved; Professor J. M. Batty for material in Chapters 2 and 6; Dr T. A. Broadbent for figure 7.4; Cambridge University Press for figure 6.10 from M. Batty, *Urban Modelling, Algorithms, Calibrations, Predictions*; David and Charles for figure A7.1 and material in Appendix 7 from I. Masser, *Analytical Models for Urban and Regional Planning*; the Elsevier Scientific Publishing Company for figure 7.1 from T. B. Smith, 'The policy implementation process', *Policy Sciences*, 4 (1973), and figure 8.3 from L. L. Roos, 'Quasi-experiments and environmental policy', *Policy Sciences*, 6 (1975); figures 4.3 and 5.1 are reproduced with permission from L. S. Meyers and N. E. Grossen, *Behavioural Research: Theory, Procedure and Design*, W. H. Freeman and Company, © 1978; figure 5.2 is part reproduced by permission of the editor, *The Geological Journal*; Gower Publishing Company Ltd for figure 6.6 and material in Chapter 6 from K. Willis, *Problems in Migration Analysis*; Methuen and Company Ltd for figure 1.2 from B. J. L. Berry, 'A paradigm for modern geography', in R. J. Chorley (ed), *Directions in Geography*; Pergamon Press Ltd for figures 2.9, 2.10, 2.11 and material in Chapter 2 from J. K. Friend and W. N. Jessop, *Local Government and Strategic Choice*; Pion Ltd and the authors for figure 6.4 from P. Smith and W. N. Morrison, *Simulating the Urban Economy: Experiments with Input-Output Techniques*, also Pion Ltd for figure A6.1 and material in Appendix 6 from *Environment and Planning A*; figure 5.2 is part reproduced from B. J. L. Berry and A. M. Baker, 'Geographic sampling', in B. J. L. Berry and D. Marble (eds), *Spatial Analysis: A Reader in Statistical Geography*, © 1968, by permission of Prentice-Hall Inc.; figure 4.8 is reproduced from D. T. Campbell and J. C. Stanley, *Experimental and Quasi-experimental Designs for Research*, © 1966, the American Educational Research Association. Reprinted by permission of the American Educational Research Association and Houghton Mifflin and Company; the editor of the *Journal of the Royal Town Planning Institute* for figure 6.3; the Tavistock Institute for Human Relations for material in Chapter 9 from A. J. Hickling J. K. Friend and J. Luckman, *The Development Plan System and Investment Programmes* (1979); figures 2.4, 2.7 and 2.8 are reproduced by permission of the editor of *The Town Planning Review*; figure 8.2 and material in Chapter 8 are reproduced from J. W. Vaupel, 'Muddling through analytically', *Policy Studies Review Annual*, 1, S. S. Nagel (ed.), © 1977, by permission of Sage Publications Inc. and J. W. Vaupel; figure 1.5 is reproduced from A. G. Wilson, *Urban and Regional Models in Geography and Planning* (1974), by permission of John Wiley and Sons Ltd; figures 2.1, 2.2, material in Chapter 2 and figure 6.9 are reproduced from D. A. Krueckeberg and A. L. Silvers, *Urban Planning Analysis: Methods and Models* (1974), by permissio of John Wiley and Sons Inc.

☐ INTRODUCTION

The objective of this book is to set out a range of established and developing methods relevant to the practice of urban planning.[1] The treatment adopted, at an introductory level, explains the principles which underlie these methods and hence seeks to promote their useful application. A detailed discussion of the theory of more general social research and policy making cannot be attempted, but it is intended that the reader will acquire a sound understanding of the application of methods in rigorous and comparative urban study and socially sensitive urban policy making. However, urban planning methods reflect the diversity of the subject and there is continued debate about their relevance and application within the statutory urban planning processes. This book does not seek primarily to justify a particular approach to urban plan and policy making, but rather to explain a useful range of concepts which will provide the reader with a firm foundation from which to select and apply appropriate methods according to need. However, we suggest that two requirements are general. The first of these relates to the need for the planner to be able to conduct good quality, relevant research into the substantive world with which he must deal, and the second is for him to understand and be able to assess the impacts and effects on the world of the policy-making processes of which he is a part.

The recent history of urban planning shows that the development of these two areas of methodology has not been equal. The importance of analysis and understanding of substantive matters – population change, migration, housing needs, employment trends, transportation and land-use relationships, as 'inputs' to the planning process – has long been widely acknowledged. In contrast, attention to policy – its relevance and effectiveness, the 'instruments' by which it is effected and so on, that is, the 'outputs' of the process – is a much more recent phenomenon among planners, indeed one that is only now generally taking place.

The text is structured in three parts. In the first part, Chapter 1 draws attention to the emergence of strategic urban plan and policy making over the past fifteen years or so and the conceptual and methodological developments. It also reminds readers of the political, administrative, professional *and* technical contexts within which urban planning is set. Chapters 2 and 3 explain and comment upon the ways in which planners have sought to develop more systematized approaches to strategic plan and policy making, in such tasks as plan design and generation, the

1

evaluation of alternative courses of action, the need to monitor ongoing change and adapt plans and policies to changing circumstances.

Against this background, Parts 2 and 3 focus upon urban research and policy study respectively. Part 2 concentrates upon how urban affairs may be efficiently and validly studied, so that planners can maximize the quality of their data and information in order that, through analysis, they may obtain explanations about urban phenomena. In this part, Chapter 4 deals with the underlying theory of appropriate research designs; Chapter 5 with aspects of the operationalization of these designs in the urban context, and Chapter 6 discusses established ways in which the particular spatial and aspatial matters of concern to urban planners can be explored, predicted and understood.

In contrast, Part 3 focuses upon urban policy-making processes and outcomes, but as with Part 2, the approach adopted makes clear the developing role of methods available to the planner and their application in systematic analysis. Chapter 7 sets out the basic organization theory and concepts for the study of urban policy and the more important problems to be faced. Chapter 8 deals with the methods by which planners may analyse and obtain insights into the process of policy formulation and its outcomes. Finally, Chapter 9 examines some of the implications of the wider use of policy analytic methods within the urban planning process.

As will now be clear, this text covers a wide field, so that not only has selectivity of material been necessary, but the depth of treatment must also be limited. There is inevitably the danger of 'a little knowledge'. It is intended that the contents will explain and illustrate principles, thereby bringing the reader to an operational threshold in a frame of mind which is, at the same time, both eager to develop a deeper understanding of the methods discussed and critical in their use. To assist further reading, each part of the text concludes with a guide to selected case study material drawn from recent urban planning practice as well as the more usual guide to selected theoretical and applied literature. Although these guides cannot be exhaustive they will provide the reader with a number of 'links' into the more specialized areas of literature. In all cases, the works cited contain bibliographies and, where these are judged to be particularly helpful, additional comment is made.

The merit of this book is derived from the foundation of knowledge upon which it stands and the citations and the bibliography record this indebtedness. It is a recurrent concern of any writer that some acknowledgement to the work of others may have been overlooked or that some viewpoint is misrepresented. Hopefully, this will not be so, but in the event, your author accepts the responsibility. Many persons, too numerous to thank individually, have contributed over the past four years, directly and indirectly, to the writing of this text. It would be, however, quite wrong not to acknowledge more personally the help of valued colleagues who have contributed much to the environment within which the text has been written – notably Michael Batty, Philip Cooke, Clifford Guy, David Hume,

Gareth Rees and Richard Spooner. The numerous drafts of the text were admirably typed by Terry Davies, and Gareth Jones was responsible for the illustrations and helpful ideas on layout.

The remainder of this introduction summarizes some of the basic thinking which guided the preparation of this text. A starting point is to suggest that the reader of urban planning literature will note that the subject not only covers a wide field, but that it reflects a long history of practical concerns and attempted remedies for urban problems. The literature is both descriptive and normative, that is, it describes real-world situations according to particular perspectives *and* offers mainly idealistic remedies as to how a better urban future might be achieved. Urban planning is indeed largely practised in terms of a repertory of conventional wisdom, much of which has been established through these practical and intuitive approaches rather than through theoretical development.

It is also important to note at the outset the influence of the extensive statutory powers granted to urban planners[2] and the extent and effect of the professionalization of the activity. Whilst this has been effective in serving rather rigid interests and pursuits, a consequence has been the strong tendency for the practice of urban planning to be regarded as an activity 'apart' from discussions as to its purposes and from its emerging theories.

We subscribe to the view that the most important general debate should be about the *purposes* of urban planning, thereby identifying the various modes in which it is possible to conceive and operate an urban planning system. A chosen mode, in turn, will constitute a paradigm, that is, a conceptual framework which, for the time being, can be used to justify the processes and actions by which the planning is undertaken. For it is only within such a framework that a satisfactory choice can be made over the use of the heterogeneous collection of methods which the activity will inevitably comprise. It is not the purpose of this text, however, to argue a detailed ideology for urban planning, for that is well beyond its scope.[3] Rather, it is to discuss a limited, though fundamental, range of methods by which urban planning may be enhanced when seen, broadly, as a problem-solving process. This is recognized as a necessarily pragmatic approach and acknowledges the inevitability of disagreement about the purposes of urban planning and hence that there will be periods of popularity for different modes and methods. The approach rests upon assumptions that in some reasonably satisfactory way society wishes, and is able, to identify *relevant* problems of concern, and can choose a mode of planning (that is a set of procedures) within which to seek their amelioration.

It is fundamental to our approach to suggest that answers to problems are more likely to be found, even though they will be partial, by as systematic an attempt as possible to understand their nature *and* the nature of the processes we choose to employ in seeking their solution. As will now be clear, this will involve distinct, but *related*, areas of methodology. First, there are methods through which an understanding of the nature of urban phenomena and problems can be achieved, and these broadly, will involve adherence to accepted rules of social scientific investigation. Second, there is methodology by which such understanding may be synthesized to lead to plan generation and policy formulation designed to bring about some desirable change through the planning system. Third, there is methodology which addresses the need to analyse policy, and which in turn will 'feed back' learning and understanding as to the relevance and effectiveness of the other areas. As we discuss in Part 1, it is the second area of methodology which has received the fullest treatment in urban planning literature. That being so, we choose to reflect upon it rather than offer detailed explanation in the first part of the text. However, if urban planning is to develop a more balanced structure as a process of urban understanding, i.e. the seeking of effective policies and learning,[4] then a fuller development of a research and a policy analytic capability are fundamental.

Such development has been implicit in the reforms that have taken place in urban planning practice since the mid-1960s – the need for a more flexible, management-like approach to urban planning, the need clearly to define the strategic, policy-based level of plan making (Structure Planning), and the widely recognized need for a more effective dissemination of data and information.[5] But, further, we will suggest that there is an urgent need in urban planning for explicit, critical and well-conducted research *both* into substantive, procedural and policy aspects of the subject. Research cannot dictate policy, but makes a fundamental contribution through enhanced knowledge of the realities with which policy must deal. Research into substantive matters can make policy more relevant and more efficient. Research can reveal the dynamic nature of important urban phenomena, ignorance of which can preclude the adoption of effective policy measures. Research, through policy analysis, can suggest new alternatives and can reveal conflict and incompatibilities. It can reveal appropriate and inappropriate policy instruments and furthermore, by serving understanding, it can help to ensure that solving one problem will not give rise to a more serious one. Yet urban research and analysis of policy are not neutral activities for, in their turn, they will be founded upon assumptions and choice about relevant issues worthy of study. It is important to recall that the use of methods can never be an end in itself.

At the outset, the meaning of certain terms should be made clear. We must distinguish first 'designing' and 'planning'. The former is used in the general, non-aesthetic sense,[6] meaning a set of procedures which set out how some particular situation may be achieved. Both terms refer, then, broadly to the same process and are distinguished only in degree. Planning and 'planning decisions' relate to situations in which the level of uncertainty,[7] or uncontrolled influence, is relatively low. In contrast, the term designing is used for situations in which the level of uncertainty is relatively high. Similarly, a distinction must be made between the use of the term 'policy' and 'plan'. Generally we use the former to refer to 'a deliberate intention', most usually expressed verbally. In contrast, a 'plan' will be more spatially specific and will usually involve a diagrammatic treatment.

Though not definitive, the distinction will avoid ambiguity arising in the course of the text.

Finally, a distinction must be made between methodology and technique. It is a feature of the growing maturity of any subject that both methods and techniques become increasingly precisely defined. In general, techniques develop first and refer to the human actions and the instruments (that is, the design of procedures) by which specific tasks are performed. Methodology on the other hand, refers to the concepts and processes by which selection is made of appropriate techniques, including an explicit justification of purpose. These concepts provide a framework within which techniques can be properly developed, selectively applied and critically evaluated.

Notes

1 Throughout the text, this term is used to refer generally to the field of study. Variants such as 'regional planning', 'town planning' or 'rural planning' are subsumed as appropriate without further comment.

2 We are, of course, referring to professional planners, elected members of local councils and government here.

3 A guide to selected literature is given at the end of Part 1.

4 So as in turn, to make revised policies more relevant and effective. Indeed, the whole planning process may readily be conceptualized as a 'learning' process.

5 These points relate to only some of the reasons for the reform of the planning system. See later discussions.

6 Where necessary, the field of study explicitly concerned with urban aesthetics is referred to as 'urban design'.

7 It may also be helpful to consider this in terms of information. A design involves relatively less information than a plan, that is, it will generally have a higher intuitive content.

PART ONE

URBAN PLANNING AND POLICY MAKING

☐ INTRODUCTION

Before discussing in an introductory way the nature of *urban* planning, it is important to make clear the meaning of planning in a more general sense. Strictly, planning means the setting out of a strategy by which some specified objectives may be met. A social interpretation by Myrdal (1968) for example, suggests that

planning... is a determined effort, through democratic institutions for collective decisions, to make... intensive, comprehensive, and long-range forecasts of future trends . . . and to formulate and execute a system of co-ordinated policies framed to have the effect of bending the foreseen trends towards realising our ideals, spelled out in advance as definite goals. (p. 251-2)

As we discuss, however, faced with economic, political and social uncertainty, planners, both generally and in urban fields, have found difficulties in making such 'comprehensive' and 'long-range' estimates with reliability. Fundamentally, planning involves a paradox. To 'plan' means to attempt to be more certain about the future, yet that future is inherently unpredictable. Also, in society generally, there is a basic ambivalence towards planning (Gabor 1963, 1969). For while it is natural for human beings to plan their future activity, for example, to make the best use of time and other resources, society does not appear to want its opportunities limited by detailed prescriptions. Fundamentally, there is a matter of selection as to what are perceived to be the *relevant* concerns of any planning activity.

Myrdal's view, however, usefully makes clear that planning involves societal choice about the future, and that choice implies political activity. In policy terms, planning is about making something happen which would otherwise not have happened or vice versa, and it is the exercise of choice in such situations that is its essential intellectual act (Davidoff and Reiner, 1962). To exercise choice, however, genuinely alternative views of the future must be presented and, in order that selection may be purposeful and deliberate, both a knowledge and understanding of the present and an explicit anticipation of the future consequences of present actions are required.

In practice, choice needs to be exercised at several levels. One concerns the purpose of planning, the criteria by which the purpose is determined and described, and by whom the criteria are selected. A second level

9

concerns the fact that most situations which require planning are, by their nature, more or less complex, and therefore choice needs to be exercised over how, of many possible ways, a particular objective can be achieved. A third area recognizes that, to be effective, planning needs to be translated into action through policies and that choice will be required as to the way in which the activity can be guided over periods of time towards the achievement of objectives. This will further require choice to be made about the allocation of the necessary resources.

The purpose of planning, in a general sense, normally rests upon two concepts which serve as rather general aims. They are not always complementary. The first, the pursuit of *efficiency*, concerns the desire for careful management of resources. This efficiency can, however, only be measured in terms of the purposes which the planning serves. As we discuss, in a social context, this can ultimately only be defined in terms of values held within a society. Efficiency has been associated traditionally with the second concept, that is *rationality*. This is usually defined in terms of 'reasonableness' in the exercise of choice, and 'comprehensiveness' by which an adequate understanding of the nature of the problems has been achieved.

Clearly, other than in trivial situations, complete rationality is impossible to obtain. The problems, for example, in acquiring a full knowledge of any human situation or social system are immense. A more commonly accepted notion is that of bounded rationality (Kaplan, 1964) which essentially focuses upon the reasonableness or fairness of decision making. In practice, this involves the provision of relevant information to decision makers about what exists in the world and what may be expected under certain *specified* conditions. In turn, this allows 'political' decisions to be made.

Experience of planning has shown that a strategy which is based upon knowledge and understanding is more likely to be sound than one based on speculation and intuition. Planning has therefore become synonymous, not only with the preparation of a strategy, but also with the acquisition of an adequate base of information and intelligence which makes understanding possible. However, it is also this understanding that permits the identification of problems and therefore the formulation of objectives. This raises an important issue, because what is *sought* in a given situation not only provides a context for its study (and hence understanding), but it also moulds perceptions by which the *relevant* concerns to a given problem situation tend to be determined. Planning has additionally acquired the connotation of guiding a selected strategy towards some desired objective over time. This may be achieved by influence and persuasion or by direct control, such as statutory powers.

As a result, the activity of planning can be readily conceptualized as some kind of process with discrete stages, though as we will discuss, this has too frequently led to the assumption that these stages are independent of each other. In turning to discuss the nature of urban planning we can usefully begin by examining how the activity has been increasingly systematized under an emerging 'process' view.

□ 1
THE PLANNING PROCESS

Changing attitudes in urban planning

Urban planning has, for a long time, been seen implicitly as a 'process'[1] of professional activity though, until the mid-1960s, it was practised principally as an art form within a traditional design context. Its purpose was seen mainly in the promotion of new development that was aesthetically pleasing and which complied with certain standards of layout. This purpose was broadly carried forward from the public health and housing reforms of the previous century enforced through an extensive set of statutory controls. Gradually, this pursuit has developed into a more general concern for amenity set in a context of rather covert assumptions about 'service to the public interest'. An inevitable development was that this pursuit of amenity became increasingly concerned with attempting to ensure that the hindrances and annoyances created by the actions of one individual, or group, or social sector, minimally imposed upon the interests, that is, the amenity of others. Urban planning, then, became concerned with attempting to resolve conflict over needs and actions between members of society.

In order to provide guidance, and indeed to justify these pursuits, physical land-use plans in a variety of forms have been employed. Their rationale lay broadly in a belief that it was possible to achieve pleasant and efficient environments through control over physical layout. This general approach was supplemented by a further belief in the relevance of a 'set of standards' which could be used to specify suitable guidelines for that layout. The origins of this stemmed from the work of the urban reformers, philanthropists and 'utopians' of the nineteenth and early twentieth centuries.[2]

As urban planning became more comprehensive, largely through the acquisition of greater statutory powers[3] and growing confidence on the part of planners, a further pursuit emerged. This was a search for urban efficiency defined in functional terms, that is, a concern with the operations and workings of the urban system as a whole. To this was linked a traditional, though somewhat latent, concern about the 'efficient' use of resources and particularly land. This aim has also been pursued through extensive physical statutory control. Increasingly, however, shortcomings were revealed. First, there was shown to be an inadequate understanding of the complexity and dynamic nature of urban issues. Second, there was a

11

growing awareness of the problems of achieving a rationality in plan and policy formulation given the plural nature of society's needs. Third, there was concern about the inevitable re-distributional social effects of planning policy making, particularly as planning became more broadly felt.

In pursuit of amenity and efficiency, urban planners have traditionally sought to exercise control over the development process and thereby to intervene in human affairs through a variety of design and enforcement mechanisms. The difficulty with the pursuit of amenity is that it is, in any context, a heavily value-loaded concept and the implied premise of 'service to the public interest' has been increasingly criticized. Planners have not found it easy to answer such criticism, for the pursuit of amenity requires both the identification of communal desires (including the identification of benefits and dis-benefits in society) and some form of debate which can allow collective responsibility to be taken for the planning actions (Friedmann, 1973). This has largely defied urban planning, not surprisingly, for communal goals can only be so imperfectly stated, or else be so general, as to be of very little practical use. A second, related point affecting both the search for amenity and efficiency alike, is that the urban planners' traditional approach essentially assumed not only the relevance of a reliance on physical control and a 'standards' tradition, but also the feasibility of obtaining consensus in producing acceptable plans conforming to the 'general good' (Cross, 1972).

On the subject of the search for urban efficiency, economists pointed out that urban planners were traditionally largely ignorant of the operation of market forces and thereby produced side-effects that were not anticipated. They, moreover, shifted costs and benefits in unpredicted ways among society. Equally, sociologists pointed out that over-concern with the physical environment and narrow pursuit of 'efficiency' led to relative neglect of the welfare of large sectors in society. Thirdly, political scientists became increasingly concerned with the apparent lack of sensitivity to political needs in the developing, but primarily, technical (or professional) plan-making process and lack of involvement of the polity in that process.

A criticism of the 'standards' set to guide development, covering fields such as housing, education, recreation, shopping and transportation is that they were based upon very little empirical analysis (Stewart, 1972). The standards generally represented a 'utopian' view, that of a high, if not idealistic standard, which might possibly be achieved in an affluent region or district, but one that was extremely unlikely to be achieved generally. In practical terms, it became clear that the 'standards' approach could be reasonably successful only over long periods of time and as long as there was a vigorous new development programme. In the 1950s and 1960s in Great Britain, the approach seemed appropriate with expansionist policies for the re-building of cities, a rising population and growing material prosperity.[4] A consequence, however, was that urban planning became pre-occupied with new urban order and, to a large measure, neglected the problems of the existing city, other than to adopt policies for large-scale, obsolete housing clearance and commercial city centre re-building. More fundamentally, because of the lack of empirical study, there has been valid criticism that the 'standards' represented the interests, cultural values, attitudes and biases of the urban planners themselves, who tended to act in the mistaken belief that they were planning for everybody (Gans, 1969).

A further, and important, challenge was that traditional urban planning contributed, *in itself*, very little real improvement to amenity in an overall sense, rather it *re-arranged* the incidence, benefits and opportunities among the urban population, and that this re-distribution has not been equitable (Harvey, 1973). Similar criticism has been levelled too at the search for functional efficiency for, in traditional land-use planning terms, this has rested upon the assumption that complex, human activities could be provided for through spatial order, that is, land-use zoning. It is questionable that the urban system actually does work more efficiently, in total, when stratified in this way, and urban amenity is not necessarily enhanced. Moreover, the assumption tended to divert attention away from seeking *reasons* as to why urban activities should be socially incompatible and therefore apparently need to be so stratified.

A recent view is that the traditional approach has rested upon the concept of functionalism, that is, urban phenomena were seen principally from the point of view of how they function, and therefore as how they *support* the system of which they are a part (Sayer, 1976). The approach has tended to assume that urban symptoms, such as 'malaise' for example, are untreatable and, moreover, it has meant that subsequent policy making, given a dynamic social and technological world, has only tended to replace one set of symptoms with another.

Over the past fifteen years, these developing criticisms, in varying ways, have brought about both a questioning of the conventional assumptions underlying urban planning (Cullingworth and Orr, 1969) and a variety of changes in its practice. These can be identified, first, as the move away from purely physical land-use criteria for plan making towards the more broadly based set of economic and social criteria in strategic, or Structure Plan making. This largely followed the Planning Advisory Group (PAG) Report (1965)[5] and the subsequent enactment of its recommendations in the 1968 Town and Country Planning Act. Second, there has been an explicit, though not entirely successful, move towards a more political or participative element in plan and policy making after Skeffington (1969) and, third, a move towards planning as 'urban managerialism' involving a more corporate view of (mainly) local authority functions following Bains (1972). The managerialist view is well described in Amos *et al.* (1973), though the conflict between need for participation and the growth of corporate organizations is an area of critical concern (Cockburn, 1977).

In general, the questioning has focused upon three levels (Batty, 1976b). The first, a question of 'what' should be planned, for the traditional concern with the built form *per se* had given way, in part, to a much more fundamental concern with the nature of economic, sociological and physical phenomena that give rise to that form. Second, questions were raised as to 'how' urban planning should be undertaken and particularly how relevant problems 'or objectives' should be defined and treated. A third level of questioning sought to examine 'by whom' and 'on whose behalf' urban planning should be undertaken so as to make more explicit the conventional assumptions about the relationship between the 'professional' planners and society, the 'client'.

Remedies to the apparent shortcomings of the planning process have been sought in two ways. First, there were attempts to define more *comprehensively* the underlying concepts and scope of urban planning. Second, there were searches for ways by which, through the adoption of systematic methods and procedures, both in analysis and policy formulation, urban planning could be made more *efficient* and thereby more purposeful. A lack of clarity on these issues in urban planning literature and a failure to grasp some important implications of these developments in the urban context, led to confusion and a largely irrelevant debate about the nature of the changes being experienced. This debate has mainly been conducted at methodological and procedural levels and has given rise to a notable polarization of views within the profession. It has focused particularly upon the supposedly alternative intuitive/speculative and rational/deductive approaches and has contributed considerably to the confusion as to the 'proper' use of methods in planning practice. These major approaches are, however, not necessarily incompatible in an applied field, for much depends upon how such concepts as comprehensiveness and rationality are defined, *how* methodology is employed, and above all, on what are the perceived purposes for which the 'planning' is undertaken.

With an acknowledged risk of over-simplification, current attitudes as to the purposes of urban planning can be summarized under two headings. One, the more conventional, covert view is characterized by a belief in order and equilibrium between urban populations, their activities and environments. This is an extension of the 'utopian' view and though it may be pragmatic and partial, it seeks societal well-being by advocating environmental quality and optional arrangements of physical artifacts and human activities. This view attempts to achieve its purpose by exercising control over new development in accordance with a spatial plan. As already noted, current urban practice has moved towards the second view which is more radical and rejects the feasibility of the equilibrium assumption. It focuses upon the dis-equalities among urban populations made manifest by the identification of key issues or problems. The on-going task is to ameliorate these dis-equalities and the 'planning' is therefore explicitly re-allocative or re-distributional in its intentions and requires intervention on a broader scale. These contrasting views have been widely discussed (Gans 1968, 1969, 1973; Pahl, 1970, 1971a, 1971b, 1975; Stewart, 1972; Harvey, 1973) and, clearly, many intermediate positions are feasible in theory, though less easy to put into practice. The concept of Structure Planning (PAG, 1965) as later interpreted by government advice (Department of the

Environment, 1974b)[6], for example, required an explicit identification of key issues or problems at a strategic level in plan making and represented a clear move away from traditional thinking. However, the lack of any devolved powers to local authorities to *effect* change at the strategic level has proved to be inhibiting in facing 'key' issues such as unemployment, mobility and even housing provision.

The need for an effective planning system to 'bridge the gap' between spatial and aspatial policies (notably social policies) has been noted by several writers (Pahl, 1971a, 1971b; Harvey, 1971). This has been achieved in theory by the concept of *spatial opportunity* which relates to the effect upon the opportunities and well being of the individual of his location within the urban system – for example, his access to job or recreational opportunities. Urban plans and policies clearly affect these opportunities, though the phenomenon is rarely examined in detail in current planning practice, as we subsequently discuss. Also, as Hall (1972) has observed, the move away from purely spatial considerations paved the way not only for the broader considerations of social concerns but also for increased attention to *broader forms of planning*, notably Corporate Planning and the use of Financial Budgeting Methods (Stewart and Eddison, 1971; Cockburn, 1977).

In practice, the past fifteen years or so of British strategic land-use planning (Structure Planning) have been dominated by two principal debates about the nature and methodology of the activity. The first of these has focused upon the search for a 'new style' of plan and policy making that would break away from the inflexible development framework of the erstwhile Development Plan system. The second area of debate has concerned the application of rapidly developing systematic methods, particularly of analysis, forecasting and problem-solving to the planning process. This debate has focused upon the extent to which such methods can and should contribute to plan and policy formulation, so that, for example, planners might be better informed about the world, or better able to predict the consequences of particular actions and so on. The debates have been widely reviewed and, as Batty (1976b), Openshaw (1977) and Simmonds (1980) have shown, the underlying pursuits have not always proved to be complementary and have given rise to some notable differences of opinion among planners.

The first stage of the long period of strategic plan and policy preparation initiated by the 1968 Act is now coming to an end. The 'new methodologies' have been applied to urban Structure Plan and policy making in varying ways, as we discuss in the next two chapters. But, in looking critically at this development, it is important to bear in mind the greater freedom given to local authorities to determine for themselves the methodological basis of their plan-making activity since 1968.[7]

Given also the broad intention that Structure Planning should become a more managerial, continuous process of review and adaptation to policy (in order to avoid the limitations of the 'end state' approaches of the past), most local planning authorities have begun to formulate the organizational and procedural frameworks by which such implementation may be carried out. An essential concept in this role is that of monitoring, whose broad function is to assess on-going change, to measure the impacts experienced as a result of implementing plans and policies, and thereby reveal the need for, and requirements to be met by, the plan 'review'. There are, however, many unanswered questions as to how this will operate in practice (Bracken, 1980b).

British planners, then, have largely completed their Structure Plan making by the use of conventional wisdom and the application of plan generating and evaluation methodologies that were rapidly developed in the late 1960s and early 1970s. It is now clear that, in moving to a monitoring and review role, new insights are required, particularly to enable the planners to measure and assess the impacts of plans and policies, both in spatial and aspatial terms (Massey and Meegan, 1978; Diamond, 1979; Barras and Broadbent, 1979). Clearly, these insights will need to relate to the developing nature of the urban process and the administrative, statutory and political contexts within which it operates.

Planning process theories

In the search for more systematic ways to plan and manage urban affairs, theorists looked at the concepts of urban planning in a more general sense, and set aside the prevailing 'unique' attitude towards the urban type of planning which had originated in the design tradition. An important consequence was the adoption of the 'rational–comprehensive' approach which became established in the 1960s and has been used widely in the preparation of Structure Plans,[8] though subsequently criticized. The approach was built upon several conceptual adaptations from other fields of which the most central was the 'social problem/policy formulation model'. This essentially assumes the relevance of a goal-identification approach to social policy making (Meyerson and Banfield 1955; Banfield, 1961). Its characteristics are first, that goals and objectives of social action can be identified and formally stated. Second, that problems thereby identified are amenable to investigation and analysis. Third, that solutions to those problems can be generated out of an understanding of the nature of those problems, and fourth, that these solutions can be measured or evaluated against the stated objectives.

Before discussing this, we must note that other important adaptations included 'systems thinking' (Emery, 1969) which was used to provide a more plausible explanation of the nature of urban planning as an on-going, cyclical process within a comprehensive environment or 'ecosystem'. This approach, in effect, attempted to apply biological concepts to social organizations, a movement by no means confined to urban planning. On the policy making and implementation side, another adaptation involved the application of 'operations research' concepts (Ashby, 1964) to the mechanisms by which urban planners exercised control and management over complex urban affairs. Expositions of urban planning processes viewed from these approaches have been well articulated by McLoughlin (1969) and Chadwick (1976) respectively. An important contribution of the systems approach was that it established the principle of using a range of methods to support the whole planning process, and it stimulated the development of 'policy-making' methods as we later discuss (Batey and Breheny, 1978a). A more general, and parallel development has been the gradual application of developing systematic methods of investigation and analysis in the social sciences to provide a better understanding of urban phenomena.

Through these adaptations and developments the constituent technical operations for the application of a rational–comprehensive approach to urban plan making became more clearly defined. In A. G. Wilson's (1968, 1974) terms for example, they are classified under the headings of *analysis*, *design* and *policy*. The analysis stage comprises problem diagnosis and system modelling, as well as other analytical and predictive methods, by which an understanding of both present *and* future problems may be sought. The design stage includes such operations as the preparation of plans and the generation of alternative plans and policies. Policy includes the implementation of plans and evaluation criteria to assess the effectiveness of the alternative policies. 'Goal formulation' is fundamental to this process in order that objectives and purposes may be clearly understood.

Frameworks such as this have no doubt contributed a clearer understanding of the nature of urban planning and its constituent processes. They have focused attention upon the need for recursive thinking and the fact that urban planning must be a continuous management-like activity. But, in themselves, these frameworks only make more explicit the traditional structure of urban planning with its assumptions of rationality and comprehensiveness[9] and arguably have not made urban planning a socially more sensitive or adaptive process. An alternative position is the much more pragmatic, problem-solving view of planning that has developed from the work of Braybrooke and Lindblom (1963) and, in its most extreme form, is characterized by the term 'disjointed-incrementalism' which rejects fundamentally the feasibility of formulating any social goals. Advocates of this approach to planning argue that goal-directed, comprehensive approaches are not only unattainable, but positively harmful. As we shortly discuss, developments of this line of thinking have led to a variety of problem-solving views of urban planning.

It is a current concern that the application of particular methodologies in urban planning practice (including those of problem investigation, analysis, forecasting and predictive modelling) appear to have taken place without a critical awareness of the assumptions underlying the applicability of those methods to particular purposes. In general, there has been a tendency for urban planners to apply, uncritically, a 'standard' set of technical procedures, and indeed often to assume the relevance of 'standard' types of information without an adequate regard for purpose. Such an approach has been assumed to be comprehensive, even though it has sometimes included phenomena which were not relevant to a problem or aim, and worse, precluded others which may have been.

A further weakness of the rational–comprehensive approach is that it fails to make clear *how* the solutions can be generated from an analysis of problems (assuming that they can be reasonably defined). This is not just the technical difficulty of generating policies from partial knowledge and in a dynamic environment, or indeed, how to take into account experience, intuition and learning. It is how urban planning, as a systematic activity, can *anticipate change*, for which it is only partially responsible. This fundamentally concerns the integration of the two types of activity which any planning must inevitably comprise.

On the one hand, planners seek to make positive or explanatory statements about the nature and behaviour of urban phenomena through investigation and understanding. On the other hand, they also make normative or prescriptive statements from which policy may develop, which suggest what *ought* to be the arrangement of those phenomena, and thereby seek to create a future which is in some ways different from the present. It is, then, the synthesis of problem understanding and creative policy making that poses the greatest challenge in conceptualizing a satisfactory urban planning framework (Batty, 1974a). While the emphasis from the social sciences has been on seeking explanations through research, albeit based upon certain assumptions, there is increasing concern over the lack of corresponding research as to how such understanding may be satisfactorily incorporated into policy formulation (Donnison, 1976).

Figure 1.1 Normative and positive activity in planning

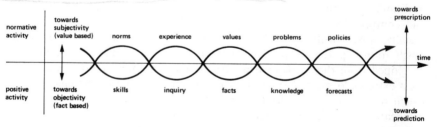

It is however perfectly feasible to postulate a framework which accommodates these processes in an applied field, though notably more difficult to operationalize into professional procedures. However, the problems of integration become rather easier to cope with if we move away from a supposedly neutral technical stance about the nature of the urban planning process and towards a more explicit social problem-solving position, that is, by a recognition of the importance of 'values'. As suggested in figure 1.1, urban planning proceeds by a particular blend of action and reaction between positive and normative processes, at a variety of levels in society, among the actors involved and according to a purpose. The traditional conceptualization of urban planning not only inadequately recognized the importance of values, but presumed a separation between these basic activities which, we argue, is illusionary.

Although analytical investigation of values poses many problems, we suggest that urban planning is best served by as systematic a study as possible of values and value systems and their relationship to activities (MacMurray, 1971). Inconsistencies may then be resolved in pursuit of specified purposes and this should lead to the identification of more explicit criteria for policy formulation. In theory, analysis of an entire value system can be postulated as feasible and it would lead to a portrayal of value hierarchies (Davidoff and Reiner, 1962). Administrative complexities, however, make the identification of relevant groups problematical, and the fact that group views do not necessarily adequately represent the views of their members is an acknowledged difficulty (Mazziotti, 1974). Assuming these can be overcome, a more fundamental issue is that knowledge of available facts is needed to determine the relative weight of particular values and this raises particular methodological issues (Kaplan, 1964).

Everyday experience suggests that personal values are influenced by our knowledge, or understanding of facts. But equally, though it is less obvious, factual statements and their analysis reflect the values of persons making those statements. This is particularly true in the attachment of importance to certain facts, choice as to what are the *relevant* facts to a given situation, and in the selection of what should be studied to yield factual information. Fact and value, then, are heavily inter-related.[10] But it is important to note that disagreement over value-based positions *cannot* be resolved by recourse to facts, that is, by any amount of empirical data. Values can only be verified and differences in belief resolved in terms of consistency within the hierarchy of other values, in other words, in terms of reasonableness (Churchman, 1968).

In practice, the planner is required to steer a path effectively between technical determinism on the one hand and the uncritical acceptance of sectoral value assumptions on the other, in such operations as the identification of relevant problems, the setting of objectives, problem investigation and the generation of relevant policies directed to secure solutions. This requires that the planner effectively embraces both *analysis*, that is the understanding of facts, and *policy*, that is the communication of values, in a relationship defined in terms of a purpose.

Etzioni (1967) postulated a realistic position between the search for full rationality and the adoption of pragmatic incrementalism, the so-called 'mixed-scanning' approach. This attempts to blend 'high-order' social policy-making processes, which set basic directions through an analysis of values, and 'low-order' or technical processes which first prepare for fundamental decision making, for example by making clear what exists in the world, what may be studied and how problems may be defined. Second, these processes are used to forecast and evaluate the practical consequences of fundamental decisions. As interpreted by Donnison (1976), this 'mixed' view involves first the identification of critical issues and subsequently the focusing of attention *alternatively* on local detail, for example, at the individual level, and on broader strategy. This alternation means that a proper synthesis of the short- and long-term technical operations and values may reasonably be achieved.

The planner's task, then, is to stimulate the debate about urban affairs so as to allow this process to develop and then to rationalize the outcome into meaningful and on-going possibilities for action. Steiss (1973) warns, however, that this role must not become simply a political role of compromise, incrementalism or 'maintaining the *status quo*' which is often the hallmark of the politician. Rather, the role should be to broaden the horizons of political and public concern by making the polity aware of its problems and the potential for at least ameliorating urban problems. Posed in these terms, urban planning can widen choice and increase opportunity in society by the portrayal of problem-solving, reformist and feasible policies. At the very least, this will cause a questioning of the nature of the *status quo* and suggest the possibility of evolutionary or revolutionary (that is, more radical) possibilities for change. In so doing, the planner uses technical operations to develop an understanding of urban processes, to identify what is possible, revealing choice, conflict and incompatibility in policies, and to objectively evaluate the consequences of alternative strategies. These operations involve both the dissemination of relevant information and understanding *and* a full discussion of values. It also requires that urban planning is conceptualized as an on-going controlling or steering process, capable of permitting policy decisions to be subjected to correction and refinement over time (Lynch, 1972).

It will now be clear that urban planning cannot be a unitary process, not only because of the need to synthesize values and technical operations, but because disagreement will inevitably arise during its course (Harris, 1970). We noted earlier that social policy making emerges from the resolution of conflict about values, and have now observed that this resolution can be helped through a proper synthesis of technical operations. However, policy making is a generator of conflict as well. Through political interaction and social adjustment, the decisions and priorities of the participants in policy making are ratified, altered, compromised, or rejected (Lindblom, 1965). Even the announcement of policy intention is a stimulus to reaction, and this suggests that policy making is an inherently political, rather than a technical process (Rondinelli, 1973). It is not surprising, then, that planners have found it impossible to be both rational and participative at the same time (Smith, 1976).

Policy, then, evolves *through* socio-political processes and this means that we must *expect* differing views as to the purpose of urban planning (as with other social policy-making fields) to predominate from time to time. The fundamental relationship is that between the planning procedures[11] and the political processes by which responsibility is taken for those procedures, but there will be any number of ways in which an urban planning process may be conceived, even within a general 'problem-solving' approach. We suggest that the development of both research and policy-making methods must recognize the range of possible modes of urban planning which compete for attention at the politico-social level. This, we briefly set out.

Modes of urban planning

Four modes have been clearly identified (Berry, 1973) and are shown in figure 1.2. The first to be distinguished is that of *ameliorative problem solving*. This mode reflects the natural tendency of human beings to do nothing until some considerable disfunction arises in society which is then perceived to be a pressing problem and which demands corrective action. Essentially, this is a pragmatic type of planning based upon reaction to past and present problems and it is characterized by the emergence of unpremeditated issues and goals. In this mode, there is a minimal attempt to foresee the future or even the future consequences.

In contrast, alternative modes can be described which are essentially based upon an *explicit anticipation* of future problems. However, the translation of problems into goals and their future specification may well be latent and constrained by the power structures in society. Nevertheless, in theory, three discrete sub-categories of 'future-oriented planning' can be distinguished, namely *system-maintaining*, *evolutionary* and *revolutionary* modes.

The first essentially involves a minimum-change approach which seeks primarily to make the best use of perceived, on-going changes. In system-planning terms, such a view corresponds to a 'deviation control' model, through negative feedback (Chadwick, 1976). The disadvantage of this mode of planning is that it readily tends towards the mere preservation of the *status quo*, and is therefore questionable in an inherently dynamic social context. The second 'future-oriented' planning mode also involves a step-by-step, or incremental approach, but one which places an emphasis upon what are called 'exploitative possibilities'. In this mode, the planning process *actively* seeks and stimulates the possibilities for change. In systems terms, this corresponds to the application of positive feed-back within the system by selected influences, thus, in effect, amplifying trends towards what are believed to be desirable objectives. This view, whilst appearing superficially to be a 'middle-of-the-road' compromise, in practice has suffered a serious deficiency. There is a tendency for only a traditional repertory of problems to be defined and thus only a constrained repertory of solutions to be exploited. This form of planning has led only with difficulty to novel, innovative problem-solving designs. A contributory reason for this, we suggest, lies in an inadequate understanding and use of the broad range (and true potential) of urban planning methods.

In contrast, the third 'future-oriented' mode of planning is completely normative and its purpose is to transform a social system by the redefinition

Figure 1.2 The different modes of urban planning

	Ameliorative problem solving	Allocative trend modifying	Exploitative opportunity seeking	Normative goal-oriented
Planning mode △	Planning for the present by reacting to past problems	Planning towards a predicted future	Planning with a predicted future	Planning by creating a desired future
Planning operations △	Analyse problems, design interventions, allocate resources accordingly	Determine and make the *best* of trends and allocate resources in accordance with desires to promote or alter them	Determine and make the most of trends and allocate resources to take advantage of what is to come	Decide on the future *desired* and allocate resources so that trends are changed or created accordingly. Desired future may be based on present, predicted or new values
Results of planning action △	Haphazard modification of the future by reducing the future burden and sequelae of present problems	Gently balance and modify the future by avoiding predictable problems and by achieving a 'balanced' progress to avoid creating new problems	Unbalance and modify the future by taking advantage of predictable happenings, avoiding some problems and exploiting others without a major concern for emergence of new problems	Extensive modification of the future by aiming for what 'could be'. New predictions by changing values or goals, matching outcomes to desires, or avoiding and changing problems to ones easier to handle or to tolerate

After Berry (1973: 16)

of fundamental values, norms and goals. This is a view which demands an explicit creative attitude to the future, and the setting out of a programme for change. Its advantage is that it accommodates both analytical, 'trend projection' and normative, 'new state' views of the future, but it suffers the disadvantage of requiring a commitment to change and a scale of decision-making which, for political reasons, is problematical. It also increases the ever-present danger of sectoral elitism, particularly by planners, in plan and policy formulation.[12]

The reason for drawing attention to the different modes of planning is not, for this text, to attempt to discuss in detail their inherent advantages and disadvantages from a political or even an operational point of view. It is, rather, to offer the reminder that such modes can be discretely identified and, moreover, that hybrid modes are clearly feasible. Second, that choice of a mode of planning is not a matter of technical or even methodological merit, rather it is a matter of perception and belief by those who are concerned with the planning activity. Third, that the mode provides the framework in which purpose and method can be properly united and thereby accommodates the otherwise difficult problem that the resulting policy and action need not be wholly rational in order to be justified. And fourth, that, for a wide range of reasons, the exploitive opportunity seeking mode would appear to be the most feasible way forward given contemporary political, social, professional and technical contexts at least in the short and middle term.

If the 'purpose' of planning stems from a societal realization of problems through perceptual processes and experience, then the technical operations of urban planning need to be sensitive to those perceptions in an on-going way and the resulting plans and policies need to be seen as fair and to effect worthwhile change. Initially, we must note that perceptions about problems and issues are formed through experience within an explicit environmental context, that is, within an all-embracing ecosystem. Berry (1973) has set out clearly a view as to how perceptions of this system influence decisions, both on *what to do*, in a policy sense, and on *what to study* in order to decide what to do, in a problem-defining or research sense. Planners, then, apply themselves to specific problems through a process of perceptual filtering,[13] by which problems are perceived and identified. These, being expressed through institutions, organizations and by individuals (including planners), are subsequently ranked in order to receive a priority of attention. This specification of relevant problems is, however, an essentially normative activity.

Perceptions, then, bias and modify attitudes about the need for action and of capacity to effect change. They are based upon mental maps of the ecosystem held by individuals and influenced by the place of the individual within that system. It is important to note that these perceptions have multiple origins, for they are generally learned through experience, that is, through periods of prior decision making and observations of its effects. Further, these perceptions are modified through interaction with values and expectations both of individuals *and* of society through its organizations and institutions. This 'collective' view is extremely important, not simply for social reasons, but because, the nature, purpose and meaning of any individual actor and his actions can only be understood in relation to a context involving other actors and actions.[14]

It is probably more meaningful to view the ecosystem not from the point of view that it is made up of objects or things, but that it is a complex hierarchy of activities and processes which are nested within systems of increasing scales. It is then clear that these can only be *understood* in an holistic relationship. At even larger scales, these activities are assembled into less stable patterns, such as, for example, social networks, which essentially consist of a hierarchy of such structures. A deeper understanding of these should lead urban investigators to the possible sources of intrinsic order and certainly the nature of disorder in society. (McLoughlin and Webster, 1970). Given the central role of value-based decision making, such policy analysis should provide insights into the most appropriate strategies for deliberate, that is planned, intervention designed to produce change which conforms broadly to societal objectives (McLoughlin, 1973).

In this approach, the role of learning is stressed and the actors' (including planners') perception of the world is made quite explicit. This blends with biological and cultural drives in society to form perceptions, usually transitory, as to the need for action on specific issues. Through learning, this is related to knowledge and attitudes to the capacity to act and effect, or at least seek, desired change. This broadly provides the context in which a feasible purpose is determined and within which relevant issues are focused upon. According to the 'mode' of planning chosen, a range of resulting impacts are possible, and these, in turn, will feed back learning and experience, thereby modifying the perceptions that initiated the process in the first place.

Recalling our earlier discussions we can therefore describe urban planning in terms of two discrete, but related, processes, that is as a *fundamentally* dual activity. On the one hand, there are processes concerned with effecting change based upon a system of values, attitudes, expectations and on-going perceptual assessments of a desirable future. These, we refer to as *effective* processes and, above all, note their important cognitive component. Whilst superior, these can only be operationally effective when adequately supported by a second set of processes. These are concerned with (i) the acquisition of knowledge and understanding about relevant urban phenomena; (ii) the way that phenomena may be expected to change over time without the influence of policy *and* (iii) as a result of the influence of planned policy, so that the likely effects of particular policies may be objectively assessed. These can be referred to as the *substantive* processes, and they are, for the most part, made up of relatively well-defined procedures. But they, in turn, can only be technically and socially effective within a purposeful framework. The mutual dependency of these processes is shown in figure 1.3, together with their constituent components and the

Figure 1.3 Dual processes of urban planning

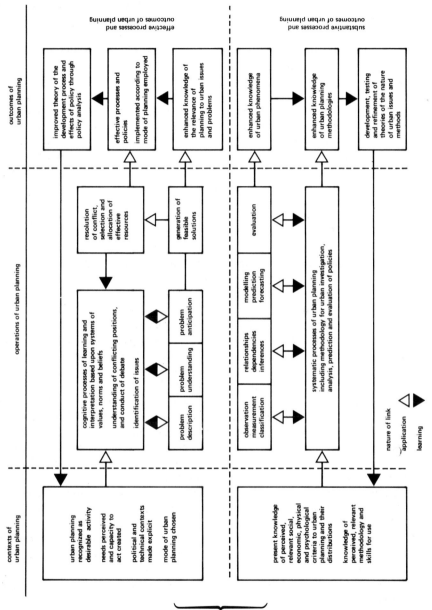

outcomes. It is also important to note that all stages will involve 'recursive' thinking though this feature is not indicated for simplicity. In summary, it is argued that planners generate plans and policies largely through continuous, cognitive processes and this should be supported to the greatest possible extent by systematic analysis, for example, through research, through forecasting, and evaluation and analysis of policy outcomes.

Key issues

The general nature of urban planning processes must now be related to the substantive issues with which planners actually deal. We have noted the important shifts of emphasis in the beliefs of urban planners as to what are their proper concerns and, particularly, that they have moved from a relatively narrow perception of the development of the built environment and its land form *per se*, to a broader attempt to understand the activities of society which cause that development to take place. At the same time, there has been a diversity of debate about the purposes of urban planning and a realization of the possible modes in which a planning system can be conceived.

The existing, and on-going, patterns of land use and development in towns and cities represent the outcome of a complex interaction of market forces and public interventions for the use of physical space. A useful starting point is to envisage this interaction in 'demand and supply' terms. On the one hand, there are the various 'demands' that human activities make upon land, for every human action takes place in an explicit spatial dimension (Lynch, 1972). Sometimes, this demand relates to an individual's needs and sometimes collectively, to groups or organizations, such as families, households, industrial and commercial organizations, social clubs, and government. In various ways, then, human activities impose their particular needs on space, and indeed on other resources, and they compete in terms of conflicting locational preferences. On the 'supply' side, there is the land space itself, with inherent[15] characteristics of land form, aspect, drainage, climate, natural beauty and so on. But most important of all, are the relative locational advantages or disadvantages of parcels of land for a particular activity in relation to other activities. Other supply factors will relate to the ownership of land, for example, in public and private sectors, collectively or by individuals, and the supply 'control' which is super-imposed by land-use planners and other public agencies in permitting specific types of development to take place in particular locations. Price will be another important factor linking supply and demand, but, of course, will not be independent of the policies of planners and the beliefs among the population at large that those policies will be effective or consistent.

A simple demand and supply model is, however, somewhat misleading for the development process is complex not only because of the variety of land-based activities, but also because of the 'linked' nature of development. So that, for example, a policy for industrial development which creates jobs

will, in turn, give rise to demand for housing, schools, roads, water supply
and any number of other requirements. The nature of these consequential
demands, all of which will meet various constraints of 'supply', is neither
constant nor always easily predicted, particularly over time. Any act of
social policy making and intervention say, to, encourage or permit
development, will generate some kind of consequential demand, or at least
'attract' demand from one location to another. Similarly, refusal to allow
development, or its discouragement by policy or even by default, may have
the opposite effect. In both types of situation, the eventual chain of
consequences may be extremely complex. Given then, the plurality of policy
making both by central and local government and other public and private
organizations in society, and the inherent complexity of urban and regional
systems, planners have to face not only the limitations of their controls but
also their partial knowledge about the system in which they attempt to
intervene. It is clear that, in order to be able to make better predictions of
the consequences of policy making, a better knowledge of the urban
development process *as a whole* is called for and of the place of land-use
planning within that process. This is particularly important so that planners
do not overclaim a role that they cannot fulfil.

The main activities within the urban system which pose their demands
upon land can be readily stated – residence, education, employment, leisure
and mobility.[16] Given the essentially dynamic nature of society, each of
these activities will impose a particular demand pattern both in space *and*
time, and optimizing policy over time is probably the greatest challenge to
any planning system. It is clear that many of the recent criticisms of the
land-use planning system, to which reference has already been made, relate
directly to the difficulty of devising a method of land-use control which, at
the same time, can provide clear and unambiguous guidance for present
development, yet remain adaptable enough to take account of the inevitable
changes in circumstances.

The activities noted above will be mostly self-explanatory, but we should
distinguish between two kinds of mobility. First, mobility can be thought of
in terms of day-to-day human movement by individuals, for example,
linking residence to employment, shopping or leisure and this, particularly,
gives rise to transportation needs. On the other hand, there is the more
general concept of mobility, that of population movement or migration,
characterized by residence-residence movements, often by households or
family groups, though this is not definitive. This type of mobility, both a
cause and effect of development, gives rise to a great deal of uncertainty in
plan and policy making. It follows that its estimation, through analysis and
theoretical explanations, is a vital task in urban policy making. Together
with the natural change of population (due that is, to births, ageing and
deaths), migration causes *structural* population change. It is important that
the urban planner understands the implications of such change for most
'derived' demands such as education needs, household formation, housing
needs, youth employment needs, car ownership levels, welfare of the elderly,

and so on, are a close function of population structure. However, this function will itself change over time, in response to cultural and social expectations and norms, exemplified by space standards for schooling, housing standards, welfare standards and a whole range of behavioural issues. These are particularly difficult to forecast for they require anticipation of social change.

Activities and their complex inter-relationships are rationalized by urban planners in order to provide a basis for plan and policy making through the study of urban systems and attempts to predict change. This 'rationalization' frequently involves moving from a broad, high-level goal-seeking position to more narrowly defined positions in facing particular issues or problems which are capable of detailed description. As part of the search for greater rationality, and in order to publicly justify their actions, urban planners have increasingly attempted to make clear their purposes by specifying broad *goals*, and from them, to seek to derive more specific *objectives* capable of guiding action,[17] but goals, and even derived objectives, have proved difficult to specify at any kind of operational level (Gutch, 1970).

Yet it is intuitively clear that some kind of 'objective' is required for at least four reasons (Perraton, 1972). The first is because of the general commitment of planning to a longer-term view of urban affairs; the second because of the emphasis in planning given to a user-orientation;[18] the third because of the need to make conflicts over objectives quite explicit; and fourth, because of the need to consider a wide range of impacts and effects of any public policy or plan. This is illustrated by figure 1.4, which shows a range of contemporary issues that have been identified by planners to be significant in the preparation of Structure Plans.

The place of goals and operational objectives in the cyclical or 'learning' process[19] of plan-making (figure 1.3) is that they are consciously *evolved through* the operations of plan generation, research and information gathering and refinement and the evaluation of the alternative policy possibilities. It seems preferable to present a rich predictive picture (as to future urban possibilities) and to allow the decision makers gradually to form and express their preferences from the alternative pictures, by adding alternatives and modifying them in the course of the dialogue (Boyce *et al.*, 1972).

In summary, the approach is one of a cyclical or re-iterative dialogue which focuses upon learning through setting out possible courses of action and their evaluation against some suitable 'performance' criteria. The technical role is one of providing the decision makers with the fullest information (Krueckeberg and Silvers, 1974). It will be clear that part of the dialogue must concern the operational objectives of the process which, in turn, will be used to specify the 'performance criteria' by which the evaluation of policies can be carried out. Care is needed, however, in specifying such performance criteria because of the existence of 'trade-offs' among the objectives and the impacts of policies on various groups and the

Figure 1.4 Problems and issues in structure plans: examples from Welsh authorities

County	Autonomous forces	Underlying causes	Problems	Issues	Development constraints	Compounded problems
Gwent	Rate of growth in national economy Structural changes in employment Decline of basic employment sector	Lack of employment growth Failure to attract jobs	Unemployment Housing demand greater than supply Housing condition	The health of the county economy Housing and community facilities Environment/ resource conservation	Lack of immediately available development land Lack of serviced site diversity Public financial resources	Population growth/labour supply/job opportunities Physical environment/ dereliction
Mid-Glamorgan	Contraction of basic industry Recession in national economy Public and private finance levels	Lack of sufficient employment growth	Lack of employment Selective out-migration Poor physical environment	The achievement of an economy free of fluctuations in employment and heavy dependence on government assistance The achievement of higher standards of living, working and recreation	Need to reclaim land for industry and housing Inadequate highway network Finance	(Not explicitly noted)
Clwyd	Rate of growth in national economy Locational disadvantages of county Policy decisions of government	Decline of basic sector Narrow economic base	Unemployment and seasonal unemployment	Strategic: population and housing, employment, transportation and environment Subsidiary: shopping, education, social services, recreation and countryside, minerals	Public sector finance	Inter-relationship of population change, employment and housing Inter-relationship of options for development

After Bracken and Hume (compiled from 1979a: 33 *et seq.* and 1979b: 33 *et seq.*)

'collective' nature of 'pay-offs' (Lichfield *et al.*, 1975). For example, it can frequently arise that tackling a 'less severe' problem as an objective can result in greater *net* benefit to society where the effects may ` be wide reaching, than tackling an apparently 'more severe', but localized, problem. The resolution of such issues goes to the heart of the decision-making debate and demands the fullest information.

The general difficulty in public policy making is that to move from objectives to an operational position, the aims must be specified not only in terms of *what* needs are to be served but also *whose* needs are to be served. Urban planners have been remarkably unwilling to make this clear. Perhaps this is not surprising, for any ranking of objectives among the sections of the population clearly involves some difficult value-based judgements and most fundamentally, an ability to measure utility.[20] So that this is not done arbitrarily, a systematic approach is to be preferred, but a simple illustration will show that it is not an easy matter.

Consider a situation with just two groups in society, A and B, and three needs for which a preference can be stated:

		Group A	Group B
	1	Road improvement	Leisure centre
Preference	2	Better housing	Road improvement
	3	Leisure centre	Better housing

It is immediately clear that information such as this can say little about *how much* preference is felt by a particular group, for Group A may have quite a strong preference for a Leisure Centre, even though it is ranked 3rd and Group B a relatively low preference for better housing, perhaps because it feels already adequately housed. It is clearly not possible to obtain any *aggregate* view over the two groups, and more groups and more options merely confuses the situation. Aggregation of preference involves logical[21] as well as measurement difficulties (see Chapter 5) and it means that rationalizing goal-type statements into objective statements in order to guide the planning process is fraught with difficulties. In practice, the decision maker is likely to proceed by some coalition of his own views of preference and values and those of the planner obtained through some kind of consultation. However, planners have found it useful, in a limited way, to use the notion of objectives to pose questions in participative exercises and to offer tentative ranking of goal-like statements to stimulate debate and invite reaction. Goal-like statements have been usefully posed in matrix form to focus attention upon apparent conflicts and incompatibilities and this has helped in the search for a reduced number of feasible options.[22]

In practice, Structure Planning has attempted to deal more explicitly with issues or problems[23] (figure 1.4). Most planning authorities have focused upon the traditional concerns of population and employment change, housing, shopping, recreation and transportation, their spatial development, implications and requirements. The treatment of broader policy issues has tended to divide planning authorities into two groups (Booth and Jaffe, 1978). Those experiencing growth have been dominated by a concern for the allocation of new development and its restraint, usually for 'amenity' reasons. In contrast, metropolitan areas and some rural areas have been dominated by a concern for their declining economic bases, their inadequate employment and housing opportunities, shortages of development land (particularly *serviced* development land), population out-migration (notably of younger people) and a lack of finance to tackle such issues effectively.[24] It will be clear that such issues and problems are both spatial and aspatial in their nature.

Important implications follow because, as already noted, the policy instruments actually available to the urban planner to effect change are, in practice, quite limited. Indeed, they can be summarized under just three headings. The first, statutory *control* over the development of land is mainly negative in its power. Such control is efficient in preventing what is thought to be undesirable, but is relatively powerless in itself to obtain what *is* desirable. The second instrument is the matter of *influence*. This is the extent to which planners can actually cause change in the development process, in both public and private sectors, for example by persuasion or by making explicit the potentials and possibilities or even by making clear future problems and any undesirable consequences of present action. The third instrument is by direct *manipulation* over public investment, such as the development of the infrastructure (roads, services, etc.) or public housing programmes, city centre renewal schemes and so on. The problem here (for planners) is that the power to exercise these functions is widely dispersed through government and local government agencies and departments. Not only is a great deal of co-ordination required through management,[25] but it is necessary to identify common purposes among these agencies and urban planners will only have a limited influence in such debate. The complexity of the links between the policy instruments, the resource objectives and the effective outcomes has been clearly illustrated by A. G. Wilson (1974). Any one policy may well manipulate, directly or indirectly, several such resource objectives, and each objective may contribute typically to several broad goals.

It is clear then that, given the complexity of the system which links policy instruments to social objectives, planners cannot expect to be able to move directly and sufficiently from an objective statement to the identification of a policy to achieve that objective. It is only in the identification of problems or issues that a *meaningful* debate can be conducted as to how the objective headings, such as those shown in figure 1.5 will apply to different individuals and households, in different income levels, in different community groups and in different locations (Wilson, 1974). And this means that a problem-solving view must prevail in the formulation of objective purposes. In summary, goals *can* provide the broad basis to establishing incentive and defining what might be done. But understanding and the

Figure 1.5 Conceptual inter-relationships of goals, objectives and policy instruments

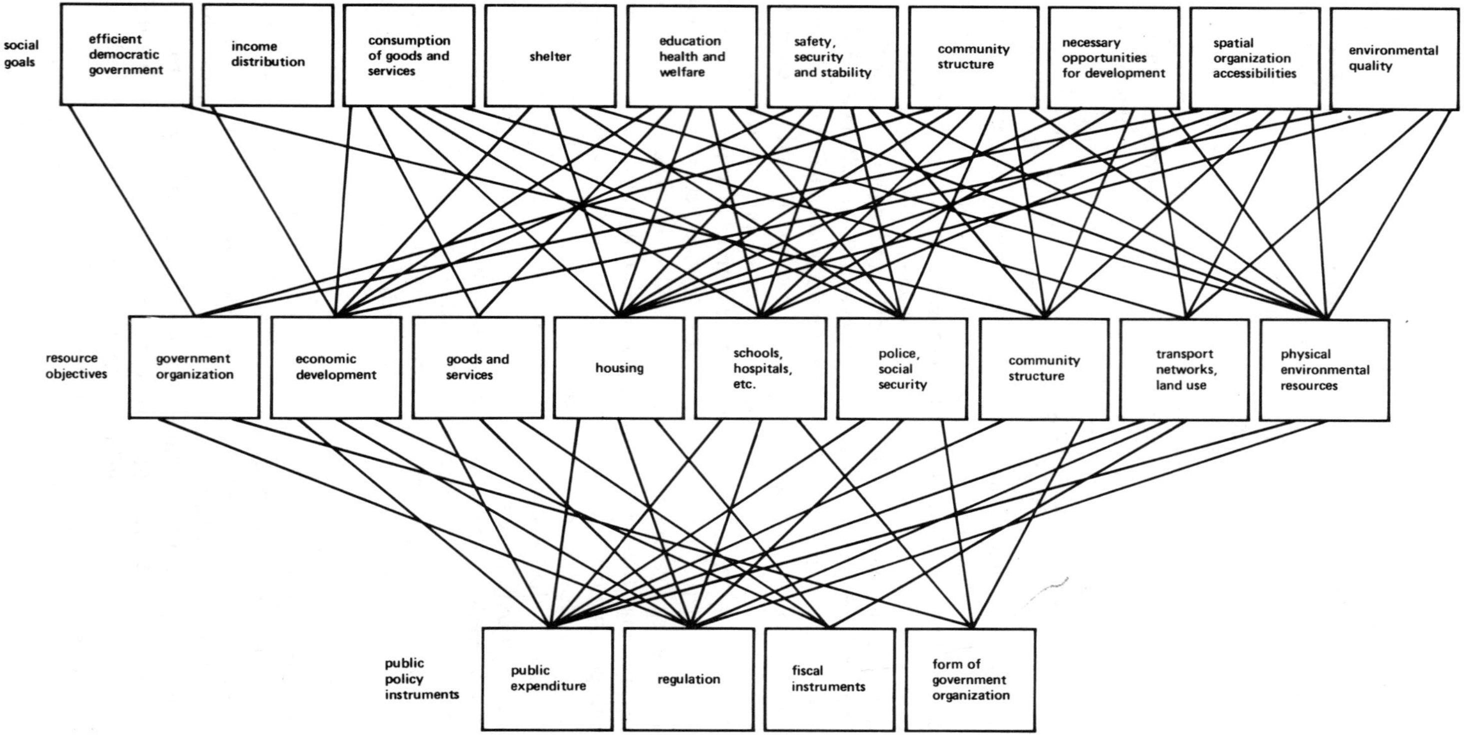

social goals: efficient democratic government · income distribution · consumption of goods and services · shelter · education health and welfare · safety, security and stability · community structure · necessary opportunities for development · spatial organization accessibilities · environmental quality

resource objectives: government organization · economic development · goods and services · housing · schools, hospitals, etc. · police, social security · community structure · transport networks, land use · physical environmental resources

public policy instruments: public expenditure · regulation · fiscal instruments · form of government organization

From A. G. Wilson (1974: 15)

synthesis of fact and values to create policies can only be undertaken, in a social context, in 'problem' or 'issue' terms. It is then clear that research to serve understanding and more systematic analysis of the ways in which the effective mechanisms of planning actually operate to intervene in the development process are vital to the enhancement of the process.

Notes

1 Geddes' well known formula – 'survey, analysis, plan' – has been a cornerstone of urban planning for over sixty years.

2 The origins of the modern town planning movement have been well documented for example, by Ashworth (1954), Benevolo (1967), Cherry (1970, 1974) and Hall (1975). The 'standards' approach is particularly characterized in the Garden Cities movement and subsequent 'New Town' development.

3 Particularly following the first 'comprehensive' legislation – the Town and Country Planning Act of 1947.

4 The PAG Report (1965) expected 'a surge of physical development not previously experienced'.

5 Examples of the influences upon PAG identified by Solesbury (1975) included Buchanan (Ministry of Transport, 1963) who called for an *integration* of transport policies with development plans; the Planning Bulletin on Town Centres (Ministry of Housing and Local Government, 1962) which stressed the need for a *comprehensive* approach; and the experience of the Liverpool Interim Planning policy (Liverpool, City and County Borough of, 1962) which was the first attempt to *re-style* the erstwhile Development Plan into a strategic form. However, also influential had been much earlier work (circa 1960) in the USA notably by Mitchell (1961) in advocating the flexibility of a strategic approach to urban policy making. Whilst Structure Planning is widely referred to as the 'new' planning system in Britain, it is worth reflecting that it is now thirteen years old by statute and over twenty in terms of its concepts. The 1968 Act was later consolidated by the 1971 Town and Country Planning Act.

6 But see also the earlier paper by Mitchell (1961) which would appear to have had an influence upon the Planning Advisory Group (PAG).

7 See the Development Plans Manual (Ministry of Housing and Local Government, 1970) and subsequent central government advice.

8 Government advice to planning authorities in the early Structure Plan period heavily stressed this model. (See the Development Plans Manual (Ministry of Housing and Local Government, 1970) and Management Networks for Structure Plans (Department of the Environment, 1971).)

9 The development of planning thinking to this position can be readily traced in Webber (1965), Hill (1968), McLoughlin (1969), Wilson (1968) and Stewart and Eddison (1971) and a discussion of the implications in Perraton (1972).

10 To effectively distinguish fact and value requires that certain philosophical assumptions are made though a discussion is beyond the scope of this text. We should note, however, that the verification of facts and the verification of values involves fundamentally different methodological approaches.

11 Judicial, administrative and technical procedures are involved. See, for example, Levin (1972) and Regan (1978) and the discussion in Chapter 7.

12 It is possible to trace the major changes in British planning ideology against this background. The nineteenth century origins of modern urban planning lay in

ameliorative problem solving. The design tradition is fundamentally normative, though sectoral. The search for rationality and comprehensiveness is an attempt to exploit opportunities, though problematical for the reasons we have discussed. Perhaps most over-riding of all, is that, since the various economic crises of the Western world in the 1970s and currently fashionable reductions in public expenditure, urban planning has been constrained to a role of 'trend-modifying' though its ineffectiveness when little 'development' is being undertaken is a major concern to many planners. For a series of essays dealing with these and related issues more broadly, see Burchell and Sternlieb (1978).

13   Sometimes referred to as the process of 'translating into objectives'.

14   This important development would however probably not have emerged so clearly were it not for the discussions about the feasibility of the 'comprehensive' approach which we noted earlier.

15   The oversimplification of this view is acknowledged for the debate as to the extent of human influence on land form, landscape and so on, which is complex and beyond the scope of this discussion.

16   The 'key issues' concept (housing, employment, transportation) is a central feature of post-1974 Central Government Advice on Structure Planning though it was implicit in both the PAG report (PAG, 1965) and the 1968 Town and Country Planning Act, later to become the 1971 Act. For 'key issue' advice see Circulars 98/74, 55/77 and 4/79 (Department of the Environment, 1974b, 1977a, 1979c respectively).

17   There was a period of considerable debate as to whether urban planning should be conceptualized as a 'goal-seeking' or 'problem-solving' process – see Chadwick (1976), Needham (1971), Drake (1975). Some of the sub-regional studies contain very extensive lists of goal-like, idealized statements which proved to be well beyond the planners' powers, influence or ambit to attain – see for example Coventry/Solihull/Warwickshire (1971) and Nottinghamshire/Derbyshire (1969) sub-regional studies.

18   For example, through the statutory public participation requirement – see 1971 Act, §8 and Circular 52/72 (Department of the Environment, 1972d).

19   A view stressed, for example, by Massey and Cordey-Hayes (1971) and McLoughlin and Thornley (1973).

20   The concept is fundamental to the body of theory known as Welfare Economics.

21   The 'logical' problem of aggregation is readily illustrated. Assume three groups, or persons, each able to express a preference for three options. They vote as follows:

		Group.A	Group B	Group C
Preference	1	X	Y	Z
	2	Y	Z	X
	3	Z	X	Y

Group A prefers option X to Y and Y to Z, and so on. A summary of preference produces: Groups who prefer X to $Y = 2$ (A and C); groups who prefer Y to $Z = 2$ (A and B) and groups who prefer Z to $X = 2$ (B and C). Logically, preference of X to Y and Y to Z expresses a ranked preference of X to Z (that is $X - Y - Z$), but aggregation over the system of preferences produces a paradox. Two groups prefer X to Y and Y to Z, which suggests a majority preference to X to Z – this is however exactly in contradiction to the preferences at the disaggregated level which shows a 2:1 preference of Z over X!

22 See, for example, Reading/Wokingham/Aldershot/Basingstoke Sub-Regional Strategy (1975).

23 The use of the (softer) term 'issues' rather than (the harder term) 'problems' appears to be quite deliberate in Government advice, for example, Circular 98/74, Department of Environment (1974b). 'Issues' might be acknowledged to be present which could be more readily ignored. The acknowledged existence of a 'problem' could carry with it a much higher level of implied commitment to do something about it. This circular suggested that authorities should focus onto the three 'key' areas of Employment, Housing, Transportation. Other issues are at the discretion of the authority. This appears to have been largely an administrative move to speed up the preparation of Structure Plans.

24 Generally, planning authorities which are faced with more predictable futures, such as those of the Home counties and Shire counties whose main aim is to restrain growth, have based their strategies on a goal-like approach to 'variations' within the predictable future (i.e. as to how much growth should be allowed or can be contained) – see West Sussex Structure Plan (1978); Other authorities in areas of employment decline, etc., have rejected the feasibility of determining goals and have placed much more emphasis on 'problems' – see Merseyside Structure Plan (1980).

25 There is considerable literature on corporate planning in Local Authorities – see, for example, Stewart (1973). Also, other 'planning' policy vehicles have been introduced in addition to the Structure Plan and Local Plan. These are Transportation Policies and Plans (TPPs), Public Transport Plans (PTPs) and Housing Investment Plans (HIPs). As a result considerable co-ordination is required between these mainly short-term, resource-based, policy documents and the Structure Plan. See also the discussion in Part 3.

2

DESIGNS AND PLAN GENERATION

The task of plan generation

The urban planner's principal task can be described as generating alternative settings of 'public policy instruments', such as a land-use plan, or a strategic policy document. The broad purpose, as we have discussed, is to regulate the spatial organization of activities and, with the help of control over public infrastructure investment and influence and control over development in the private sector, to ameliorate urban problems. The planner thereby works towards more general objectives. This 'generating' activity will normally involve the identification of urban problems and issues, their relationships to potential policy options and the construction of a policy 'package'.

Determining the land-use implications of policies is a sub-stage of this 'generation process' and involves the translation of population and employment levels, for example, into a land requirement for additional residential, industrial or commercial development with the aid of assumptions on densities, existing capacities and commitment.[1] It is then necessary to explore various distributions of this land requirement with respect to the existing built form, constraints and policy objectives. (Booth and Jaffe, 1978). The physical constraints can be readily listed as (i) land supply (a dominant feature of urban plans); (ii) existing planning commitments (which are often present though, surprisingly, rarely analysed – see Bracken and Hume, 1979c); (iii) transport and utility networks which necessarily provide major constraints on new development, and (iv) local authority development finance.

Two points must be made clear at the outset of this chapter. The first is that plan and policy *making* is the *fundamental* task of planners, so that the use of analytical, forecasting and evaluation methods must ultimately serve this purpose. This accords with central government advice to planners since the 1968 Act. The second point is that, because of urban system complexity, the main decision making difficulty that has to be faced is the overwhelming number of alternatives that can be envisaged. It has already been noted that it has been mainly through the use of 'standards' of physical layout and design that planners have traditionally reduced the number of options and thereby much of this complexity.

In generating plans and policies there is a large range of methods[2] that planners can draw upon and, in practice, they make great use of conventional wisdom acquired through experience. The methods range widely; on the one hand, 'brainstorming' approaches, that is, highly intuitive thinking, or, 'delphi' methods, using group debate and 'semi-logical' discursive approaches seeking 'middle way' answers to problems. On the other hand, there are highly systematized, mathematical methods for finding solutions to well-defined problems and a large body of guiding theory known as 'decision theory'. We do not think it helpful to enter any kind of over-simplified debate as to whether any of these approaches is 'best' for urban planning. Each serves different purposes and has different requirements, and in most applied fields some kind of blend of methods is inevitable and will make a useful contribution to the all-important synthesis of fact and value in policy making. There is also the probability, as we later discuss, that as British strategic land-use planning moves towards a more on-going managerial role, the idea of 'plan generating' may be seen as less important and this will have important implications for the way in which methods will be used in the future.

First, we draw attention to some traditional approaches. The Delphi method, often used implicitly by planners through their conventional wisdom, can usefully be made an explicit process. A recent example has been in the preparation of the East Anglia Study (1974). Here group panels were used to represent the various pressure groups and interests in the region, drawn from members and officers of the Economic Planning Council and Board, the Regional Consultative Committee, and selected experts from within and outside the planning team. A questionnaire approach was used to elicit from each panel member a 'scenario' view of what could be expected to happen in the future. Those individual findings were discussed in panel sessions and refined towards a consensus view.[3]

The method has the advantage of involving a wide range of persons, in effect, a form of participation, and it draws upon the experience of a potentially large number of people concerned about the future of a town or region. It is also useful in lessening the degree of reliance often placed upon an analysis of past trends in plan and policy making, with the attendant danger that undesirable present trends and features are simply extrapolated into the future. Though a useful approach, there are limitations. First, that opinion bias will inevitably be present, and second, that estimates of the future trends will be based more upon intuition and expectation, than on a systematic analysis of trends. This can be overcome if a considerable amount of technical literature can be read in preparation for the exercise by all those concerned. It is not to be expected, however, that such discussions should produce a consensus either as to what may be expected or indeed as to what should be done. Rather the purpose is to make use of a broad base of 'expert' opinion in identifying a probable and limited range of future expectations.

In urban planning, as in architecture, there has traditionally been a widespread use of the 'black box' approach to problem solving. Indeed, the origins of work in both of these fields has rested upon the ability of a human 'designer' to be capable of producing a solution to a problem, which has a good chance of being successful, in which at least the designer has confidence although he cannot say precisely how the solution was obtained or, indeed, why it may work. The nature of the 'creative leap' implied in this approach has been the subject of much debate. Inevitably, one suspects that there will always be much in the urban system that we cannot and will not understand and that conjecture, intuition, learning and experience will contribute to the formulation of strategies. In a social context, however, these inputs also give rise to unacceptable inefficiencies and uncertainties.

Over the recent past there has been a rapid development of interest in 'design' and 'problem-solving' methods in general. Though diverse in approach these developments have features in common, the most important of which is that they attempt to make more public the hitherto private thinking of the designer or problem solver, that is, they seek to *externalize the process.* And this can be done either through the use of words, diagrams or mathematical symbols, as we later illustrate. The reasons for this development are not difficult to find, for

the high cost of...errors, particularly in the case of complex urban systems, is a strong incentive to externalize design thought, for only in this way can it be subjected to criticism and such testing as can be carried out, before expensive mistakes are made. The rapid search for new problem solving and design methods in all applied fields is a consequence of the realisation that problems have grown too big and complex to be left to the private judgement of even the most experienced designer. (Jones, 1970)

The main operational difficulty which has to be faced in the urban context is that planners can generate, by various means, a universe of unfamiliar alternatives which are too large, complex or numerous to explore by the slow process of conscious thought. Once this point is reached the planner cannot use intuitive, or 'black-box' methods alone in making a choice because that simply re-imposes the restrictions of previous experience that he is trying to move away from. Neither can he use machines to search computationally, for these require an explicit objective to search for, exact criteria to specify the objective and precise ways of measuring and evaluating each outome. As we have already discussed such objectives are not easy to specify or measure in the urban context. Given then, that the methods planners can use will generate a large range of alternatives, the main requirement becomes one of finding systematic ways of avoiding the need to evaluate *all* possible alternatives. Such a situation is generally referred to as a *combinatorial* problem.

A useful approach to the difficulty is to divide the task into two parts. The first part focuses upon generating, or searching for, a variety of feasible solutions. The second involves devising ways of controlling and evaluating the pattern of this searching, that is, some kind of strategy control. Posed in this way intelligent, organized approaches are possible, so that the design effort which concentrates upon a strategy control provides an accurate model of the strategy itself and its relationship to the external situation (the problem) that the design is intended to satisfy.[4] A further advantage of this 'externalizing' process is that it allows each member of a design team, or group engaged in the urban planning process, to see for himself the degree to which the various actions and processes do, or do not, produce an acceptable balance between problems, possible solutions and the likely consequences of adopting one of them. It requires, fundamentally, a high degree of 'information exchange' between the participants though, in practice, political, administrative and technical constraints all too readily apply.

Using this approach, however, we can usefully discuss the planners' task of policy generation, first, by considering the difficulties associated with the inherent uncertainty of the task and second, by drawing attention to examples, show how systematic approaches have made a useful contribution through a refinement of design and strategic concepts to urban plan and policy formulation. Before doing so one further comment should be made about 'models' in the design context. Having introduced the concepts associated with a systematic approach to plan design, it is relevant to draw attention to a long history of work which has attempted to apply mathematical theory, first, to land use planning problems (Harris, 1968), and subsequently to a broader range of public policy applications (Harris, 1978), including transportation, education, and health services.

Harris (1976) has categorized the types of design problem faced by urban planners that are most amenable to a mathematical treatment by means of an operational model. One area concerns public and private urban capital investment and its relationship to future land allocation for particular uses. This is a vital area for systematic design because urban capital investment has a long life, and once physical development takes place, is irreversible. A second, broader level in this relationship concerns the overall locations of capital investment in the urban area, and the factors which influence investment both spatially, and over time. At a more abstract level, the relationship can be considered in terms of urban systems, and constructing a theoretical model of such a system is an important (indeed, often the only) way in which the behaviour of the system can be analysed and predicted. We discuss these areas in more detail later, but, for the moment, should note that the concept of a 'model', whether in a mathematical or physical form, is essentially a device to connect theory with its applications. By observing the real world, the planner or analyst may attempt to build an abstract model of some aspect of its behaviour and thereby hope to examine and test some hypothesized theory. Equally, the model can be used in an operational sense, in that, believing in the relevance of some theory to a particular situation, the planner may use the model to generate, or test out, variations of plans or policies through the manipulation of the model.

The use of models (see Chapter 6) is an important tool in the generation of plans and designs, and must be seen as complementary to other approaches to plan generation that we now discuss. However, there is an underlying problem as to how well any abstract model, whether mathematical or not, can capture the essential features of the system which it purports to represent, without its predictions being dependent upon 'other factors' that cannot be readily specified and given explicit form in the model.

Sources of uncertainty

One of the consequences of the search for more systematic approaches to urban planning has been that planners have become increasingly aware of the inherent uncertainties in their task (Lynch, 1972). The problem has been put succinctly by Wedgewood-Oppenheim (1972).

Plan makers are beset by the problems of uncertainty. These arise not only because they are concerned with the future which is difficult to control or to forecast, but because there is much in the present which they do not know or understand, which affects the success and the viability of their plans for the future.

It is also clear that the traditional approaches to planning that we discussed earlier, have tended to obscure this uncertainty, for example by extensive use of the 'standards' approach, and through over-simplistic assumptions in making forecasts of such issues such as population and employment change (Chapter 9).

There is a further vital issue concerning uncertainty. As we have discussed, plan and policy making in a social context cannot optimize, that is, identify singular objectives capable of precise achievement. A more realistic concept is that of 'sufficing' (Simon, 1957), that is, to seek only a sufficient amelioration of problems and to make modest improvements in desirable directions as an on-going task. Given that there are so many variables in the urban system that cannot be predicted with certainty, and a general desire to provide only for more immediate needs, the concept is relevant. It relates to the basic ambivalence in plan making, noted in Chapter 1, that planners seek to reduce present levels of uncertainty in order to make plans but, in our society, cannot rigidly plan for the future. Even quite modest attempts to forecast the future can be totally overtaken by changing events well beyond the planners' ambit of control. Any policy then needs to possess some degree of flexibility to cope with inevitable change.

Flexibility in policy making is, however, a difficult aim to operationalize though the concepts of *sensitivity*[5] and *robustness* provide important approaches which have been widely applied in operational research and management. In theory, these concepts can be extended to any field of analysis in which parameters of 'reasonable expectation' can be assessed, and fairly full statements made of the probabilities associated with the range of expectation for each contributory assumption. Statistical methods can then be used to estimate limits of 'reasonable expectation' over the policy as a whole.[6] There are clear difficulties in applying this to the urban context, mainly in making sufficient simplifying assumptions about the system being represented, the forms of the probability distributions, and, particularly, in making assumptions as to the independence of the constituent topic estimates. A variation is Robustness theory which essentially refers to the extent to which a set of policies, adopted at one moment in time, leave as many options as possible for future decision making (Gupta *et al.*, 1968). This theory usefully requires the setting out of criteria by which assessment may be made as to how best to strike a balance between the need for current commitment to action to deal with a specific problem, and the extent to which those actions can be limited or chosen so as to allow the maximum of flexibility for future choice.[7] For example, it may be thought desirable to forgo deliberately some immediate benefit in order to leave an option 'open' for a future decision when the problem can be seen more clearly and a 'better' choice made. This raises the concept of 'opportunity cost',[8] namely, that the cost of having choice in the future must be weighed against the value of the immediate benefit that has to be forgone.

In our context, two general points should be noted. The first concerns the role of the policy maker. Robustness has to be viewed not only from the standpoint of how options should be kept open, for example, what cost in present benefits has to be forgone, but also whether the remaining options do, in fact, *extend the policy-makers' freedom of choice* in ways that are of some real value to them (Friend and Jessop, 1976). The second point is that examination of robustness, through sensitivity analysis and assessments of the need to keep future options open, may lead decision-takers to the view that their *initial assumptions* were not correct and, therefore, a complete rejection of a set of alternatives is possible. If so, such a rejection must be seen as part of a wider evaluation of plans, policies and the planners' role in their preparation, though there may be political and cost difficulties to be faced. In other words, a critical examination through the use of robustness principles will extend the range of alternatives which must be considered, including perhaps not having a plan, or at least a very minimal one. The search for flexibility may bring changes in the range of alternatives which ought to be considered and this may well have implications for *statutory* urban planning. The argument can be extended to suggest that 'flexible' policy making and statutory regulation are indeed incompatible (Eddison, 1971; Regan, 1978).

The various uncertainties which contribute to the difficulty of making a clear statement of preferences in urban planning have been classified and discussed under three headings by Friend and Jessop (1976). The first heading concerns the nature of the external planning environment; the second concerns the assumptions about the future intentions of the planners or, more particularly, the planning organization or authority; and the third concerns the appropriate value judgements which, as we have already discussed, must be applied in the selection of a preferred policy from among a number of alternatives. The practical issues which urban planners face include, for example, external uncertainties such as national and regional economic performance, financial and fiscal measures by government or expenditure patterns in society. Related field uncertainties arise, for example, because government, as well as carrying out its planning functions will also be making selection and choice over other, but related, policy areas in housing, transportation, education and health at central, county and district levels. Sources of value uncertainty (Chapter 1), for example, will include the whole range of perceptions about the nature and purpose of urban planning, and it is important to remember that value-based uncertainty will exist both at individual, person or household level and at an aggregate, group or society level. There is, moreover, unlikely to be consistency between these levels.

It is not to be expected that any sensitivity analysis can do other than make a contribution to systematic policy making, for the limiting factor will be that the quality of information which emerges can only be as good as the quality of the subjective estimates of uncertainty that are fed in. For reasons already discussed, it is to be expected that assessing the range of 'reasonable expectation' for each of the contributory estimates will be a subject of disagreement between those engaged in the planning process. Although this disagreement may be narrowed through further analysis of the sources of the information or through debate and processes of mutual adjustment it is not practical to expect the elimination of *all* subjectivity and discretion in the chain of reasoning. It is also clear that the problems of uncertainty must be judged in relation to the degree of commitment or irrevocability associated with a particular choice by planners and policy makers.

Friend and Jessop's classification of uncertainty makes clear that three approaches to improving the planning process exist. In brief, that uncertainty in knowledge about urban affairs must be tackled through better research; that uncertainty as to appropriate value judgements must come through a better understanding of policy-making processes;[9] and that there remains a continuing need to reduce the uncertainty related to the interaction of the many policy vehicles and policy departments which affect urban affairs through better management of the planning process.

One further essential point to note is that, whilst there may be ready agreement that any one, or more, of these needs is desirable, it is less intuitively obvious that they are not independent. Moreover, the way in which the decision-making process operates in practice can effectively preclude ways in which these uncertainties may be reduced. Uncertainties thereby become compounded[10] (Friend and Jessop, 1976). On the role of the planners, Friend and Jessop point out that their powerful role in urban decision-making means that they can exercise considerable discretion in reducing the level of uncertainty by pre-judgement about alternatives and the acceptance of assumptions which they may prefer to be implicit and covert. This can happen to such a degree that only a single recommendation may be preferred, or at most a very limited set of alternatives, and guidance to the decision makers may have restrictive sectoral consequences.

With these cautionary comments in mind, we first turn to consider some basic theory upon which planners have attempted to generate their plans and policies more effectively and conclude with a discussion of the past fifteen years or so of Structure Planning experience.

Decision theory

Decision theory is a formalization of the problem involved in making optimal choice in a given situation[11] (Arrow, 1964). Though the strict application of decision theory to urban planning is somewhat problematical, its conceptual framework is useful because it helps to clarify the requirements for decision making, both for the planning process as a whole, and for its various constituent parts. For example, the theory emphasizes the essential act of choosing; the necessity to clarify options; to evaluate the possible outcomes; and to blend these tasks with the various probabilities with which the constituent events may occur. Broadly, then, decision theory makes clear the need for three positions to be defined: (i) a position of knowledge as to possible options; (ii) a definition of values associated with those options; (iii) a way of dealing with uncertainty. This final point is crucial for the 'correct' decision in any context must ultimately be dependent upon the set of (probably) transient values associated with the various options. In short, decisions will always be less than optimal not only because of imperfections in the decision-making process, but inevitably due to the passage of time.

A decision-theory approach, then, is about making an assessment of the likely outcome of selecting the various possibilities among particular courses of action. Some of these may be obvious and easy to predict; some difficult; some desirable and some undesirable; some exclusive; some compounding; some will inhibit other possibilities and some will increase the opportunity for other future possibilities.

There are a number of branches of the theory which are of relevance to urban-planning situations. For example, Game theory deals with decision-making situations where two or more *competing* decision makers are faced with choice in taking some finite action in a situation where some knowledge of the alternative outcomes is available. In more complex situations, the choice of a certain course of action may lead to any one of several subsequent states in such a way that the actual state resulting from the choice is outside the control of the decision maker. This can readily happen, for example, if, following one person's choice, another decision maker can influence the outcome, or if a chance event can occur, or if not enough is known about the real world processes to be able to determine just what may happen (Singleton and Tyndall, 1974).[12]

Criteria for applying decision theory can, however, be quite simply stated, such as 'how certain is it that a particular option will come about' or 'if it does, what does it contribute to welfare'? It is clear that the first step in this process is to find some way to maximize knowledge about the certainty of a particular outcome, thereby minimizing uncertainty. But further, decision theory is concerned with analysing *how* appropriate choices can be made in situations where alternatives actually exist. This requires that some consistent form of comparability between alternatives must be possible, requiring measurements both of facts and values, and the ability to relate these to the future uncertainties. The main decision-making objective, then, is to remove as much ambiguity as possible by analysis, prediction and evaluation leaving a minimal residual uncertainty which has to be accepted as in the nature of the human world. Shortly, we discuss how improvements to traditional 'design' methods and the application of 'strategic choice' to urban plan and policy making have built upon the principles of decision theory. Before doing so, it is appropriate to introduce briefly the basic concepts of decision models.

The single most widely used model framework is the decision tree. Assume an urban system comprising just two elements, such as land use and transportation, and that there exist just three new development possibilities for urban expansion, (i) continuous expansion, (ii) nucleated expansion and (iii) star-shaped expansion, and two possibilities for transportation: (i) a radial highway pattern and (ii) a grid highway pattern. The whole development situation can be summarized as figure 2.1, and the decision tree describing these various possibilities can be readily set out.

Such a system can clearly be extended, and each combinatorial possibility can be uniquely identified.[13] Even with few variables the number of possible outcomes increases rapidly so that, with say, 4 elements and 4 options for each, there are 256 options. In practical terms, real decision areas will usually be more complex than this and an obvious need is to focus attention systematically in some way onto the feasible options which can be subject to research and analysis, prediction and evaluation. It is likely, for example, that some outcomes will be infeasible because of inbuilt conflict among the elements.

In figure 2.1 the assumption has been made that the choice over each step in the tree (or 'policy option graph') is independent of the others. In practice, in a social context this will rarely be so. For example, improving access to a given area through road development will normally tend to increase development pressure on land. Factors or issues may be linked causally, or functionally, or even inversely to each other. Moreover the nature of those linkages may be due to political, economic, technological or social reasons. In fact, it is often the knowledge of the nature of these links which enables an important reduction to be made in the number of options which need to be systematically evaluated, and to do this it is not even necessary to fully understand the causes of these links. Historical study of the patterns is vital however, for it can reveal particular persistent combinations of events. Research may not be able to suggest why this is so, but will suggest, that, in the absence of change in policies or circumstances, they are most likely to persist, and simple probabilistic statements can be made about that likelihood.

It is ideal if these can be stated formally, for example on a scale from absolute certainty of an event happening ($p = 1$), to an absolute certainty of

Figure 2.1 Decision tree of development alternatives

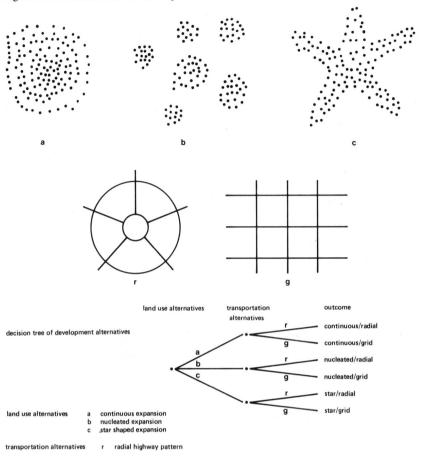

From Krueckeberg and Silvers (1974: 64–5)

it not happening ($p = 0$).[14] If q represents the probability of non-occurrence then $p+q$ will always be equal to 1. Moreover the laws of probability state that for any two or more consecutive occurrences, their combined probabilities will be the product of the probabilities of the separate occurrences. This principle allows us to extend the concept of the decision tree.

Assume that, through empirical study of consumer preference covering two possible dwelling types (A or B), two levels of housing density (high (H) or low (L)) and two different site layouts (mixed (M) or segregated (S)), the data in figure 2.2 (a) are obtained. The *joint* outcomes and their associated probabilities can then be readily calculated (figure 2.2 (b)). The most probable overall outcome is for dwelling type A, high density and with a segregated layout (AHS). Some outcomes are clearly extremely improbable.

Figure 2.2 Decision tree of preference probabilities with and without independence of factors

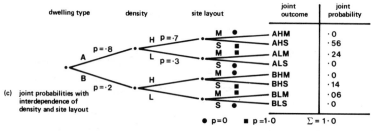

dwelling type preference		density preference		site layout preference	
A	·8	H	·7	M	·4
B	·2	L	·3	S	·6
	1·0		1·0		1·0

(a) preference probabilities

(b) joint probabilities assuming independence

● p=·4   ■ p=·6   Σ=1·0

(c) joint probabilities with interdependence of density and site layout

● p=0   ■ p=1·0   Σ=1·0

After Krueckeberg and Silvers (1974: 71, 73)

We have, however, assumed independence of the decision stages. But supposing that it were known, that site layout preference is not independent of density preference, so that a choice of a mixed layout is *conditional* upon, say, a choice of low density. Such interaction can be represented in a simple binary matrix, as

		Site layout	
		Mixed (M)	Segregated (S)
Density	High (H)	0	1
	Low (L)	1	0

and the decision tree can then be modified to take into account this new information (figure 2.2 (c)). The immediate effect is to reduce the number of 'feasible' outcomes and, in this case, to increase the certainty of the most probable outcome. What are the implications? First, that the tree is a useful way of setting out an alternative set of policy combinations which can help focus attention onto most likely or most plausible outcomes. Second, that if information is available on the frequency of an event, or on the preference of one strategy as against another, a probabilistic approach becomes possible and so reduces the complexity of the number of alternatives that must be evaluated. It is important, however, to note that the *order* in which the policy choices are set out in such a tree, where interdependence is assumed, is itself making an assumption of a dependent relationship structure among the choices. An alternative ordering of the choices will produce a different set of outcomes, and empirical knowledge will certainly be required as to the validity with which the real world structure is embodied in the model. Although, ideally, probabilities are expressed in numerical terms, this will not always be so. In Part 3 of the text we discuss how the general decision tree approach can nevertheless provide useful guidance in policy analysis even though full quantification is not possible.

Turning now to deal more practically with the ways in which planners have sought to systematize the generation of urban plans and policies, we can distinguish two broad approaches. They can be regarded as general methods. The first has been a systematic development of the traditional *design* process in urban planning. It essentially involves the analysis of problem structure in order to formulate a framework for the design of a solution.[15] The second approach, *strategic choice*, has sought to cope particularly with the inherent uncertainties in urban-planning policy making. In contrast, this approach is basically logical rather than computational. We briefly describe each in turn.

Plan design

The essential principle is to seek a better application of design methodology to problem solutions by focusing attention onto system or problem *structure*. In effect, the designer uses this structure to articulate and discover, or at least work towards, the solution to his problem whether the problem is to design a piece of furniture, house or city. In the urban context, two variations can be identified, exemplified by Potential Surface Analysis and Markov theory design process. In essence, the approach (Manheim, 1966, 1967; Alexander, 1964; Chadwick, 1976) assumes the structure of a problem to be a nested hierarchy of sub-problems. A solution to the problem is then reached by first solving the sub-problems at lower levels in the hierarchy and then by merging these partial solutions, the designer moves to the top of the hierarchy gradually solving his overall problem. An important contribution of this thinking is that it makes clear that the nodes of the structure of a problem (which represent persons or issues, or factors pertinent to the problem) in fact define the structure and that the links between them (representing a communication, or a causal relationship) define the relative importance of the nodes in the design process. Alexander

(1964) points out the implication, which such an approach makes very clear, that if two issues (or persons, or factors) are linked in a design in some way, then any action to affect one will have implications for the other and may make it more difficult or more easy to deal with the other. Such pairwise analysis will also readily identify conflicts. In this way, the relative weighting of the factors in any design can be a reflection of the problem structure and can be derived as a part of the design process itself (Churchman et al., 1957; Churchman, 1961; Schlager, 1968). The design is, therefore, fundamentally not dependent upon the preconceptions of the designer.

A useful technique is to present a problem as a *linear graph* in which the nodes (joints between links) represent requirements and the links represent some form of interconnection between respective pairs of requirements. In its simplest form, the approach assumes that the 'final' solution can be obtained by a linear synthesis of the solutions of the sub-problems, which gives rise to a 'tree-like' design process. Critics have argued, however, that such an approach too readily oversimplifies the nature of complex problem situations, such as the urban system. An improvement (Alexander, 1965; Davis and Kennedy, 1970) is to view the problem structure as a 'semi-lattice',[16] and this distinction can be readily illustrated.

Assume a hypothetical problem associated with the design of a district shopping centre. At some stage in the design just four particular factors are involved (figure 2.3 (a)). The design problem may be posed as a 'tree-like' structure, using the notion of sets. At the first stage, the design attempts to rationalize the requirements of the car users and their accommodation in the scheme and, in parallel, the needs of those using public transport and their accommodation. Later in the design these 'sub-designs' are rationalized into a final scheme. However, this structure has pre-supposed an interdependence of the factors which in reality is probably unrealistic. For the extent to which one mode of transport is accommodated would probably influence use of the other. This suggests that the problem could more realistically be represented as figure 2.3 (b). Here it is clear that interdependence of factors 1 and 3 must be resolved at an early stage in the design, and, moreover, that at the next level in the design the synthesis of 1 and 3 will affect all following stages (123), (134) and hence (1234). Clearly, the idea can be adapted to more complex situations by extension of the lattice. The important point is that the approach requires knowledge of, and makes use of, the interconnectivity among the structural components of the problem.

The use of this concept is well illustrated in the Hertfordshire County Structure Plan (1976), which builds upon Alexander's broad approach to work up internally consistent policy packages from a set of individual policies and a matrix representation of their degree of interconnectedness. In other words the approach is a structuring of the design problem which identifies a whole range of constraints and policy requirements and seeks to group them hierarchically into a smaller number of sub-sets by resolving

Figure 2.3 Comparison of (a) tree and (b) semi-lattice structures in design and problem solving

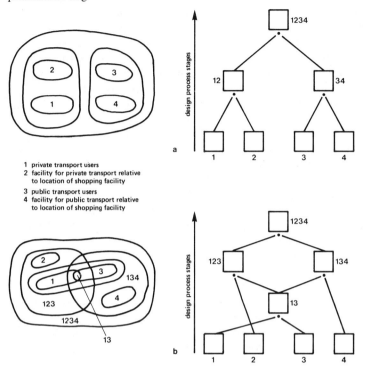

1 private transport users
2 facility for private transport relative to location of shopping facility

3 public transport users
4 facility for public transport relative to location of shopping facility

a

b

the most important areas of inter-policy conflict. Political judgement can then effectively be made to secure a preferred final option.

Potential surface analysis attempts to apply a systematic design approach to the generation of *explicitly* spatial plans. Broadly, it attempts to make more sensitive the sieve map technique traditionally used by land-use planners (Keeble, 1959). This approach to plan generation identifies the various constraints on and encouragements (the factors) to development of particular types in particular locations and plots their spatial distribution. By superimposing these plans, for example, as transparencies, areas of land *un*constrained by any factors and therefore suitable for development could be readily identified. Equally, 'sensitive' areas unsuited to development could be identified. The 'factors' need not necessarily be limited to physical features, such as land form or poor drainage, but could represent locational issues such as good access to road networks and job opportunities, or subjective issues such as high landscape quality. Though widely used,[17] the 'sieve' approach has several serious disadvantages, the most important of which are that it treats the factors as equally important in the argument and does not permit any cumulative consideration of factors or 'trade-offs' between them. The method works even less well with an increasing number of factors and is generally insensitive. Moreover, it does not readily allow the consequences of various policy options to be systematically examined and therefore cannot effectively serve an evaluative role.[18]

The potential surface analysis approach was developed (Chadwick, 1976) to overcome at least some of these difficulties in both the generation of spatial plans and policies and the evaluation between alternatives. In principle, the approach seeks to value each factor on some kind of scale from 'good to bad', or 'very important to unimportant', thereby avoiding at least some of the arbitrary, traditional judgements about factors. This has meant that local variations in the attachment of importance to some factor can be taken into account in the design process. The same argument, by extension, means that over the design or plan as a whole, *relative* importance can be attached to some factors as opposed to others. Also, by varying the weights (values) by which this importance is expressed, a degree of experiment becomes possible thereby allowing the possible consequences to the plan and policy making of these variations to be measured, or evaluated. This can be done for two reasons. The first is in order to explore the sensitivity of a particular policy to the underlying assumptions which are, of course, represented in the weights, and second to explore how different in reality plans or policies would be, if different assumptions are made in the plan-making process. In other words, planners can make some kind of assessment as to whether the alternatives that they generate really do have alternative spatial implications.

Most attempts to apply potential surface analysis start from the calculation of a set of scores for each of the factors, or issues, across some geographical grid, often comprising 5 km or 1 km squares covering the study area.[19] The smaller the scale, the greater the sensitivity of the analysis, but the greater the amount of data that must be handled and the complexity of the final analysis. The factors that have been typically used in Structure Planning are illustrated in figure 2.4. Each tract (square) of land is then awarded a score on a suitable scale for each of the factors in the analysis, ideally through empirical survey work. So, for example, the landscape quality of each tract is assessed, say, on a survey point scale ranging from 'very high', 'high', 'just above average', 'average', 'just below average', 'low', 'very low'. Almost all of the 'measurements' used in this kind of analysis will involve such subjective judgements. The essence of potential surface analysis is then to combine systematically the scores for each tract of land, to produce an overall score for its 'development potential'. Factors that contribute to that potential such as access to services will have positive (or high) scores, and factors which are thought to detract (or ought to detract in the policy-making sense) will have negative (or low) scores.[20]

In making any attempt to combine scores, some consideration must be given to the relative importance of one factor as to another. This importance is represented by a cardinal 'weight', which is derived from the objectives and can thereby be used to modify the (standardized) scores. The main problem concerns the subjective judgement required to do this.

Worcestershire

1 Conservation and attractive villages
2 Archaeological remains
3 Utility services
4 Minerals
5 Recreation and Leisure
6 Transportation
7 Forestry
8 Hospital and education services
9 Shopping
10 Atmospheric noise pollution
11 Nature conservation
12 Landscape
13 Agriculture

Staffordshire

1 Landscape quality
2 Agricultural land
3 Residential environment
4 Noise and air pollution
5 Urban sprawl
6 Access to countryside
7 Reclamation of derelict land
8 Access to jobs
9 Access to road network
10 Access to public transport
11 Servicing restraints
12 Building restraints
13 Access to labour
14 Access to shops

Stoke

General
1 Service costs
2 Access to public transport
3 Access to private cars
4 Building constraints
5 Land reclamation

Residential
1 Access to public open spaces, recreational and community facilities
2 Access to local services
3 Access to district services
4 Proximity to industry and main roads
5 Landscape quality
6 Past planning policy

Industrial-manufacturing
1 Slope of land
2 Access for large vehicles
3 Access to rail facilities
4 Proximity to existing housing
5 Landscape quality
6 Past planning policy

Industry-service
1 Access to railway passenger services
2 Landscape quality

Oxfordshire

1 Conservation of agricultural land, forestry and mineral resources
2 Conservation of areas of historic and natural history interest
3 Access to job opportunities
4 Access to service facilities
5 Access to labour supplies by industry
6 Environmental quality

West Berkshire

For residential areas
1 Cost of water supply*
2 Cost of sewage*
3 Cost of drainage*
4 Loss of agricultural land*
5 Accessibility to work place
6 Accessibility to shops*
7 Cost of gas supply*
8 Cost of electricity*
9 Loss of mineral reserves*
10 Impact on landscape*
11 Residential environment
12 Historic areas
13 Site access to existing road*
14 Public transport parking and environmental impact of traffic movements

For industrial areas
1 Accessibility to workers
2 Accessibility to transport facilities
3 Impact on residential areas
4 Site developments
5-14 All above which are marked*

Wolverhampton

1 Access to employment
2 Loading of radial road routes
3 Townscape value
4 Open space potential
5 Residential environment value
6 Agricultural value

From Booth and Jaffe (1978: 451)

Leaving the matter wholly to the plan makers leaves much to be desired and, indeed, invites a considerable degree of self-justification of the resulting plan or policy. A better, though by no means perfect, way is to canvass opinion widely[21] among professionals, politicians and lay people as to the relative importance of the factors and the validity of the scales which are used to perform the measurement. The overall process then can be summarized as figure 2.5.[22]

Figure 2.5 Summary of development potential calculation

Obtain for each spatial tract, a score on a suitable scale for each factor to be considered	→	Transform all scores to a suitable standardized scale, say 0–100	→	Apply numerical 'weights' to the standardized scores to rank the importance of the factors	→	Aggregate the resulting 'scores' for each tract to indicate the 'development' potential

For each geographical tract, a single development potential score will result, which arguably, represents the sum of development potential relative to all other geographical tracts and which can be mapped. There are, however, problems. The first is that, as the potentials are assessed within the context of one plan-making process, there cannot be comparability of the potential scores either nationally or within regions. Secondly, the scales used in measuring each factor's contribution to the potential is linear which may be unrealistic. Third, the factors are assumed to be independent, so that cumulative potential will often fail to be adequately represented. The same point will also mean that pay-offs are obscured, that is, the extent of realization of potential in one factor may inherently affect the scaling of another. The method assumes that any proposed development will not, in itself, affect the potential of any other possible sites for development which means that the method cannot take into account the advantages or disadvantages from the agglomeration of land uses and developments. Despite these difficulties, the method can provide useful insights. For example, the potential surfaces for a given geographical area can be calculated for a base date, and by making assumptions about the way alternative policies may work, for a range of future dates. Each alternative policy can have a set of 'weights' associated with it which, by experiment, can reveal the effects of those policies. This would suggest that the method is of use both in 'generating' a range of solutions, and in 'evaluating' solutions to enable a choice to be made.[23]

When used to generate alternatives, potential surface analysis may produce a vast number of possibilities. The problem, as always, is to select from among the alternatives a few which are genuinely different to each other, from which a selection can be made. Sensitivity analysis is useful here in assessing the extent to which the alternatives are indeed independent of each other, and of one or more of the factors upon which the method is based. The calculations can be in a number of ways manipulated subjectively so that the effects of judgement can be examined. These cannot be set out in detail here and readers are referred to the cited literature.

We turn now to consider a further development of the problem structure approach to urban plan generation. In this, Batty (1971, 1974a) proposes an operational approach to design which treats the hierarchical problem structure implicitly rather than explicitly, to obviate some of the practical difficulties which arise in any fundamentally hierarchical approach to the design, whether in the form of a tree or indeed a semi-lattice. First, there is an inevitable loss of information in defining a complex problem by a simple hierarchical structure. Second, there is difficulty in the choice of an appropriate technique for decomposing the problem into its constituent parts. Third, (and in a social context arguably the most important), there is the problem of defining the relative weight of influence of each design factor in the final solution; and fourth, most design problems do not have very clearly articulated hierarchical structures.

The approach is developed from social psychology. Consider figure 2.6 (a), which represents five people in a problem-solving situation having different attitudes towards that problem, perhaps as a group of planners. The figure is drawn as a directed graph so that, as we noted earlier, the links represent the channels between the designers which are 'open', that is, operational. Thus, not every person in the group has ready access to every

Figure 2.6 Convergence of values in the design process

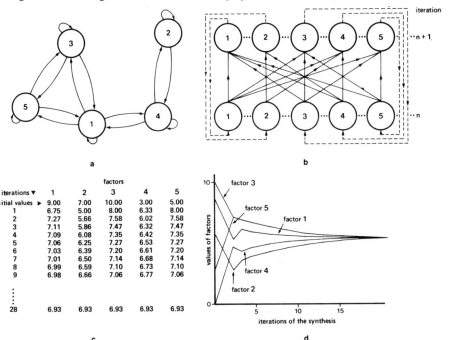

| iterations ▼ | factors | | | | |
	1	2	3	4	5
itial values ►	9.00	7.00	10.00	3.00	5.00
1	6.75	5.00	8.00	6.33	8.00
2	7.27	5.66	7.58	6.02	7.58
3	7.11	5.86	7.47	6.32	7.47
4	7.09	6.08	7.35	6.42	7.35
5	7.06	6.25	7.27	6.53	7.27
6	7.03	6.39	7.20	6.61	7.20
7	7.01	6.50	7.14	6.68	7.14
8	6.99	6.59	7.10	6.73	7.10
9	6.98	6.66	7.06	6.77	7.06
⋮					
28	6.93	6.93	6.93	6.93	6.93

c

d

From Batty (1971: 438)

other member of the group, and this would represent organizational constraints. If it can be assumed that each member of the group is prepared to compromise in his views on how the problem may be solved then a convergence process model of designing can be constructed. It is intuitively obvious, that, given this assumption, step by step, a single unanimous agreement will emerge. This can be demonstrated and proved by a branch of probability theory, known as Markov Theory.[24] The process can be simply illustrated. Figure 2.6 (b) shows graphically the communication and compromise channels among the actors, and it will be helpful to add some numerical values to this example.

$$D_1 = 9.0$$
$$D_2 = 7.0$$
$$D_3 = 10.0$$
$$D_4 = 3.0$$
$$D_5 = 5.0$$

At each step of the process, a designer takes the average of his own attitude plus the other attitudes that have been communicated to him. This process can be represented by simple difference equations in the following form, letting n represent the present attitude and $n+1$ the new attitude.

$$D_1(n+1) = \tfrac{1}{4}\{D_1(n)+D_3(n)+D_4(n)+D_5(n)\}$$
$$D_2(n+1) = \tfrac{1}{2}\{D_2(n)+D_4(n)\}$$
$$D_3(n+1) = \tfrac{1}{3}\{D_1(n)+D_3(n)+D_5(n)\}$$
$$D_4(n+1) = \tfrac{1}{3}\{D_1(n)+D_2(n)+D_4(n)\}$$
$$D_5(n+1) = \tfrac{1}{3}\{D_1(n)+D_3(n)+D_5(n)\}$$

The successive steps in the process can be traced through figure 2.6 (c) and the whole process of convergence can be represented as a graph (figure 2.6 (d)). Batty argues that such a group convergence process is highly applicable to problems of design, and can be readily adapted to relate to design situations in which there are conflicting *factors*, rather than conflict among actors and their attitudes as introduced here. Exactly as convergence has produced a 'rationalization' of attitudes to a problem, so the model can reproduce the essential processes involved in, say, allocation of land between competing and conflicting demands.

It will already be clear that, in examining the structure of problems in order to postulate efficient ways in which solutions can be found, the use of graphs is particularly important.[25] It may be helpful to reproduce some typical design situations as graphs to show the principle.

Five classes of design problem are distinguished in figure 2.7, namely:

(a) *Completely connected graphs*: Such a design problem is one in which every factor is directly related to every other factor.

(b) *Strongly connected graphs:* This class involves problems in which every factor is related to every other, but these relationships may be indirect.

(c) *Unilaterally connected graphs*: Such problems contain factors which are only related to other factors in one direction. In terms of a communications network, this means that certain messages cannot be transmitted to points in the network.

(d) *Weakly connected graphs*: In this class of problem, relationships between some factors do not exist in either direction.

(e) *Disconnected graphs*: Such graphs can be partitioned into two or more non-interacting parts. In design terms, this implies that the design problem can be solved as two or more separate problems.

Figure 2.7 Classes of design problems

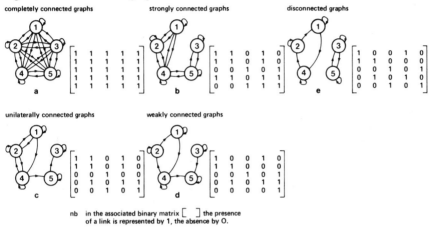

nb in the associated binary matrix [ ] the presence of a link is represented by 1, the absence by 0.

From Batty (1974a: 300)

It will immediately be clear that (a) is rather an unrealistic design problem, and that nearly all real problems will have some kind of constraints. However the type (a) graph is in fact a representation of the technique of sieve mapping and, as noted earlier, it suffers as a method because it treats all variables simultaneously and neglects the need to weight the relative influence of one factor to another. In the social world, most non-trivial design problems will fall into categories (b) and (c). The important point is that, using this graphical network notation, the relative weighting of each factor in the final solution can be seen to be a function of the *structure* of the network.

If each factor represents some spatial parameter to development, say, land availability, drainage constraint, area of dereliction or obsolescence (high cost of renewal), high quality landscape areas, and so on, then the links in such a network can be summarized as a binary matrix (figure 2.7). The Markov approach to design operates so that, at each step in the process, a new factor is formed by taking an average of all the factors which are related to it. Thus, in figure 2.8 the new value for factor 1 would be an average of itself and two other factors (2 and 4). Each contribution can be summarized as the Matrix A' and an associated graph.

Figure 2.8   Factor contributions to a design problem

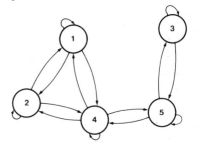

$$\mathbf{A'} = \begin{array}{c|ccccc} & 1 & 2 & 3 & 4 & 5 \\ \hline 1 & \frac{1}{3} & \frac{1}{3} & 0 & \frac{1}{3} & 0 \\ 2 & \frac{1}{3} & \frac{1}{3} & 0 & \frac{1}{3} & 0 \\ 3 & 0 & 0 & \frac{1}{2} & 0 & \frac{1}{2} \\ 4 & \frac{1}{4} & \frac{1}{4} & 0 & \frac{1}{4} & \frac{1}{4} \\ 5 & 0 & 0 & \frac{1}{3} & \frac{1}{3} & \frac{1}{3} \end{array}$$

After Batty (1974a: 297)

Each row of the matrix $\mathbf{A'}$ is, in effect a *steady state vector*, which simply summarizes the proportions of *relative weight* of each factor to the total designing process.

The importance of this to design, as Batty shows, is because this vector can be calculated for any network associated with any design problem. Indeed, the design problem need not be quantifiable as the steady state vector depends on the *network* structure, not the *factors*. Furthermore, insight can be gained into the design process by looking at the vectors generated from networks reflecting different problems and development processes.

There are broadly two ways in which this process has been applied to urban policy making, both explored by Batty (1974b, 1976a), although they can only be discussed briefly here. The first concerns the use of such design networks in the context of measuring and evaluating the (possibly) conflicting attitudes of the various actors within the planning system. In this, the 'graph' represents the inter-communication channels between people or organizations and the nodes represent those people or organizations. The application of the method analyses the design process by which agreement may be reached on particular policy issues, and ultimately can reveal the nature of power structures in a society attempting to deal with planning-like situations. The second application is to use the approach to generate more systematically spatial arrangements, by taking into account a large number of interactive constraints and potentials. In effect, the method becomes an extension of potential surface analysis. Using data drawn from the Severnside Feasibility Study (1971), Batty has explored the way in which such a systematic design method can be employed. The range of factors pertinent to the study were traditional including: accessibility to road and rail networks, proximity to labour supply, value of agricultural land, need to protect areas of valuable minerals, woodland, areas of high landscape value, land with drainage or other physical problems, and so on.

Strategic choice

This approach to plan and policy generation has been designed to confront the problems of uncertainty, partial knowledge and the unpredictable outcome of social policy making. It tackles these difficulties, in sequence, by identifying (i) the range of possible directions that could be taken; (ii) the uncertainties that make it difficult to choose a single plan with confidence; (iii) the actions that can be taken to reduce uncertainty; and (iv) the decisions which can be made so as to leave as many options open as possible.

The strategic choice model of Friend and Jessop (1976) builds upon decision theory using an operations research approach to urban decision making. The basic principles of this approach have been widely reported and can be elucidated by considering the following example.

Figure 2.9 A land development problem as strategic choice

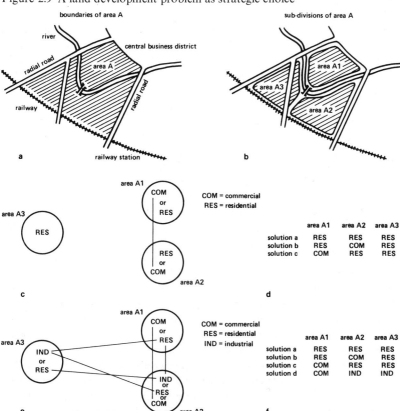

From Friend and Jessop (1976: 143–4, 146–7)

The example concerns the policy-making problems associated with the development of a hypothetical tract of urban land which it is assumed is derelict and therefore ripe for comprehensive renewal. The assumption is that the land, A in figure 2.9 (a), is bounded by two radial roads and a railway. In order to consider the possible options of allocating the land between different categories of land use, the assumption is also made that the site falls naturally into three sub-areas (figure 2.9 (b)).

It is supposed that, initially, only two categories of land use are being considered; *commercial* (shops and offices), because of demands for expansion arising from the central business district, and *residential*, because of a deficiency of satisfactory housing over the town as a whole. Assuming that it is difficult to combine both uses within the same area, the problem to the local planners is one of deciding whether each of the three areas should be zoned as predominantly commercial or predominantly residential. It is also assumed that future demand for expansion of the central business area makes it wasteful to zone more than one of the two remaining areas for commercial use.

Such a situation can be posed symbolically (figure 2.9 (c)). This diagram simply indicates that there is a choice of commercial or residential use in each of areas $A1$ and $A2$, but that the option of commercial use in area $A1$ is considered incompatible with the option of commercial use in area $A2$. In the language of the technique known as 'Analysis of Interconnected Decision Areas' (AIDA) (Luckman, 1967), the diagram is referred to as an *option graph* and the line linking areas $A1$ and $A2$ an *option bar*. This effectively bars the specific combination of the commercial option in $A1$ with the commercial option in $A2$. Each of the areas in the diagram is termed a *decision area*, in that it represents a particular field of choice for the planners – although for the moment there is no choice in area $A3$. In this initial example, each decision area corresponds directly to a particular area of land – though the idea of a decision area can be applied more widely to the representation of fields of choice other than those which are directly concerned with land use. There are then three possible solutions to this simple problem (figure 2.9 (d)).

The planners and policy makers concerned in formulating proposals for the development of the area may be able at this stage to express some preference between the alternative solutions, based on their own perception of the most appropriate system of values to be applied. For example, planners might have a clear preference for solution a, because it goes furthest towards a solution of the local authority's housing problem: however, local commercial interests might argue that solution c provides for extension of the existing commercial area and would be in their interests. The policy makers might well then be subject to pressures of various kinds from the local commercial interests, and so the planners might not feel confident that their own preferences would ultimately be endorsed by the Council. In other words, the local planners, despite their own preferences as a group within the government system, might feel some uncertainty as to the value system with which they ought to conform in putting forward proposals for area A. Planners can resolve this by taking soundings among the elected members.

However, consider now the addition of further uncertainty. Suppose that the possibility of an inner bypass road has been raised, and one possible alignment passes through area $A3$. This might make industrial development of either $A2$ or $A3$ a possibility. But suppose also that the local planners are working to a brief which imposes severe restraints on the adjacency of housing and industry. A new diagram (figure 2.9 (e)) can be drawn summarizing this situation. It incorporates four new option bars ruling out the combination of industrial development in any one area with residential development in any adjoining area. By a process of logical elimination it is possible to show that of the twelve possible combinations of commercial, residential, and industrial zonings in the three areas (figure 2.9 (f)), no less than eight must be excluded because of the various restrictions that have now been imposed. Of the remaining four solutions, three are identical to those which were considered before the possibility of industrial development arose, but a fourth solution is now added, though if the planners wish to consider industrial development at all in area A, they must permit it in both areas $A2$ and $A3$ in combination with commercial development in $A1$. This might then raise the question as to whether the planners' initial brief might have been unnecessarily restrictive, and that development of light industry next door to a housing area might be permitted, or perhaps a mixed residential and commercial zoning might be possible in one or more of the three areas, and so on.

The planners' problem, so far quite simple, now becomes much more complex. The value of the strategic choice approach is that it accommodates this complexity by allowing a full range of the policy options (or action sets) to be specified for such a situation. Returning to Friend and Jessop's example, figure 2.10 summarizes the options available. The first three action sets correspond to the options of full commitment to solutions a, b and c, respectively (figure 2.9 (f)). On the other hand, the option of full commitment to solution d cannot be available before a decision on the bypass line is obtained. Action sets 4 to 10 each involve specific land use commitments in two of the three areas only, while action sets 11 to 15 each involve commitment in one area only. Under action set 16, all options are left open and no commitments at all are made for the time being.

Which action is chosen will depend primarily on the intensity of the various pressures acting upon the planners to commit themselves. For instance, if they were being pressed particularly strongly by local commercial interests for a clear policy on the zonings of land for commercial expansion, they might be inclined to select one of the seven action sets ·2, 3, 7, 8, 9, 10, 14 or 15. Each of these includes a firm commitment to allocate land for commercial development. By contrast, if they were subject to particularly strong local authority pressure to start work on design and land-acquisition for new public housing schemes, they would choose differently, and so on.

As an example of how a tabulation of the action sets makes clear the various options, figure 2.10 can be rearranged (figure 2.11). Here, it is assumed that the planners now see some advantage in making an immediate selection of one area for commercial development, and also an

Figure 2.10 Development action sets

	Commitments now			
Action Set	Area A1	Area A2	Area A3	Solutions remaining open
1	RES	RES	RES	(—full commitment to a)
2	RES	COM	RES	(—full commitment to b)
3	COM	RES	RES	(—full commitment to c)
4	RES	RES	—	a only
5	RES	—	RES	a or b
6	—	RES	RES	a or c
7	RES	COM	—	b only
8	—	COM	RES	b only
9	COM	RES	—	c only
10	COM	—	RES	c only
11	RES	—	—	a or b
12	—	RES	—	a or c
13	—	—	RES	a or b or c
14	COM	—	—	c or d*
15	—	COM	—	b only
16	—	—	—	a or b or c or d*

*Conditional on location of by-pass

From Friend and Jessop (1976: 148)

Figure 2.11 Degree of commitment alternatives in strategic choice

Degree of response to pressure for commitment Commercial	Housing	Firm allocations of land	Action set	Full solutions available
Full	Full	One area for COM and two for RES	2 or 3	b only c only
Full	Partial	One area for COM and one for RES	7 or 8 or 9 or 10	b only b only c only c only
Full	None	One area for COM but none for RES	14 or 15	c or d* b only
None	Full	Two (or more) areas for RES but none for COM	1 or 4 or 5 or 6	a only a only a or b a or c
None	Partial	One area for RES but none for COM	11 or 12 or 13	a or b a or c a or b or c
None	None	No areas either for RES or for COM	16	a or b or c or d*

*Conditional on by-pass decision

From Friend and Jessop (1976: 150)

immediate selection of one area, or perhaps two areas at most, for housing development.

Given a full specification of possible action sets what criteria can be suggested so that a preferred option is taken? Friend and Jessop suggest three. First, the 'response-to-pressure' criterion. If an action set A permits exactly the same choice of full solutions as another, B, but satisfies the pressures for commitment less fully, then A should be rejected (i.e. other things being equal, response to pressures for commitment is a good thing). Second, the 'preferred-full-solution' criterion. Thus, if an action set A satisfies the pressures for commitment to exactly the same degree as another, B, and permits the same choice of full solutions except that one or more solutions permitted by B are replaced in A by other solutions lower in the order of preference, then A should be rejected (i.e. other things being equal, it is a good thing to go for full solutions higher up the order of preference). Third, the flexibility criterion. If any action set A satisfies the pressures for commitment to exactly the same degree as another, B, and permits the same choice of full solutions except that it *omits* one or more full solutions allowed by B, then A should be rejected (i.e. other things being equal, flexibility is a good thing, even to the extent of retaining extra options which at present do not appear very desirable). If these principles are then applied to the contents of figure 2.11 we obtain the following action preferences:

By the response-to-pressure criterion:

> reject action sets 7, 8, 15   (prefer action set 2)
> reject action sets 9, 10   (prefer action set 3)
> reject action set 11   (prefer action set 5)
> reject action set 12   (prefer action set 6)
> (leaving action sets 1, 2, 3, 4, 5, 6, 13, 14, 16)

By the preferred-solution criterion (accepting the order of preference between solutions as a > b > c, etc.):

> reject action set 3   (prefer action set 2)
> reject action set 6   (prefer action set 5)
> reject action sets 9, 10 (prefer action set 7 or 8)
> reject action set 12   (prefer action set 11)
> (leaving action sets 1, 2, 4, 5, 13, 14, 16)

By the flexibility criterion:

> reject action sets 1, 4   (prefer action set 5)
> reject action sets 11, 12 (prefer action set 13)
> (leaving action sets 2, 5, 13, 14, 16).

This process, one of *partial preference ordering*, leaves five short-listed action sets (2, 5, 13, 14 and 16). To permit further selection, these three criteria of response to pressure, preferred full solution, and flexibility are no longer enough in themselves, and it becomes necessary to make further assumptions as to the balance to be drawn between the criteria. These will certainly involve political implications. For example, what is it worth to the policy makers to satisfy immediate pressures for commitment, or how strong are the advantages of keeping options open? As Friend and Jessop discuss, these are questions whose answers probably lie well beyond the immediate bounds of the situation that has been described.

In Friend and Jessop's text, this and other examples are fully explored, together with the rules and procedures. In effect, the process is one of attempting to simulate a complex pattern of changing events and influences, which rather than seeking to find some 'complete' solution to a problem, in practice, concentrates upon the search for an acceptable partial solution, and at the same time does not foreclose the possibilities of adapting to further options when more information, or better understanding of changing circumstances is obtained. It is argued that by such an approach the requirement of flexibility in plan and policy making can be attained and can be related to the all important political judgements, yet set within a 'process' view of planning which is fundamentally continuous in its nature and not 'end state'.

In summary, this approach involves (i) the use of the AIDA representation as a means of clarifying the relationships between different areas of choice; (ii) the idea of a distinction between full solutions and more limited 'action sets' which may leave the planner with a degree of flexibility in the face of uncertainty; (iii) a method of reducing the list of alternative action sets through the use of separate criteria of response to pressures, of preferred full solutions, and of flexibility; (iv) and is a demonstration of the way in which the context of choice may be changed by the enlargement of the initial planning perspective (Friend and Jessop, 1976).

It must be made clear that the example given and our discussion so far has only dealt with a limited number of alternative options, and has not yet introduced any methodology for measuring the costs and benefits occurring to individuals or groups from the solutions. Clearly, the approach can be extended to do this and examples will be found in the cited Structure Plans. The strength of the AIDA approach appears to lie in making explicit the priority ordering of the decision areas so that the options open at 'secondary' levels are constrained by choices at the 'primary' level. This is well illustrated in the West Berkshire Structure Plan (1977). For example, the scale of economic growth will constrain the spatial distribution of development which in turn will constrain the scope for transport policy.

The strategic choice approach has been widely applied to a number of levels in plan making from local (as in the example) through Structure Planning to regional planning. We briefly refer to two useful examples. First, the East Anglia Regional Strategy Team's report, Strategic Choice for East Anglia (1974). The main headings under which the 'operations' of the strategy are formulated relate first to resources. The strategy seeks to minimize both resource costs of development and construction and its on-going public sector running costs, to minimize the overall amount of land to be taken up for development, and conserve the region's environmental resources. The second heading is to maximize the contribution which the region makes to the national economy, both by supporting the economy through infrastructure investments (roads, etc.) and by shielding or buffering the region from impacts occurring in the national economy which would be detrimental to the regional economy. The third heading relates to improving the quality of life by maximizing choice of employment through residential location, and setting suitable standards for public sector services. A related objective is to attempt to share improvements in the quality of living fairly between different sectors of the population and between different parts of the region.

The synthesis of these broad objectives through a strategic choice approach led the team to identify the choice of developmental strategies which, to a greater or lesser degree, might work towards these objectives. The report spells out in detail the implication of and conflicts within such a series of objective statements and chooses a strategy by an evaluation of the extent to which that strategy reasonably meets their objectives. Our earlier comments (Chapter 1) concerning problems and goals must however be borne in mind and this will become relevant in any examination of strategic thinking in response to goal-oriented objectives. Nevertheless, there is much in the study of a systematic nature which will be helpful to others as a case study.

The second example is the West Berkshire Structure Plan. The benefits of the strategic choice approach are seen in this study (Bather et al., 1975) as: (i) being able to marshal and organize a range of specialized techniques for dealing with specific aspects of analysis *within* the context of a coherent process (thereby enabling the outputs to be related in a systematic way). This is particularly true of scenario (delphi) type approaches to plan generation through the identification of the Interconnected Decision Areas (that is, through the use of AIDA); (ii) being able to articulate the assumptions and judgements entering into the analysis in a way which allowed them to be debated, particularly in the political forum; (iii) having the means to see the analysis in a dynamic context within which assumptions and judgements might change at any time necessitating a response in terms of the analytical framework; (iv) having a relatively simple framework within which to relate the various strands of work in a systematic and explicit way, right through to the 'policy design' process; (v) being able to start with a manageable number of key issues and gradually building up the complexity of the analysis by recycling and 'progressive reformulation'; (vi) having the means of moving from the technical, often numeric aspects of plan making to verbal expressions of policy in a consistent, formalized manner, thus avoiding undue reliance on intuitive processes in 'policy design'; (vii) having the ability to manage uncertainties not only within the *plan-making* process but also in the *plan-implementing* process, thus allowing the work to be progressed and yet identify areas where extra resources are required to examine uncertainties (this then becomes the organizational framework for plan production); and (viii) by being explicit and systematic about cyclical thinking, it is possible to reconcile this need with the real organizational constraints imposed by the need for a linear approach to much of the work. This means that deadlines can be met, and reports issued at appropriate stages to indicate commitment and elicit input from other sources at crucial stages.

In the West Berkshire plan, six decision areas were identified under headings of constraints, shortfalls, uncertainties, employment and population and finally the role of the county. As in conventional planning practice, population and employment were taken as the areas of initial focus, options were drawn up on the level and type of population and employment growth. At this early stage, councillors and outside bodies were involved in the objectives and constraints from which the option bars (lines joining pairs of incompatible options from different decision areas in the AIDA system) could be defined. In some cases, this generated the need for more analysis. As Booth and Jaffe (1978) summarize, from the restricted set of possible option combinations, a preferred strategy was selected and combined with five options on the county-wide spatial form, ranging from centralized to dispersed settlements. By the use of more objectives and a policy impact matrix, a coarse evaluation could be carried out in order to reveal the implications of the alternatives. The remaining decision areas concerned the elucidation of the detailed spatial form, and by a coherent use of objectives, development potential and dominance analysis, a set of four integrated employment and residential settlement patterns were obtained and the implications for secondary choice drawn out. In general, the flexibility of the approach allows for a number of routes to the solution, but opens the weakness of too great a dependence on explicit but informal judgement without adequate support by analysis. In particular, the identification of incompatible parts of policy choice needs to be based on an understanding of the interaction between decision areas as well as the use of appropriate objectives.

The strategic choice approach has been subject to modification for a variety of levels of decision making, and computing software has been developed to deal with the numerical difficulties of attempting to cope with more inherently complex urban and regional situations. An important development, which has achieved practical application is the Decision Optimizing Technique (Openshaw and Whitehead, 1975). This is characterized not only by extending the Strategic Choice approach into more complex decision situations, but more fundamentally, by allowing consideration of the performance of plan or policy options *over time*. In other words, it addresses the consistent problem faced by planners as to how to optimize present decision making in the almost certain knowledge that events and circumstances will change. Clearly, the frequently made assumption that a fixed strategy can hope to remain relevant over a period of time is a highly doubtful one, and as Openshaw and Whitehead (1978) comment, is based more upon considerations of convenience and expediency on the part of plan makers, rather than empirical evidence. However, as we discuss in Part 3 the need for methods by which the planners can systematically study this evidence of policy performance and its contexts, is only now becoming widely recognized.

Proponents of the Decision Optimizing Method argue that it can provide an explicit and integrated framework within which (using the military analogy) the various tactical aspects of plan and policy making can be examined and forecast, and their impacts and influences upon the overall strategy of the plan can be systematically explored. Each strategic option can therefore be evaluated, at least to some degree, in terms of its anticipated performance over time and in a changing environment. In other words, tangible information as to the expected 'sensitivity' or 'robustness' of the plan can be achieved. One broader outcome of this development is that the traditional distinction between plan-generating activity and plan-evaluating activity is shown to be spurious as we discuss in Chapter 3.

It is not possible, given the nature of this text, to delve deeper into these methodologies, and the reader is referred to the cited literature. Some final comments must however be made about the use of the systematic approaches that have been outlined. Such methods can provide only an *aid*, however important, to the planner in formulating his plans and policies and it is crucial that our earlier discussions on the nature of planning are borne in mind. Plan making is fundamentally an art which blends imaginative insights and judgement with systematic methods of analysis, prediction, forecasting and evaluation. The processes described here have proved to be useful in widening that imagination, in revealing more fully the range of choice and to help the planner understand the nature of the processes in which he is engaged. The second point, also related to our earlier discussion, is that the planning process that we have discussed has developed in an era when the 'proper' role of urban planning has been seen largely as the control of the distribution of new development and therefore fundamentally assumes a situation of continuous urban growth in order to make that control effective (Massey and Meegan, 1978). Recent questioning of the pursuance of economic and material growth, changes in world and national economies and re-distributional influences in society suggest that the traditional plan generation methods of planning may need to be re-thought or at least supplemented, in the near future. There is also a further contributory reason, which is that the current round of Structure Plan making in Britain, now almost complete, is likely to be followed by a 'monitoring and updating' type of planning (that is, a more incremental approach) which will involve less attention to 'plan generating' methods as such, and greater attention to the analysis of policies and an evaluation of their effect and impacts. The implications of this we consider in later chapters, together with the use of modelling and simulation approaches, which have been particularly concerned with the translation of generated policies into probable spatial distributions.

At this stage it is worth reflecting that planners traditionally allocate the various development activities through spatial standards,[26] largely on the basis of adaption to the existing urban structure, but independently of each other (Booth and Jaffe, 1978). This means that by assessing the spatial implications each topic (employment, housing, shopping and transportation) separately, the implicit assumption is that the other factors are fixed. This is clearly not so in reality and modelling approaches offer ways of dealing with this fundamental problem. These approaches are, however, poorly developed in practice,[27] a phenomenon which has been the subject of much debate.

A final comment in this chapter must draw attention to the problems faced by planners under the post-1968 Development Plan system in having to give much greater attention to the wording and communication of policies, rather than being able to rely largely upon a spatial Development plan to communicate their intentions. Little guidance was available to the planner in undertaking this particular task of Structure Planning and it remains to be seen how effective the various wordings of the policies prove to be when subjected to the judicial and administrative realities of a statutory development controlling process. There is clearly a learning role here which will have implications for the ways in which policies are amended and communicated as a result of the reviews over the next decade. Some further comments on this will be found in Chapter 7.

Notes

1 Not all Structure Plans go through the process of translating policy decisions into spatial (land-use) strategies. See for example the East Sussex County Structure Plan (1975), and Teesside Structure Plan (1974).

2 The case studies cited at the end of the next chapter will amply illustrate this variety.

3 The idea of inviting scenarios, in the form of intuitive or 'heuristic' statements, is widely used in public policy making fields (Kahn and Weiner, 1967; Brech, 1963; Chadwick, 1976). Scenarios enable the analyst and decision maker to obtain imaginative insights into problems, likely future events and the branching points in the decision making processes dependent upon particular choices of action. The approach is intended to overcome widely acknowledged psychological problems such as 'self-imposed' barriers to thinking; the belief that there can only be one answer to a problem; a desire to 'conform' to the assumed thinking of others, that is, by 'conforming', or even through a fear of being shown to be wrong.

4 The essential operational requirement is that the model requires a 'language' to describe the relationship between the strategy and the design or planning situation, and this is often referred to as a 'meta-language' (Matchett, 1968).

5 Also referred to as 'risk analysis'.

6 The research implications of this line of thinking we discuss later. It has lead to a variety of attempts to develop integrated forecasting systems for planners, for example, dealing with population/employment change and urban policy making.

7 A specific technique such as Critical Path Analysis is useful in applying these concepts for it can embrace general theories of decision and of welfare.

Measurement problems, particularly of welfare, however, reduce its value to urban plan and policy making generally, though limited application in more discrete 'problem' areas such as housing development and transportation planning are quite common.

8   This is, of course, a well developed body of economic theory.

9   Value uncertainties, in particular, may be *latent* – that is, they may only emerge in response to the preparation of a policy. See the discussion in Chapters 7 and 8.

10   For example, a demand for more research could drive an issue further into institutional or departmental processes and thereby perhaps preclude open 'political' debate. Demands for more policy guidance might tend to place an issue further into the political arena where different perspectives and pressures might be brought into play. Demands for more co-ordination might serve to widen the range of interest about the issue both from planning professionals and elected members, and so make it even more difficult to promote a meaningful dialogue and obtain agreement as to a policy (Friend and Jessop, 1976).

11   Formally, a decision problem comprises four parts:
   (i) choice of an *objective function* defining the relative desirability of different outcomes;
   (ii) specification of policy alternatives available to the decision maker;
   (iii) specification of a *model*, that is, the empirical (real world) relations that link the objective function and the variables, and
   (iv) *computational methods* for choosing among policy alternatives one which performs best as measured by the effective function.
   Strictly decision theory is only the final part of this process, but is commonly broadened to embrace these four stages in social applications.

12   Such a situation is the subject of *stochastic* decision theory and fundamentally involves a probabilistic approach to assessing the consequence of any decision act. Understanding of even more complex situations can be obtained by the use of simulation techniques within a decision model – see Scott (1971), Newell and Meier (1972), Ripper and Varaiya (1974) and a review of these methods in the urban context by Bracken (1978).

13   The number of outcomes will be given by $a \times b$, where a represents the number of ways for the first choice and b the number of ways for the second choice, and so on.

14   In practice this means that p must lie between 1 and 0, that is $0 < p < 1$.

15   One aspect of which is to build upon a branch of mathematical theory known as Markov theory.

16   The debate as to how to conceptualize the morphology and development processes of complex entities such as urban systems is, however, far from resolved. See Harary and Rockey (1976).

17   Indeed, the approach in general underlies much of the planners' conventional wisdom.

18   The Nottinghamshire–Derbyshire Sub-regional Study (1969), however, provides a good example of an attempt to achieve this. However, where the same factors are used for generation *and* evaluation there is a considerable danger of circular reasoning and self-justification.

19   It should be noted that the incidence of the grid mesh and the reality of the spatial distributions on the ground means that the location of the grid itself can influence the results (Chapter 5).

20   In order that the raw data source can be combined it is first necessary to transform each scale of measurement to some standardized scale. Often such a standardized scale ranges from 0–100 so that the lowest raw score value is set to 0, the highest raw score value to 100 and all intermediate raw values are recalculated on this new scale.

21   Through a questionnaire approach for example, perhaps combined with 'Delphi' methods (see earlier in this chapter) or other participative exercises.

22   The clearest explanation of the sequence of events in a potential surface exercise is still to be found in the Coventry/Solihull/Warwickshire Sub-regional Study (1971).

23   Examples are cited in the guide to further reading. The point is further discussed in Chapter 3 in dealing with evaluation methods.

24   Markov chains are a subset of a set of stochastic processes (known as Markov processes) in which the outcome of any independent trial or event depends only on the outcome of any directly preceding trial in the chain or sequence (Feller, 1968). The basic feature of a Markov chain is a transition probability, P_{ijt}^k, which identifies the probability of movement from any state, i, to any other state, j, for any sub-group k, of the population in time interval, t. It is possible to define the set of probabilities in terms of a transition matrix in which

$$\sum_j P_{ijt}^k = 1.0, \text{ where } P_{ijt}^k \geqslant 0 \text{ for all values of } i \text{ and } j.$$

Kemeny and Snell (1960) provide good definitions and explanations.

25   There is indeed a well developed branch of mathematics, known as graph theory, which covers this field.

26   These include, for example, average household size; shopping floorspace/serviced population; industrial workers per hectare (for different industry groups); hectares of open space per thousand population; and so on. Numerous examples will be found in the case studies cited.

27   A good example, however, is in the Hertfordshire County Structure Plan (1976) which uses an activity allocation model to explore the interactions between population and growth of service and basic employment (see Chapters 5 and 6).

□ 3
EVALUATION AND
⊘MONITORING

The need for evaluation[1]

It has been shown in the previous chapters that the traditional concept of urban plan making gave way to a cyclical view of the nature of the process, in which continuous refinement is the key (Boyce *et al.*, 1970). The process involves a gradual refinement from broad issues to a narrower range of feasible options. Each cycle builds upon the lessons of the previous cycle and this permits alternatives which clearly fail as feasible plans or policies to be rejected and those which appear to be the most promising to be further refined. Thus, the evaluation of some alternatives will lead to the searching out of better ones (Lichfield *et al.*, 1975). Eventually, a decision can be taken on a preferred option though this final stage cannot normally be performed as a 'technical' operation, but must involve judgements of a political nature. In this chapter, we explain the concept of evaluation and discuss the various methods that planners have found useful in choosing among the vast variety of plans and policies that they are able to generate. However, it will be clear that the 'continuous process' view of urban plan making involves wider implications for this 'refining' role and this leads to a concluding discussion on the concept of monitoring.

The conventional view of evaluation is that it is concerned with making objective assessments of particular consequences of alternative proposals. Four points must be noted at the outset. Evaluation must take place at a number of different stages in the process in order to contribute to 'continuous refinement'. Second, as urban planning is complex, there is a need for evaluation methods which do not oversimplify planning issues, and which strike a balance between the unwieldy character of too much information and the inadequacy of too little (Perraton, 1972). Third, evaluation is needed to set out the implications of different courses of action in a communicable and intelligible form so that decision makers can make a reasoned choice (Boyce *et al.*, 1972). Fourth, there must be an evaluation of the 'distributional effects' of the plan and policies upon the welfare of groups[2] in society (to identify those that 'gain' and, by implication if necessary, those that do not). This will of course be related to the resource costs of the alternatives.

It is important to be aware, however, that political decision makers will generally reserve the right to interpret 'technical' evidence on the advantages and disadvantages of alternatives in their own way (Lichfield *et al.*, 1975). This means that planners cannot assume that the particular set of alternatives which they submit for decision will necessarily contain one which is even acceptable. In practice, close involvement of both officers and members in the various cycles of plan generation can avoid this situation, but can create other difficulties. The presentation of alternatives ought to make clear the options that society is being asked to forgo in the light of the decision makers' preference, though he may well prefer those options to remain undisclosed. This touches upon a sensitive part of the relationship between planner and decision maker. What is likely, in practice, is that the planner will tend to generate only a limited range of options with little of substance about their different potential impacts. Equally, whilst evaluation properly requires a clear specification of the assumptions which underlie the planners' alternatives, he may well prefer these to remain covert to avoid doubt being cast on his 'technical competence' and thus diminish the arguments put forward in favour of *his* preferred alternative (Lichfield *et al.*, 1975).

Inevitably, then, evaluation will reflect the 'values' of the planners and politicians. Three general difficulties stand out (Breheny, 1974). Evaluation by politicians tends to be dominated by a concern with very short-term, expedient measures, and particularly those that may have some bearing upon re-election, rather than strategic issues. Evaluation by planners tends to be heavily influenced by their sectoral values and judgements which preclude the consideration of an adequately wide range of alternatives. Particular options may well be foreclosed. Third, a wider involvement of the public, through participation in the evaluation and choice over alternative policies involves some difficult communications problems and much (possibly ineffective) use of time.

Breheny (1974) suggests that these factors have inexorably led to only one land-use strategy being seriously considered in many cases. As yet there is no ready answer to this problem though, as we discuss in Part 3, research through policy analysis which places emphasis on the policy *outputs* of the planning process, rather than the technical inputs would appear to have much to offer (Barras and Broadbent, 1979). Finally, by way of introduction, we must note a further practical and very general problem. Given the cyclical, 'learning' nature of the generation-evaluation process, it will be obvious that planners cannot hope to systematically evaluate *all* feasible options, not simply because of technical inability, but because any attempt to be comprehensive lengthens the planning process and ensures that the policies will be out of date before they are even begun to be implemented. Given a dynamic environment, can planners ever hope to formally design alternative strategies in sufficient detail for effective evaluation to be done? It is frequently argued that what is needed is an approach which, while permitting a gradual refinement and 'focusing in' on the most promising plans and policies, does not entirely preclude a return to an option that might have been earlier discarded. For example, circumstances may change during the planning process; or quite probably, the criteria that the plan is designed to satisfy may change; or evaluation may shed such light onto apparently favoured alternatives that they become less attractive (Breheny, 1974).

Given that complete re-checking of all alternatives generated at each stage of the refinement process is quite infeasible, some compromise is called for. A useful approach, which is founded upon the tendency for alternatives to have a number of elements in common,[3] is for one example of each 'family' rejected at each stage of the evaluation process to be carried

Figure 3.1 Generation–evaluation process with clustered options

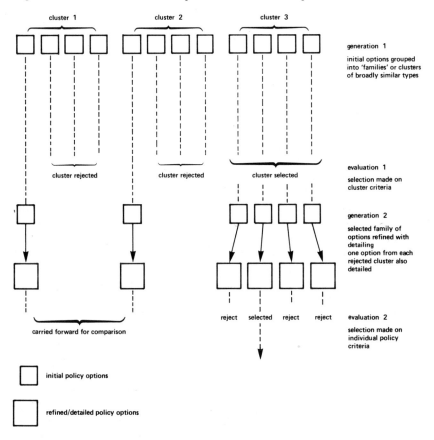

forward and included at subsequent stages of evaluation. This reasonably satisfies the requirement that sight is not lost of potentially alternative approaches throughout the whole evaluation sequence. It ensures that decision makers are made aware of the possibility of significantly different alternatives, yet systematically reduces the number of alternatives which have to be considered (figure 3.1).

Although useful, this model still oversimplifies the process, for, as we shall now discuss in a review of the various methods used in urban plan evaluation, there is a general combinational problem to be faced. This will involve trade-offs[4] between alternatives, assessment of opportunities that have to be forgone, and the need to take into account the incidence of benefits and dis-benefits that may be extremely difficult to quantify.

Traditional approaches to plan making have been frequently criticized for their poor integration of evaluation methods into plan and policy generation, so that, for example, evaluation has often been left too late in the process for it to make an effective contribution to subsequent decision making. It has frequently been seen as a once-for-all choice between (supposedly) alternative feasible policies or plan approaches (Lichfield et al., 1975). Indeed, it is a quite recent phenomenon that any systematic evaluation should be made of alternatives, for traditional land-use planning rested upon the assumption that plan design or generation in itself was efficient enough to produce satisfactory, even optimal outcomes. In order to exploit the 'learning' potential of a cyclical link between generation and evaluation it is necessary to be sure that the alternatives generated will consciously reflect, as far as possible, the treatment of the objectives in the evaluation. This is necessary in order to attempt to identify the 'best' and 'worst' features of the plans.

For this to be feasible, the objectives of the plan or policy and the constraints[5] acting upon the situation have to be translated into operational criteria, which the plan seeks to achieve and against which the evaluation can measure achievement. As Lichfield et al. (1975) warn, it is important that these criteria are established early in the process, because plan design and evaluation will yield information that will inevitably lead to the modification of these criteria. It will be clear that the criteria will normally be expressed in terms of objectives to be achieved, or problems to be solved. The 'goals versus problems' argument in planning has already been commented on, but we should note here that the contrasting views have influenced the ways in which evaluation methods have been developed. These we discuss shortly. Performance criteria, then, need to be explicitly established as part of the debate on the purpose of a particular planning exercise, and this will involve both normative standpoints and empirical study on the part of the planner.

It is in the identification of these criteria, however, that the most sweeping criticism of traditional evaluation approaches lies. In particular, that planners have rarely attempted to consider spatial welfare criteria[6] (Breheny, 1974). The concept refers to the relative advantage gained by an individual or organization because of its geographical location relative to other locations. Such 'spatial opportunities' can be readily seen in terms of job or shopping opportunities; opportunities to enjoy health, school or open space facilities by individuals; industrial linkage opportunities by industry, or opportunities of easy access to markets for products. Equally, the concept can be extended to consider spatial disutility, such as traffic noise, industrial pollution or traffic congestion. Harvey (1973) has shown

how welfare theory may be used to derive measures of positive and negative ←
income to individuals through these concepts.

In considering plan impact, it is clear that planners should be aware of
how people derive utility from their environment and the impact which
plans or policies may have upon the distribution of that utility and
opportunities (Booth and Jaffe, 1978). Proponents of the welfare view argue
that some kind of welfare income measurement is vital to a proper
evaluation of the redistributional effects of urban policies. This can be
attempted through the use of 'indicators' as we discuss later.

However, evaluation, in theory, can be undertaken from group through
to individual levels, though there is much uncertainty as to how various
methods can be applied to different levels. It has been found quite
impossible to establish meaningful sectoral objectives at a sub-regional scale
because of the difficulty of identifying valid groups with similar preferences
at this level (Breheny, 1974). Nor does it seem logically consistent to try and
evaluate a general sub-regional strategy through a disaggregated tracing of
local-scale sector costs and benefits. Equally, evaluation of small group, or
even individual impacts can clearly only enter the evaluation debate at a
very local level, where specific proposals can be meaningfully assessed.

An evaluation of distributional effects comprises four general tasks
(Booth and Jaffe, 1978). First, the choice of criteria for grouping
individuals; second, a means of tracing the incidence of gains and losses
between groups in respect of the policies; third, a means of 'weighting' these
gains and losses to reflect the relative importance attached to the various
groups; and fourth, attempting to measure the strength of preference for a
particular proposal. This task can be subdivided for it will involve both an
attempt to measure the physical effects of the plan (for example in
measuring journey to work time, improved access to a wider range of job
opportunities, or improved visual amenity); and an attempt to measure the
evidence of relative value placed upon these 'benefits'.[7] The general
'technical' problem is in finding common units of value to measure such
costs and benefits and thereby 'trading-off' the gains and losses in an
assessment of overall impact.

Among other things, these tasks imply the need for early collection of
data concerning the criteria for distinguishing between groups of individuals, the number of persons in each particular group, and the spatial
location of those groups relative to the project. In this way, attention can
be given at the earliest stage to methods of tracing the incidence of
advantages and disadvantages.

In sum, evaluation involves identifying, as well as possible, the probable
impacts of alternative plans and policies, assessing the relative importance
of those impacts (for they will certainly not be regarded by planners, public
and politicians as of equal importance) and relating these to resource needs,
costs and availability over the period of the plan. Given this broad purpose,
and the levels at which evaluation can be carried out, no single set of
criteria and no method is generally applicable. Rather, the methods which

have been developed are partial and can only be used selectively, with careful regard to their underlying assumptions, and with considerable discretion. The methods are not optimizing, that is, they do not point unequivocally to a 'best' answer, for the 'performance criteria' by which the alternatives can be evaluated are not easily specified and there will be problems in defining and measuring the incidence of benefit and dis-benefit among society.

Plan evaluation methods

Land-use planners have traditionally used a 'checklist' approach to evaluation, comparing the emerging plans and policies with lists of criteria that they hoped the plan would satisfy. This process was rarely practised systematically and the 'trade-offs' between options, and the opportunity costs associated with one option as against another were barely recognized. The checklist approach placed great emphasis upon the planners' ability to intuitively generate suitable 'objective criteria' and the decision makers to judge the overall 'worth' of a particular selected strategy. The objective criteria, though often implicit, related to, for example, the allocation of land to house the population at acceptable density standards; the provision of employment, shopping and so on; the securing of appropriate levels of amenity and visual well-being; the development of an efficient transportation network and so on. Of course, these criteria feature strongly in contemporary planning practice, though the essential difference is that the inter-relationship between their respective achievements, the resource costs, more general welfare costs and the tangible and intangible benefits are more generally recognized.

   A good example of the traditional approach, with a convergence towards a plan which maximizes its achievement on a number of conventional criteria was the Central Lancashire Study[8] (1967). This study also introduced a broad 'sieve' type approach to evaluation to drop options which performed badly and gradually refined the 'best' option according to the (independently treated) criteria. It will be clear, however, that such an approach has severe limitations posed by its inability to cope with conflicting objectives, which thus must be wholly resolved by professional and political judgement. A refinement is to be found in the Roskill Commission Study (1971) into the siting of the Third London Airport. This attempted partially to systematize the rejection of options which performed relatively poorly compared with others, by the use of a system of 'scores', and thereby objectively reduce the number of options which had to be considered in detail. However, these approaches reveal distinct limitations as methods to evaluate plans where a diverse and conflicting range of criteria need to be taken into account.

   Two general approaches have dominated the search for improved ways to evaluate urban plans. The first, cost–benefit analysis[9] seeks to measure and evaluate systematically the incidence of benefit and disbenefit (costs) from a given plan or policy as it affects a given set of groups in society. The method requires two fundamental conditions to be met, not easy to achieve in practice, particularly in public sector policies. First, it is necessary to ensure that a sufficiently wide range of alternatives are analysed in order to assume that the policy which maximizes net benefits is in fact among those considered. Secondly, in theory, it is necessary to assume that the items of cost and benefit which are included in the analysis do effectively represent all the gains and losses of every member of society whose well-being might be affected by the implementation of the programme (Chadwick, 1976). It will be intuitively clear that such measurements are difficult to attain not least because of the need to deal fully with the opportunity costs[10] of a particular plan. There are also other general problems. First, it is necessary to assume a 'lifetime' for the plan or policy over which it will yield benefits to society and also over which its costs have to be borne. This is referred to as the 'discounting period'. Second, the benefits and costs ideally need to be measured on the basis of the preferences of individuals or groups who may be affected, and objective measures of these preferences need to be derived from evidence of people's behaviour rather than from their stated preferences *per se* (Lichfield *et al.*, 1975).

Third, the measurement of the costs and benefits is a difficult and error-fraught process, not least because cost–benefit analysis is essentially a process of economic optimization, and therefore needs to reduce all items to a common 'metric'. In effect this means a money value.[11] Several quite fundamental problems immediately arise. For example, the social worth of a policy must be judged by its contribution to raising some aggregate level of benefit over a group of people, so that they are 'better off', perhaps in terms of an improved environment. Clearly, many features of plan and policy making contain elements which do not normally form part of the 'market' transactions of life and for which the attachment of a money value may be almost meaningless. Indeed, critics of the use of such economics-based concepts argue that it is precisely those elements of policy making which are important to public policy (including land use planning) because of the shortcomings of the 'free market' operations (Chadwick, 1976). Reliance on monetary values also means that an evaluation exercise will be highly sensitive to underlying assumptions.

Fourth, there are equally difficult problems of 'weighting' the costs and benefits among individuals to represent the importance that they attach to the effects that the plan or policy may have upon them. This raises the unresolved question as to whether a technique which is mainly concerned with economic efficiency, can in fact be extended to consideration of equity.[12] There is also the problem of overlapping and conflicting objectives.

The most extensive use of cost–benefit analysis in recent years was that of the Roskill Commission[13] into the location of the third London airport, and the surrounding debate critically exposed the problems that we have noted above (Lichfield *et al.*, 1975; Self, 1970). As a result, the formal use of cost–benefit analysis has been minimal in the evaluation of strategic plans.[14]

Perhaps the most basic criticism of cost–benefit analysis is that it denies the value of any kind of political choice as to the preference of a particular policy. Cost–benefit analysis in its strictest form therefore conflicts sharply with a view of planning as involving the exercise of political choice. In an attempt to broaden the application of the principles of cost–benefit analysis to urban planning, Lichfield (1962, 1969, 1970) developed the concept of the planning Balance Sheet. This seeks an objective approach to the effective evaluation of alternative policies and plans, but in a way that avoids the need for monetary quantification of all elements in the accounting framework, yet can consider the incidence of costs and benefits upon different groups in the community.

The Balance Sheet is constructed as follows (Lichfield, 1962, Lichfield et al., 1975). The first task is to identify the various groups who play a role in establishing and implementing the various plans and policies. These are termed 'producers/operators', and each is, as far as possible, paired with the appropriate groups of individuals who will be consuming the goods and services which are generated by the plans and policies.[15] Each linked, or associated, pair of producers and consumers is considered to be engaged in either a notional or a real transaction. These 'transactions' are not necessarily confined to goods and services in the traditional marketable situation, and can extend for example to amenity consideration, physical disturbance effects, indices of accessibility and so on. The balance sheet then aims to produce a comprehensive set of social accounts in a descriptive, rather than an analytical framework. As well as the 'transactions' which cover all the 'outputs' of the planning process, estimates can be made of the resource costs which are necessarily incurred in the plan and their distribution among the groups involved. Though there will be 'transactions' within the matrix which cannot be quantified, the requirement that each potential interaction is considered ensures that no such interaction is overlooked.

The Planning Balance Sheet, then, contains both 'hard' and 'soft' data, that is both numerical values and statements about the plan; it identifies the various 'sectors' within a community who are potentially affected by the proposals, both beneficially and adversely; it identifies the various consequences of the proposals and how these relate to the objectives and preferences of the sectors of society; it requires that units of measurement are made explicit where this is possible. It is argued that, in focusing upon the groups, their probable benefits and losses, and the interaction of the proposals and their respective welfare, a more meaningful approach to evaluation is obtained compared with, for example, optimizing methods such as cost–benefit analysis. The Balance Sheet, then, recognizes the political nature of planning decision-making by accepting that choice must be made in consideration of a very diverse set of elements in the 'account'.[16]

Criticism of the Balance Sheet has focused mainly upon the absence of efforts to weight the various impacts and effects of the policies upon the sectors of the community (Hill, 1972). As discussed earlier, in dealing with systematic methods of plan generation, any application of weighting involves value judgements, which are difficult to quantify and which lead to combinatorial problems in their application. However, Chadwick (1976) suggested that the explicit requirement for political judgement by the Balance Sheet approach is better than attempts to systematize the process of optimizing further, by, for example, the introduction of complex value-based weighting systems. This has been a matter of considerable and unresolved debate.

A contrast to the cost–benefit approach which essentially focuses on problems, are the 'goal achievement' methods of plan evaluation. These contrasting approaches reflect the more general debate of the late 1960s and early 1970s about the nature of urban planning. Although both approaches have common origins in the basic planning checklist approach and economic theory, the goal achievement methods represent a distinct school of thought in planning evaluation work. The basic approach is to attempt to determine the extent to which alternative plans will achieve a pre-determined set of objectives or 'goals'. Thus, it is the progress towards or retrogression from these specified goals or their constituent objectives that are taken as indicative of the advantages and disadvantages associated with the alternative plans and policies.[17]

For reasons that we have discussed in Chapter 1, the specification of general goals of planning has proved elusive and, in practice, the application of goals achievement evaluation methods has had to focus on much lower-level objectives to attain practical measurement. There are four main characteristics of the approach (Lichfield et al., 1975). First, goals or objectives are always formulated, in a preliminary fashion at least, in advance of both the design or generation of alternative plans and any analysis of their consequences. It is of course to be expected that such goals may become modified through the learning process of plan-making. Second, in practice, the goals have related to a broad range of criteria from aesthetic and environmental objectives, political aims as well as the more conventional economic criteria. Advocates of the approach argue that this means that the method is superior to, for example, cost–benefit analysis in accommodating a wider range of criteria as the basis for evaluation. The third point is that all goal achievement methods are designed to compare mutually exclusive plans only, that is, the plans being considered do represent alternative ways of tackling a particular situation. Fourth, the criteria used are invariably assigned a 'weight' which attempts to reflect the relative importance of each criterion to the achievement of the goals. This is usually achieved through a prior ranking of the criteria according to their presumed importance before any comparative analysis of consequences. However, this is clearly a meaningless exercise unless some regard is had to the different levels of objective achievement and the feasibility of measurement. Thus, the relative value to be attached to each goal has to be established in operational terms. The evaluation is then made by assessing to what extent each alternative course of action can satisfy each of the goals which are now expressed as operational objectives. It can be readily visualized that a matrix can most effectively summarize this situation, and goals achievement methods are normally treated in this form. Row and column summation can then be used to assess overall performance on each goal for each alternative. The columns of the matrix normally represent the alternative plan or policies, and the rows represent the aims or objectives to be satisfied. It follows that the objective measures of performance for each alternative are placed into the cells.

In practice, the goals achievement approach has been used in a variety of ways. At the simplest level, it is really little more than a modest extension of the 'checklist' approach to evaluation and involves a systematic ranking of alternatives with respect to the various objectives to be satisfied. Inspection and comparison may then suggest which is the preferred option. A more systematic approach is to employ some kind of quantitative assessment of the objective achievements, or scores, which can themselves be refined by weighting to represent the relative importance of the objective measures. The alternatives can then be ranked, that is placed in an ordinal scale according to their relative success in meeting each objective.[18] The preferred plan is selected by a summation of rank scores, which can be modified (multiplied) by the objective weights. However, the process of ranking makes the selection dependent upon *relative* performance between the alternatives as opposed to the performance scores on each objective.[19]

An example of this approach is to be found in the London Docklands Study (1973)[20] and is presented in unusual detail in which principles are made very clear. In contrast, however, to a true 'goals evaluation', this study is more pragmatic and represents a problem-solving approach to evaluation, but through the use of objective criteria, including maximizing job opportunities, costs of overcrowded housing and so on. In this particular study, some forty problems formed the objective criteria, for which eighteen feasible alternative strategies were evaluated including their respective resource costs.

It will be clear that any evaluation requires that the alternatives really are distinct and produce *significantly* different distributional effects through their policies both in respect of the objectives and among the groups in society who are affected. It has been a frequent criticism of planning that minor variations on a particular theme, chosen either through political or technical predetermination, tend to detract from one of the principles of good planning practice, namely the presentation of choice. Hill's (1968) approach is notable for its attention to the use of a hierarchy of goals, that is, ranging from the most general to the most specific within one evaluation, so that 'lower' order objectives are evaluated in terms of the degree of achievement attained within a framework of 'higher' order objectives, or ideals, particularly those which relate to equity considerations and concepts of 'social justice'. Also, the matrix can be used to explore the alternative distributional effects of the gains and losses which might result if one strategy is preferred as against another. In other words, the method can assist the planner to trace the incidence of benefits and costs among the specified group though, as we noted earlier, this may raise political issues which planners and decision takers would prefer to remain covert. There is also the fundamental point concerning who is to determine these preference weights, particularly if decision takers are unwilling or unable to commit themselves to making such equity considerations public.

Both Goals Achievement and the Balance Sheet are comprehensive approaches to evaluation. Each in their way, seek to either optimize or to assist in the finding of a best policy or plan according to a full range of criteria extending across the physical, social, economic and even political dimensions. Although widely used, particularly in the late 1960s and early 1970s, the methods rest upon a fundamental belief in the feasibility of such comprehensive treatment. Moreover, it is clear that Structure Plans are strategic policy documents for which no single objective criteria can possibly be found. Critics, such as Barras and Broadbent (1979), have pointed to the impracticability of these approaches and have demonstrated the need for a much more partial treatment of the concept of evaluation, placing more emphasis upon the quality of the *outputs* of the planning process, particularly at the stages involving policy, its formulation and implementation, rather than seeing the process as a technical 'optimizing' operation, however manipulated. They have also suggested that planners should concern themselves much more explicitly with the *spatial* effects of policies (Breheny, 1974). These important themes we return to and develop in Part 3 of the text.

Evaluative indicators

It is relevant at this stage to consider the concept of 'indicators'[21] by which the outputs of plan and policy making can be assessed. The approach (Crowther, 1971) is to use a set of evaluation indicators to measure various spatial characteristics of urban structure, so that the performance of the different structures forecast for alternative plans and policies could be compared. Initially, these indicators related mainly to measures such as residential density and accessibility to various urban activities, such as jobs and shopping facilities. It is these concepts of accessibility which link this approach in theoretical terms to our earlier discussion of the distributional effects of plan and policy making and the need to evaluate these effects. From the outset, then, this approach attempts to evaluate plans and policies *directly* by means of substantive content, a point of criticism of the evaluation methods discussed earlier, which dealt only 'indirectly' with these substantive and distributional effects.[22]

As Breheny (1974) makes clear, the contribution of the approach to solving social objectives lies in explicit measurement of accessibility to various urban resources and the potential it provides for disaggregating such measures to account for different socio-economic groups. Although urban development models[23] can be used to predict the outcome of various alternatives, they cannot, of themselves, judge between those alternatives. However, a set of indicators which measure hypothesized system performance under different policies relating to spatial structure can be used in both a positive (what will happen if...) and a normative (what ought to happen...) manner.

The use of indicators for evaluation have been developed mainly through work on urban modelling, though the concept of an 'indicator' (Chapter 8) has been rapidly broadened to the more general role of continuous monitoring. For example, research observations are indicators of past and present phenomena, planners' standards and criteria are indicators of the desired performance of plan and policies, whereas forecasts are, in effect, indicators of projected performance of phenomena. As far as evaluation is concerned, it is the indicators relating to the 'standards and criteria' that are important in comparison to those related to forecasts. Evaluation, then, is a matter of establishing objective criteria and assessing the extent to which the planned alternatives (as 'forecast') will satisfy these criteria.

The concept of using explicitly spatial indicators can be considered under two headings. The first is to measure accessibility (or spatial interactions) between various urban activities; and the second is to use the concept of 'space' indicators, such as density of development. Some examples (Echenique et al., 1969a)[24] of types of indicator relevant to urban policy making will make this clear. Consider a 'Social Interaction Indicator'. This could represent the opportunities of making social contacts. It can be measured in terms of distance within which residents can reach a given number of other residents via the transportation network. An 'Employment Opportunities Indicator' may represent the accessibility of employment opportunities to residents. Again, it is measured in terms of the distance within which residents can reach a given number of job opportunities. Similar indicators can reveal accessibility of services, open space or leisure activities to urban residents. A slightly different concept is involved in an 'Employment Clustering Indicator'. This may represent the degree to which employment clusters together, and is measured in terms of the distance within which employment can reach a given number of employees. Clearly, many similar spatial considerations can be represented, including residential density, cost of land and even cost of road maintenance.

For each indicator, a realistic target is set and can be used as the basis for comparison with the real world measures of the plans to be evaluated. But, in generating such indicators, a number of assumptions must be made concerning the way in which the parameters of these empirical measurements are obtained. This is beyond the scope of the present discussion but is explained and illustrated in Echenique et al. (1969b) in a study comparing three New Towns (Stevenage, Hook – not built, and Milton Keynes) with an established urban area (Reading). The latter, in effect, providing a datum for the evaluation.[25]

Whilst obtaining objective indicators for the performance of plans and policies for specific criteria is fundamental to evaluation and monitoring, attempts to extend the concept to some kind of overall index of performance, that is a movement towards comprehensiveness, have suffered from the same problems as the more traditional evaluation methods already discussed. Notably, the lack of empirical evidence upon which the 'weights' are determined and further the sensitivity of the overall scores to these weights rather than the original indicator values.

It will be clear, however, that the idea of using indicators for evaluation relates well to the 'cyclical' concept of plan and policy making, involving generation, evaluation and refinement. First, it provides tangible measures of performance by which alternatives can be compared, and therefore accepted or rejected; second, it provides measures by which any improvement achieved in a later stage of the cyclical process can be evaluated relative to earlier attempts providing that the objective criteria are meaningful and their relative importance can be agreed (Perraton, 1972). This of course is what the political input to the plan and policy generation process is about and the use of indicators offers a flexible and realistic approach to evaluation providing objective information to decision makers as to the consequences and achievements that can be expected in selecting one course of action as against another (Breheny, 1974).[26]

The approach is quite straightforward to apply in terms of the traditional spatial concepts of planning, relating to density, accessibility and so on, and recent examples in Structure Planning are given in the bibliography at the end of this chapter. In extending the concept to evaluate distributional effects there are some difficulties, for it is necessary to disaggregate the indicators in order to evaluate the performance of a plan or policy in relation to *each* defined sub-section of a community. The difficulty (Perraton, 1972; Breheny, 1974) is that, while it is fairly easy to generate quantitative indicators which can measure the overall performance of an urban structure (such as density), it is far more difficult to generate socially meaningful indicators. For this requires an in-depth knowledge of the preferences, needs and priorities of different groups and the effects of policies upon them, a point which relates fundamentally to the discussions of urban research needs and urban policy analysis in Parts 2 and 3 of this text.

One final aspect of plan evaluation which has latterly received considerable attention is the application of the so-called 'multi-objective' or 'multi-criteria' planning methods. Their development (Cohon, 1978; Nijkamp, 1980) stems directly from an increasing recognition in both economic and social theory that an over-simplistic analysis of complex and pluralistic real world problems arises through the use of 'single' design or evaluative criteria. It is frequently the case that there is no readily specified single function which can adequately suggest when a plan provides an optimal solution especially when the plan itself is trying to satisfy conflicting criteria that defy measurement. Typically, as we have seen, this problem arises in our field because of the importance of values and value-based preferences as design criteria. Equally, any system of evaluating alternative strategies cannot be very satisfactory if it does not directly face this problem.

For example, as Nijkamp (1980) has shown, a widely used, traditional measure of the economic health of a country or a region is income *per capita*. In effect, this uni-dimensional criterion is used as a proxy for a wide variety of other factors, but clearly will only provide a very rough approximation to other contributing variables to human welfare, which might include residential living conditions, or the quality of working life, access to facilities or mobility. Thus,

the increased attention to the distributive and qualitative aspects of human well-being and the call for a greater responsibility of man for his surroundings (e.g. environmental management or resource management) have led to a need for a broader view of welfare or well-being (including also non-monetary and qualitative elements). (Nijkamp, 1980:20)

As a result, during the last decade or so, there has been increased interest in the possibility of developing a multi-dimensional criterion for welfare, which might include *inter alia*, such elements as income levels, economic growth, environmental quality, distributional equity, access to and quality of public facilities, mobility, and so on. This possibility has given rise to the idea of welfare profiles (Nijkamp, 1977, 1979a), which, it is argued, can more adequately represent the multi-variate elements that constitute welfare. Also, the construction of such 'profiles' enables a distinction to be made in the way in which the welfare which might result from a given plan or policy is assessed for different areas, or different groups of people (for example, in different socio-economic strata). An important underlying construct of this process is the social (or socio-economic) indicator, which, as we discuss in Chapter 8, is fundamentally designed to overcome the inadequacies associated with uni-dimensional measures.

The concept of the welfare profile is, then, mainly aimed at providing a systematic framework within which the various contributing indicators can be coherently related to each other. By way of example, the following list represents a set of components which can typically contribute to the construction of a multi-dimensional welfare profile (after Nijkamp, 1980).

W_e = the *economic* profile encompassing *inter alia* income, growth, investments, differentiation of economic structure, consumption levels, degree of economic specialization, etc.

W_s = the *social* profile including *inter alia* the quantitative and qualitative state of the labour market, degree of social stability, social and public facilities, levels of health care, housing quality, etc.

W_p = the *physical-geographical* profile related to location patterns, residential densities, industrial location and land use, transportation facilities (public and private), etc.

W_m = the *environmental* profile, incorporating *inter alia* ecological quality indicators, levels of pollution, quantity and quality of natural areas, levels of congestion, etc.

Within each profile, sub-profiles may then be constructed for the constituent groups of a population, for specified geographical areas and for different periods of time. Analysis of the profiles focuses upon measures of discrepancy between them and a wide variety of methods have been suggested (Cohon 1978, Nijkamp, 1980). Perhaps the most promising of these, as far as urban plan evaluation is concerned, is that of *multi-dimensional scaling*, which essentially transforms the data so that a set of weighted outcomes is obtained, which then allows the various plan alternatives to be directly ranked according to their aggregate performance across the profile criteria. There is, as yet, little practical work upon which an assessment of the methods utility in urban plan evaluation can be made, though the theory has been developed in Nijkamp and Soffer (1979).

If multiple criteria for evaluation can be established, it becomes possible to postulate the use of multi-objective design or problem-solving methods for complex situations. These are also currently being developed in the environmental context (Cohon, 1978, Nijkamp, 1980) and again serve to remind us that plan generation and evaluation cannot be regarded as distinct activities. In brief, multi-objective planning models seek to solve conflicts and inconsistencies in design and problem-solving situations, where such conflicts occur at different levels among the actors involved. As Nijkamp and Rietveld (1979) explain, multi-objective decision models are based on the assumption that the absence of a common denominator (or single objective criterion) for policy making leads inevitably to conflict among the performance levels of the various policy criteria. The conflicts may emerge from several sources, as for example (Nijkamp, 1980):

1   A conflict between various objectives to be achieved simultaneously by one decision maker or decision committee (interior conflict), e.g. the aims of maximum income and maximum leisure time.
2   A conflict between various decision makers or decision units regarding the achievement of one or more policy objectives (exterior conflict), e.g. the claims of environmentalists versus those of the supporters of economic growth.
3   A conflict between different levels in the policy and decision hierarchy (multilevel conflict), e.g. diverse interests of a central government versus regional authorities.
4   A conflict between the achievement of short-run results versus long-run goals (intertemporal conflict), e.g. the divergence in interests of the present generation versus those of the future generation.

A variety of mathematical algorithms are available for the solution of multi-objective problems and these, in outline, focus not upon the achievement of a single objective function, but rather upon the marginal changes in the output variables (measures of achievement) as a result of marginal changes in inputs (the resources), and the effect of the weighted conflicts specified in the model. Interpretation of the results in turn focuses mainly upon an examination of the sensitivity of the solution or solutions to the system of constraints and conflicts and the marginal changes in the variables.

Monitoring

Within the cyclical model of the planning process, it will be clear that there is a close relationship between the functions of plan or policy generation, evaluation and monitoring. Finally, in this chapter, it is necessary to briefly discuss the emergence of monitoring as a distinct concept in the planning process and this, particularly, will set an important context for the following parts of this book. For the moment we should note a considerable weakness in planners' contemporary attitudes to monitoring. In Part 3 of the text an explanation will be given as to how an explicit consideration of policy performance should become a central feature of urban plan monitoring activity.

The concept of the rational-comprehensive planning model (Chapter 1) made explicit that monitoring[27] is an essential feature of any on-going controlling process. In theory, effective monitoring requires three functions to be fulfilled. First, there must be some clearly specified intentions set out by the plan or policy. Second, the circumstances which the plan or policy addresses must be capable of observation in some way; and third, there must be a facility for communicating information about the difference between what is intended in the policy or plan and what is observed by decision makers. In practice, then, monitoring implies the regular, deliberate and systematic collection and analysis of information (McLoughlin, 1975). Moreover, in a social context, monitoring must include commentary on policies and emerging opinion and values (so that policies may be reviewed) that will necessarily extend well beyond the limited boundaries of the urban policy makers' agency, for example into the housing, education, or social service fields (Vickers, 1970).

As McLoughlin (1975) makes clear, the demands placed upon monitoring relate directly to the mode of planning employed (Chapter 1). The incrementalist planning model requires short-term, problem-oriented information. The comprehensive model is very demanding of information simply to maintain its broad perspective, and many planners would argue as to the impossibility of any practical monitoring function fulfilling such a role (Lee, 1973). 'Mixed scanning' offers a more realistic position, demanding two kinds of information from monitoring. First, a continuous and course-grained look at a necessarily small range of matters which are judged to be particularly relevant to the plan or policy. Second, a set of deeper studies of issues which are judged to be important from time to time.

It is suggested that the credibility of strategic planning as a concept will be revealed by the effectiveness of its monitoring abilities. As Haynes (1974) points out,

> while the quality of planning could once be legitimately judged in terms of its physical outcomes as such...the shift in emphasis towards a continuous and adaptive process-oriented mode demands that its validation be sought in operational flexibility. The effectiveness of a planning system must be judged by its *continuing* ability to influence change towards desired ends, *and its responsiveness to pressures to alter those ends* in conformity with evolving societal goals [italics added].

Effective implementation is clearly crucial, but more so the need to learn through monitoring from the attempt to implement policy and thereby subsequently adapt policy to on-going objectives.

There is, as yet, relatively little systematic guidance available to planners on how monitoring might be carried out, though Haynes (1974), Harris and Scott (1974) and Floyd (1978) have provided useful reviews of underlying concepts and there is a small body of operational literature.[28] Official guidance has been very limited, for example the 1971 Act does not mention monitoring at all, simply placing a duty on a local planning authority 'to keep under review...matters which may be expected to affect the development of their area or the planning of its development' (section 6(i)) and the Development Plans Manual[29] provides little further guidance other than to offer that monitoring is 'continual survey aimed at discovering and measuring significant deviation from a plan and its underlying assumptions'. The general tenet of government advice is very much one of advising against the setting-up of expensive or sophisticated systems of monitoring, and it is very much up to local planning authorities to devise an effective framework for their monitoring programmes.

However, certain principles to guide the development of these programmes can be set down at this stage. The first requirement is that monitoring must relate to the stated objectives or the purposes of the plan or policy. Here, immediately there is a major difficulty, in that many Structure Plans for example appear to have been prepared without effective monitoring in mind. This is despite clear advice from central government (Department of the Environment, 1977b)[30] which makes the single point that 'policies and general proposals should be expressed in a form which *will facilitate* monitoring and review'. One difficulty is that the policy statements are often worded so as not to create inflexibility, but it then becomes extremely difficult to establish the effective criteria upon which monitoring can focus. A potentially greater difficulty is that many policies are political in their nature and therefore the monitoring function itself may require normative positions to be adopted. Indeed, this point begs the fundamental question about the whole nature of control which, through the political system, strategic planning is actually 'allowed' to achieve. Different political considerations will clearly permit or inhibit different approaches to monitoring, a point we discuss later in Part 3.

The second requirement is that monitoring must relate to the substantive issues with which the plan and policy is concerned. Here topics such as population change, employment and industrial change will be familiar enough and their measurement will present fewer difficulties though the need for *comparative* study must be an over-riding concern in the collection of data, and will require constancy in the definition of variables and terms, and so on. The third requirement of monitoring is that it must relate to the artifacts that the plans or policies have sought to develop or provide, including, for example, such 'indicators' as the number of houses built. These are sometimes referred to as the 'inputs' of the policy effectuation (Batey and Breheny, 1978a) and the difficulty to be faced here is one of establishing some form of common currency to enable comparative study to be carried out, and to make an assessment of achievements. Financial accounting frameworks will probably provide the most systematic methodological basis. The fourth requirement of monitoring is almost certainly the most problematical, for monitoring must relate to the 'benefits' (or the 'dis-benefits') that are received by the subjects of the plans or policies. These will comprise, for example, residents (both as individuals and groups), industrialists and so on. These benefits may be usefully referred to as 'outputs' and their assessment will involve the use of social indicators[31] and welfare criteria. The idea of linking such monitoring programmes to community performance surveys is being explored (Mobbs, 1975; Floyd, 1978) and this is one example where a technique already practised in the plan-generating process may prove to be helpful. The main point to be made under this requirement is that monitoring and participation are closely related, and that effective participation programmes will increase the relevance of monitoring. It follows then, that monitoring, through these programmes, will almost certainly require a greater effort in field involvement by planners than did the plan generation participative programmes.

The fifth requirement is that monitoring must relate to the way in which the strategic land-use planning policies and their implementation will interact, in turn, with the resource allocation policies in fields firstly such as Transportation and Housing (TPPs and HIPs), and secondly, to local investment programmes, for example, in dealing with industrial policy and development. This point can be extended to suggest that monitoring should be concerned with learning about the nature and efficacy of the *linkages* between the various agencies responsible for strategy and resource allocation (Thompson, 1975), and this has already been the focus of some forward thinking about the nature of monitoring.[32]

The sixth and final requirement, and in some ways the most crucial area, is that monitoring must be used to observe the technical and political *processes* of decision making and relate these in turn to the desired *and* undesired outcomes of the policies. This raises again the point made earlier about the extent of 'control' permitted or expected of land-use planning within the political system. It also raises the problem of conflict among the decision-making levels, particularly within local government given the heterogeneity of objectives among its departments (Stewart, 1973). This requirement has undoubtedly been made more complicated by the post-1974 two-tier planning system of Counties and Districts, adopted for most of Britain.

It will be intuitively clear that no single operational framework can be designed to cover these monitoring functions and that, like the plan-making process, monitoring will be many-faceted. This means, for example, that procedures based upon large-scale information systems will be inappropriate, for the problems of both acquiring and integrating large amounts of data would not only be expensive but, more significantly, could not adapt to the diverse objectives of the monitoring programme. Monitoring will clearly involve many different tasks and a highly selective approach is indicated. But in order that the tasks are purposefully carried out, and so that comparative analysis can take place, some kind of organising framework is highly desirable. This can only be effectively developed when there is a clear understanding of the purposes that the monitoring is to serve. It is suggested that its main objective must not be simply to measure changes in circumstances, though that is an important first step. It is rather to attempt first to *explain* those changes through analysis of the impacts to the policies through the political decision and resource allocation procedures and thereby to recognize the inherent uncertainties due to imperfect knowledge and control. It is then clear that the skills and attitudes used in plan generation will not serve this purpose.

The need for comparative study raises some important implications for the practice and particularly training of planners, not only because of the need to be proficient in social research methods, for example in measuring phenomena and assessing attitudes or welfare, but also to seek understanding through policy analysis of the effects, impacts and efficacy of plans and policies.

The discussions of this and the previous chapter will have shown that urban planners have developed a variety of systematic techniques for the generation and the evaluation of plans, and, in general, most Structure Plans have been prepared by feeding objectives straight into these 'technical' processes. This has normally, though not always, produced alternative physical land-use strategies. But, as Barras (1978b) makes clear, the nature of these techniques have encouraged definition of objectives which emphasized factors most appropriate to treatment by these techniques. Examples have been accessibility and quality of environment, and there has been a considerable danger of circular reasoning. In contrast, distributional issues and objectives, for example, as to who benefits in plan and policy making, and the relationship of factors such as housing quality or types of employment skills to social structure, have been obscured.

Later structure plans, following the selective 'key issues' advice of 1974, have given more attention to selected issues. Even so, two features stand out. The first is that the plans have been produced with a relative lack of locally based empirical work on substantive issues. This suggests that local planning authorities have not, in general, recognized the need for, or have been unable to undertake, or even initiate, on-going local research into selected issues. A particular weakness, again, is the absence of any attempt to identify distributional effects of policies. Second, an emphasis upon generation and evaluation techniques has obscured the need for greater attention to processes and methods of policy formulation within an explicit recognition of just what powers are available to planning authorities to effect change (Barras, 1978b). These over-riding needs are addressed in the following parts of the text, which, though they will not provide immediate answers, will suggest the principles and methods by which planners will be able to take a more effective role in the conduct and management of urban affairs.

Notes

1   The term must not be confused with 'valuation' which concerns the assessment of the financial value of property, etc.
2   Evaluation of planning policies cannot expect to deal with individuals in society. Even group impacts may be difficult to assess because of interactions and cumulative effects (Lichfield *et al.*, 1975).
3   So that they can be regarded as 'family-like'.
4   Most land-use planning evaluations to establish community preferences, are based on welfare economics concepts, particularly the so called 'Kaldor-Hicks' optimum – namely the sum of those made better off should exceed the sum of those made worse off. This is, however, easier to state than to measure.
5   It is worth noting in passing, that rarely are constraints in urban planning *absolute*. They are normally relative and frequently heavily value-loaded. That is, there is often only an *a priori* assumption that certain types of development, for example *cannot* be carried out. Most constraints are therefore capable of being overcome 'at a cost', though in practice planners frequently pre-exclude a wide range of options for quite normative reasons. 'Threshold' analysis is relevant here, see Kozlowski and Hughes (1972).
6   Referred to also as 'spatial opportunity' or 'place utility'.
7   A similar treatment will be required for dis-benefits or costs of others disadvantageously affected.
8   Matthew, Johnson-Marshall and Partners (1967).
9   This technique came to prominence during the 1950s as a means of choosing a particular form of an investment project so as to achieve the greatest amount of economic benefit from it. Its origins, then, lay in the context of the theory of the firm and profit maximizing. The approach was subsequently extended in an attempt to appraise the social and economic worth of large-scale public sector investment projects.
10   These it will be recalled, are the 'costs' of the possible alternative uses of the resources to be consumed in the plan programme which have to be forgone.
11   Advocates of the approach, using utility theory, suggest that such benefits and costs can be 'measured' by the quantity of alternative goods and services which would give the same amount of satisfaction to those affected. This is a difficult argument to put into practice, however.

12   That is, to the fairness and justice of the incidence of the costs and benefits of a proposal on different groups in society.

13   See the Commission into the Third London Airport (1969, 1970, 1971).

14   Under most restricted circumstances, the principles involved are widely used particularly in 'budgeting' situations. For example, cost-effectiveness analysis uses similar principles where a fixed amount of investment funds have been allocated to a project and it is necessary to determine the best way to utilize the total budget. Cost minimization is a related technique which is concerned with finding the 'least-cost' way of undertaking a particular project, such as accommodating a peak transportation problem. Applications of these methods are well described in literature dealing with public sector projects and programmes, often under the heading of Plan and Program Budgeting Systems (PPBS). A useful urban introduction is Krueckeberg and Silvers (1974). In passing, it is worth noting that PPBS is not without its critics, particularly concerning the denial of political judgements inherent in the application of financial accounting frameworks to social policy making (Wildavsky, 1969).

15   By convention, the producers/operators are listed on the vertical axis of the Balance Sheet.

16   The Balance Sheet concept has been widely applied by planning authorities, particularly in the early Structure Plan-making period.

17   The development of the goals achievement approach was heavily influenced by experience with transportation planning in the 1960s. But whilst the specification of general goals in this field was feasible (Boyce et al., 1970) the extension of the approach to broader urban concerns has been problematical. The pioneer work for the goal achievement method of urban plan evaluation was carried out by Hill (1968).

18   In practice, three types of scaling measure have been used – cardinal, ordinal and normalized ordinal (Booth and Jaffe, 1978). The first requires the definition of a precise performance measure for each alternative strategy. The difficulty is the familiar one of quantification. The second is most frequently used (for example in the Staffordshire and Leicestershire Structure Plans) in which the alternatives are ranked with respect to each objective. The theory is discussed in Holmes (1972) though one drawback (Kettle and Whitbread, 1973) is that it is neither possible to say by how much a particular strategy is better than another, nor to comment on the trade-offs inherent in choosing one strategy rather than another. Ordinal evaluation techniques tend to give insufficient weight to strategies with a medium-to-good performance against all objectives and too much weight to single-purpose strategies with an excellent performance against a few objectives. The third alternative, normalized ordinal evaluation, is intended to overcome the principal weakness of ranking (Leicestershire and South Hampshire Structure Plans are examples). Here, a relative measure of performance is attained by awarding points on a scale. A useful discussion of the methods will be found in the Stoke Structure Plan.

19   This process is well described in Boyce et al. (1970) and is also used by Schimpeler and Grecco (1968).

20   Travis Morgan and Partners (1973).

21   Or 'objective indicators'.

22   This approach has been pioneered by Echenique et al. (1969a); Crowther (1971) and Breheny (1974).

23   These we discuss in Chapter 6.

24   Other examples will be found in Booth *et al.* (1970a) and Porzecanski (1972).

25   See also a study of Cambridge by Booth (1970b).

26   It should be noted that the development of 'social indicators' is widely based. For example, see Social Trends (HMSO) as an example of the use of general indicators of social well-being intended as a basis for the monitoring and assessment of public policies (Chapter 8).

27   Or 'negative feedback' in systems planning terms, i.e. to regulate the system.

28   See for example, McLoughlin (1975), Wedgewood-Oppenheim *et al.* (1975), Riera and Jackson (1971) and Barnes (1976).

29   Ministry of Housing and Local Government (1970). See also Circulars DOE 98/74 (1974b) and 55/77 (1977a); DOE Structure Plan Notes 1/75 (1975d) and 1/78 (1978a).

30   Department of the Environment Circular 55/77 (1977a).

31   As advocated by Department of the Environment Structure Plan Note 1/75 (1975d). See also the earlier discussion in this chapter.

32   See, for example, Floyd *et al.* (1977).

☐ GUIDE TO FURTHER READING

(Full references are given in the Bibliography.)

1 The planning process

Faludi (1973) *A Reader in Planning Theory* is recommended as a comprehensive introduction to the debate about the underlying theory of urban planning. The contributory essays to this volume explain the diversity of this debate from rational/comprehensive to extreme incremental positions, and include 'compromise' arguments already cited in this text – the 'mixed-scanning' view of Etzioni and the 'procedural' view of Davidoff and Reiner. Readers will find Lasserre (1974) *Planning Through Incrementalism* helpful, and much of relevance to urban planning on the theories of public policy making will be found in the Open University Course Unit (1974) *The Administrative Process as Incrementalism*, particularly the contributions of Dror (originally published 1964 and 1968) and Lindblom (originally published 1959a).

A good introduction to the broader issues of urban policy-making in the British governmental context is Levin (1976) *Government and the Planning Process*. The theoretical concepts which underlie the making of collective choice in a society are introduced by Smith (1977) *Human Geography: A Welfare Approach* in presenting a social welfare view of urban issues. See also Walker (1980) *Urban Planning and Social Welfare*.

Thorough treatments of the theory and nature of comprehensive urban planning processes will be found in Chadwick (1976) *A Systems View of Planning*, and McLoughlin (1969) *Urban and Regional Planning: A Systems Approach*, the former more theoretical, the latter with a greater emphasis upon the substantive topics and issues with which urban planning is concerned. The rapid changes in urban planning thinking during the 1970s have been widely discussed and, as yet, no single thorough treatment discussing this period of development is available. However, a review by Batey and Breheny (1978a and 1978b) provides many insights in respect of the development and use of methods with extensive referencing.

Literature describing the statutory and non-statutory context of urban planning is readily available together with the many discussions of the conflicts and tensions that arise in attempting to satisfy the conflicting requirements of a statutory planning system. These include the requirement for central approval of Development Plans, and the desire by planning authorities to achieve, at the same time, an adaptive and flexible system of plans and clearly specified, unambiguous and consistent advice to guide the development process. See particularly Cullingworth (1979a) *Town and Country Planning in Britain*, and papers by Boynton (1979) *Planning Policy – Its Formation and Implementation*, Eddison (1971) *Statutory Conflict*, Bor (1974) *The Town and Country Planning Act 1968*, and Smart (1977) *The Future of Development Plans*. Cullingworth (1979a) op. cit., also provides an excellent summary of official advice, statutes and most important circulars, etc. A collection of short papers on the history of statutory Town and Country Planning (1909–1971) can be found in the May 1974 edition of the Journal of the Royal Town Planning Institute.

2   Designs and plan generation

On the application of human thinking processes to problem solving in general De Bono (1971) *The Mechanism of Mind* and Polya (1957) *How to Solve It* are good introductions. A wide variety of intuitive and systematic approaches to 'planning' the future are discussed in two texts by Jantsch (1967) *Technological Forecasting in Perspective* and (1969) *Perspectives of Planning*. The use of Delphi methods of forecasting future urban change is well illustrated in Hall (1973) *Urban Europe 2000: Progress of a Research Project*. A further collection of papers are: *Hall* (1974) *Futurology: Planners, Forecasts, The Public and The Future*; Vickers (1974) *Projections, Predictions, Models and Policies*, and Earwicker (1974) *The Future of Planning: An Exploration Using Future Techniques*, all in the Journal of the Royal Town Planning Institute (1974) 60, no. 4.

Texts dealing with 'Delphi' and related methods are Delbecq *et al.*, (1975) *Group Techniques for Program Planning*, and Linstone and Turoff (1975) *The Delphi Method: Techniques and Applications* (see also the Guide to further reading in Part 3). Case studies are given in Sackman (1975) *Delphi Critique: Expert Opinion, Forecasting and Group Process*. Ways to exploit human creativity in problem solving are described in Osborne (1957) *Applied Imagination: Principles and Procedures* and Gordon (1961) *Synectics: The Development of Creative Capacity*. The subject of design methodology has a large literature and a good review which provides insights into the application of methods and underlying theory is Moore (1970) *Emerging Methods in Environmental Design and Planning*. Illuminative treatments of systematic design methods are March and Steadman (1971) *The Geometry of Environments* and March (1976) *The Architecture of Form*. Recent work in the field of large-scale systems models that relate to social situations are well documented in Sage (1978) *Methodology for Large Scale Systems* and a more advanced treatment by Warfield (1977) *Social Systems: Planning, Policy and Complexity*.

As an introduction to decision theory and the mathematics of problem solving we recommend Singleton and Tyndall (1974) *Games and Programs: Mathematics for Modeling*. A great deal of relevance to urban planners will be found in introductory books on decision theory and management by Moore and Thomas (1976) *The Anatomy of Decisions* and Kaufman and Thomas (1977) *Modern Decision Analysis*. The founding work for the Strategic Choice approach and a standard reference is Friend and Jessop (1976 – first published in 1969) *Local Government and Strategic Choice*. A related text which deals with the approach in the context of corporate management in local authorities is Friend, Power and Yewlett (1974) *Public Planning – The Intercorporate Dimension*. The following papers will provide much helpful guidance in the application of the method: Hickling (1974) *Managing Decisions: The Strategic Choice Approach*; Sutton, Hickling and Friend (1977) *The Analysis of Policy Options in Structure Plan Preparation: The Strategic Choice Approach*; and Sutton (1976) *The AIDA Program: A User's Guide*. More general reviews of AIDA and its application are Bunker (1973) *A Review of AIDA and Strategic Choice*; Bather *et al.*, (1975) *Strategic Choice in Practice*; Hickling (1978) *AIDA and the Levels of Choice in Structure Plans*. This latter paper also deals with some derivatives, though the Decision Optimizing Technique and its application is fully described in the following papers: Openshaw and Whitehead (1975) *A Decision Optimizing Technique for Planners*; Openshaw (1975) *An Alternative Approach to Structure Planning: The Structure Plan Decision-Making Model*; Openshaw and Whitehead (1977) *Decision Making in Social Plans: The Dot Methodology and a Case Study* and Openshaw and Whitehead (1978) *Structure Planning Using a Decision Optimizing Technique.* The Development Potential Approach is well documented in Batty (1974b) *Plan Generation: design methods, potential surfaces, lattices and Markov chains*; and Smith (1974) *The Use of Potential Surface Techniques in Sub-regional Planning*, with a critical review of the approach by Jaffe (1975) *Use of Potential Surface Analysis in Structure Plans.* All the texts and papers cited above contain extensive bibliographies which will guide the reader to more specialized literature.

The 'cyclical' approach to plan-making was pioneered in such studies as the *Nottinghamshire–Derbyshire Sub-regional Study* (1969) which illustrates the principles of the approach well, and there are numerous Structure Plan examples which have followed its broad principles.

Since the publication of the 1968 Town and Country Planning Act, which formally introduced the 'new style' of plan-making, there has been considerable government advice placing emphasis upon the use of systematic plan-making methods, an emphasis upon policy formulation, and the need to consider plan and policy generation and evaluation as a cyclical concept. This advice includes Department of the Environment (1971) *Management Networks: A Study for Structure Plans*; Department of the Environment (1975a) Structure Plan Note 6/75 *The Generation of Alternative Strategies in Structure Planning.* The substantive issues with which Structure Plans should be concerned is spelled out in the Development Plans Manual (Ministry of Housing and Local Government, 1970) and in Circular 98/74 (Department of the Environment, 1974b). Most Structure Plans deal with population change, employment, housing, shopping, transportation and recreation, and are generally concerned with the level, allocation and restraint of growth. Problems and issues which will be commonly found in case studies include an inadequate supply of resources, particularly land and public sector finance, urban decay, declining economic base, population out-migration, unbalanced settlement pattern. Numerous examples will be found cited in the reviews of Booth and Jaffe (1978), Barras and Broadbent (1979), Bracken and Hume (1979a, 1979b). In general, the 'shire' counties have a greater concern for the allocation and restraint over new development (for example *South Hampshire Structure Plan*, 1974; *Hertfordshire County Structure Plan*, 1976), whereas the Metropolitan areas' concern is focused upon their declining economic bases and inadequate housing and/or employment opportunities (for example *Merseyside Structure Plan*, 1980; *Mid-Glamorgan Structure Plan*, 1979).

There is generally an inadequate treatment of inter-relationships among substantive issues, though the *Greater Manchester Structure Plan*, 1979 and the *Merseyside Structure Plan*, 1980 contain examples of inter-relationship exercises, the latter through the use of social area analysis (see chapter 7). This latter is also one of the few examples of a Structure Plan which explicitly discusses the impact of policies on vulnerable social groups, though a general requirement for Structure Plans to consider 'social distributional' effects is given in Department of the Environment (1975a), Structure Plan Notes 6/75. This advice also includes guidance on the level of complexity and precision which can reasonably be expected in plan-making. See also Langley (1979) *The Social Impact of Structure Plan Policies.*

In addition to the plans already cited in the text, the following are recommended as case studies with respect to different approaches to plan generation. A broad approach through development potential assessment is illustrated by the *Oxfordshire Structure Plan*, 1976 and the *West Berkshire Structure Plan*, 1977 extends the concept to assess different categories of potential development such as residential and industrial.

The use of 'design' approaches through identification of constraints and policy requirements is well illustrated by the *Hertfordshire County Structure Plan*, 1976 and the *Greater Manchester Structure Plan*, 1979. The *Dudley Structure Plan*, 1974 is an interesting example of a systematic attempt to test the effects of alternative policies. This uses a decision-tree approach covering twelve policy packages dealing principally with choice about the character of the town, employment and economic growth. Other policies, for example, relating to services and shopping and transportation are dependent upon choice made earlier in the hierarchy of policy making.

Very few plans, in practice, place much emphasis upon the previous 'inherited' policies from earlier plan and policy making. *Teeside Structure Plan*, 1974 and the *Powys Structure Plan*, 1979 are examples where the effects of previous policy making upon present policy making is explicitly acknowledged. Grampian Regional Council (1976) is a good example of a systematic attempt to analyse 'inherited' policies.

As noted elsewhere in the text, the AIDA approach is well exemplified in the *West Berkshire Structure Plan*, 1977, *Cheshire*, 1977 and *Coventry*, 1973, Structure Plans.

For a more detailed guide to the uses of systematic methods in these Plans, see Booth and Jaffe (1978), Barras and Broadbent (1979) and Bracken and Hume (1981).

3   Evaluation and monitoring

Evaluation has been the subject of a great deal of urban planning literature, and there is a single text devoted exclusively to it, namely Lichfield *et al.*, (1975) *Evaluation in the Planning Process*. This is recommended as the next reading for the serious student. It includes both an explanation of principles and illustrative case studies from regional to local scale. Many of the texts cited in the previous section on systematic plan generation also contain useful material on evaluation, for example, Friend and Jessop (1976) *Local Government and Strategic Choice*, Sutton *et al.*, (1977) *The Analysis of Policy Options in Structure Plan Preparation: The Strategic Choice Approach*. On the emerging concept of flexibility, Whitehead (1974) *Flexibility in Structure Plans* provides some conceptual insights and the question of robustness is broadly introduced by Rosenhead *et al.*, (1972) *Robustness and Optimality as criteria for strategic decisions*, whereas practical problems for urban planners are discussed in Department of Environment (1976) *Development Plan Evaluation and Robustness, Application of an Analytical Program and a Review of Measures of Performance*. This includes a computer program for use in evaluation exercises to test for the robustness of plan and policies. The questions relating to different measurement systems and the weighting of the objective criteria are discussed in Holmes (1972) *An Ordinal Method for Evaluation* and Kettle and Whitbread (1973) *An Ordinal Method for Evaluation: A comment*.

Official advice on the use of evaluation methods has been considerable, for example: Department of the Environment (1972b) *Notes on Structure Plan Evaluation* Structure Plan Notes 7/72, and (1972a) *The Use of Evaluation Matrices for Structure Planning*, Structure Plans Notes 8/72; Department of the Environment

(1974a) *Evaluating the Effectiveness of Alternatives in Structure Planning*, Planning Techniques Paper 1/74. Directorate of Planning and Regional Strategies (Department of the Environment) (1972c) *An Approach to Structure Plan Evaluation* working note 82; Directorate of Planning and Regional Strategies (Department of the Environment, 1973b) *Decision rules in Structure Plan Evaluation*, working note 94.

There is a large, widespread body of literature on traditional methods of plan evaluation. Friend and Jessop (1976) and Booth and Jaffe (1978) both include case study material from selected plans in their discussions. On the 'refinement of plans and policies' theme through evaluation, see the *Oxfordshire Structure Plan* (1976). The generation of new strategies through evaluation of earlier possibilities is made clear in the *Leicestershire Structure Plan* (1974) and the *Staffordshire Structure Plan* (1974). On the approach to objective achievement, the *Norfolk Structure Plan* (1977) illustrates a broad, informal approach; the *Teeside Structure Plan* (1974) illustrates an approach based on a clearly identified set of issues and the *Dudley Structure Plan* (1974) a similar approach placing greater emphasis upon constraints. Practical material relating to the problems of obtaining objective measures and scaling can be found as follows. Cardinal measures are used in the *Staffordshire Structure Plan* (1974), and the more frequently used ordinal evaluation is illustrated by the *Stoke-on-Trent Structure Plan* (1974), *Leicestershire Structure Plan* (1974). The use of normalized ordinal evaluation is illustrated in the *South Hampshire Structure Plan* (1974). In Sutton *et al.* (1977) *The Analysis of Policy Options in Structure Plan Preparation*, there is a good account of the potential for the evaluation and refinement of strategic options though, as we comment in Part 3, there is so little known about the probable performance and durability of policies that *any* systematic analysis is problematical. A guide to the attitudes of planners towards the different use of methods in the face of economic decline is Batey (1978) *Factors Affecting the Choice of Strategic Planning Methodology in a Stagnating Metropolitan Area: A Case Study for Gtr. Manchester*. Other relevant references on this theme will be found in the guides to further reading in Part 3.

Recent work in the field of multi-objective and multi-criteria plan design and evaluation is clearly set out in Cohon (1978) *Multi-objective programming and planning*, Van Delft and Nijkamp (1977) *Multi-criteria Analysis and Regional Decision Making*; while Nijkamp (1980) *Environmental Policy Analysis: Operations Methods and Models* is a more advanced treatment.

PART TWO

METHODS FOR URBAN RESEARCH

☐ INTRODUCTION

In the preparation of Structure Plans, local planning authorities have largely drawn upon data obtained through 'national' agencies. These include various government ministries, particularly for data published in respect of industrial development and employment, and transportation, and other government agencies such as OPCS,[1] notably for data on population distribution and change, migration, housing and household composition, and so on. These data are used mainly at an aggregate level and, indeed, are produced to serve a wide variety of purposes. To obtain greater detail it is necessary to supplement these data by whatever local studies the planning authority is able to conduct.[2]

One traditional area of locally based data gathering is that relating to the various dispositions of land uses in an area and the rate of land development. This has normally been done through occasional field surveys though, more recently, systematic data processing of applications and consents for 'planning permission' linked to the recording of development actually being carried out through building control records has provided a 'continuous' data base.[3]

Other well-established areas of 'local' data gathering including house condition studies, shopping behaviour studies, and tourism and recreational studies. Planners gather their data from a wide range of disparate sources and the quality varies enormously. Some data may be recent, other data considerably out-of-date. These, however, are well recognized problems. On the whole, local surveys are used in a descriptive mode, from which only very general attempts are made towards 'explanation'.[4] It is therefore a matter of concern that much of this work makes very little contribution to the development of theory that can serve the wider practice of urban planning.

Several writers have noted the extent to which the supplementation of published aggregate data by local survey is unbalanced (Broadbent, 1979; Bracken and Hume, 1981), though there have been notable exceptions. Local population censuses have been conducted by a number of local authorities where they believed that the abandonment of the 'intermediate', national 1976 census created an unacceptable 'data gap'.[5] But, in general, local surveys on population, housing, employment, and so on, have supplemented the 'demand' side of planning data and information. That is, they have served the calculation or estimation of such matters as jobs need, household formation rates, traffic demands, shopping floorspace demand, recreational facility demand and so on. Much less attention has been focused upon the estimation of the 'supply' side of land availability for particular developments, and other resources including levels of public and private sector finance or the capacity of the construction industry.

As already noted, Structure Plans have been produced with an emphasis very much upon 'demand' estimation by making assumptions about, *inter alia*, population growth and levels, economic activity and unemployment rates, retail spending levels and so on. These are translated directly into land needs by spatial standards (such as industrial floorspace per worker) though many of these standards are highly arbitrary and rarely derived from empirical study. Moreover, they tend to remain fixed over time.

In moving towards the continuing review of Structure Plans, the monitoring of real world changes in events and the many influences of planning policy, and the preparation of various types of local plan to implement the strategies, it is clear that planners need to seek new directions in several important respects.

Planners will increasingly find that aggregate, published data will serve their local needs and this monitoring role inadequately, and the importance of obtaining good quality 'local' information will increase. There are several reasons. Aggregate data are coarse and do not reveal the locally significant changes in events which it is necessary to understand in order to make, and keep relevant, local policy. Aggregate data tend to be infrequently published, such as the census each decade, and cannot therefore reveal short-term changes. Also, the degree of 'explanation' offered by analysis of such data is necessarily limited because of its general and widely serving nature. In short, the need for explanation linked to policy analysis (as discussed in the next part of the text) must replace the present heavy emphasis upon mere description. These changes will also bring a need to broaden the information[6] base beyond the present reliance upon 'hard', factual data (important though that will continue to be) about jobs, traffic flows, homes and numbers of people, to integrate a more extensive range of 'soft' data (less quantifiable information) about attitudes, values, priorities, political pressures and above all, the effects and impacts upon people of the policies that planners implement.

One aim of this text is to explain the methodological basis by which this transition can be made and it is convenient to divide the treatment into two parts. First, Part 2 of the text explains how planners can improve their research skills and use established methods to maximize the quality and relevance of their local information bases. Given, however, the complexity and breadth of the urban scene, it is clear that a highly selective approach is called for, and this implies the need for some fine judgement to be exercised about the problems, issues and topics that it is *useful* to study. It also implies the need for careful identification of appropriate methodology that will yield essential insights, yet be realistic in regard to available time and resources. It is suggested that these judgements can only be made in the light of a firm grasp of available research methods, their potential for yielding valid data and likely resource demands. Above all, a clear understanding of principles will mean that valid data and information are the more likely to be obtained and serve not only a wide audience through a dissemination of results, but contribute to the development of theory about real world events. In this way, the practitioner will acquire not only a repertory of useful methods and a sufficient knowledge of basic principles to make correct use of them, but he will also be able to understand the research and analytical literature of others. It follows that a more extensive repertory of skills and a deeper understanding of correct application can be gradually acquired.

Chapters 4 and 5 deal with these principles and discuss their application to the needs of urban planning. Chapter 6 deals with the ways in which data and information can be obtained and manipulated by modelling and simulation methods in order to develop theoretical explanations about urban phenomena, which in turn can lead to an ability to predict urban affairs and thereby inform the preparation of policy.

Later, in Part 3 of the text, a complementary treatment is given to the analysis of urban policy itself. This will include a consideration of the role of analysis and research in the formulation and implementation of policy.

Notes

1   Office of Population Censuses and Surveys.
2   The increasing importance of local survey data is widely acknowledged. See, for example, Dugmore and Gilje (1979) and Eversley and Cope (1978).
3   For an example of a systematic approach to continuous land use monitoring, see Wakefield District Council (1979).
4   For a useful guide to the range of topics, methods and scope of these surveys in Structure Plan work, see the Directory of Local Authority Surveys (Department of the Environment, 1979a).
5   For a discussion of one well-conducted example, see Rowbotham and Holmes (1977).
6   There is evidence of both official (i.e. governmental) and unofficial recognition of the planning research implications. See, for example, Duncan and Johnson (1978).

□ 4
RESEARCH THEORY
AND DESIGNS

Data needs, sources and classifications

Since Geddes first formulated a 'systematic' approach to urban planning, 'survey-analysis-plan', planners have properly regarded the acquisition of an adequate body of data, suitably transformed into relevant information, as of paramount importance. The problem in urban planning is not so much the acquisition of enough data, but rather of obtaining data of adequate *quality*. It is a popular misconception that urban understanding can be achieved in some way by the mere accumulation of factual information. Rather, understanding is served by the development of, at first localized then more general, theory which can be confirmed by real world observation. Such development requires, not only good quantitative and qualitative descriptions, but also an ability on the part of the researcher to make comparisons among the phenomena, particularly over time. It follows that an absolutely essential ingredient will be that of standardization, both of descriptions and procedures, in order that one set of findings may be readily and objectively compared with others. Descriptions, however, need to be 'explained' by the use of theory, which for us will be drawn from fields such as location analysis, economics, sociology, political science and environmental psychology. This theory is not an optional extra, it is the foundation upon which a better understanding of the nature and possibilities of urban planning may be sought.

There are however, considerable problems. First, most urban phenomena do not lend themselves readily to systematic study and quantification. It is not easy to formulate widely applicable methods and the development of theory is often problematical. Analytical methods only produce valid results under quite precise circumstances, and as these are not easy to define operationally in the urban field, a close regard for the 'rules' cannot be overstressed. Second, almost every study will require some adaptation of methodology to suit its particular circumstances. The educational implication is that the analyst or planner can best equip himself by a thorough grasp of proven methods as the only basis upon which he may satisfactorily make his adaptations. A checklist approach, for example, is useful and enables selection of a method to be made from an established and well understood repertory. There is always a danger that, because of ignorance, lack of critique or sheer expediency, methods are overlooked which could better serve the purpose, or the usefulness of those methods which are used is over-claimed. But equally, it is also important that the planner does not limit himself simply to those areas of study for which established methods of inquiry and policy making are to hand. After all, the development of any subject is best served by an exploratory attitude to new fields of study and innovation of methods, through a critical approach and a firm grasp of the rules of proven practice.

The application of knowledge to problem solving requires specific, but different skills and abilities from investigation and analysis. The urban planner needs a highly developed cognitive ability, that is, an ability to perceive, define and work towards the solution of what are, by any standards, complex problems (Amos, 1973). This will clearly involve a heuristic or learning element, and a recognition of the social and political processes involved in policy making. The ultimate reason for undertaking urban research, namely to better inform policy making, needs to be borne continuously in mind.

The role of data in the planning process serves three broad purposes. The first is to secure *distributional* information. This has two meanings. A statistical distribution refers to the way in which a group of data scores are 'distributed' around, say, an average value. We may, for example, measure average family size in a neighbourhood and find that there is a small distribution of values. We would infer that there is little variation in family size in the neighbourhood. Second, there are explicit spatial distributions, such as population density, or density of manufacturing employment in an industrial region. In general, these distributions serve a descriptive purpose, and comparisons are clearly possible between areas.

The second purpose in collecting data is to obtain information about *relationships*, and again these may be spatial and aspatial. Here the possible list is extensive, but examples include measuring a relationship between traffic speed and road accidents, between population structure and household formation, between industrial investment and unemployment, education levels and job opportunity, or housing conditions and income levels. The relationship may be explicitly spatial, for example as to how the distribution of employment is related to the distribution of housing, or similarly housing to shopping facilities. Measurement of relationships serves both a descriptive and an analytical purpose so that valid inferences may be made, possibly to establish dependency of one variable upon another and ultimately causality. Simple descriptive, inferential and bi-variate statistical methods will be used.[1]

The third purpose in using data is broader and represents a more recent development in the field of urban planning. It is summarized by the term *indicator*. Here, data are analysed to provide information about various human needs or problems, such as poverty, social deprivation or stress, housing conditions or unemployment. These criteria are, however, not readily capable of direct measurement. Usually, the problem is a compound one, and its presence is 'indicated' by factual measurement of related, more clearly defined variables. For example, poverty may be 'indicated' by a co-existence of low income levels, high rents, poor education levels and poor job opportunities. Clearly, judgement is required in relating the importance of an 'indicator', however measured, to the problem to which the indicator is used to draw attention. Data for such purposes has been widely gathered in recent years both from censuses[2] and empirically in the field by planners. A useful range of approaches is to be found in the literature on Social Area Analysis,[3] and it is under this heading that multi-variate statistical methods are widely employed.[4] In general, as yet, the use of indicators serves only a descriptive function in urban planning. They can, however, be employed in dealing with both spatial and aspatial matters.[5]

To be useful, data must be manipulated from their original state of *facts*,[6] into more meaningful states of knowledge, namely information. In turn, information is refined by conscious selection and interpretation into even more meaningful states of knowledge, that is, intelligence (Catanese and Steiss, 1970). The essential tasks involved in this process are that the data must be defined and collected; manipulated by analytical and predictive techniques; classified and ordered; and interpreted as to meaning. In an urban planning situation, there will also be an important communicative phase involving planners or analysts and decision makers. It will be clear that a wide range of communicative and analytical processes are involved.

One specialized area that must be noted is the concept of urban 'information systems' and brief comment can be usefully made at this stage. Such systems have become popular in recent years with the widespread use of computers, and the associated ability to store large amounts of data. The systems are essentially management devices for storing, updating and retrieving selected data, and which can allow a variety of 'searches' of the data to be made by the analyst. The concept of the data bank is not simply one of enabling the analyst to retrieve particular information from an extensive library of data, though that is useful. Two further features should be noted. The first is that the data system, if well designed, will not only allow for frequent up-dating of information but also allow for the re-classification of material consistent with changing needs. Secondly, the system allows relevant, associated data to be retrieved for two or more topics in a way that is not readily possible if the source data remain in separate files or records. The term *relational* sums up this possibility precisely.

Data storage and retrieval systems are widely used to store land-use, population, employment, household and housing data and such systems can be directly interrogated by the analyst. Much preliminary descriptive analysis can also be done by means of package programs available in computer libraries.[7] More generally, on the subject of urban planning information, comprehensive guides to useful sources have been published by White (1974) and Catanese *et al.* (1979), and the various updated research registers of the Department of the Environment, the Royal Town Planning Institute and Social Science Research Council provide a great deal of relevant information concerning these sources. The General Information

System for Planning (1972) report not only deals with sources but introduces the political and socially sensitive issues concerning privacy and the necessity of limiting access to certain types of information. A good example is that of local authority housing and tenure records, and it must be noted that it is generally data at the household level that gives rise to the greatest problems of privacy in the urban planning context.

Whilst the data needs for any individual piece of work will necessarily be specific, a general framework is of help in developing a systematic approach. Four main headings are involved in such a framework (Catanese and Steiss, 1970). The first, *data identification* involves preparing an inventory of the data believed to be desirable. The second, the *data identifiers* is to associate a particular item of data with the spatial, personal or organizational taxonomies within which the datum will be used. These will include such 'classifying' devices as areal and grid locations, other geographical bases such as addresses, classifications of people, occupations or activities and so on. Once these are decided, the third heading will involve *data assembly*, for example as in a file. This heading, in effect, concerns the matter of flexibility. All data-classifying structures or taxonomies impose limitations on the way in which the data may be retrieved and used. An efficient data assembly design can do much to facilitate retrieval, even if the form of that retrieval cannot be envisaged when the data file is created. New computing systems offer greatly enhanced file and data handling potentials to all social policy fields where, traditionally, there has been a problem of large-scale data handling. The fourth heading, that of *data privacy*, has been noted already. As there are no general rules it can only be suggested that the planner needs to be aware of the various legal restrictions and conventions which apply in a society.

In terms of concept, it will be clear that the need to develop suitable classifications for using data pose the greatest challenge. They are indeed quite fundamental to the development of theory *and* practice in any field of study, for without them there can only be the record of individual occurrences. Using classification, an order is imposed on observations, enabling analysis to take place. Certain points must be noted. The first is that a classification system is wholly within the control of the practitioners in any field. Over periods of time, planners have developed classifications for land use, occupations, urban activities, development types, household types, housing types and so on. The list is extensive. Each has been developed because it is believed to be useful in developing an understanding of the real world. But, dependent upon its design, an existing classification can hinder or assist a new investigation. A system of classification designed for one purpose will not necessarily be suitable for another, though the advance of knowledge in a subject will generally be helped by a consistency in the use of its data and information classifications. Therefore, whilst a classification system should not be accepted as sacrosanct, neither should researchers or practitioners indulge in *ad hoc* classification according to the whims of their successive investigations and interests.

Consistency can best be served by careful regard to the rules by which classifications may be made. In brief, there are two routes, one derived from conventional logic (Stebbing, 1970), the other from set theory (Stoll, 1961). In whatever way data classifications are devised, however, it is important to note that their utility cannot be assessed independently of the purpose they are designed to serve. Neither can any system serve all possible purposes with anything other than a low level of efficiency (Harvey, 1969). Therefore devising a suitable classification in any field of study will involve the researcher in some fundamental decisions.

Urban study clearly reveals the possibilities and limitations of the two routes. In the *logical division* (or deductive) approach, a universal set is partitioned into sub-sets according to logical principles and well-defined rules, and these sub-sets will then comprise mutually exclusive classes. An example is a classification of occupations. The universal set is 'all occupations', and this starting position assumes that such a universal set is itself relevant to the field of study. Well-established criteria can then be used to guide the development of the classification (Sneath and Sokal, 1973). These criteria can include, *resemblance*, that is that the objects classified show certain affinities; or an *homologous characteristic*, that the objects have a common origin, or a common line of *descent*, namely that the objects possess a similar evolutionary history. The former is the most widely used, so that for example occupations can be sub-classified into discrete types – manual, skilled or professional. In turn, each sub-set can be sub-classified by the identification of attributes at a more detailed level, for example – (skilled) mechanical engineer, electrical engineer, civil engineer and so on. Clearly, such 'tree-like' classifications abound and form the basis of most available data. The important point to note is that at each successive step in developing the classification the properties of the objects are used to deduce a 'sensible' partitioning, and the classification which results reflects very much this choice.

As the classification becomes more and more extensive, however, it becomes increasingly difficult to correct any mis-judgement made at an earlier stage of development. Thus, there are dangers in this method of introducing mis-classification through a lack of sufficient information about the whole set. At an early stage in the development of most disciplines, such classifications are commonplace, but as the theory of the discipline develops, these classifications are often found to be increasingly inefficient, and as they reinforce traditional thinking they can inhibit methodological advance. In urban planning, traditional land-use classification falls into this category and is widely recognized now as representing a far too simple view of the richness and complexity of urban activity.

The alternative route to classification is arguably less precise, though more realistic, and owes its origins to recent developments in mathematical routines. They allow a more systematic approach and have been developed particularly in sociology and human geography studies. The approach involves an 'inductive' grouping procedure which searches for regularities among the phenomena being examined and for significant inter-relationships. In other words, no underlying structure is assumed to exist and therefore significant properties do not initially have to be known. The major difference between the methods in practice is that, in logical division, the starting point (or universal set) is specified by definition, whereas, in grouping the set emerges empirically from the data. In the study of urban phenomena, for which there is often large amounts of data but which is poorly explained by developed theory, this second method would appear to have much to offer. Typical of this approach is cluster analysis (Johnston, 1978; Everitt, 1974) which essentially involves generating classifications and typologies from large sets of data.[8] As yet, however, these methods have to prove their utility and there is criticism that the resulting typologies are highly sensitive to the mathematical algorithms which are used.

Principles of social research

In urban study, as in other social fields, a researcher faces a range of difficult problems in the use of methods, and his findings may contain all kinds of inadequacies. Without a clear understanding of these, he will not only delude himself and probably others, but may mislead policy makers into wrong, expensive and socially harmful actions. A close regard for the principles of research design will minimize these dangers.

Urban study may be divided into two broad areas. *Descriptive* investigation seeks simply to measure, record, classify and categorize phenomena. *Analytical* investigation goes further, for example, by making comparisons, measuring differences, and verifying or rejecting hypotheses that significant relationships exist among the phenomena studied. It is also fundamental to distinguish clearly between experimental and non-experimental approaches to research. It is a characteristic of social fields of study that investigation is mainly carried out by the latter. Essentially, it means that the researcher is limited to observational rather than experimental data. As later discussed, there are experimental possibilities in urban study, and 'hybrid' research can be conducted using quasi-experimental methods and simulation and modelling techniques. But, for the most part, the urban researcher is faced with less than ideal scientific circumstances.

Research procedures can be looked at from two conceptual viewpoints (Ackoff, 1953). The more traditional view is of a *problem-solving* process, though many social scientists prefer a view which emphasizes the interactions between individuals and environments, that is, of a *communicative* process.

A detailed discussion of these views cannot be attempted, but it is relevant to draw upon some essential features. In the problem-solving approach, the main concepts and operations relate to: (i) knowledge of a problem; (ii) conceptualization of a design method to investigate it; (iii) creation of a situation in which the subject is to be observed;[9] (iv) recording and analysis of data; and (v) selection of a course of action directed towards solving the problem. Some, or all, of the stages may have to be repeated if this process fails to find a satisfactory outcome.

In contrast, the communicative approach identifies: (i) the consumer (for whom the research is undertaken); (ii) the researcher; (iii) the observer (for the researcher may employ others to make the observations); and (iv) the subject(s). These headings represent roles rather than individuals and indeed may involve groups of persons.

Both approaches suggest that good research should proceed by well-defined and logical stages according to a clear design or plan and with a careful regard for the actors' roles. They provide useful operational checklists from which the specific rules for the conduct of particular pieces of research may be systematically formulated.

The scientific approach

The purpose of science is

to establish general laws covering the behaviour of empirical (real world) events or objects with which the science is concerned, and thereby to connect together knowledge of these separately known events and to make reliable predictions of events as yet unknown. (Braithwaite, 1960)[10]

A widely accepted model is that scientific explanation proceeds by creating a consistent hierarchy of statements, from *factual statements* to *empirical laws*, and thence, at the highest level, to general or *theoretical laws*. The initial factual statements are derived from analysis of data about the real world, and by following a process of logical generalization, science is able to offer validly supported explanations. It can, however, do this best for real world phenomena whose behaviour are invariate and which are therefore capable of study by means of replicative experiment.

There are two main schools of thought concerning the underlying processes of science. The first, in brief, is that 'truth resides in nature' and can only be found through the empirical observation of the world, that is, through the senses. The alternative, more widely accepted view, is that such insights provide a basis for stating what *might* be true. This, in turn, provides the incentive and a framework, or paradigm, for finding out as far as possible what *is* true. Science then, is initially as subjective and as psychologically conditioned as any other branch of human endeavour (Chorafas, 1965), but it is also subsequently a critical and analytical activity, seeking proof, objectivity and explanation. There are two 'routes' by which a scientific law can be established according to these schools of thought. One, the *inductive* route, rests upon the premise that it *is possible* to proceed from the observation of numerous particular events to generalized statements, that is, to inductive theory. This may, if widely accepted, be formulated as a scientific law, but as it is possible for quite false conclusions to be drawn, even from correct premises, the approach is often considered to be not truly scientific (Popper, 1957). However, inductive logic *can* yield hypotheses from which testable consequences may be deduced.

The second, deductive route, proceeds from some *a priori* premise to statements about particular events or sets of events, typically as in the so-called 'hypothetico–deductive' system (figure 4.1). This consists of a set of hypotheses which are arranged in such a way that, from some of the hypotheses as premises, all other hypotheses logically follow, for the essential characteristic of deductive logic is that if the premises are known to be true, then so are the conclusions (Braithwaite, 1960).[11] A weakness, however, is that the deductive system *by itself* can neither prove anything that is not already known, nor say anything about the truth or validity of the initial premise.

Figure 4.1 The hypothetico–deductive route to scientific explanation

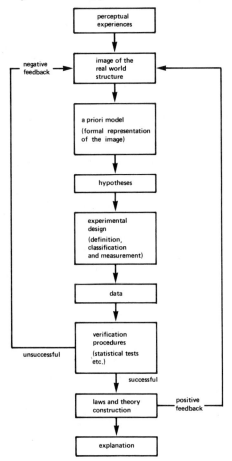

From Harvey (1969: 34)

The starting point for the deductive system is an initial statement or hypothesis, which is accepted *for the time being* as true. Even if there is no established scientific knowledge about a particular urban situation, there will exist all manner of opinions, hunches, attitudes and values which can influence the initiation of the research. Data about the empirical world is then used to test this hypothesis, which can lead to verification through the use of deductive forms of inference, but only to a certain degree of confidence. The data from the observations are in effect a factual statement, and several such statements related to each other lead to tentative theory, or an *empirical law* (Meyers and Grossen, 1978).

This newly deduced state of affairs may correspond to events already observed, or, alternatively, *new* observations and experiments may be required to test the deductive predictions. In the former, we say that the theory has served to explain known facts, whereas in the latter, the science has succeeded in predicting novel occurrences.

Even though it is through deductive processes that the tentative theories are tested, induction still plays an important part in the articulation and verification of such theoretical structures (Harvey, 1969). Verification is an absolutely essential part of scientific method, but theory cannot be verified or confirmed other than by inductive inference, which means, in effect, that theory can never be completely validated and, at best, can only ever rest upon the evidence available. As a result, alternative explanations and interpretations will always be offered. In that true verification cannot ever be absolutely achieved, substitution of the concept of falsification (for verification) brings a more rigorous procedure (Popper, 1972). Science proceeds, then, according to this more strictly logical view by conjecture (induction) and the *refutation* of hypotheses.

The comment that alternative explanations will always be possible has raised the behavioural view of science.[12] This emphasizes that the researcher's systems of personal values will have influenced the initiation of the research, guided progress and affected the interpretation of the results, particularly as to the readiness with which explanations may be accepted as having validity. In consequence, results can only be meaningfully understood by reference to this system of values.

In applying the scientific model to such fields as urban study, there immediately arises a number of quite fundamental issues.[13] Some of these are more theoretical, while others relate to the methodology of science. In general, there are two main schools of thought. One, classical empiricism, states that there can be no difference *in principle* between the study of social phenomena and the study of any other natural phenomena. Scientific rules and methods, particularly of controlled inference and verification, are therefore equally relevant (Schultz, 1970). A criticism, however, is that assuming the equal relevance of scientific method, it is difficult to explain why the social sciences should lag so much behind the natural sciences in their development (Ryan, 1970). Sometimes it is argued that the subject material of the social sciences is inherently more complex than that of the natural sciences and a further distinction can be made between the complexity of subject matter and concepts (Kemeny and Snell, 1972). Whilst it is commonly accepted that social sciences such as sociology, political science and economics, are more conceptually puzzling than the natural sciences, the view does not explain why social science has induced a confusion which natural science apparently has not (Ryan, 1970).

The second school of thought, in contrast, states that the phenomena studied by the social sciences are different *in kind*, not merely in the degree of complexity because human beings endow natural phenomena with some kind of 'meaning'. For example, while a particular human action may be empirically observed and recorded, the action may have been performed for a variety of purposes and, therefore, have various 'meanings' according to the actor. In general, actions are therefore capable of interpretation in a variety of ways. The aim of science is, then, not so much to establish 'regularities', but rather to establish the rules of 'significant action' (Ryan, 1970), which can explain these behavioural aspects. It follows that a more philosophical, probabilistic approach must be employed. However, a distinction as to the nature of events does not *by itself* invalidate the relevance of similar methodology, although it may mean that there will be differences in the way in which inferences are drawn.

This latter point suggests that the empiricist and humanist views of science can be somewhat reconciled by a third, more holistic, view. This starts from the premise that the theories of *both* the social and natural sciences are the products of particular societies and there is a set of socially-generated 'rules' or 'guidelines', that is a paradigm, which governs the way in which particular aspects of both physical and social worlds are studied (Kuhn, 1962). These 'guidelines' may shift from time to time, which usefully explains the sometimes quite marked changes in the direction of scientific enquiry. It also explains why a form of determinism does not take over in the study of human affairs, for otherwise, if empirical study of the human world gives rise to social theory, logically that theory should influence and hence determine human behaviour. A common sense view of the world suggests that this simply does not happen.

In operational terms, the paradigm serves two purposes. It explains the purposes of the research and further, by providing a framework (however temporary) capable of description, it delimits a study area and commits researchers to the same 'problems, rules and standards' (Haggett, 1967). It therefore constitutes *a priori* assumptions that shape the general approach to investigation by scientific methods (Krausz and Miller, 1974). This approach does not require that specific scientific methods are *equally* applicable to all types of subject or discipline, but does enable selection of appropriate, valid methodology to be made according to purpose. It follows that, *de facto*, some disciplines will be more scientific than others, though the pursuit of objectivity will be a common aim. However, whilst this is easily stated, it is notoriously difficult in itself to define.[14]

By focusing attention onto a small range of problems, paradigms permit investigation in detail and depth, though in so doing they tend to reinforce a *status quo* view (Kuhn, 1962). They can therefore stifle innovation and experimentation with new ideas. Ideally, they should be as subject to change as all other notions, and exhibit at a more general level the same processes of definition and re-definition that are appropriate for the more detailed processes of the scientific approach (Krausz and Miller, 1974). We must expect paradigms to be subject to quite dramatic change for, in the behavioural sciences, they will be affected by the very discoveries of the research. Even a quite cursory review of urban literature will show how dramatic shifts of emphasis or 'fashion' occur as analysts and planners respond both to developing methodologies and perceptions about real world events worthy of study. The 1950s, for example, were characterized by a considerable interest in the New Towns, neighbourhoods and social structure; the 1960s by Transportation and its land-use relationships, the 1970s by a re-discovery of the problems of the Inner City; and Regional economic problems may well prove to be the 're-discovery' of the 1980s.

One further point must be made concerning paradigms. In urban study, with complex and dynamic subject matter, there are massive data-handling problems and, to deal satisfactorily with these, a framework of paradigms is vital since, otherwise, all available facts may seem equally relevant to a given problem (Haggett, 1967). Within the paradigm, selection of *relevant* data is possible and the problems of unselective and unrestricted fact gathering on the one hand, or of limiting a study to facts that are readily obtained, on the other hand, can be overcome.

Theory and causality

It has already been noted that the development of urban knowledge depends not on increasing quantities of data, but upon explanation made possible by the development of theory. A subject without theory is all fact, because facts, or observations, are then only what is *believed* to be correct. The factual burden of a discipline, then, ought to vary inversely with its maturity. Moreover, a lack of satisfactory explanations means that over-attention tends to be directed to 'effects' and not to 'causes', for the latter can only be explained in terms of theory (Berry, 1973). In using knowledge as a basis for policy making this is a matter of the greatest importance, for any intervention to guide social change which is not based upon an understanding of 'cause' is likely to be highly suspect.

It is relevant then to note briefly the process of theory formulation. It is, in effect, a process of abstraction or generalization (figure 4.2), in which inductive or deductive forms of inference can be used as appropriate to the nature of the science. Theory consists of at least two main components (Meyers and Grossen, 1978). The first comprises the *postulates*, which are a set of analytical statements derived from empirical data. These form the foundation of the theory from which *theorems* (that is, refined statements) may be deduced. The second component is the *rules of correspondence*, which essentially concern the relationship between the postulates (and theorems) and their empirical (real world) equivalents. It is the hypotheses which form the link and which can be tested to establish the validity of this relationship (figure 4.3).

Figure 4.2 The process of theory formulation

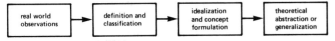

Figure 4.3 Component stages of theory formulation

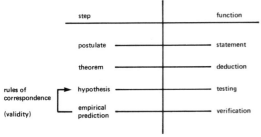

After Meyers and Grossen (1978: 5)

A theoretical explanation is only of practical use if it can be interpreted with reference to the real world phenomena. This 'correspondence'[15] is vital, not simply for interpretation, but for the verification of the theory as well. But as theory can only ever be an abstraction, there must always be a distinction between the abstract language of the theory and the operational language that we use to describe the real world phenomena that the theory purports to explain. Ultimately, this correspondence can only ever be a matter of convention and agreement through definition of terms and it is not, therefore, a simple matter (Blalock, 1974).

Urban study has not yet reached a mature state in developing theoretical explanations. It is, therefore, necessary to use loosely connected notions as theories, and the distinction between postulates and theorems may be blurred. In such situations, it is useful to group these notions for more limited purposes under the heading of *concepts* (Meyers and Grossen, 1978). These are abstract statements about some aspect of reality, which either attempt to describe that aspect through observation, or preferably attempt to describe the inter-relationships or regularities about the reality. These statements can also be descriptions of the processes by which research into the reality might proceed. Where a concept has been deliberately invented for some specific purpose, for example, 'socio-economic status', then the term *construct* is sometimes used instead (Krausz and Miller, 1974).

As concepts are abstract, as with all theoretical constructions, it is necessary to find some empirical 'correlate' capable of being measured if the 'theoretical' statements are ever to be verified. The process of choosing observable indicators for the concepts is one of the major problems in the conduct of urban research. Finding a suitable correlate to measure, say 'unemployment', or even a 'household' is not straightforward (see Chapter 5) and more complex issues such as 'deprivation' or 'social mobility' present even greater difficulties. Refinement can come through research, however, for at a later stage a classification of concepts may emerge (Merton, 1968). At the initial stage, concepts must often be 'borrowed' from other work, or even generated out of attitudes and values on the part of the investigators. Once a satisfactory language is found, that is, a means of expressing the 'correspondence', these concepts can guide the research. In particular, hypotheses can be generated and tested by experiment or observation, through the collection of data, by analysis, and processes of logical inferences. The connection between theoretic and empirical worlds may, however, not be revealed in a unique manner for there will always be some uncertainty arising from limitations in the clarity of the language used to express concepts and define the terms. But as the research matures, ambiguities will be revealed by refinement, restatement and refutation, and the hypotheses, if validated, may then become theories.

It may be useful at this stage to be reminded of the purpose of urban study. It is to explain, rather than simply to describe, urban phenomena and human behaviour. More precisely, it is to produce theoretical statements about the regularities in urban systems, for it is through such discovery that *causal* explanation is possible. This, logically, can lead to prediction (Krausz and Miller, 1974), and the ability to predict is, after all, the fundamental planning skill. Distinguishing 'true' causal situations is fundamental to urban research, and hence to policy making, but it is far from easy.

First, it should be noted that as causality is itself an abstract concept, it cannot be proved by direct, empirical observation and that it is only ever possible to *infer* a causal relationship. A causal relationship is one in which there must be present the essential ingredient of 'producing' (Bunge, 1979). For example, if a change in some phenomenon X is produced by a change in another phenomenon Y (which could be a policy), then a causal relationship may be inferred. This situation must clearly be distinguished from that in which the changes merely happen to follow on another, or indeed, where they are associated but without the necessary condition of one producing the other.[16]

In practice, a number of problems have to be faced. It is never possible to say with absolute certainty that Y is the sufficient and sole influence affecting X, for no guarantee can ever be given that *every* influence has been observed. A probabilistic approach is therefore necessary. Second, the relationship between phenomena is often asymmetrical. Y may cause X, but X may not necessarily cause Y: indeed, reciprocal causation in the human world is very rare. Fortunately, in most areas of urban study, the temporal sequence will be self-evident, as will the direction of the relationship, though the isolation of 'cause' and 'effect' is not an easy matter.

Third, in order to make an empirical evaluation of the causal relationship between any two variables, it is necessary to make simplifying assumptions about other variables, or influences. Indeed, the whole purpose of any scientific approach is to 'control' these other variables. In the study of social systems, the extent to which this can be done is limited, partly governed by available research designs as we later discuss, but more so by the complex nature of the real world itself. In such situations, models are particularly relevant (Simon, 1957) and they serve two purposes. First, they enable the researcher to select a *limited* number of specified variables for study, and those that remain can be subsumed as 'error' effects. Once the simplified system is understood by means of the model, additional variables can be added, which will make the model a closer replication of reality. Second, because models are abstractions, they are a convenient way of overcoming the difficulties already noted arising from the different language of theory formulation and empirical observation.

Design and validity

A design stage will be essential to all investigation. There are usually three operational phases: (i) the formulation of the problem, (ii) the idealized research (or investigation) design, (iii) the practical research design (Ackoff, 1953). The first seeks to specify exactly as possible the nature of the problem. The second specifies the optimum procedure that would be followed if there were no practical restrictions, and the third translates the idealized design into one that is capable of realization within the practical limits of the research situation. The practical design, in turn, will usually comprise: (i) a *sampling design*, dealing with the methods by which the subjects are identified and chosen, (ii) *the statistical design*, how the observations are to be made and the data analysed, (iii) the *observational design*, dealing with the conditions under which the observations are to be made, and, more generally, (iv) the *operational design*, concerned with the choice of appropriate techniques for the sampling, statistical and observational designs.

No blueprint can be given which can set out the appropriate procedure for all urban investigations. Almost every inquiry will contain unique events, but an investigation based upon logical, consistent and systematic rules will be superior to an investigation based on none, and will build upon accumulated knowledge. A 'checklist' approach is useful, drawing upon a repertory of accepted practice. From this, inappropriate methods may be rejected which will ensure a more rigorous approach than one in which the researcher builds his own design from limited knowledge. Setting out the idealized research design enables the researcher to evaluate the efficiency of his potential practical designs.

The most important single design criterion to be faced concerns validity and two aspects must be distinguished (Campbell, 1957). *Internal* validity is that without which any research or experiment is uninterpretable, that is, literally meaningless. In contrast, *external* validity concerns the extent to which results can be generalized to a wider context. These aspects of validity interact. For example, efforts to improve internal validity (for example by making a study more detailed) may well reduce the possibility of generalization. And, as a great deal of urban data are drawn from samples, which in any event limits generalization, the attainment of valid data is of the utmost importance.

A helpful approach is to set out the factors which can jeopardize validity (Campbell and Stanley, 1966), that is, increase error. The following criteria should be noted:

1   *Historical Effects* are the specific events which occur to any subject *during* an investigation (whether a survey or an experiment) and which change its characteristics in some way.
2   *Maturation Effects* result from the passage of time *per se*, for example, effects due to the ageing of the subjects. If values, attitudes, or opinions were being measured it would be expected that these might change simply due to passage of time. This effect becomes the more important if the time scale of the research is extended.
3   *Testing Effects* occur directly as a result of the research itself. In dealing with a human subject, for example, both inquirer and subject will learn from each other during an investigation, and this will condition subsequent research. This 'learning effect' is a common source of difficulty.
4   *Instrumentation Effects* result, for example, from changes in the calibration of a measuring instrument, substitution of different observers, alternative definition of variables in dealing both with inanimate phenomena or human subjects, any of which can produce unwanted errors.
5   *Statistical Effects* arise from a number of sources. They often arise when the subjects of an investigation do not form an adequately representative sample, or where, in an experimental situation, they *are not allocated randomly* into groups for study.
6   *Biases* arise notably in experimental designs when the *selection* of subjects from the study groups takes place differentially. Effects 5 and 6 are to some extent inter-related and can be dealt with by the careful use of randomization procedures as discussed shortly.
7   *Mortality Effects* are caused by the differential loss of respondents or subjects during the research. Again this particularly affects research conducted over longer time periods.

Finally, there is the complicating factor that any two or more of these jeopardizing effects may occur simultaneously. A particularly common co-effect, for example, is that between the 'membership' of study groups and the 'maturation' of their respective members.

In measuring a phenomenon, X, internal validity concerns those factors which directly affect the accuracy with which our 'observed' X represents the 'true' X. In brief, internal validity is maximized by careful attention to the principles of research design and, secondly, by the correct use of statistical theory and procedures.

External validity concerns not the relationship between the 'true' X and the 'observed' X, but that between the 'true' X and the more general population X'. In other words, it concerns the representativeness of what is actually studied about a subject to the wider population of that subject, for example, to what extent the results of a study into shopping behaviour in one town might be generalized to behaviour in a region. It therefore concerns the extent to which the behaviour and characteristics of X' can be explained by the observations X, and what residual effects must be assumed to be attributable to other (unobserved) influences. This can be summarized as

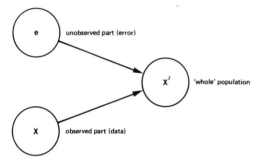

A great deal of urban investigation requires that inferences are made about a larger population from a study of some part of it, that is, from a sample. This process of generalization – induction from the particular to the more general – is not strictly logically justified for, in effect, it requires extrapolation into a realm which is not represented in the sample. In practice, however, it can be done by *assuming* knowledge of the relationship based upon not only the research but also accumulated experience (Campbell and Stanley, 1966). But, while tentative pronouncements can be made and hypotheses can be generated which may be subsequently verified or disproved, positive, logically deductible assertions cannot be made. Neither, therefore, can claims be made to establish absolute causality. This is an important point for, in urban planning, as in other applied fields, there are many examples where research has tended to over-claim results both in respect of generalization and of causality.

External validity, then, is particularly important in an applied subject. The main problem is that of 'controlling' for the influences of the larger population upon that part which is actually studied. Validity will be satisfied when successive investigations (or experiments) yield similar results and/or can be confirmed by similar work of others, though this must not be achieved at the expense of internal validity. In practice, it means that strict control must be exercised over the conduct of the research and particularly the problem of 'reactivity'.

If an inquiry or experiment is repeated on a human subject in some way, then the very conduct of the research will alter the subject's responses concerning the variable. Also, the attitudes of the researcher may be affected. Different results will be obtained in successive investigations, simply due to this reactive effect. It is then extremely difficult to generalize, for it cannot be inferred with any confidence which responses are truly representative of the larger population. This sensitivity will also vary between subjects and the topics studied. For example, there will be interaction between criteria, that is, asking a question about one topic may influence the subject's views about a related issue. Secondly, 'reaction' may affect the selection of the subjects and this makes generalization even more difficult. Thirdly, there will be a general, cumulative learning effect for experiences are not 'unlearnt' by a human subject and this must be recognized in the interpretation of results. This latter problem is extremely complex because the learning effect may not even be due to the research being conducted at all but from some other, extraneous source.

Difficulties may also arise from the realization on the part of the subject that he or she is in the artificial setting of an experiment or investigation, and it follows that his behaviour and responses to the inquiry may be quite different from his 'normal' feelings. He may, for example, respond more freely, enjoying the attention of the researcher, he may try to give answers which he feels will please, or be reluctant to give his opinions to a stranger. He may even act an imaginary part with varying degrees of seriousness. Such problems are very difficult to handle satisfactorily in urban inquiry. Randomization of subjects may help, but some bias towards particular sub-strata of the population is almost inevitable. One answer, of general applicability, is to extend the period of study and repeat the research. It then ceases to become such a 'special event' and reaction for this reason may be less marked. On the other hand, the research will impose further on the subjects and this may increase their reaction.

It follows that any researcher needs to be well aware of the many problems which can affect his practical research design. Against this background, the methodology for some relevant research designs for urban study can be set out in greater detail. These will cover exploratory study, experimental, quasi-experimental and non-experimental designs in that order.

Exploratory study

At the outset of research, the inquirer often knows very little about his subject. The subject area may be perceived poorly and with misconceptions, and there may even be difficulty in defining the 'terms of reference'. There will certainly be some difficulty in distinguishing important from non-important issues, and therefore the researcher will be unable readily to formulate hypothetical statements for testing significant events or variables and their behaviour.

In this situation, an exploratory investigation is most helpful. It concentrates on obtaining information about a broad range of issues which appear to be relevant to the problem. The best starting point is to consult a wide range of literature of general relevance to the subject. Very little urban research is genuinely *de novo*, and a common failing is a tendency to skimp preparatory, broad reading of published work in a misplaced enthusiasm to plunge into data collection. The importance of a thorough review of literature in the chosen area of investigation cannot be over-stressed. It enables the researcher to build upon the accumulated knowledge of others, it reveals how they approached similar problems and their successes and failures, and it provides insights about the subject as perceived by others. This latter point is important for it can help to overcome the initial limitations imposed by the researcher's preconceptions and prejudices. The review will often give useful guidance about the potential use of methods.

Once the subject area has been delimited, a useful next step is to review a wide range of relevant data and information. In urban studies, this usually means sources such as the Census, central and local government reports, and so on. Much clearly depends on the nature of the investigation, but the emphasis should be on exploring the general characteristics of the subject which will provide the framework within which the more detailed and rigorous research can properly be specified. Extreme caution must be taken in drawing any inferences or conclusions from exploratory data, particularly since standardized methods will not have been used.

Experimental design

In contrast stands an experimental design and, although this has only very limited direct application in urban research, there are two reasons for setting out the principles. First, it represents a model for rigorous, desirable forms of investigation which can provide useful guidelines for all research designs and, secondly, there are quasi-experimental possibilities in urban study, and limited experimental possibilities through simulation and modelling.

It will be helpful to start with the concept of the ideal experiment. A variable (the dependent variable) is identified whose behaviour is to be studied. The fundamental assumption is then made that this variable is influenced by another variable or set of variables which is/are the possible causes of the behaviour of the dependent variable. These, causally prior variables, are the independent variables, although their identification is frequently difficult in social research. The experimental design attempts to isolate the effects of one or more independent variable upon a dependent variable, and this permits inferences to be made directly about their relationships. These relationships may, for example, be linear or non-linear, symmetrical or non-symmetrical, exponential or of some higher-order function. In this process, the most important conceptual point is that as it is never possible to have *total* knowledge of all independent causes in a situation, it is always necessary to assume some error influence in the making of inferences.

Suppose we obtain a statistical measure of relationship between two variables (X and Y), for example, by a correlation coefficient. What may be inferred? The measure *may* indicate a causal relationship and, if so, we can state that, 'allowing for errors, X is wholly explained by Y'. Then any policy, for example, which sought to influence X by acting upon Y would be more or less successful, subject to the size of error influence. Such a simple situation is, however, unlikely in any social context. Most likely there will be numerous Ys all affecting X, and *each* will have an associated error component, in other words, a typical multi-variate situation will be present. Furthermore, it is highly probable that these various Y terms will be inter-related among themselves.

It is equally possible that the observed relationship between X and Y in our simple case is 'spurious', that is, they may *appear* to be inter-related but this is simply because both X and Y are, in fact, dependent upon another influence(s), Z, which is unknown and is therefore unobserved.

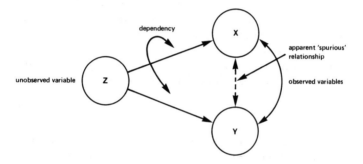

Attempting to manipulate Y through X, for example by means of a policy, will now be much more problematical. There may be an effect, through Z after a time lag, but the period of this may be quite unknown.

Central to the idea of experimental research is to design the process in such a way as to minimize to the greatest possible extent the error influences in observation and measurement. These errors, in fact, arise in one of two ways. *Random (or stochastic) error* which arises in almost all research design from the inherent nature of the methodology is accommodated by stating inferences to explicit levels of certainty by the use of statistical tests. *Systematic error* (also called *bias*) arises largely from inadequacies in the application of methods and is therefore amenable to reduction, or even elimination, by careful design research. The initial difficulty is to distinguish these contributors to the 'total error effect' from each other. This is not easy in urban research because of the potentially large number of unknown, disturbing influences. Research design is therefore a matter of coming to terms with the problem.

The most important principle is that of randomization[17] which is used to distribute the unknown error effects *randomly* throughout the measures, thereby removing the possibility of systematic error. This principle is effective for errors arising from either one or a number of sources and, indeed, does not even require a knowledge of the sources. The principle is extremely useful, indeed, it is a more efficient and practical device than attempting to hold all variables constant in an experimental social research context, even when these variables are known (Blalock, 1970). The approach, then, is to keep under rigid control those variables about which enough is known to do so effectively, and to randomize the influence of the remainder. At the analysis stage, the probable influence of this randomization can be readily assessed through statistical tests.

Figure 4.4 Simple experimental research design

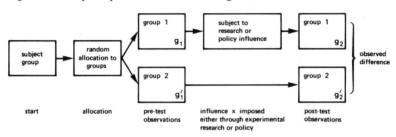

Bearing in mind the need to control for internal validity, an idealized, experimental-type research design can be illustrated as figure 4.4. This might typically apply to a situation where an influence (such as the manipulation of a variable as in an experiment or the impact of a policy change) upon a subject group can be identified. Measurements are taken both before (pre-test) and after (post-test) the influence. Although something of an ideal, such a design is able to 'control' for all the major factors which may jeopardize internal validity. Randomization of the membership of the two study groups will control any group membership bias; historical effects are controlled in that effects which produce a $g_1 - g_2$ difference will also produce a $g'_1 - g'_2$ difference. Maturation and testing effects should appear equally in both groups, and statistical effects are controlled, for both groups are randomly assigned. Comparison of $g_1 - g'_1$ and $g_2 - g'_2$ difference reveals any mortality effect.

An extension of this type of design allows control to be exercised over external validity. This can be made clear by a design such as the Solomon Four Group Design (Solomon, 1949) shown as figure 4.5.

The study population is now randomly allocated into *four* groups. In effect, the previous design is now paralleled by another test which does not include the pre-test observations. The additional subject groups are not therefore subject to the 'learning effect' of the research itself. Meaningful differences can now be measured by comparison, in turn, of $g_1 - g_2$, $g_2 - g'_2$, $g_3 - g'_3$, $g_3 - g'_1$, each of which will produce controlled, that is valid, data in respect of the influence X. Further, any pre-test influence effect will be revealed by comparing g_2, g_3 and g'_2, g'_3. Tests for significance cannot be undertaken on all six sets of observations in figure 4.5, but the respective *pairs* of observations may be tested, for example, by analysis of variance.[18] These tests are summarized in figure 4.6.

Figure 4.5 Four group experimental research design

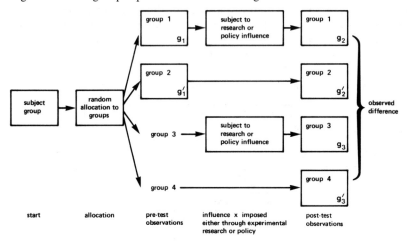

Figure 4.6 Possible tests for significance in experimental design

subject to ▶ ▼	influence of x	no influence of x	
pre-test	g_2	g'_2	test for effect of pre-test
no pre-test	g_3	g'_3	
	test for influence of x		

Here the main effect of X can be estimated from the column mean scores and the effect of pre-testing from the rows. Also, a comparison of the cell mean scores will test for the *interaction* of the influence X and the conduct of the research. These tests provide the information necessary for the researcher to be able to generalize with confidence.

It will be clear that the experimental approaches require full control over the scheduling of the experimental influence and over the randomization of subjects. Correct temporal sequences must also be identifiable or at least inferred. Such designs could then provide high-quality information but usually, in urban study, these criteria cannot be fully satisfied and it is necessary to adopt a somewhat less rigorous procedure. Nevertheless, it is useful to use experimental designs as ideal frameworks for research in order to make clear to the researcher the specific variables that his *design fails to control*, for the resulting error influences will increase the number of interpretations possible from the results.

A brief hypothetical example in the urban context may clarify these principles. Assume that an authority is interested in improving the take-up of housing improvement grants, either because they believe it a good thing that the housing stock is improved, or because they are interested in finding out just what improvement in take-up could be achieved by spending money on promotion. The willingness of groups of residents to take up grants is affected by a wide variety of factors, affecting both individuals and households, socio-economic status, income levels, housing conditions, and so on. There will be general factors at work influencing people's attitude to improvement and using grant money. Faced with this situation, a planning authority can use an experimental approach, though there will necessarily be some relaxation from a true experimental situation. The main requirement is to isolate the effect due in one group of residents to the promotion of improvement grants from the general effects upon the population. Ideally, an experimental situation can be constructed by taking a group of subjects (residents) living in improvement-ripe housing, randomly allocating half to a control group who receive no promotional publicity, and the other half to an experimental group who do receive publicity. Observation over time as to how many grants are taken up by each group would demonstrate the effect of promotion, and all other influences could be assumed constant for both groups. The difficulty, however, is that the approach would presume an *independence* of communication between the groups. This might be achieved if the subjects were relatively few among a large population, but in a dense urban area this assumption could not hold, and an alternative approach which dispenses with the random allocation can be used.

Here the independence criterion can be satisfied, at least reasonably, by dividing the groups spatially. The experimental group being residents in one part of a town, say, and the control group being residents in another part, *matched* as far as possible for age, income levels, condition of houses and so on. Again, selected publicity, for example, by house-to-house visits, letters, may produce a response in the experimental group. Clearly, any general publicity, even through local press coverage, would have to be restricted. Provided care is taken, a number of similar applications are possible, in housing studies, or transportation, and sufficiently matched groups between towns can sometimes be achieved to provide useful 'experimental' type data.

In effect, the experimental Pre-test/Post-test Control Group Design (figure 4.4) is used but without the randomization of the subjects. When subject groups are *given* to the investigator, such as groups of residents, the interpretation will clearly require more assumptions to be made, though the more similar the various groups can be made in their recruitment then the more effective the design becomes. If it can be *assumed* that a reasonably random allocation has been achieved, then the design controls for the main invalidating effects of history, maturation, testing and instrumentation. If the observed differences for the experimental group between pre-test and post-test *are greater than* those for the control group, it is probable that those differences are genuine (Campbell and Stanley, 1966).

Quasi-experiment

A more widely applicable design is that of the quasi-experiment such as the simple time-series study shown as figure 4.7. Here, it is assumed that observations of a subject *can* be made at intervals over a period of time, but

Figure 4.7 A quasi-experimental research design

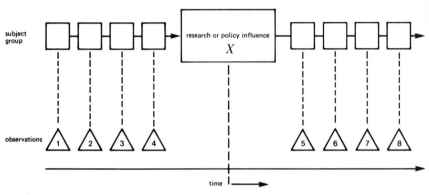

random allocation of the subject into control and experimental groups is *not* feasible. This is a very common situation in urban study for, in analysing the effects of planning policy, it will normally be the case that the policy affects a whole population in some way and allocation into separate groups who are affected and not affected is impracticable.

The essence of this design is to establish a clear understanding of a pattern of change over time, both before and after some scheduled event. Interpretation of the results then focuses upon the differences between observations 4 and 5, *and* the general pattern over the whole measurement series. The effect of influence X, perhaps the policy influence, can then be isolated, though with some reservations. Typical findings from this kind of approach are illustrated in figure 4.8. It would be reasonable to infer that X indeed had some influence in the outcomes A and B, and with less certainty in cases C, D and E. Cases such as F, G and H would provide no such evidence.

Clearly, the extent to which a particular quasi-experimental design satisfies or fails to satisfy the jeopardizing criteria for validity will depend upon the circumstances of each piece of research. One general aspect, however, can be noted. In the urban context, researchable phenomena often reveal themselves only after periods of time have elapsed, that is, with a time lag. Particular care is needed to interpret successive post-test results, and this is further complicated by the presence of cyclical changes or seasonal changes. To adequately control for these the overall time scale of study may need to be long.

Figure 4.8 Some possible outcomes for a quasi-experimental research design

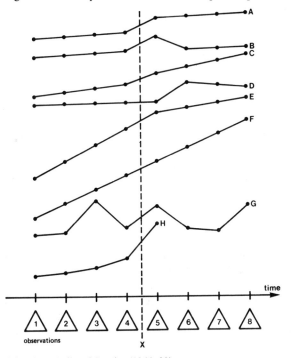

After Campbell and Stanley (1966: 38)

A good example of the many possible applications of this type of design is in measuring the effect of the opening of a new hypermarket on consumer shopping behaviour. The 'normal' behaviour of residents of an area is observed over a period of time (say through sampled survey interviews) so that general trend changes occurring due to disposable income levels or car ownership rates are observed. At point X the new store is opened and the post-test observation may reveal not only the immediate response, but more importantly how that response is affected by passing time for, in such a case, it may be several months before a new 'stable' pattern is established. Comparison of this situation with the pre-test measurements enables useful inferences to be made about the effect, in this case, of the opening of a new store. It will also be apparent that such a design can be useful in a *monitoring* role within the planning process, though an essential part of the design is to *anticipate* events so that a satisfactory set of pre-test data can be acquired.[19]

Non-experimental design

It will frequently be the case that even quasi-experimental approaches to urban research are not possible, or even desirable, and recourse will be made to non-experimental designs. These are particularly appropriate for situations in which there are difficulties in identifying and disentangling the variables for study and the way in which they act upon each other.[20] In these situations, there is often inadequate information about temporal sequences and 'cause and effect' are particularly difficult to establish.

Three general points must be noted. First, non-experimental designs use data obtained through observation of the real world (as from censuses and surveys) much of which is obtained for a variety of general purposes. The data then, are often 'non-specific' in contrast to the data obtained through an experimental approach. Second, it will be necessary to make many more, less plausible, assumptions to set up the research and this means that there will be greater difficulty in drawing satisfactory inferences, particularly causal ones. Third, compared to any experimental approach, a larger number of variables must be brought into the investigation to give it explanatory power and, in turn, this will mean that simpler assumptions will have to be made about how the variables fit together (Blalock, 1972a). In non-experimental research, more use will have to be made of statistical probability theory in order to handle the greater number of the unexplained influences and associated random and systematic errors. Findings will then have to be stated, not in terms of laws, but rather in terms of probabilities and with a due acknowledgement of assumptions. And because these influenced by the very conduct of the investigation and randomization necessarily amenable to randomization. Further, as the subjects of the research cannot be isolated from their social environment, they will be influenced by the very conduct of the investigation and randomization cannot help at all with this.[21]

Faced with these problems, how may we proceed to a non-experimental research design? It will be helpful to reconsider the two-variable situation, X and Y, and to ask the question:

what are the necessary conditions which have to be established in order to say that X (independent) causes Y (dependent), and thereby to be able to say with some certainty that any manipulation of X will cause some equivalent change in Y?

Four types of influence can be distinguished (Kish, 1965). The first relates to the particular variable X (or several Xs) that we are able to identify accurately from our knowledge of the subject area and which we believe to be directly influencing Y. Such variables are the primary focus of the research, and if we are attempting to measure the impact of a policy, then the input will be a variable of this type. The term 'manipulated' can be used for, in effect, such variables will be the equivalent of an experimental influence noted earlier. Diagrammatically, we have

Second, it is possible to envisage an X-type variable, X_2 (or group of such variables) about which we *do* possess knowledge, but which, for a variety of reasons, we do *not* seek to manipulate. This knowledge, however, enables us to take account of their influence, that is, to 'control' for their presence.

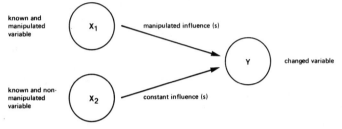

In general, the object of the scientific approach to research is to bring as many of the independent variables as possible into either of these X_1 or X_2 categories.

Next, there will be a potentially large group of influences of which we will have no knowledge. A third category of independent variables, X_3, then, can be envisaged. These cannot be identified but it can be assumed that they will have an influence upon the dependent variable, Y. This type of influence will often produce changes in the dependent variable, the subject, during the conduct of an investigation and can be very troublesome. Adding to the diagram we get the following picture.

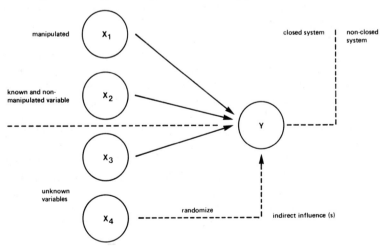

The fourth type represents influences which have an *indirect* relationship between X and Y. These are very common and are often systematically related or partially related to 'known' X influences. The presence of these influences will clearly cause problems in a policy sense, because they jeopardize the extent to which manipulation of Y through X_1 will be efficient and predictable.

In sum, the ideal design will be where no X_3 or X_4 influences are present, that is, we will have a typical isolated system to study. It means that the relationship betweeen X and Y can be examined by manipulating the X_1 influences and holding constant the other (X_2) independent influences, observing the effect on the chosen dependent variable. But, in most urban research, X_3- and X_4-type influences will dominate the initial framework of any investigation. The overall aim of good research design is then to try to convert these influences into X_2-type influences.

It is, in fact, the same conceptual approach to dealing with the measurement error problem, for it is the type X_3 and X_4 influences which give rise to most of the errors in research, particularly systematic ones. Randomization changes type X_4 errors into type X_3 errors, so that at least inferences can be made about the independent/dependent variable relationships through statistical tests.

There is, however, an important qualification. Converting type X_4 influences into type X_3 influences by randomizing will not be successful if the X_4 influences are *themselves* related to other types of independent variable, namely the X_1 or X_2 influences. There will also be problems where two or more X_4 variables are present, for if they are heavily inter-related the problem of multi-collinearity[22] will arise.

An example will make clear some real-world equivalents of those concepts. Assume that we are interested in population migration into a town. Clearly, everyday knowledge will suggest this may be a complex matter in which there are many influences at work. Migration will, however, be specified as the dependent variable, Y, and one may hope to establish statistically a relationship with possible 'causal' independent variables. Assume for the moment that data are available about changes in the number of migrants over time (from, a census for example) and that other time-series information relating to rates of housebuilding, industrial and commercial investment, levels of employment, the socio-economic structure of the area and the land release policy of the planning authority are available. It can be readily hypothesized that these may be influences affecting migration, and these variables must form the X_1 types. That is, each can be readily identified, and as data are available, the relationship between migration and each variable can be quantified by a statistical measure, as we shortly discuss, by 'holding' the other influences constant in solving the equations. They are treated then as type X_2 influences. In other words we can identify one variable (or a group of variables) to be manipulated in turn to observe the effect upon the dependent variable (X_1), and treat others as controlled (X_2).

It must of course be assumed that there will be many other influences at work, about which we may have only a very hazy idea. Levels of mortgage availability, individual perceptions of the attraction of the area, domestic linkages, and so on all of which may clearly affect people's tendency to migrate. Also, we may have no information about distance moved, and so on. These will fall into the X_3 and X_4 categories. What can be done about them? Mainly two things. First, as far as possible, the possibility of systematic bias must be eliminated among these variables. For example, variations in the availability of mortgages might affect owner occupiers' propensity to migrate in contrast to those occupying rented accommodation. Thus, our 'explanation' of migration could be heavily biased if the areas for which we have data contain a preponderance of one category of tenure or another. In testing the relationship say between industrial and commercial investment and migration as an $X_1 - Y$ relationship from the data (holding the other 'known' variables constant as X_2 types), we would want to ensure that there was no systematic error due to tenure. This could be achieved by ensuring that the areas for which we have data are merged in such a way that the proportion of tenures is similar for all areas, and so on.

Secondly, careful preliminary study, and particularly a search of the literature of other research attempts in the same field, should reveal the possibility of any large, single, independent influence. The more these can be treated as explicit variables, and hence controlled, the fewer and less disruptive will be the residual influences. Pilot work can also help to overcome this difficulty. Whilst clearly, this example is oversimplified, and there will remain potential difficulties from the non-independence of the independent variables (that is, they will be to some extent inter-related among themselves), the foregoing will have suggested a basic sequence to be followed in setting up such a research design.

Firstly, as many type X_2 variables as possible are obtained by careful classification of subjects, definition of variables and the acquisition of valid data (see Chapter 5). Secondly, as far as possible, individual subjects are randomly allocated in the study, helping to turn any type X_4 influences into type X_3. Thirdly, recognizing that the design will, in any event, be less than perfect both for conceptual and measurement reasons, tests of statistical significance are applied to the findings to establish confidence levels.

Randomization is an important research device but it cannot eliminate certain types of error (Blalock, 1970). To understand this we should remind ourselves of the two types of causal inference. Firstly, there are inferences which attempt to generalize the findings, sometimes called 'forcings' and which relate to external validity.

Secondly, there are the inferences that we make about the subject but within the bounds of the immediate system which we are studying. Randomization can only help deal with the latter. More general, exogenous influences can, in fact, only be controlled if their existence is known and they can be converted into type X_2 influences. Careful exploratory investigation and attention to the simplifying assumptions necessary in all research can ensure that these external influences are not overlooked and left as dominant.

We have noted the extreme difficulty in determining any causal relationship in non-experimental research. It is fortunate, however, that we can usefully consider a relationship between any two variables quite independently of any causal notion (Blalock, 1972a). We can examine the relationship simply in terms of *co-variations* and use the notion of prediction to measure the relationship. The concept of causality can then be conveniently ignored. How can the behaviour of one variable be predicted from another? This can be illustrated with a simple case involving three variables, *X*, *Y* and *Z*. Assume that data has shown that *X* is highly co-related to *Y* and *Z*, through say, a correlation coefficient.[23] Diagrammatically,

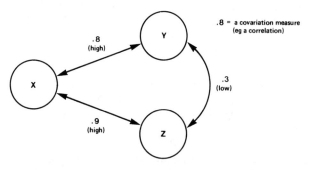

We must not infer any 'direction' to the relationship, hence the double arrows, and must also normally assume that there will be unknown influences at work giving rise to errors. The causal possibilities are three-fold. One is that *X* causes *Y* and *Z*; or *Y* causes *X* and *X* causes *Z*; or even that *X* causes *Y* which causes *Z*, but this latter is less likely. However, we first concentrate on predicting or estimating the relationship between the variables. There are two main considerations. One is to find out as much as possible about the relative strengths of the relationships through the use of statistical procedures such as correlation or regression and the second is to assess the probable error. In general, we must not expect to be able to say how much error *in total* exists in any given measurement. What we have to do is to concentrate on making realistic assumptions about *how* the error effects are working to influence our results (Blalock, 1972a). The most important of these are that we must assume that the error influences are *independent* of each other, and that if there are *many* error effects they will tend to cancel each other out. This assumption is plausible if it is further assumed that any one very large single error effect ought to be known either from general knowledge of the subject or from exploratory investigation.

The main point to note is the principle that, by such a research structuring (given appropriate data), the influence of one variable on another (or others) may be measured and, further, that the significance of this influence may be assessed by the use of statistical tests. The approach requires that assumptions are made about the *ordering* of the variables, that is, which are to be treated as independent or dependent, and that, if necessary, by re-ordering, a complex system can be systematically treated. The principles by which such a non-experimental situation for four variables can be analysed is set out in Appendix 2.

There are a wide range of situations in the urban context to which such research designs can be applied. At the conclusion of this part of the text, a guide is given to selected examples which will not only reveal the detail of the application, but lead the reader through a sequence of simple to more complex illustrations.

Causal inference

There remain the problems of drawing inferences from these research designs. Is it possible to interpret results in terms of a true causal structure? Probably not, for, as we have noted in studying the human world, the error effects and interdependencies among variables normally mean that alternative explanations cannot entirely be ruled out. It is, of course, particularly important that a causal relationship is not imputed where none really exists. There are several common situations in which causal inferences may falsely be drawn. First, noted earlier, is that of *spurious correlation*. Given a three-variable situation, for example, an apparently clear relationship might be found that Z is closely related to Y, and Y is closely related to X. Such a finding is ambiguous, however, for either of the following causal situations might be present: $X \to Y \to Z$ or $Z \leftarrow X \to Y$. The first interpretation is that X is a direct cause of Y and an indirect cause of Z. The second, equally possible, interprets X to be the direct cause of both Y and Z. In this event, the apparent correlation between Y and Z is spurious. We could hold X constant in our research in order to find out if Y and Z *are* related, but, in a practical situation it may not be easy because X may be partially a direct cause of Z, which will confound the attempt (Blalock, 1972a). The number of situations in which spurious measures can appear is very large, even for a system with few variables. It is also important to note that regression coefficients are a more useful device than correlation coefficients in measuring a relationship because they say something about the *direction* of the relationship. Provided the data are valid this may help establish a causal structure. There is a further statistical reason why they are to be preferred. In attempting to hold selected relationships constant, the value of a correlation coefficient can be reduced because the *total* variation in the independent variable, relative to the relationship with its dependent variables, will be affected. As a result there is a considerable danger of self-justification from findings based upon correlation measures alone.

Brief further comment should also be made about the problem of multi-collinearity noted earlier. In the study of social systems, there often arises the situation in which two or more independent (possibly causal) variables, X and Y, are themselves highly inter-related. Diagrammatically,

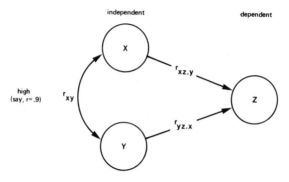

In this situation, the partial values $r_{xz.y}$ and $r_{yz.x}$ representing the respective and simultaneous influence of X and Y on Z may become extremely sensitive to sampling errors in the data.[23] The higher the value for r_{xy}, the more difficult it becomes to interpret meaningfully the XZ and YZ relationships. Indeed, the use of regression to solve such a situation ideally assumes that X and Y are quite independent of each other. This problem is best avoided by careful research design in which independent variables are defined and selected in such a way as to maximize the distinguishing characteristics between them.

Finally, in this chapter, attention must be drawn to two specific problems in the conduct of non-experimental research which are particularly relevant in the urban context. The first concerns 'the fallacy at the wrong level'.[24] Most urban research is conducted at the level of a spatial scale. The problem is that, in moving from one level or scale to another, we are likely to affect the manner in which the various disturbing, external influences operate upon both independent and dependent variables. For example, at the small scale it is more likely that random external influences will not cancel out and therefore it is less tenable to presume that randomization is an effective device. Further, the criteria by which we define variables may change in moving conceptually from one level to another.[25] For example, will measures made at an enumeration district level be equally meaningful for our purposes when aggregated to a higher level, such as that of a district or a county?

Comparisons *between* different scales bring similar problems of inference (Harvey, 1969) either as a *contextual* relationship, that is, where comparison is made from 'higher' to 'lower' scale, or the converse, referred to as an *aggregative* relationship. Drawing inferences in these situations requires making further assumptions about the similarity of conditions at the various scales and the appropriateness of the research methods used. This particularly affects data collection methods (Chapter 5), for it is often found that data collected at one scale, and for one purpose, are inappropriate for a different scale or purpose.

The second problem is a measurement difficulty, and can be stated more briefly. Urban planning research often takes place over considerable periods of time and it is therefore quite possible for a variable, assumed constant, say, as defined for an exploratory investigation, not to be so when observed over a longer period of time. This is particularly a problem with 'indicators' such as poverty, immobility and so on, and as noted shortly, changes may be brought about by the conduct of the research. This is considered more fully in following chapters.

Notes

1   The research approaches discussed necessarily involve the use of some basic statistical concepts and methods. Given the nature of the text it is not possible to cover these in detail, neither would that be appropriate for there are many excellent texts available. A familiarity with more basic skills must therefore be assumed, though notes in Appendix 1 will provide some guidance. Given the extensive range of social statistics that are arguably relevant to urban study, advice is offered in these notes as to those with which the urban analyst should be familiar at the introductory level. A checklist is given against which the reader may compare his knowledge. Any unfamiliarity should be covered by a careful reading of one of the cited texts, to build up a repertory of useful concepts and methods.

   Secondly, experience has suggested that a common problem facing planners is that of choosing a 'social statistics' text which introduces the material in a personally acceptable form. It is suggested that the reader chooses carefully and is prepared to search for a text in a style that suits him. Some texts, for example, are more descriptive, some more explanatory, some inherently more mathematical or theoretic, and some in the form of a programmed text with exercises. Some recommendations are given in the Guide to further reading at the end of Part 2.

2   Particularly at Ward Library Level.

3   See, for example, Johnston, 1978; Robson, 1971; Webber, 1975.

4   Notably factor analysis and derivatives (see Johnston, 1978).

5   See Chapter 8.

6   A 'datum' can be defined as a unitary relationship, that is, a one-to-one relationship between an observation and some real world phenomenon.

7   Such as SPSS (Statistical Package for the Social Sciences) or GIMMS (Geographic Information Manipulation and Mapping System). Output information can be presented in a variety of ways, through tabulations, mappings, diagrams and video-displays. This is a specialized field for which there is an extensive literature. See, for example, Baxter, 1976; Waugh, 1973; and White, 1974.

8   There is, however, a broad range of development in such fields as Social Area analysis (Robson, 1971, 1975), and migration (Bracken, 1976), and more generally in urban activity system analysis. Some useful case studies are cited in the Guide to further reading.

9   In a non-experimental situation the research will 'move into' a study area rather than 'create' it as for an experiment.

10   Readers wishing to consider this statement in detail are referred to standard texts such as Braithwaite (1960) or Nagel (1961).

11   The aim of science, then, is to cover the greatest possible number of empirical facts by logical deductions from the smallest possible number of hypotheses or premises (Chorafas, 1965).

12   A viewpoint much stressed by writers such as Churchman (1968) and Kuhn (1962).

13   We cannot, however, attempt here a discussion of the epistemology of social science. Readers may care to refer to a standard text such as Brodbeck (1968), or the discussion in regard to Human Geography by Harvey (1969).

14   The traditional view of objectivity rests upon the agreement of several observers, that is, *consensus*. A better answer though more complicated, is found not so much by examining the objectivity of a statement in itself, but rather by examining the inferences derived from the entire conceptual framework, or paradigm, in which the statement is set (Meyers and Grossen, 1978).

15   The term 'text' (Harvey, 1969) is sometimes used to describe this correspondence.

16   For example, night follows day, but clearly does not 'produce' day.

17   The principle owes much to the work of Fisher (1973) in the context of experimental research design.

18   See statistical notes, Appendix 1.

19   A guide to further examples of the use of quasi-experimental research designs in the urban planning context are given in the Guides to further reading for Parts 2 and 3.

20   Given the general lack of good quality historical data in urban planning studies, this is a common situation.

21   See the discussion in Chapter 5.

22   See statistical notes, Appendix 1.

23   See statistical notes, Appendix 1.

24   A particular case of this, where the researcher attempts to make inferences from knowledge about 'group' behaviour to that of an 'individual' is referred to as the 'ecological problem' or 'ecological fallacy'.

25   A good example of this is the way in which migration motivation varies from local to international scale (Clark and Rhind, 1975).

5

RESEARCH CONCEPTS
AND OPERATIONS

Variables and observation

Observation is the activity concerned with the correspondence between a real-world event and what is perceived and interpreted via the senses. In terms of objectivity, it is an imperfect process and optical illusions are a familiar reminder of this. Psychological research has demonstrated clearly the influence of prior experience on perception. Consider figure 5.1. At first glance, this appears to be an arrangement of marks, but which, for many people, will transform into a rider on a horse. Once 'recognized' the image tends to persist. In a similar way any interpretation of events through perception will be 'learned' in the context of circumstances in which the observation takes place (Bruner and Minturn, 1955).

Figure 5.1 Perception and learning

From Meyers and Grossen (1978: 12)

Any researcher must then come to terms with his own perceptions of the complex, real world, which enable him to formulate concepts, and which in turn permit understanding. In particular, we should note the transient nature of these concepts and the fact that it is only an assumption that objects and people do have properties that remain constant enough for us to measure them. Unless we do this, we can never generalize beyond the single and unique event. As Blalock (1972a, 1974) reminds us, certain of these assumptions will be more realistic than others. Some objects may, for all practical purposes, be assumed to have constant properties over long periods of time; but the properties of others, such as poverty or mobility may change almost as rapidly as we measure them, or may change precisely because we measure them.

The practical aim of observation is to obtain a set of valid information which will satisfy the investigation, without procuring so much that the researcher becomes swamped by it. This selective process can be likened to 'filters' (Harvey, 1969). In an exploratory study, for example, the researcher chooses a 'coarse' filter, obtaining broad, general information, though this will only poorly serve explanation. To explore the data in depth and search for regularities and patterns, 'less coarse' filters are used, of increasing selectivity as the researcher understands more about his problem. In this way, the volume of information is reduced but its quality is increased. Finally, at the highest level, the researcher can test hypotheses by choosing the 'finest' filter available. At this level, however, the higher quality data will be quite specific to the task set, and data collected for one purpose is unlikely to be very useful for another.

The satisfactory definition of terms is often given inadequate attention, and indeed is sometimes overlooked in the haste to acquire information. There are two types of problem. The first is that of language. A defined word or term is really nothing more than a convenient shorthand for a much longer statement.[1] In practice, this statement will embody a number of criteria,[2] specifying:

1   What is to be observed.
2   Under what changing and unchanging conditions the observations are to be made.
3   The operations that are to be performed.
4   The instruments and measures that are to be used.
5   How the observations are to be made and treated. (Ackoff *et al.*, 1962)

As Harvey (1969) comments, 'the important thing is to follow the rules in each set of circumstances, and not to be mesmerized by any one particular system of definitions set up with rather special circumstances in mind'. Definitions, then, should not be regarded as sacrosanct, nor treated lightly, but should be questioned as to their adequacy for each investigation. It is, however, important that the researcher records the 'rules' by which he has defined a variable for the advice of others.

The second problem, particularly in the social field, is that the definition of terms cannot be held independently of the researcher, or of the operations in which they are used. For example, in the attempt to fit observations to defined categories, the definitions may well be changed because the researcher will, even at that time, be forming new percepts about what he is studying. With the more original areas of urban investigation this matter is a very real difficulty, though a careful preparation of the research design will minimize the problem.

The central operational concept in making observations is that of the *variable*, 'a property or characteristic whose degree or form varies across a set of objects in a given situation' (Kohout, 1974).[3] For example, the variable properties of 'person' are sex, age, race, socio-economic status, income level, preferences, and so on. The essential starting question is how adequate are the *assumed* concepts for any particular investigation which is, after all, a unique event. It is fortunate that, in most applied studies, urban planning included, a great deal may be safely assumed. Defining a person's properties such as age, income, occupation and so on, usually involves simply deciding upon a unit of measurement. For example, as to what are the most suitable sub-divisions of age for a given population study. But other variables will present greater problems. Characteristics such as status, race and intelligence have less-established definition, and reference will be necessary to contemporary research and publications, in order to obtain acceptable norms of both the concept *and* its definition.[4] Some terms may even be unique to the investigation, such as an index of preference.

Important decisions must also be made about the necessary detail of an investigation. Data may usually be aggregated into higher-order classifications, but not the converse, and this suggests attempting the maximum detail possible – but what is that? Increased dis-aggregation in survey work can only be obtained at the cost of increased design work, survey effort, analytical complexity and data processing time. It is also worth noting that the marginal cost of obtaining additional information in an investigation may be quite small, and certainly less than a specific investigation for this additional data. However, extending an inquiry can bring problems. The investigation may be prolonged overall, with a detrimental effect on the validity of the 'main' data, and second, if the study involves an interview survey, an extended questionnaire may induce antipathy or even hostility on the part of the respondent.

We should, at this stage, re-consider the matter of control and particularly the four 'types' of variable commonly found in most types of social inquiry (Chapter 4). First, there are *independent* variables. These relate to the phenomena which we are trying to study, and they are also referred to as 'predictors', 'experimental' or 'explanatory' variables. In an analytical investigation, the researcher will be concerned to ensure that these variables are treated systematically so that their particular effects can be observed and measured, as far as possible in isolation. The second type, the *dependent* variables, correspond to the effects of a particular action or a predicted outcome. These variables are the subject of the statistical tests (for significance) which can determine the strength of their relationship to the independent variables and to each other. Third, there are the *controlled* variables. As already noted, the main objective of systematic research design is to reduce as much as possible the influences which are not under the researcher's control and which therefore have unmeasurable influences on the results. If this can be controlled, it is possible to fulfil the condition of 'other things being equal'. Three possibilities exist. First, by selecting certain variables for a particular study, we automatically exclude others, such as a particular sex, or age group in a population. Second, where exclusion of an unwanted variable influence is not possible, it can be 'held constant'. For example, variations over different days of the week in shopping behaviour, can be controlled by limiting a series of the reasearch studies to the same day in each week. Third, if it is difficult to hold a variable constant, it can be controlled through randomization. Here, we deliberately manipulate a variable so that its influence is made as random as possible in relationship to the other variables in the research.

Fourth, there remain *uncontrolled* variables or influences which include all the influences which cannot be measured, observed directly, or controlled. These can give rise to serious errors in the interpretation of results. They can be usefully divided into two categories, one more inherently difficult to treat than the other. The least problematical, the 'error influences', arise mainly from deficiencies in sampling and measurement. The correct application of statistical methods will minimize their effects. The more problematical are the so-called 'compounded influences'. These literally have an unknown influence on the results and the researcher must attempt to eliminate their effects as much as possible, even though he may not know directly of their precise nature, by anticipating their presence through the literature of others and by exploratory study.

In order to ascribe quantitative values to variables, it is necessary to move from a conceptual to an operational level, through the set of procedures called 'measurement'. We noted earlier a definition of data and how data are manipulated from their original state of facts into more meaningful states of knowledge and intelligence. It is, however, extremely important for the validity of this process that the measurement concepts inherent in our data are themselves understood.

Measurement and scales

Measurement is the attachment of defined units to observed phenomena and their attributes. Its purpose is to facilitate unambiguous communication about a set of observations, and this usually, though not necessarily, involves quantification. The extent to which some types of variable can be quantified is, however, limited, such as 'amenity' or 'environmental quality'. This often produces a particular unnecessary argument, often found in urban planning, between those who believe that phenomena which can be quantified are in some way fundamentally different to those which cannot. To the latter, the term qualitative is often given, and their measurement will be necessarily that much more subjective. But the essential point is that quantification is simply a way in which the *quality* of observation can be enhanced, descriptive power increased and ambiguity reduced.

There are four *scales of measurement* (Stevens, 1946): (i) the *nominal* scale, (ii) the *ordinal* scale, (iii) the *interval* scale, and (iv) the *ratio* scale. At the most simple level, symbols or numbers can be allocated to each category of variables, and will yield a nominal scale. Persons may thus be 'labelled' by sex, as male or female; groups of children categorized as a, b, c, d; land uses can be given names; as indeed are people. Nominal scales are important ways of classifying data about distinguishable events or objects and their variable characteristics and they are a prerequisite to all kinds of study.

An ordinal scale enables the categories to be placed in some kind of order. It is a process of *ranking*, or a *dimension*. A simple example is numerical values in an ascending or descending order, or a symbolic system such as an alphabet. When measurement is recorded along a dimension, the differences in the measure become quantitative as well as qualitative. Although the actual unit of measurement is irrelevant to this operation, ordering will be controlled by the use of mathematical operations statements such as 'greater than' ($>$) or 'less than' ($<$). Thus, if a is greater than b, and b is greater than c, the ranked dimension is a, b, c, though the choice of symbols is only a matter of convenience and convention. Such variables are referred to as *ordinal* and the corresponding operational device is an ordinal scale. However, it has limitations. It can provide information as to which of the two variables is greater, but no information can be obtained about how much more or less one variable is to another. If five persons are ranked a, b, c, d and e in their preference for, say, a policy or a house design, and the scale is arranged so that a expresses the greatest preference and e the least, we can say that a has a greater preference than b and so on. What we cannot say is that a's preference exceeds b's by more, for example, than c's exceeds that of d. Each arrangement is also an independent operation. If the preferences of *two* groups of people are ranked, useful 'greater than' or 'less than' information can be obtained within each group separately, but ordinal scaling does not permit comparison to be made between the two groups.

A great deal of useful urban data is based upon ordinal scales and, in particular, 'attitude' measurements. For example, a respondent might be asked to give a view about some planning issue according to the following specification:

Strongly agree	Agree	Slightly agree	Indifferent	Slightly disagree	Disagree	Strongly disagree
3	2	1	0	-1	-2	-3

The values which are attached enable the replies to be ranked, but they cannot be used in arithmetic operations without the need of further information. Ordinal scales are also useful where measurement relates to a succession of events, such as the completion of house building programmes, but though this makes clear a temporal order, it does not in itself say how much later one event is followed by another.

Adding the concept of the *interval* means that variables can be conceived as classifying observations into an ordered series with equal and therefore consistent spacing. A simple example of an interval scale is temperature.

The scale satisfies the criteria for both nominal and ordinal types of scaling but, in addition, requires that the specified values are of equal interval. Even so, there is a limitation on the information which can be inferred from such a scale for there is no fixed point or zero. This means that comparative conclusion is not possible.[5]

Finally, the *ratio* scale satisfies all the previous requirements for the other scales and in addition has a fixed point or 'zero' reference.[6] In measuring age, we may legitimately say that a person of 20 is twice as old as a person of 10, and it is only with a ratio scale that such comparative conclusions are possible. For more complex measures, in which ratio scales are combined, such as speed (distance divided by time), these ratio characteristics are maintained.

Three general points should be noted about these scales. The first is that it is relatively easy for the researcher to confuse them, particularly where several scales are used in one investigation, say, combining factual and attitudinal data. Second, it is often not possible to determine the scale of measurement simply from an examination of the data and this creates particular problems where the data are from a secondary source. It follows that, in publishing work, the researcher should inform others of his scaling. Third, whilst the rules for defining the scales are quite precise, it is possible for both partial and hybrid types to exist (Kaplan, 1964).

One further topic under the heading of measurement is that of transformation. Measures, like words, may be put into a variety of forms without loss of information content. For example, a Fahrenheit scale may be transformed into a Centigrade scale, kilometres to miles, and so on. This is achieved by a set of prescribed operations which relates to the correspondence between the scales. It is often the case that an alternative way of presenting a measure can improve understanding and assist analysis. This is particularly true when several types of measure are to be compared. For example, it is often helpful to subtract a constant from a set of data values to simplify mathematical operations. The relative distribution of the data is unaffected by this, as is the variance. In effect, the origin of the scale is shifted, and the values are rescaled from it. Also, data are often transformed from absolute values to frequencies or percentages to permit comparison. Relative measures such as ratios may be calculated for the same purpose and ranking is yet another simple, common transformation.

A transformation is chosen in order to obtain a distribution more amenable to analysis or interpretation, but this is conditioned not only by the type of scale involved but also the type of operation which is being performed on that scale (Schuessler, 1971). It is important to distinguish *scale operations* such as ranking, counting and measuring, from *comparative* or *scale relationships* such as differences, ratios and inequalities. As far as the operations are concerned, ratio scales are subject to greater transformation restrictions, interval scales rather less and ordinal scales the least. Indeed, for the latter almost any operation may be performed on the values providing that the rank order is preserved. For relationship type transformations, the converse situation applies, ratio scales being the least restricted and ordinal scales the most.

Error, validity and reliability

No measurement is quite free from error which is, in effect, a measure of failure (Kaplan, 1964). To minimize error it is necessary to be able to recognize the various types of error which will most probably arise in urban study. It is also important that the researcher not only finds out as much as possible about these error effects but also makes this information known as part of his findings. The concepts of error and validity are clearly related.[7]

Errors arise from a number of sources. First, there is the inherent imprecision of the measuring 'instruments' and the way in which variables are defined. The term 'instruments' refers not only to the familiar devices, but also the procedures that are followed in carrying out measurement. This imprecision is called the sensitivity of measurement. It is, for example, not a technical limitation in the narrow sense that prevents the measurement of social class. Rather it is a matter of adequate conceptualization and definition.

The second source of error is that of reliability which concerns the extent to which the 'measurement remains constant when it is repeated under conditions which we take to be constant' (Kaplan, 1964). Repeated measurement, under even most closely controlled situations, rarely produces identical results. There are usually *random* influences or fluctuations at work, and under less controlled conditions, *systematic* errors will occur as well. Random errors are those which arise both in positive and negative directions, and therefore tend to cancel given an adequately large number of occurrences. They are, therefore, particularly difficult to trace, being in effect 'unobservable', but are less troublesome if truly random. They arise because they are embodied in the theoretical concepts of measurement. Systematic (or cumulative) errors normally arise from operational inadequacies in the research procedures rather than conceptual inadequacies. Common sources include inattention to 'rounding' values in calculations, or failure to use an adequate number of decimal places in calculation. They also arise through 'leading' a subject in an interview situation, or through badly calibrated measuring scales.

In much social investigation, the investigator himself will introduce both random and non-random fluctuations as he carries out his investigation. His investigation will teach him something about the subject, but equally the subject (either as an individual or a group) will learn about the investigator's intentions and also something about itself. This means that it will generally be impossible to repeat an investigation under similar conditions and the concept of reliability is jeopardized. Even the prior announcement that a survey will take place about some issue may affect attitudes of the potential repondents, and it is highly possible that they will be affected in some non-random, systematic way. For example, a particular sub-group, say those with higher education levels, may hear of the intentions of the researcher and this may influence their responses as a group. Distinguishing the presence of pre-existing error effects (those which would exist in any event without the investigation) from those which arise from the conduct of the investigation also adds a further difficulty.

Errors in quantification can give rise both to under- and over-enumeration, and also tend to be systematic rather than random. Even in quite simple counting tasks it is possible to fail to observe and record every unit. Traffic and pedestrian counts are good examples especially when the pattern of movement is complex. In sample survey work, non-response to questioning or failure to reach selected subjects will lead not only to under-enumeration but almost always to systematic error. Over-enumeration is likely to arise from double counting, which is a particular problem with inadequately defined classes or sub-groups for study. These errors are also systematic, but may be reduced by a thorough appreciation of the problems of quantification, the careful delimitation of classes and categories of what is to be observed, and the use of standardized measures and procedures. In distinguishing error sources, it is useful to recall that validity is dependent upon reliability, for if a measure has a high degree of validity then it must also be reliable, but if the degree of reliability is limited then a limit will be set to the degree of validity attained.

One further benefit arises from the use of standardized procedures, namely, that the concept of replication may be satisfied. Examples include interview data collected from respondents, each of which has been placed in as nearly an identical situation as possible. Each interview relationship must be treated in the same way, for example, in the way that questions are posed, and so on. Standardization of sample procedures will ensure that no ambiguity arises in the drawing of statistical inferences, and standard criteria for data analysis can be set out. If the need for replication can be satisfied, it should mean that any two analysts confronted with the same data should come to the same conclusions. This means that it will also be possible to generalize from the particular study to a wider environment.

It is a characteristic of urban study, as with other social fields, that this quest for replicative study is rarely pursued. There appears to be an almost myopic belief in the supposed adequacy of a single investigation, and it is the lack of properly conducted replicative study which accounts for the paucity of theory. There are, however, obstacles in achieving true replication which must be noted. First, the subject will most likely change in some respect during the conduct of the study. For example, if an enquiry were interviewing groups of residents in a local area, experimental replication would be achieved only if, for successive interviews, the same group could be assembled. Even then many other parameters will not remain constant, some of which we consider below. Whilst this is easy to see in respect of the human subject, the same is also true of the physical and economic 'environments' as well, though the sensitivity to change will probably be less. The question to be answered for the *practical purposes* of our inquiry is, are we dealing with a situation stable enough over time for these external influences to be assumed constant.

Second, as no human subject is entirely insensitive to being the subject of an inquiry about which he has knowledge, any attitudes, opinions, expectations and values will be changed by the very fact of the inquiry itself. Any attempt at replicative inquiry with human subjects must come to terms with this problem. It must be assumed that both the inquirer and the subject(s) will have learned from the conduct of the investigation. A very common situation is where a person may formulate some apparently very strong opinions simply because he is asked about some issue. Successive inquiry in this situation must try to take account of this 'learning effect', though it can also be used to heighten interest in a topic.

Third, the attitudes of the investigator will also change during inquiry. An unexpected characteristic of the subject may be observed which may cause a substantial reformation of attitudes, opinions and values, and even, through the re-arrangement of priorities, change the objectives of the investigation. These changes are particularly difficult to observe because, in effect, they require critical self-monitoring on the part of the researcher.

Fourth, there is the problem that, given that the subjects of an investigation will not be isolated, they will be influenced by changes in their general environment and by each other. In other words, in dealing with human behaviour and attitudes, for example, the general changes occurring all the time in society will be represented in the inquiry. These changes, which may occur slowly, will show up as 'error' effects and it is necessary to be able to distinguish them from the other types of error arising from measurement inadequacies and the sampling procedures.

Survey principles

The purpose of a survey is to obtain data with the maximum of reliability and validity, though, as there will always be some 'error', a more practical approach is to try to minimize the amount of error. The main considerations in the design of survey work relate to: (i) the object of the survey, (ii) the choice of subjects, including their spatial distributions, (iii) the selection of variables and characteristics to be measured, (iv) selection of the subjects, how many and in what distribution, (v) the method whereby the survey is to be conducted, (vi) the design of the 'instruments' for the survey, (vii) the design of procedures for the conduct of the survey, and (viii) decisions about the temporal (time series) relationships.

All survey design involves compromise, particularly where comparability with previous work is sought, notably in the choice of variables or the type of questions used. Usually, with hindsight, previous approaches, questions, definitions, and so on, are shown to have been inefficient. Not to improve the conduct of an inquiry by incorporating the lessons of previous work negates the accumulation of knowledge. Yet such modifications will jeopardize the extent to which comparability with previous work can be made and careful choice is called for to make the best of this conflict.

An initial distinction must be made between primary and secondary types of data. The former are acquired through the use of some kind of empirical, survey work; the second from published sources, or the work of others. Our main methodological concern is the former but, as the use of secondary data is commonplace, we should note certain potential problems. One is that sufficiency of definition, measurement, validity and reliability often has to be assumed. Good quality data make these matters clear, but regrettably much which are published does not. Sometimes, even information about the spatial bases and temporal periods is inadequate. While such data may be useful in exploratory study, it is only with additional corroboration or by the making of additional assumptions that they can be used in comparative and systematic analysis.

Turning to discuss the acquisition of primary data, a distinction must be made between interactive and non-interactive (or 'passive') inquiry. This concerns essentially the relationship between the investigator and his subject(s). Investigation of a non-living subject will be passive, as will that of a human subject who is *unaware* of the inquiry, for example, aspects of aggregate human behaviour such as the study of traffic flows or pedestrian movements. Time-lapse photography and other devices may be used in this context. In many instances in urban study the 'subject' will in any case be inanimate, for example, the flow of goods, or land uses, or housing conditions, and the resulting data will be factual though it may be of a probabilistic type. While there will be problems in explaining behaviour from the analysis of 'passive' data, the data itself are not biased by the subject's knowledge that he is part of an investigation. This means that the data may be more valid, though lack of explanatory power limits its usefulness.

In contrast, in interactive types of survey the acquisition of valid data depends upon the communicative process established between the investigator and his subject. In this process, each will respond to the other, and there will be a mutual learning effect. In order to maximize the reliability and validity of data, it is extremely important that the investigator obtains knowledge of the way in which the conduct of the investigation has influenced the responses that the subject gives. A further distinction can now be made between factual and attitudinal data and, although the division is sometimes rather arbitrary, a different technical approach is required for each.

At this stage we should note that simple checks can be built into survey design. For example, the reliability of factual questions can be checked by posing two separate questions so that their answers should be consistent. In dealing with the human subject this may have to be done covertly, for repeating a 'question' (which after all in an experimental situation is the usual method of ascertaining reliability) may either be invalidated by the learning effect or can even produce hostility from the subject. If he feels that a question is repeating ground already covered, he is most likely to assume incompetence on the part of the interviewer rather than appreciate the problems of interview reliability. Validity can be measured by designing an inquiry in such a way that the data can, in part, be checked against other known data, such as from the Census. For example, an age and sex distribution can be checked and, if in approximate agreement, assumptions could be made more generally about the validity of the survey.

The importance of thorough pilot work must be stressed. The pilot is conducted at a much smaller scale to test out the methodology of the main study, and, as we discuss, is obligatory if questionnaire design is involved. It will often reveal serious shortcomings in a proposed survey design, particularly that of unexpected interpretation.

A distinction must also be made between *cross-sectional* and *longitudinal* designs. The former are the most common but also suffer from the greater number of deficiencies. The subject is studied and data obtained, at one point in time, typically through a census of some kind. No attempt is made to follow the behaviour of the subject over a period of time and such a design cannot say anything about cause and effect relationships. Indeed, there are serious difficulties in exploring any inter-relationships. Data from cross-sectional investigations are often reported in the form of cross-tabulations and correlations between the variables, but explanations will be strictly limited. For example, in most urban investigations there will be phenomena which are well-represented in the data and others which are relatively scarce, and at the outset this may well be unknown. As the analysis attempts to establish relationships among the variables, it will be found that the incidence of infrequent occurrences imposes a limitation on the depth of analysis possible.

As there is no temporal order in a cross-sectional survey, it is difficult to control adequately for the inter-relationship between variables. This is a particular difficulty with respect to the explanatory variables, although occasionally a pseudo-temporal order may be found. An example is the National Census where the incidence of migratory moves by households during the periods up to one year and up to five years before the census dates are recorded. Such information must not be confused with genuine time series information. It is frequently necessary to compare data from two cross-sectional designs and if care is taken this can approximate to a longitudinal design, particularly in respect of factual data. This, however, will only be valid if the definitions, measurements and circumstances of the two sets of observations are identical.

In contrast, a longitudinal design sets out to make valid inferences about the dependent and independent relationships among a given set of variables. Longitudinal designs are, in effect, characterized by 'before and after' treatment. The subject or subjects are observed on at least two occasions, possibly more, under as identical a set of conditions as can be achieved. An experimental or quasi-experimental approach is then possible in which the effect of various influences can be tested and explained with statistical significance. The design enables a researcher to control for a large number of variables and, in particular, he can design the investigation in such a way as to be able to infer what would have occurred in the event of the subject *not* having been affected by some particular influence.

It is often the case that the phenomena under study vary considerably in their incidence and this raises problems in making correct inferences. A *factorial* design can help in this situation, in that subject selection can be manipulated so as to obtain a reasonable number of responses for *each* characteristic being studied in the survey data. Rare occurrences and rare combinations of phenomena ideally will appear as frequently as the more typical cases, though careful subject selection is necessary. The cost of this approach is that the random selection of the subjects is sacrificed.

Once the type of general approach has been decided, the choice as to the specific survey method will be from: (i) direct subject observation, (ii) direct subject interview, (iii) indirect interview by person employed by researcher, or (iv) self-administered survey. These methods may sometimes usefully be combined as, for example, when an inquiry is initially sent to the subject by post (self-administered), and subsequently a researcher calls to collect the answers, obtaining additional information and/or checking its accuracy. Such procedures can greatly improve the response rate for an inquiry, though usually at considerable manpower cost. As far as direct (passive) observation is concerned, little needs to be said. Provided that adequate attention is paid to the questions of definition and measurement, and the procedures later discussed are followed, few difficulties should be encountered. Surveys involving other then simple direct passive observation, however, give rise to some difficulties. In these there will be at least three interactive variables: (i) the respondent, (ii) the researcher, and (iii) the instrument (that is the questionnaire, interview schedule or recording procedure). Each of these, as well as the ambient interview situation, can have an important effect upon the validity and reliability of the results.

We deal first with the interview survey. This can yield a high response rate because the subject is approached personally and a rapport can be established. It means that control can be exercised over the actual respondent, sensitive issues can be tackled, as can complex issues which require explanation. Disadvantages include the near certainty that some interviewer bias will occur, and that the method can be costly in man hours for a given amount of information. There will be difficulties in standardizing the interview procedures where many interviewers are involved, and this will be made even more difficult if the geographical area to be covered is large. It is probable that there will be some problems of non-response, particularly for certain types of respondent, such as for working households or for persons who are away from home for lengthy or irregular periods, and avoiding this kind of bias can be expensive in repeat visits. 'Street' type surveys, where the interviewer selects at random from passers-by, will produce a different type of bias arising from the sectoral nature of the choice.

Interview designs can be usefully sub-divided into standardized, semi-standardized and non-standardized types (Burton and Cherry, 1969). A standardized interview is used when the same information is to be collected from each respondent. This requires ideally that the answers of all respondents *must* be comparable and classifiable, and that differences in responses reflect actual differences among respondents, and not, for example, differences in meaning which respondents have attributed to the same questions. The use of the standardized interview requires three conditions to be fulfilled. These are, first, that respondents have a sufficiently common vocabulary so that it is possible to formulate questions which have the same meaning for each of them; second, that a uniform wording for all respondents can be found for any subject matter, and third, that if the meaning of each question is to be identical, and since all preceding questions constitute part of the context, the sequence of the questions must be identical. There is also the implicit assumption that the requirements of these three separate assumptions can be met, for example by means of piloting and pre-testing of questions and questionnaires.

The standardized interview is most appropriate where (i) data are to be collected from groups which are significantly homogeneous; (ii) about subjects which can be expressed fairly easily in non-specific language, and (iii) covering matters which are factual or at least relatively non-emotive. The advocates of the semi-standardized interview method argue that if questions are to have the same meaning for each respondent, they must be formulated in wording that is *appropriate* for each respondent. Here, the interviewer operates not with a pre-determined schedule of questions, but a list of required information. A compromise situation is frequently used in which a schedule or questionnaire is used, though the interviewer may choose to question the respondent in any sequence. The non-standardized interview, sometimes called an 'open interview' is not formally structured and is most commonly used in exploratory situations. It can provide useful background information, particularly at a preliminary stage in an inquiry, but it does not yield comparable data. All interview situations ideally require the use of trained (or at least well-briefed) interviewers and Burton and Cherry (1969) categorize the desirable requirements.

In contrast to the interview, there is the so-called self-administered survey. The respondent is required to complete a form, say, which has been posted or given to him, but without any immediate guidance or advice. The advantages of this type of approach are that a wide geographical area may be covered and a larger sample achieved for a given cost. The organization of such a survey will usually be simpler, for there will not be an interviewing team to be briefed and organized. Perhaps the most important single advantage is that self-administered surveys avoid interviewer bias and do not require a relationship to be established between respondent and inquirer. There is also the advantage that the survey can be seen as anonymous by the respondent. These advantages, however, are obtained at a cost for there are major disadvantages. The most important of these is that the response rate will often be very low, even when replies are pre-paid, and this counteracts the apparent advantage of a large survey for minimum cost. Unfortunately, sample size cannot simply be increased by circulating a larger number of questionnaires in the first place, because non-response is almost always heavily biased towards particular sub-groups of respondents and the resulting errors are nearly always systematic.

Two particular aspects of non-response cause the greatest difficulty. First, because response depends upon the active effort of the subject he must feel in some way that it is 'worth his while'. If, as is common in urban investigation, any benefits to the individual may be perceived only obscurely, if at all, it is only a social motivation which will prevent him throwing the questionnaire away. Persons who have no great interest in the subject matter, or who hold no strong views, may simply not bother. Worse, they may pass the inquiry on to someone whom they think will be 'interested' and who may have very strong views about the matter. He is quite likely to enjoy the opportunity to respond, perhaps twice! In general, therefore, no control can be exercised over who will actually respond. Second, in a postal inquiry we rely upon the intelligence of the respondent to read, understand and respond, assuming he wishes to do so. The approach is clearly biased against persons of lesser intelligence, poor ability in reading and comprehension, and so on. Self-administered inquiry avoids interviewer bias but is heavily affected by respondent bias. Non-response may be partially overcome by follow-up letters or personal visits or telephone calls, or even money inducements, though, in all cases, the timing of such reminders is critical (Scott, 1961). Some bias inevitably remains which is difficult to assess, though it is often suggested that *late* 'responders' and 'non-responders' may be similar in their characteristics.

The questions which can be asked in self-administered surveys are limited both in type, depth and number. No control can be exercised over circumstances in which the questions are answered, or indeed their order. Given that the response to one question may very much influence the subject's attitude to a subsequent question, additional uncertainty is introduced. Conversely, there is a danger of 'leading' or influencing the respondent through poor ordering of questions. In principle, the problem could be overcome by randomizing the order of questions, but this may introduce problems of comprehension for the respondent who may well dislike 'jumping' from one subject to another and back again. Some compromise has therefore to be sought, the effect of which can never precisely be evaluated.

In an inquiry, it is important for the survey designer to remember that every question, every response, indeed every part of an interview or question schedule will affect the overall attitude of the respondent and contribute to his willingness and his ability to answer successive questions. The maintenance of a positive attitude on the part of the respondent is not easy, and it will be enhanced by careful attention to such factors as initial explanation, layout of questionnaire, friendliness and courtesy of the interviewers, and so on.

Survey design

The subjects and their various characteristics to be studied need to be precisely and unambiguously defined and classified, and some general guidelines may be helpful at this stage. We might, for example, classify the subject material relevant to urban planning under three general headings such as (i) the physical environment, (ii) the built environment, and (iii) the social environment. These will have explicit spatial dimensions, and can be further sub-categorized. The purpose of using such a system is to develop a hierarchy of suitable subject definitions and to avoid ambiguities.

Among these classifications will be subjects which have acquired an established, clearly defined meaning. For example, under the heading of the physical environment we may cite climatic events, land form and slope, land drainage, and agricultural land uses. With the traditional emphasis in planning upon the built form, classifications have been developed in urban land uses and some such systems are of considerable detail. Here, the researcher is not faced with problems of the conceptualization of the subject, but rather with finding the best way to operationalize his idealized survey design.

On the other hand, in studying aspects of human behaviour in the urban context, more conceptual difficulties arise concerning the satisfactory definition and communication of terms. Collective expressions such as 'households', 'shoppers' or 'motorists' need to be defined as unambiguously as possible. This is not easy and some of the problems may be seen in an example. A private household[8] may be:

1   A one-person household, viz. a person who lives alone in a separate housing unit (as defined) or who occupies, as a lodger, a part or the whole of a separate room or rooms in a part of a housing unit but does not join together with any of the other occupants of the housing unit to form part of a multi-person household as defined below. Or:

2   A multi-person household, defined as a group of two or more persons who combine together jointly to occupy the whole or part of a housing unit, and to provide themselves with food *or* other essentials for living. The group may pool their incomes and have a common budget to a greater or lesser extent in different circumstances. The group may be composed of related persons or unrelated persons or a combination of both, including boarders but excluding lodgers. (*Boarders* take meals with the private household and generally are allowed to use all the available household facilities. *Lodgers* however are sub-tenants who have hired part of the housing unit for their exclusive use. They may or may not have meals regularly with the household, but they are distinguished from boarders principally by the fact that they do not automatically enjoy the use of all available household facilities.)[9]

In most cases the selection of a given subject will also be conditioned by the location of the investigation. For example, getting a truly representative sample of 'shoppers' and 'non-shoppers' in a main street will clearly be difficult and lead to bias. Indeed, any locational basis for subject *selection* will exclude the non-user. If we are, for example, seeking a sample of motorists, do they actually have to be at the wheel of the car to be so classified? If we are asking questions about use of a car, then perhaps car *owners* may be a suitable classification basis, and they can reliably be asked questions about car use, whether we question them in their home, at work, or on the road. On the other hand, if we are interested in attitudes to other road users, or some similar behavioural aspect of driving, then clearly asking questions in a place or time other than whilst active in the task will produce potentially different responses.

Many of these issues will apply also to the definition of the variables (the characteristics of attributes of the subjects) and there is a further point (Harvey, 1969). In any survey, important decisions have to be made on which variables to include in a survey and which to leave out, and clearly, this can only be done in the light of the objectives and the resources. Equally, the choice of variables cannot be made independently from the choice on the spatial base of the survey, for there will be difficulties in comparing data about a given set of variables based upon one spatial basis and another. Most surveys will involve some kind of sampling. For this, we need to have knowledge of what we are sampling from, that is, the whole population[10] assembled in a list with either spatial or at least nominal characteristics. Examples include a list of households in an urban area, lists of persons, lists of enumeration districts, lists of 100 metre squares for an urban area, or even a grid reference system for an urban area. Frequently, the 'whole population' of entities cannot be defined, for example, if we wish to investigate, say, traffic congestion or delinquency. Fortunately, valid sample data may still be obtained even though the whole population size must be assumed. Further assumptions of a different type have to be made, for example, in measuring phenomena such as traffic flow, or flow of goods between industries. Here the 'frame' will be conceptually more difficult, and there will be both a spatial and a temporal dimension to define. The most important point is that the frame, however defined, must allow each entry an exactly equal chance of appearing in the sample survey, and the units must be selected in such a way that no systematic bias occurs. The frame needs to be as up-to-date as possible, and without any duplication of entries.

The principle of the sample frame can be extended to two (or more) dimensions to allow spatial sampling. For example, an area of land may be regarded as the whole population and a set of samples drawn from it to represent characteristics distributed over the surface. There are a number of ways in which land use surveys can be conducted (Berry and Baker, 1968; Harvey, 1969; and Haggett *et al.*, 1977) using (i) points, (ii) lines (or traverses), and (iii) areas (or quadrats). The simplest method is to use random numbers by pairs to identify point locations on a grid superimposed over the study area (figure 5.2 (b)). However, this brings disadvantages for, if some of the phenomena being studied are relatively rare, then a very large number of points has to be taken to allow those rare characteristics to be adequately represented. There may also be rather obvious operational difficulties in actually locating the survey points on the ground, even sometimes of gaining access to the precise location.

Figure 5.2 Types of sample frame

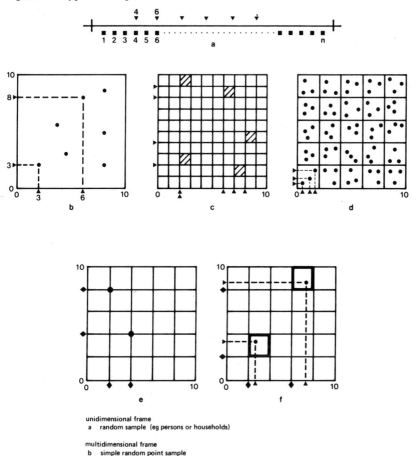

unidimensional frame
a   random sample (eg persons or households)

multidimensional frame
b   simple random point sample
c   simple random area sample
d   areally stratified random sample
e   systematic random sample
f   nested (two-stage) random sample

After Krumbein (1960: 361), Berry and Baker (1968: 92–3) and Harvey (1969: 364)

Nevertheless, if the method is feasible it is an efficient design and relatively simple to interpret the data produced. The difficulties can often be met by traverse or area sampling (figure 5.2 (c)), and occasionally, in order to improve the distribution of the data points, area and point methods may be combined (figure 5.2 (d)). Here the land is divided by areas and a sample point is chosen from each, in a form of spatial stratification. The essential distinction for the survey is between a random and systematic sampling base, though where there is an explicit spatial dimension they may usefully be used jointly. A further alternative, though more complex, is to use quadrat sampling which concerns theorizing about the probability function of the data points in the respective quadrats into which the study area is divided.[11] If the phenomena being studied are randomly distributed throughout the sample survey frame and of roughly equal occurrence, then any sample design will produce useful data and the obvious choice is the simplest method. When this is not so, particularly where linear and other trends are present, more specialized techniques are required.

Figure 5.3 The data cube

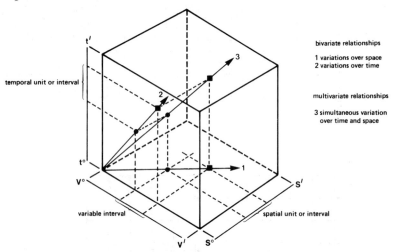

In recognizing the utility of time series data, we have not yet commented on the definition of the time interval or time unit which may be employed, nor indeed have we dicussed the inter-relationship of temporal and spatial concepts in the process of measurement. These issues can be most effectively illustrated by the concept of the *data cube* (Berry, 1964; Chorley and Haggett, 1967; Harvey, 1969). For the most part, urban data comprises three dimensions. The first corresponds to the phenomenon itself, its capacity to take on a range of values (without which measurement is irrelevant) and which represent its characteristics. This measurement, however, relates to both the space in which the phenomenon occurs *and* the changes which occur over time (figure 5.3).

Simultaneous study of these dimensions can cause difficulties and it is often helpful to decompose the 'cube' into three bivariate components. For example, a phenomenon can be studied over time holding its spatial distribution constant, or the spatial patterns in the distribution can be studied at a single point in time. Third, the behaviour can be held constant and measurement made of changes in spatial distribution over time. If the information which enables us to study these inter-relationships is itself compatible in terms of validity, reliability, measurement and its spatial and temporal units, then multi-dimensional aspects can be studied. In that choice as to spatial and temporal units has to be made as part of the survey design, it is important to note how such comparability can be satisfied. First, however, we must note a complication. If we consider the spatial dimension, we will find that the choice of spatial unit will affect the validity

Figure 5.4 The problem of choosing an 'observational' base

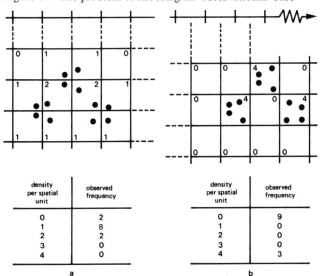

density per spatial unit	observed frequency
0	2
1	8
2	2
3	0
4	0

a

density per spatial unit	observed frequency
0	9
1	0
2	0
3	0
4	3

b

of the measure itself, that is, they are not independent. In the same way, validity of measurement is not independent of the time unit chosen for the survey. Two simple examples will illustrate the problems. Many of the phenomena of interest to urban planners have an underlying dimension, that is, a pattern of distribution over the land surface. Indeed, without these regularities, the phenomena could not be studied systematically at all. Equally, many phenomena exhibit regular temporal patterns such as trends, though they may be linear, non-linear, cyclical, or irregular. In figure 5.4, a particular choice of spatial unit is superimposed in two ways on a phenomenon which *itself* possesses a regular spatial pattern. The accident of interaction between the survey or 'observational' structure (the grid), and the distribution of the phenomena can lead to widely different results. Figure 5.4(a) suggests that the distribution is fairly even over the observation surface. On the other hand, figure 5.4(b) appears to say that the phenomenon is highly clustered, and indeed in nine out of the sixteen spatial units observed, no trace of the phenomenon appears at all.

In practice, choice over the spatial base for surveys varies, often quite arbitrarily, for example including enumeration districts, grid squares or street blocks. It has to be recognized that the choice over spatial unit usually involves compromise, particularly over the level of spatial disaggregation, and it requires a cost/effectiveness judgement on the part of the researcher. However, it is important that care is taken not only to determine a base which fulfils the requirements of adequate spatial detail, administrative efficiency, ease of definition, and so on, but also that it does not inhibit the validity of the measures, or worse, impose a pseudo-structure of its own on the data. The choice of the observational base, then, is neither simple nor neutral.

Figure 5.5 The problem of interval measurement over time

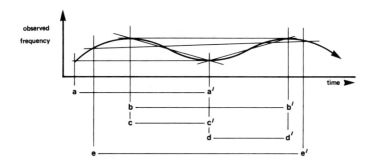

An underlying temporal dimension presents a similar problem. Consider figure 5.5 and a cyclical phenomenon. If observations are limited to time points $a - a'$, no change in trend may be inferred; equally, with observations at points $b - b'$, though neither gives any valid information about the average frequency of occurrence. Observations $c - c'$ mislead by implying an overall decline, and $d - d'$ the converse, while $e - e'$ suggests steady upward growth. The reader can, no doubt, readily add any number of other possibilities. The immediate answer is to make more observations, say a, b, c', whereupon a better representation of the trend is obtained. The extent to which valid data can be obtained is not just a function of the number of observations but of their temporal coincidence with the fluctuation of the phenomenon itself. In general, the danger of assuming trends from a few datum points needs to be carefully observed. There are also well established branches of statistical theory for dealing with cyclical or periodic events.[12]

As far as simple observational (i.e. passive) surveys are concerned, again little needs to be said. Providing attention is paid to the concepts that have been identified, few problems should arise. For the active types of investigation there are important further matters to be discussed.

If the number of subjects and their geographical distribution permits, the researcher can personally conduct interviews. He can then effectively control the whole conduct of the inquiry and deal unambiguously with unexpected situations that may arise. This is sometimes taken as obviating the need for him to fully think through the investigation design in detail. There is then a tendency for the investigator to 'make it up as he goes along', not so much in blatantly adding or deleting sections to his inquiry, but rather in the way that answers are interpreted. Any researcher is, after all, likely to have certain preconceived views about what he is hoping his survey will reveal. A real danger is that the investigator may interpret any ambivalent or uncertain responses in favour of either his own personal opinions or in favour of his research expectations. This is a particular danger in measuring attitudes or aspects of behaviour. A number of effects are possible. For example, a researcher may have a strong expectation as to his findings. Through a variety of causes, including perhaps an inadequate research design, he obtains a greater number of indeterminate responses than he feels his approach justifies. He may be under pressure to obtain results, or may simply be genuinely disappointed, and he may search the ambivalent and indeterminate responses for evidence in support of his own expectations and bias the results. Second, if through poor question design he finds his approach ineffective, he may tend to rephrase the questions, or even just to add intonation to his voice, hinting additional information to the subject. Any such extra 'help' is likely to introduce bias in favour of the researcher's expectations.

A similar situation may arise where interviews are carried out by persons employed by the researcher, but here the problem is not likely to be *their* expectation of the responses, for the researcher might not disclose these to the team, rather it is that the interviewers will form their own attitudes and opinions to the questions during the survey. They may, for example, have no views, or just weakly held views at the outset, which may be transformed into strong views. Again, this may influence the interpretation of ambivalent responses or lead the subject. These effects can be summarized as below.

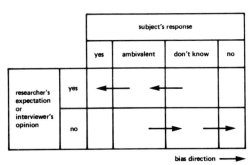

To minimize these problems several points should be noted. First, all persons involved should be aware that the problem may arise and, as far as possible, adopt a neutral position. Second, the opportunity for such bias increases greatly as the number of ambivalent or indeterminate responses rises, and as far as possible the range of response cells, categories and classifications of answers should cover all expected responses. The importance of pilot work here cannot be overstated. Third, interviewers should be instructed to 'refer back' ambivalent or inconclusive responses to the organizer, limiting interpretation to one person. Fourth, interviewers should keep strictly to the agreed formula for posing questions. Particularly, they should resist the admittedly strong temptation to help out a subject who is in difficulties in understanding a question, but the resulting embarrassment often pushes the interviewer into a highly biased amplification of the question. Again, good pilot work can do much to both train interviewers and identify possible problem areas.

The organization of the actual survey will require careful briefing of the investigators, particularly if they are very numerous, and if there is a wide geographical distribution there will be problems of co-ordination. Agreed procedures must be followed in such cases as non-return of questionnaires, misinterpretation of questions, or substitution of one sample unit for another, any of which can give rise to serious bias. Further, there must be agreement as to how to treat missing cases, for example, how many return visits should be made to absent households, and so on. As noted earlier, non-response is invariably not random and it is particularly important for it to be minimized. Where the survey covers several areas with different general characteristics, it will also be important to try to ensure an even response in all districts to avoid a non-random bias against a particular area. A quality control check should be made on a survey team in the form of a sample check by a supervisor, or the researcher himself, repeating selected operations, and if the sample is large, and/or relatively inexperienced persons are employed, such a check is vital. Questionnaires and data will need to be read and checked for 'missing cases' and omissions, any clearly erroneous information, mis-interpretation of questions, and obvious measurement errors. In that any survey will require a unique design, as well as noting the more general concepts already discussed it is suggested the reasearcher reads as widely as possible in preparation for survey work, particularly well conducted case studies. These will be invaluable in preparing the researcher for the methodological and procedural problems.

In one particular type of survey it is essential that the researcher conducts his own inquiry. This is the exploratory situation noted earlier, which often forms the outset of a particular investigation. The emphasis is upon obtaining data of a general, descriptive nature about the opinions, attitudes, values, expectations, and so on, of the subjects. The information is used in turn to construct a more rigorous subsequent investigation. Regrettably, in much urban study this distinction is not always clearly observed. Typically, a formal interview can degenerate into an unstructured chat, which may well provide new and interesting insights but which will make analysis and valid interpretation quite impossible.

We should introduce now the problems to be faced in designing the instruments of the survey, assuming that the subjects have been defined and located. For passive inquiry, the design of the recording sheet to be completed by the observer will be a straightforward matter.[13] For the active type of inquiry there are particular difficulties in the wording of questions to be asked. Arguably, it is the most difficult part of survey design. It is best approached by noting that each question has a communicative function which is broader than the immediate subject content of the question itself. Indeed, questions, words, intonation, and phrasing, all convey an impression by the interviewer which builds up to an overall influence upon the respondent (Oppenheim, 1968). What guidelines can be offered? First, note must be made as to the subjects. They may be adults or children, working people or pensioners, women or men, residents or visitors, and so on. We may have some experience of their relative ability to respond to questioning and this must influence question design. A review of literature is particularly useful here and will throw light upon the problems and difficulties which others have faced in similar situations.

Questions should avoid technical language or jargon and should be direct, exactly to the point, and short. Unfamiliar words must be avoided and it is important to note that words sometimes have local meanings. In general, a questionnaire designer should try to put himself in the position of the respondent. He should try out questions on his colleagues, or better still, on persons similar in class, occupation, intelligence levels, and so on, to the prospective subjects. Pilot work is extremely important for even experienced investigators can be surprised at the interpretation which can be placed upon apparently quite straightforward questions.

Although the ordering of the questions is important in any survey, it is particularly so in respect of attitudes. Two points should be noted. First, each question and its response will contribute to sustaining the relationship with the subject throughout the inquiry. The subject's involvement in, and attitude towards, the inquiry can be nurtured by careful ordering of the questions. Easy questions should come first, allowing the subject to develop his confidence in responding, and it is important to proceed quickly to what the subject expects the questions to be about. Care in presentation is necessary to prevent the subject from becoming self-conscious if unable to answer questions, and it is useful to include straightforward, factual questions at the end which will leave the respondent in a state of mind of having been able to supply answers. The second point is that questions should be ordered so that the subject cannot anticipate subsequent questioning and be led into responses that he might not otherwise have made.

As far as the design of questions is concerned, we must consider the two types. *Factual* questions seek a precise piece of information, though as we have noted, 'facts' can be difficult to define and rest only upon common acceptance of terminology. However, if care is taken with definition, factual questions are straightforward to design. In urban study, they frequently relate to characteristics such as age, sex, marital status, family size, income, house type, car ownership, and so on, and the data are often used to classify the subject groups for analysis. Factual questions can relate to behaviour at a particular point in time or to specific periods. For example, 'how often in the last month have you visited the supermarket?' and, in drawing conclusions, generalization must be made as to how typical is this behaviour over longer periods. The longer the period that is *specified* in the question, the less likely it is to obtain a valid measure, for the ability to recall actions in detail is limited even over quite short periods. If an accurate record over time is required, the alternative is to use the diary method. Here the respondent is asked to keep day-to-day records of aspects of behaviour, such as shopping trips or car use. This approach can yield very accurate data, but there may be difficulties in recruiting satisfactory subjects, particularly in some population sub-groups, and the failure to make regular records will almost certainly be biased. A troublesome problem is that some subjects may be tempted to fill in missing parts of the diary from memory just before completion.

Attitudinal questions attempt to find out information about attitudes, values, aspirations, hopes, wishes, views and the like. They give rise to greater design problems. The first problem arises in the definition of the terms, even before the problems of communicating the questions can be tackled. For example, we may try to find out if a group of subjects find some particular situation satisfactory, say pedestrianization of a shopping street. How can this be done? First, we must define the situation in our own terms, and unless we do this satisfactorily we cannot communicate it to others, let alone interpret any information the respondent may give. Attitudes must be measured in terms of a scale which will enable us to distinguish meaningfully the various responses which we obtain. In reply to our question, we might adopt a simple attitude scale as noted earlier which could yield valid data. Even so, it is important that our criteria are well understood and that, as far as possible, the intentions of the respondent can be unambiguously interpreted.

Some general issues should be noted before a further discussion of attitude inquiry. Questions can be classified as 'closed' or 'open'. The former require either a factual answer, such as age, or occupational group, or a reply in terms of some pre-selected, discrete criteria, such as yes/no, or frequently/occasionally/never. In an open question the interviewer records the reponse in the terms of the respondent, which the researcher must interpret. Open and closed questions are generally not compatible in the same survey for the subject may not distinguish clearly between them. Also, open questioning requires considerable experience and can only really be effective when conducted over a group of subjects by a single researcher.

As far as possible, questions need to be presented in a neutral mode, that is they should not suggest the investigator's own point of view[14] or indicate that a particular opinion is being sought. Questions may inadvertently imply approval or disapproval to the subject, and if he is anxious to please or embarrassed, his response may be affected. One form of question, often encountered in planning type surveys but better avoided altogether, is predictive questions, 'What will you do next Saturday?', or 'How will...?'

In general, people are very poor predictors of their own behaviour and events often bear little correspondence to expectations, and answers will usually amplify any expectation. A preferred approach is to use valid behavioural data from a similar situation and attempt to make assumptions as to its applicability to the particular area of interest.

Two types of questions deserve special mention, namely 'prestige' and 'sensitive' questions, and both give rise to serious under- and over-statement. With the former, the respondent may feel loss of prestige or embarrassment if he answers truthfully, for example, if he admits being dismissed from employment. For similar reasons, a person may increase his income or reduce his age. He may disguise being unable to answer the question at all by a false answer. Sensitive issues such as income or co-habitation require special treatment. Responses to an income question can sometimes be obtained by broad-band answer categories posed in the form 'do you earn more or less than £90 per week?' rather than 'what are your weekly earnings?' Questions about personal behaviour should neither suggest disapproval nor patronize.

If the survey schedule is long, 'filter questions' can be used to sub-structure the inquiry. For example, a question such as 'do you have any children?' enables the interviewer to include or avoid a whole sub-section of a survey on that topic. Switching, however, needs to be managed smoothly, for a poor performance on the interviewer's part may well be reflected in the responses of a less than confident subject.

Attitude measurement

It remains in this section to return to the problems associated with attitude measurement. In trying to measure opinions, values or beliefs about planning and planning problems, at the simplest level the researcher may simply ask for opinions from a selected stratum of a population. This will be akin to exploratory study and, while it may provide useful information, it will do little systematically to advance knowledge. Ideally, one would like to be able to apply the same measurement rules as for factual data. The major difficulty, however, is a psychological one, namely of defining the presence of the attitudes that are sought, for they may be latent and only expressed in response to an inquiry. An attitude then can be thought of as a tendency to act or react in a certain way when confronted with a stimulus (Oppenheim, 1968). Given this situation, measurement is only possible by making certain assumptions. The first is that attitudes can be ranked on a dimension or scale, ranging from strongly held positive and negative positions, through an indifferent neutral position. For simplicity, most scales are linear and although readily comprehended have limitations. The second assumption is that attitudes are often realized, though not necessarily so, among *groups* of people. However, this assumption must take into account not only that attitudes are transient, subject to quite dramatic change, and may be inefficiently expressed, but that they are often formulated by reaction to a situation and are therefore very susceptible to the influence of other people's attitudes.

To establish a scale of measurement, we first find out the range of views and opinions held on a topic, usually by pilot study. This range can then be used to construct a scale, though assumptions have to be made about linearity and relevant intervals of measurement. Again, pilot study will help determine the latter, and will enable a check to be made on the subject's perceptions of the researcher's intentions and their interpretation.

Attitudinal surveys proper are usually conducted by in-depth interview which serves two purposes (Oppenheim, 1968; Hoinville and Jowell, 1978). The first is to explore the origins, complexities and ramifications of the attitudes in question in order to decide more precisely what is being measured. The second is to obtain attitude expressions from the respondent in a form that enables construction of the scale. In practice, the scale is often constructed partly in advance of and partly after the inquiry.

In posing the questions, a deliberately non-neutral stance is adopted. The questions must be as informative as possible and have a specific aim of maintaining the interest of the subject and stimulating response. Oppenheim suggests that familiar language is the most important single requirement. In a sense, the subject should not think out his replies too much, for we are more interested in spontaneous reaction. Complex, formal questioning or use of unfamiliar language will inhibit the achievement of this objective. It is usual to measure attitudes by the use of *sets* of questions rather than a single question on each topic, and these will help define the scale. This also means that any bias which might arise from the interpretation of any one question will tend to be cancelled out when questions approach the topic from different angles, with different wording and reactions. Ideally, the underlying 'common' or 'true' attitude will be constant in the responses and can be identified. The underlying assumption, then, is that there is such a thing as a 'true' attitude which is stable enough to be measured. By using sets of questions, provided they all relate to the same attitude, it is possible to maximize the more stable component while reducing the instability due to idiosyncrasies on the part of both the subject and the conduct of the inquiry. Reliability is, however, invariably lower than with factual inquiry.

The validity of attitudinal questioning is limited by the lack of criteria (Oppenheim, 1968). It would be ideal if there were groups of people with known attitudes so that it would be possible to determine whether or not questions can discriminate between them. But by their nature these groups are extremely difficult to define. The purpose of trying to measure attitudes is to establish possible links with behaviour, but at best there is only likely to be a rough correspondence, and behaviour cannot necessarily be predicted from attitudes.[15]

For the actual scaling of responses there are a variety of methods commonly used, such as Likert, Guttman and Thurstone scales.[16] The general approach can be made clear by an example. Guttman scale analysis is essentially a means of examining the inter-relationships among a set of attitudinal responses according to certain properties which define the scale. In order to do this (as with other scales) particular criteria have to be met. In this case, the scale must be unidimensional, that is, all component items must measure attitudes towards or away from the same single underlying object. Neither the substantive nature of this object nor the unit of analysis is critical to the method. Guttman scaling employs a cumulative approach which implies that the component items can be ordered according to some criterion such as difficulty, or strength of attitude, and that a subject who responds positively to a given statement will also respond positively to less difficult or less strong statements. For example, we are interested in the attitude of a particular group of residents in a town to the recent pedestrianization of a shopping street. Each respondent is presented with the following set of statements to which he can agree or disagree.

A: Pedestrianization is worth the cost of the scheme.
B: Pedestrianization makes shopping easier.
C: Pedestrianization is good for traders and shoppers.
D: Pedestrianization means a better environment for shopping.
E: Pedestrianization means less noise and danger.

Each of these statements is clearly concerned with the measurement on a single scale, namely the attraction of a pedestrianized shopping street. Also, the statements have been placed into an order, so that in effect more people are likely to 'agree' with statement E than statement A. This ordering can either be done prior to the survey by the researcher according to his preconceptions of the problem, or *after* the survey according to the proportion of the respondents who agree or disagree with the statements. Technically, an ordinal scale has been constructed with a 'cutting point', that is – agree/disagree. For each statement, we are interested in which side of this cutting point the response lies. Should the ordering be substantially different from what is expected, the researcher will be wise to reconsider his initial understanding of the problem.

The degree to which a group of responses is both unidimensional and cumulative is determined by the extent to which 'agreements' on any statement are associated with 'agreements' on all statements which have been ranked as less demanding. Similarly, the scale will be unidimensional and cumulative in so far as 'disagreement' for any statement is associated with disagreement on statements which are judged to be *more* demanding. In theory, according to Guttman principles, perfect unidimensionality and cumulativeness would be indicated by the following pattern of responses.

These six scale types exhaust the possible combination of perfect responses. Empirical data, however, is unlikely to conform to this perfect pattern, and the Guttman test of scaleability[17] is to compare the data with this scale-perfect model and measure the deviation or error. These errors are accumulated and statistically tested to see how nearly the data are unidimensional and cumulative.

Statements

Scale type	A	B	C	D	E
5	1	1	1	1	1
4	0	1	1	1	1
3	0	0	1	1	1
2	0	0	0	1	1
1	0	0	0	0	1
0	0	0	0	0	0

1 = agreement
0 = disagreement

Sampling principles

In many areas of investigation, a *whole population* cannot be investigated. It may be undefined, or too large or too inaccessible to be studied in its entirety. By studying a part we hope to be able to obtain knowledge and draw inferences which can be generalized to apply to the whole population to some degree. Sampling theory concerns the development of ways in which this partial information may be acquired efficiently and with validity. If the whole population is unknown it is necessary to make assumptions as to how much of it the sampled part represents, but, if known, a *specified* portion or fraction can be studied.

Every sample design will yield data the representativeness of which to the whole population is limited. This arises partly from inevitable deficiencies in the procedures by which the sampling is carried out, but also from the inherent 'error' of sampling method. This, *ceteris paribus*, is closely related to the *size* of the sample. A larger sample will give more accurate results than a smaller one, but will need more resources to carry out and will cost more. Careful evaluation of the 'worth' of the accuracy of the information relative to the resources necessary to produce it is an essential, though often difficult, stage of sample design.

The design for a particular use of sampling depends upon four general factors (Harvey, 1969). They are: (i) the purpose of the investigation; (ii) the nature of the phenomena being investigated; (iii) the mode of inference envisaged (for particular forms of statistical inference require particular kinds of sampling procedure); (iv) the cost (in time, manpower and money) incurred. The first three are important to the accuracy or *validity* of the sampling procedure, while the fourth raises more general concerns.

If the subject matter being investigated is uniform in the distribution of its characteristics, almost any sample will give representative results. For example, laboratory experiments on blood can be conducted from any single drop. This is because the circulatory system is a closed and therefore isolated system and we can rely on the characteristics which we wish to investigate being uniformly distributed through mixing in the fluid. But ideal sampling situations are rare in non-experimental investigation, and we must therefore have the closest regard to an appropriate choice of sample design in order to obtain as representative a set of data as can be achieved.

In general, a representative sample is defined as one which is relatively free of *bias*. Freedom from bias (perfect representativeness) is an idealized situation, but it is useful as a yardstick by which the sufficiency of a particular sample design may be assessed. This bias is often referred to as 'sample error', because it is error which arises from the inherent nature of the sampling process. There is no way in which this error can be known in advance, for to find it, after all, would require knowledge of the whole or 'true' population, and the main reason why we use sampling methods is to avoid having to measure this true population.

In addition to sample errors, 'measurement' or non-sampling errors such as interviewer bias will arise. Any results obtained from sampling will therefore be subject to a total error which will comprise two components, sample and non-sample errors and, in many practical situations, they are confused. If the reasonable assumption is made that these types of errors are independent of each other, the total error is a function of two independent sources and cannot be substantially reduced unless *both* types are simultaneously controlled (Blalock, 1970). This is of great importance for sample design. There is little point, for example, in increasing a sample size beyond a certain point in order to reduce sampling error, when a non-sampling error may remain unaffected, and relatively large. Similarly, a researcher will be wasting his time if he designs a sample survey which pays great attention to minimizing non-sampling errors, if, in doing so, he has to use so small a sample that he incurs large sampling errors. Good sample design is a matter of balancing the estimated effects of such errors, and their probable effect on the total design.

Two procedures[18] can be identified of particular relevance to urban planning, namely *purposive* (or non-probability) and *probability* sampling. In the former, the subject is not chosen systematically and, therefore, no guarantee of randomness can be given. Such sampling is often used in exploratory investigation where general, or initial, knowledge about a phenomenon is required and where accuracy is not critical (Haggett *et al.*, 1977). Examples include 'case studies' (Chapter 7) where an area, say part of a town is chosen for study with the assumption that it can yield useful data that are 'typical'. Such data are useful to support or contradict initial inductive conceptualizations about a particular problem, at which point much research begins (Harvey, 1969). However, the lack of control and absence of randomization means that only tentative generalization is possible and inferences can be drawn only to a very limited extent. Nevertheless, with care in the selection of the cases, possibly with deliberate, haphazard selection of cases or sub-groups (as opposed to true systematic random selection), the quality of such samples can be raised to a useful level. Improvement can sometimes be achieved by sub-division, which may allow a characteristic otherwise obscured in a large body of data to be revealed.

In probability sampling, sample selection is done systematically which ensures randomness and enables the investigator to specify the probability with which any item is chosen for inclusion in the sample. He can therefore estimate the accuracy of his sample for any given sample size. If the sample is obtained truly randomly, it will yield an *unbiased* estimate of the true population, and the properties of the normal distribution will enable an estimate to be made of how good this sample estimate is. However, some bias will remain, even in probability sampling, due to effects such as measurement error and non-response in survey work.

Probability sampling can be carried out in a variety of ways. If the subject is randomly distributed then most forms of sampling are appropriate and simple random sampling is the most straightforward to use. However, if some linear trend exists within the true population, either spatially or temporally, or both, then it is preferable to use either stratified or systematic sampling. If it is feasible, the former normally yields the more efficient results (Berry and Baker, 1968), but if spatial autocorrelation[19] is present, a more specialist method may be necessary (Haggett *et al.*, 1977).

Given clearly defined objectives for a survey, a sampling design will usually involve the following practical stages: (i) the preparation of a sample frame; (ii) the selection of the sample units; (iii) the conduct of pilot trials; (iv) the conduct of the main survey; (v) the analysis and presentation of findings.

The sample frame is a suitable classification of the true population from which the sample is selected. In probability sampling, it is of vital importance that the frame should be complete, so that every identifiable element or unit which has relevance to the sample has an exactly equal chance of being chosen for inclusion in the sample. In practical terms, the compilation of a satisfactory frame is problematical. Often it is necessary to use some previously published data as a frame, and this may contain a number of inadequacies, notably, by being out of date. For example, the National Census uses a sample frame of households,[20] and this needs to be brought up-to-date by the removal of households from dwellings which have been demolished, by adding households in new constructions and the new households in dwellings which have been sub-divided, and so on. Acquisition of such updated information can be difficult and costly. A number of sources may need to be consulted and this raises additional problems of overlaps, varying base dates and missing cases. Often compromise is needed, weighing up the advantages to be obtained from an improved frame against the cost of its acquisition. It must be noted that inadequacies in a sample frame are usually *not* randomly distributed among the characteristics of the population being studied and may lead to serious bias in the sample.

The actual selection of the sample units may be made in a variety of ways. An important general point is to stress the need for consistency and a clear, defined approach which should be carefully recorded. Unless this is done, subsequent investigators and analysts will have difficulty in the interpretation of the results.

Types of sampling[21]

The basic principle of simple[22] random sampling is to select a sample of n units from the true population N in such a way that every unit has an equal chance of being chosen. This is frequently achieved by the use of random numbers and a suitable sample frame. This process is usually done without *replacement*, that is, when an item is chosen for the sample it is removed from the frame and cannot be chosen by chance again. Any repeated random number is, therefore, ignored.

We should, at this stage, introduce some conventional notation. Capital letters are used to refer to the characteristics of a population and lower case letters refer to those of its sample. As sampling is used to say something about the characteristics of a population from a study only of a sample of it, we need to distinguish the *true* characteristics of the population from the *estimate* of its characteristic. The latter is denoted by the symbol ˆ. We can define the following basic measures for a population X and between two populations X and Y:

	Population		Sample
	True	Estimate	
Total	X	$\hat{X}$	x
Mean	$\bar{X}$	$\hat{\bar{X}}$	$\bar{x}$
Ratio { of totals	$R = X/Y$	$\hat{R} = \hat{X}/\hat{Y}$	$r = x/y$
{ of mean	$R' = \bar{X}/\bar{Y}$	$\hat{R}' = \hat{\bar{X}}/\hat{\bar{Y}}$	$r' = \bar{x}/\bar{y}$
Numbers of items	N	$\hat{N}$	n

An estimate of a population is not useful unless its precision can be indicated. In other words, how closely does the 'estimate' represent the 'true', but unobserved population, a difference referred to as the standard (or sampling) error. Sample design aims to minimize this error.

If the sample chosen is a truly random one, that is, one without *bias*, then distribution of values will accord closely to that of the normal distribution. In this case, the main factor influencing the relationship between sample values and true population values will be the size of the sample. Thus, for any two samples taken from the same population, it is probable that the values from a larger sample will be a 'better' estimate of a population parameter than from a smaller sample. In other words, the larger the sample the less variability there will be in the sample proportions, and this is because the more extreme values become *relatively* less important in a larger sample.[23]

A mathematical value for the relationship between the variance of the sample means and the number of items in the sample is found by dividing the variance of the individual items in the sample by the number of items in the sample, that is, $\mathrm{var}_n = \sigma^2/n$. The standard deviation, σ, of the distribution of sample means with n items per sample may also be readily obtained and is more often referred to as the *standard error of the mean*. It is roughly equivalent to the standard deviation of the population divided by the square root of the number of items in each of the samples. It has a number of uses (Cochran, 1977); it is used (i) to compare the precision obtained by simple random sampling with that obtained by other methods of sampling; (ii) to estimate the size of the sample needed in a prospective survey; and (iii) to estimate the precision actually attained in a completed survey. Its central value lies in the fact that, if it can be assumed that the distribution of the population is normal, then the distribution of sample means will also be normal,[24] and according to the properties of the normal distribution an estimate can be made of the accuracy with which the sample mean is a reflection of the true population mean. This measure of the precision of the estimate is expressed in terms of *confidence limits*. Thus, it is probable that 67.3% of sample means, for example, will lie within one standard error of the true mean, and approximately 95% within two standard errors, and so on.

The corollary of this is equally useful, for, given a sample mean of n items we can say that the population true mean is unlikely to differ from this sample mean by more than $\pm 2(\sigma/\sqrt{n})$, at an approximate 95% level of probability. Similarly, extension to three standard deviations will increase the probability to a 99.7% level of certainty that the difference between sample and population true means will be closer than $\pm 3(\sigma/\sqrt{n})$. These expressions indicate the limit of precision for a given level of probability, which means that, in a *majority* of cases, the differences between sample and true means will be less than that indicated. Appendix 3 shows an example using these principles which demonstrates the determination of a sample size to obtain a result within a specified range and for a given confidence limit. Sample size is chosen, therefore, with regard not to the size of the population but to the accuracy with which it is required to estimate a given population parameter. A given level of accuracy demands a given size of sample and there is no amount of statistical manipulation which can change this. Equally, an estimate of a population true mean from a sample can only be given in terms of a range of values and an associated confidence level. It will now be clear that sample size can only be determined in the context of the total investigation design which will include decisions about confidence limits and the levels of accuracy required of the data.

We should note a further reminder that the confidence limits are based on probability theory. It is quite possible for the true population mean to be outside the specified limits from the sample mean. For example, given a confidence level of 95%, it is probable that once out of twenty times the values obtained from the sample will *not* be typical of the assumed population. How can this situation be indicated? The answer can only be found in the comparison of two or more samples taken from the same population, which means that a single sample in any situation must be regarded with caution. The 'Standard Error of Difference' can be used to assess the possibility that the observed difference between two samples (or two experiments) may be due to some real difference in the populations of the two samples, or to a chance difference arising simply from the random selection of samples from the *same* population.[25]

Normally, the sample standard deviation, *s*, is used as an estimate for the true standard deviation representing the distribution of the whole population. However, when sample size is small, this is unreliable and an adjustment needs to be made. This is also illustrated in Appendix 3.

We have so far made assumptions about the normality of the distribution of sample means, but it is frequently the case in urban investigation that there is marked non-normality, usually in the form of pronounced positive skewness. Often, a large number of small values are obtained and fewer large ones, for example, samples of numbers of shops by size, or even towns, produce such data. This situation may also arise as a consequence of using a very small sample. The main concern is what happens to confidence probabilities when we sample from such skewed populations. This can best be discussed under the heading 'sampling for proportions'.

Here, sampling is used to find out what *proportion* of a given population possesses some specific characteristic. A binomial[26] type of distribution is one in which each member of the population will either possess a certain characteristic or not. Such data can arise, for example, from asking dichotomous-type questions requiring yes/no answers. Alternatively, they can arise when an original continuous measurement of some variable has a discrete classification imposed upon it by the researcher. A good example is age measurement and a subsequent 'cutting point' separating two discrete groups, say, ages under 15, and 15 years and over.

Given that a member of a population can either possess a characteristic (*p*), or not (*q*), we can identify

	Population	Sample estimate
With characteristic	N_P	n_p
Without characteristic	N_Q	n_q
	$N_P + N_Q = N$	$n_p + n_q = n$
Proportions {	$P = N_P/N$	$p = n_p/n$
	$Q = N_Q/N$	$q = n_q/n$

The standard error, which for a normal distribution is given by $\sigma/\sqrt{n}$, is now given by $\sqrt{npq}$. This expresses the error in absolute terms in relation to the number of items in the sample, where *p* represents the probability of a member of the sample possessing the characteristic and *q* the probability that the member does not. In practice, the values in a binomial distribution are most readily expressed as proportions of percentages so that the standard error formula of the sample proportions is s.e. $= \sqrt{(p\%q\%/n)}$.

For example, if a survey shows that $p\% = 40$ (therefore $q\% = 60$) and the sample size, n, is 50 items, we may readily find the standard error as

$$\text{s.e.} = \sqrt{\left(\frac{40 \times 60}{50}\right)} \rightarrow \text{s.e.} = \pm 6.93\%$$

Confidence limits are established in the normal way. In this case at the 95% level of probability, (2σ), the true population value will be $40 \pm 2(6.93)$, that is between 26.14 and 53.86. An increase in the size of the sample, say to 100, will reduce the limits,

$$\text{s.e.} = \sqrt{\left(\frac{40 \times 60}{100}\right)} \rightarrow \text{s.e.} = \pm 4.9\%$$

and at the same confidence level the true population value will lie between 30.2 and 49.8.

As before, this process may be used to find the necessary size of sample required to give a standard error of a specified value and an' example is given in Appendix 3.

Instead of sampling randomly, it is possible under certain circumstances that the sample frame itself can ensure randomness in the way the units are ordered within it. If this is so, units can be selected regularly from the list. Thus, to obtain a sample of say 5%, or 1 in 20 of a population, we might choose to begin with the 7th item in the list, and continue with the 27th, 47th,..., which is systematic sampling. This method of sample selection is much simpler than random sampling and is frequently used where the source list, the 'frame', can be assumed to be reasonably random. Many of the common lists in use in social investigation, such as alphabetical lists of surnames, house street-numbers, names of streets, and so on, are often reasonably random.

However, two situations may be met in practice in which systematic sampling can cause serious bias (Blalock, 1970). First, the units in the frame may be arranged in the form of a trend, which means that the random choice of the first item drawn may cause bias, particularly if the sample fraction is small. Thus assuming a sample fraction of 1/100, if the first item were chosen as the start, then 101, 201, and so on, very different overall scores may be obtained than if a start were made with, say, item 99, then 199, 299...If the 'frame' is arranged, say, in some order of ranking from 1 downwards, then the second choice of starting value 99 would cause under-representation of the high value units, and so on.

A second problem arises where the 'frame' possesses some periodic or cyclical characteristic. If this happens to coincide with the sample fraction serious bias can result. For example, in a housing development survey every eighth dwelling unit may be, say, a larger family unit. If the sample fraction happened to be 1/8, and by chance the first item chosen happened to be a large unit, then *all* sample units will be large units. Similarly, an 'even' sampling fraction combined with the normal practice of 'odds and evens' in house numbers will cause a sample of dwellings only to be taken from one side of the street. These situations can be overcome by changing the sample fraction, and/or by making several different random starts. Providing that care is taken to check for these unwanted sources of bias, systematic sampling offers some advantages of simplicity over random sampling selection and is frequently used in urban study.

It is often useful in urban research to sample a body of data in subsets, or groups, with a separate sample drawn from each subset, referred to as *strata*. To be valid, certain conditions must be met. First, the strata must not overlap, that is, the sum of the number of items in the strata (the strata populations) must equal the number of items in the whole population. Second, the samples must be drawn from each stratum *independently*, so that the selection of the sample units in any one stratum does not influence in any way the selection of the units in another stratum.

As with all sampling methods, the main purpose of stratified sampling is to obtain an estimate of some parameter of the population, such as mean or variance. With stratified sampling, however, there are in effect two 'populations', namely the stratum population and the overall population, and both, together with appropriate standard errors, may be estimated from the strata samples. In effect, there are three levels of measurement: sample, stratum, and whole population. If h denotes a particular stratum, N the whole population, N_h the stratum population and n_h the sample units obtained by sampling a stratum, then we may readily find for stratum h, the true stratum mean as

$$\bar{X}_h = \sum_{i=1}^{N_h} x_{hi} \Big/ N_h \quad \text{and the sample mean as} \quad \bar{x}_h = \sum_{i=1}^{n_h} x_{hi} \Big/ n_h.$$

To obtain estimates from stratified random sampling two further factors must be considered. The *stratum weight* represents the proportion of the total population which is represented by a particular stratum, and it enables compensation to be made for the influence of variations in this proportion between the strata. It is obtained by dividing the stratum population by the total population, as $w_h = N_h/N$. Similarly, the *sampling fraction* represents the proportion of the sample to the stratum population from which it is selected. It is defined as $f_h = n_h/N_h$. This fraction may be kept constant for all the strata in a survey, or alternatively may be made to vary between the strata. This distinction must be recognized in the calculation of the estimates, particularly those for the whole population. If the fraction is constant,[27] the numbers in each sample will vary, for the strata populations will usually be of different sizes. This may mean that some samples are extremely small and give rise to unacceptable sampling errors. The alternative (apart from an unnecessary increase in the sample fraction over the whole survey) is to vary the sample fraction in each stratum. In this case, the numbers in each sample are kept constant, and any otherwise small sample increased to a satisfactory size. The abandonment of a constant sampling fraction, however, adds complexity to the calculation of the estimates. As before, an illustration of principle will be found in Appendix 3.

In practice, stratified sampling is used for two overlapping purposes (Blalock, 1972b). The first is to find out something about the meaningful sub-divisions of a population. For example, if specified sub-divisions of a population are known to exist, and are thought to be meaningful to an investigation, stratified sampling produces useful estimates of the population in its sub-divisions. For a human population, for example, these may relate to age and sex. In effect, stratified sampling is a way of using simple sampling techniques to simultaneously investigate homogeneous sub-sets of the population. Similarly, stratified sampling may be used where there are well-defined spatial sub-divisions for the data, such as local authority areas, community districts or enumeration districts, and this often brings administrative convenience for each 'area' may be separately administered in the inquiry. This will be particularly useful where the geographical area to be covered is very large. Stratified sampling is also useful where it is necessary to vary the method of sampling between the strata, for example, so that private and non-private households (institutions) may be treated differently, or county and district authorities may be separately sampled.

The second purpose is essentially concerned with the use of stratified sampling theory in order to obtain estimates of the characteristics of a whole population. The problems of determining strata size and their selection have so far been ignored but, clearly, they will affect the precision of the overall population estimates. In many cases, the strata into which a population may be divided will be self-selected by the nature of the population. Data about households, for example, may be readily classified by dwelling type, house, flat, maisonette, or a facility such as hot and cold water, bath, and so on. Human population data can be readily classified by age, sex, occupation. Often, these sub-divisions have been established by definition and convention over long periods of time and there will be little difficulty in deciding the strata.

In a less traditional investigation, this will not be so and the earlier discussion concerning the definition of variables should be borne in mind. The important point so far as the sampling method is concerned is that when the division into strata is made, then the stratum to which a particular variable belongs will not be known until the data are obtained. This means that the strata sizes cannot be known in advance, and the confidence levels of an intended sample can only be made on the basis of an *estimate* of the sample size of each stratum.

Sometimes it will be possible to obtain a reliable indication of this from previous work, or from the nature of the population itself. Thus, we may fairly readily estimate the age structure in stratified groups of a human population, given certain assumptions from our general knowledge of mortality rate. Where this is not possible, pilot work will be necessary.

Broadly similar considerations apply to the selection of the number of strata. Sufficient stratification must be used to obtain information about each meaningful group, but increased stratification reduces the size of each stratum and therefore increases sampling errors, especially if there is interest in estimates of the whole population. Some compromise is invariably required. In general, stratified sampling will produce a smaller variance for the estimated population means or total than will a comparable random sample, though certain conditions have to be met and various statistical measures are available to estimate the gain which can be obtained.[28]

Two further methods of sampling should be mentioned briefly. If the geographical area is large or the population widely dispersed, the work involved in conducting a random sample can be reduced by *quota* sampling.[29] This is often used in opinion polling and market research enquiries. The population is pre-stratified and a quota set, say 100 interviews per stratum. Typical stratum bases are age, sex, race and occupation. The inquirer chooses his own subjects until he has completed his quota, but the calculation of estimates from quota sampling raises problems and the usual methods of calculating sampling errors cannot be used with the same reliability as for random· sampling proper. Much depends on the way in which the quota sample is conducted and particularly upon the size of each stratum sample. Poor results are often obtained because of extremely small sample numbers, apart from the more general problem associated with interview sampling. Quota sampling is useful to obtain a general indication of attitude without the cost of producing a sampling frame as, for example, in an exploratory type of investigation, but otherwise it cannot be recommended.

A second alternative is cluster sampling. In stratified sampling, the population is divided into strata and a sample is drawn from *each* stratum. But, in some situations, it may be preferable to regroup the strata into so-called clusters and the samples are then taken from these clusters. An example may make this clear. We may have a situation in which no satisfactory sampling frame exists for, say, a region. But lists of households or populations may exist for each of the towns within the region, and we may proceed by obtaining strata within each town and selecting, randomly if possible, clusters of such strata, from which we may (randomly again) draw our samples. The aim is to select clusters that are as heterogeneous as possible, but are small enough to reduce the survey costs, particularly those of preparing the sample frame, for the conduct of interviews over a wide geographical area. In general, the use of cluster sampling will produce larger errors than an equivalent size simple random sample, but will cost considerably less. The question of which should be used is, therefore, dependent on the object of the survey and the resources available.

Notes

1 Some difficult philosophical questions are involved as to how such longer definitive statements can actually be validly derived. See Nagel (1961).

2 The criteria will in fact correspond to certain rules – the so-called rules of correspondence noted earlier. For a discussion of these see Braithwaite (1960) or Harvey (1969).

3 In other words, something defined and which can take on at least two 'values' in a given situation. If something cannot so vary, it is referred to as a 'constant', though at a metaphysical level even the notion of constant may be questioned. We should remind ourselves of the universality of change and the potential need at least to reconsider carefully terms of reference in each investigation. For practical purposes, we must assume that objects do remain constant enough to permit study.

4 It will be clear that objects and variables can be ranked in a hierarchy of common acceptance.

5 Whilst there is a measurement of $0°$, this is an arbitrary value midway between $+1°$ and $-1°$. It does not represent absence of temperature, and a statement such as '$60°$ is twice as warm as $30°$' is therefore invalid.

6 This can be identified in logic with the absence of what is being measured.

7 A measure is said to be valid if it measures what it *purports* to measure (Jahoda, 1970). Whether it does so can be established in a number of different ways, but, in general, validity is largely a matter of definition, and of 'empirical connections' (Kaplan, 1964), and it is measured in terms of error.

8 A collective or institutional household is separately defined as comprising persons 'living in hotels, boarding-houses, colleges, schools, hospitals, military installations, penal establishments', who are subject to a common authority or are bound by a common objective and/or personal interest and characteristics. These are also commonly referred to as 'non-private' households.

9 Even defining a 'dwelling' is problematical – see, for example, Wheller (1975); or EEC Conference of European Statisticians (see Benjamin, 1970).

10 By 'population' we refer to the entirety of any defined subject. The term is not limited to a human population.

11 A good discussion will be found in Wilson and Kirby (1975).

12 See Wonnacott and Wonnacott (1970) for an introductory text, or Box and Jenkins (1976) at a more advanced level.

13 The probability that some form of machine processing of data will be used should be borne in mind, in which responses will be coded and (commonly) punched on to standard 80 column computing cards. The layout of the survey sheet can do much to facilitate this process, and the researcher should take advice on this. Survey sheets can sometimes be self-coding, that is, data are recorded in such a way as to be directly readable by the punch card operator, or even for the survey sheets themselves to be 'machine-readable', as with Optical Mark Reading. Here, data are marked by soft pencil in appropriate answer boxes directly on the survey form, and are read directly by the computer input device. Although this procedure can be most effective, an important checking stage is omitted, and any investigator, particularly if others are making the observations and encoding the data is wise to make selected quality checks on the accuracy of these processes.

14 In social research, under carefully controlled circumstances, 'leading' questions

can be useful in probing an issue, but, in general, any tendency to 'lead' must be avoided.

15   The converse is also problematical and, at present, obscure. One possible approach is through the concept of construct validity which involves the identification of relationship networks which link attitudes and behaviour, though this is beyond the scope of this text. For the present we must rely on in-depth study with free-answer questioning, and accept limitations of reliability and recognize that it will serve only an exploratory purpose.

16   Reference to these are given at the end of Chapter 6.

17   The operations used in this process are rather lengthy and researchers can make use of one of the computing packages with a Guttman facility, for example SPSS.

18   A useful classification of sample designs has been given by Galtung (1969).

19   Spatial autocorrelation concerns the problem that inefficiencies in sampling designs frequently give rise to non-independence of the 'residuals' in a statistical analysis. It then becomes difficult to infer accurately the proportion of variation among the data which can be explained. Changes in geographical zoning are a common source of difficulty.

20   Commonly used sample frames are the property rating lists of Local Authorities, and the valuation lists maintained by the valuation offices of the inland revenue (hereditaments). The latter is used for the National Dwelling and Housing Survey, (Department of the Environment, 1978b).

21   In this section, we use the terms mean, variance, standard deviation and 'normal' distribution without definition. Readers unfamiliar with their meaning should refer to the Statistical Notes – Appendix 1, and Sampling Example – Appendix 3.

22   Also referred to as 'unrestricted random sampling'.

23   This can best be imagined by a situation in which, say, a population is sampled firstly by a single sample, then three samples, and then ten samples. If we plot the distribution curves for the means (arithmetic averages) of these samples, we would obtain the following distribution. It would be expected that there will be less scatter of these sample means as the *number* of samples taken is increased.

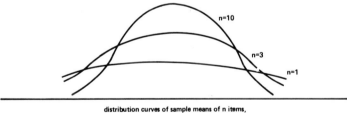

distribution curves of sample means of n items,
where n=1, 3, 10

24   The sample mean *may* be normal even if the population distribution is not normal.

25   The Analysis of Variance is also a useful test of comparison, but more complex. See statistical notes – Appendix 1.

26   Strictly speaking, the binomial is only an approximation to the distribution for a finite population, though this will not raise problems in this discussion. See statistical notes – Appendix 1.

27   Often referred to as sampling with proportional sample size.

28 Note should be made of the special care required to determine appropriate strata limit values for *continuous* data.
29 A discussion of the comparison between quota and other sample methods is given in Stephan and McCarthy (1974).

6

URBAN SIMULATION AND PREDICTION

Models of urban activity

In the discussion of research methods so far, it will be clear that the essentially spatial dimension to the planner's area of interest has been largely assumed. In order to apply knowledge and understanding to the formulation of planning policy, this spatial dimension needs to be treated explicitly. In summary, planners are mainly concerned with three aspects of spatial organization (Masser, 1972). First, they are interested in the patterns of location of particular types of urban activity within a limited area, such as employment, shopping, or residential location. Secondly, planners are concerned with the flows between different parts of the study area and the ways in which consumers respond to alterations in, for example, the transportation facilities that are available. Third, these locational patterns and flows of people and goods must be interpreted in terms of their effect upon the environment for some part of the study area.

It is this interpretation that will guide development through the preparation of plans and policies and their implementation. An essential task here will be to make forecasts and future estimates of the levels of these activities and the way in which these estimates may be influenced by the plans and policies. The 'role' of forecasting is discussed in the following part of the text, but for the present, it is essential to note that forecasts can only be built upon understanding, because of the assumptions about future change which are necessarily involved. The use of various simulation approaches to urban study that we now discuss are primarily research methods, that is, they are designed to serve understanding rather than directly inform the formulation of policy. This point must be clearly understood because there is considerable evidence in practice of many such methods (particularly forecasting methods) being used directly to attempt to 'predict' a future state of affairs when, for example, policy effects and the underlying assumptions of the prediction are barely recognized, let alone understood.

A brief comment about the term 'predict' is appropriate. The word will be used in the research sense. That is, a quantity (say of people, jobs or houses) may be 'predicted' in the analysis of a given situation by reference to other variables. For example, it may be found that, when office development takes place in an area, immigration of people takes place. Analysis might reveal the nature of the relationship so that for other assumed levels of office development, appropriate migration flows can be *predicted*. The researcher's task is then to test this prediction against newly acquired data at a later point in time, or perhaps against a similar situation in another location. Confirmation that the prediction is correct or reasonably so, confirms an understanding of the relationship which in turn can lead to a theoretical statement. The phrase 'conditional prediction' is often used and reminds the researcher that his predictive model itself will be based upon any number of assumptions about the correspondence between his model and the real world that he purports to represent.

If the understanding is confirmed by further study, the relationship may be expressed as a law. Prediction then essentially concerns the idea of testing and verifying assumed relationships. It is vital to distinguish its use from that of forecasting, which is essentially a matter of conjecturing about possible future events. This distinction will become clear over the remainder of the text.

An important way in which complex situations can be studied and understood is by the use of some kind of simplified model designed to reproduce the behaviour of what are *judged* to be the most important elements within the system to be studied. Simulation,[1] which includes modelling, is essentially a research tool by which experiments can be conducted on a system which is not itself otherwise amenable to an experimental research approach (Chapter 4). Essentially, the model allows the researcher to examine a 'what would happen if...?' situation.

The modelling and prediction of population change is a useful topic with which to introduce this chapter. First, an understanding of some aspect of population change is a basic factor in all urban plan and policy making, and second, the topic has long been subject to a systematic treatment by urban planners and several methodological concepts can be introduced. It is possible to distinguish aggregate and dis-aggregate approaches; the former treating a human population as a whole, say for a region or nation, whereas the latter is concerned with the population broken down into components, such as age and/or sex groups, or in terms of spatial sub-distributions, say, parts of a town. A further disaggregation would be to deal with households and their behaviour.

There are two, simple, aggregate predictive methods. Trend methods are applicable where it can be reasonably assumed that recently experienced change will persist. The most widely used method is that of the linear model, $y = a + bx$, in which time is represented as the dependent variable y, population is the independent variable x, and the regression coefficient, b, represents an annual increment.[2] The constant, a, represents the 'base' year, or datum from which the prediction is made. The model fundamentally requires that the underlying reality is in fact linear and may be expected to remain so.

The simple linear population model then is readily represented as

$$P_{t+n} = P_t + b(n),$$

in which P represents a population,[3] t represents a moment in time, n represents a time interval and b represents the interval increment of change. The first task in predicting change will be to 'calibrate' the model, that is by calculating b for a known period. If P_{t-n} represents data from an earlier Census (n years earlier) and P_t a present Census, we can readily find the annual increment over the period from

$$b = \frac{P_t - P_{t-n}}{n}.$$

Prediction for alternative intervals can readily be made either graphically (as figure 6.1 (a)) or by simple calculation. Of course, the trend may well not be linear, and it may be more appropriate to assume a geometric or exponential form (figure 6.1 (b)), particularly for longer periods of time. The rate of change is not now assumed to be constant.[4] The model now becomes

$$P_{t+n} = P_t(1+r)^n,$$

in which r represents the rate of growth. Given historical data, r can be readily calculated as

$$r = \frac{1}{x}\left(\frac{P_t - P_{t-x}}{P_{t-x}}\right).$$

As this form of growth tends to infinity, an alternative is to make use of the 'capacity' idea. Here, it is assumed that some ceiling to growth applies at some point in the future. This might apply if certain limits were imposed on the development of an urban area. This approach is briefly illustrated in figure 6.1 (c) in which the future capacity is denoted by k, that is as a stable state. Prediction is now made by assuming that the population at any moment in time can be predicted by estimating first the value for k, and then subtracting from it a portion, as it were, of increased capacity, so that the *proportion* of capacity which is not used at each increment over time is held to be constant. Denoting this proportion as c, a formula may be written

$$P_{t+n} = k - [(k - P_t)(1+c)^n].$$

Again, given data for an historical period, the value of c may be readily calculated as

$$c = \frac{1}{x}\left|\frac{k - P_t}{k - P_{t-x}}\right|.$$

Yet a further refinement of the exponential form is more complex in that it is assumed that at some point in time, 'inflexion' takes place and the trend reverses. The result is an S-shaped, or Gompertz curve[5] shown in figure 6.1 (d). There is evidence that over long periods of time this model is highly realistic for population analysis and derivatives are frequently used by demographers.[6]

Figure 6.1 Linear and non-linear population prediction

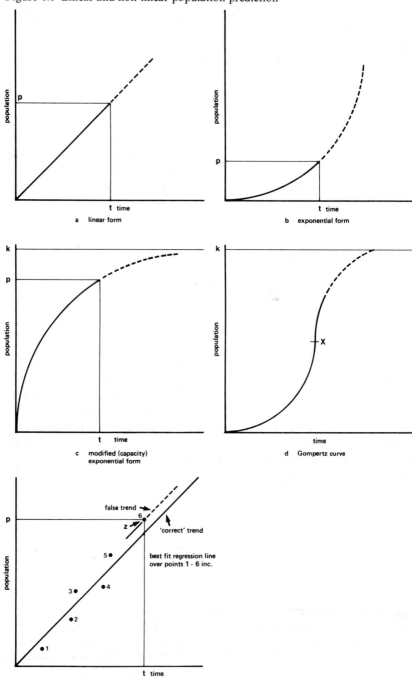

The so-called 'ratio' methods provide an alternative basis for analysis and prediction of aggregate population change. Here, one area, say a town, can be predicted as some function of change in another area, say the country in which the town is located, and for which change can be more reliably estimated. The latter area is usually referred to as the *pattern*, and the 'dependent' area, as the *study* area. Again a simple example will make the principle clear, and, in its simplest form, we assume that a given study area will share a constant proportion (or fraction) of the population change in the pattern area. In other words, the *ratio* of the two areas will be a constant. In notation, we write

$$\frac{S_{t+n}}{P_{t+n}} = \frac{S_t}{P_t},$$

where S is the population of the study area and P is the population of the pattern area. The estimating model is simply a re-arrangement of this expression, so that,

$$S_{t+n} = \left(\frac{S_t}{P_t}\right) P_{t+n}.$$

In practice, the method is totally dependent upon the plausibility with which the estimates of the pattern area can be made, and the constancy or otherwise of the relationship. The ratio approach is in fact a re-statement of the linear model, $y = a + bx$, where a is assumed to be zero; the independent variable x is the size of the pattern population and the coefficient b is the ratio of the study and pattern population size.

As the model is widely used to predict population change, some important features must be noted. For example, figure 6.1 (a) shows a prediction based simply on a trend measured between just two points.[7] It is, however, preferable that any trend estimation should be based on several data points and, as will be clear in figure 6.1 (e), it is unlikely that such a trend line will actually go through the most recent data point (z). Prediction is therefore correctly carried out, not by fitting the trend to this final data point, but from the true linear trend among the data points. This will require a *best-fit* estimate to be made for the most recent period of known data, t, as a correct base. The approach also means that confidence limits for the prediction can be correctly stated. A further point is that the calculation of a best-fit linear trend is not dependent upon having historical data at equal time intervals, so that 'missing' Census and irregular survey data can be readily accommodated.

A better analysis of population change is obtained by dis-aggregated methods,[8] which are particularly appropriate for urban study and policy making, in that many of the needs and problems of an urban population relate directly to its age and sex structure. The 'components of change' that are taken into account relate to births, deaths and migration. This can be summarized as $P_{t+n} = P_t + B_n - D_n + M_n$, where B_n represents the number of births over a period n, and D_n the deaths. The term M_n represents *net* migration over the period and is itself defined as $M_n = IM_n - OM_n$ where IM_n is the number of in-migrants to the area and OM_n the out-migrants from the area.

This general form can be further disaggregated into age groups and sexes. Each age group, by sex, may then be treated independently in the population. For example, a *mortality rate* expressing the probability of death occurring to a given age group (or cohort) of males over a specified period of time as that group ages, can be multiplied by the estimated numbers of males in that age group. The result will be an estimate of the numbers of deaths, and by subtraction, the predicted number of survivors is obtained. Similarly, a *fertility rate* expressing the probability of births occurring to a specified group (or cohort) of females over a period of time

Figure 6.2 (a) An age and sex structure pyramid of a population (England and Wales 1978, estimate). (b) A diagram of a simple cohort survival model

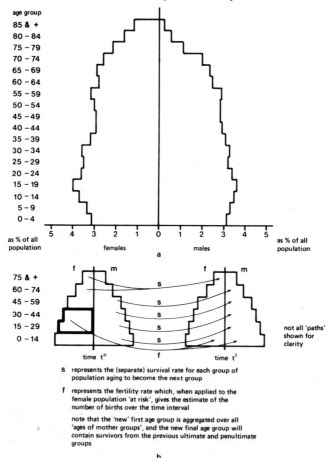

note that the 'new' first age group is aggregated over all 'ages of mother groups', and the new final age group will contain survivors from the previous ultimate and penultimate groups

After Krueckeberg and Silvers (1974: 278)–(b) only.

will produce an estimate of numbers of children likely to be born. When this approach is extended over several age groups in a population, we refer to it as a cohort model.[9] In its simplest form the model assumed zero net migration for each cohort. This model is widely used and figure 6.2 summarizes its main features. Each cohort is 'survived' into an older cohort by applying an appropriate survival rate (or mortality rate). Similarly, a new infant cohort is generated and is estimated by applying fertility rates to the fertile female age groups.[10]

The model is primarily an analytical model capable of yielding high quality estimates of the rates of change being experienced in a local area, where for example two intervals of census data are available. Given knowledge or estimates also of birth and death rates the model can be used to generate estimates of net migration flows by age.[11] More commonly, the model is frequently used to make future forecasts by applying 'trend'-based assumptions of birth and death rates[12] to a given population producing estimates of population structure, five, ten, or more years ahead. But migration assumptions, which often dominate this exercise, not only tend to be based upon inadequate empirical work in the local area, but are often made without consideration of the possible effects of planning policy.[13]

At this stage, it is important to refer to matrix mathematical methods which, following work by Keyfitz (1968) and Rogers (1966, 1968, 1975) have been widely applied to situations such as the analysis of population change. Essentially, matrix methods allow a disaggregated survival simulation to be repeated in a single operation rather than as a series of independent linear statements for each element or cohort. A grasp of these principles is essential for the reader to cope with the wider applications that will be found in the literature, and an elementary example is set out in Appendix 4. It will be clear that such a model offers extensive possibilities for experiment of the 'what would happen if...' type, though careful recording and tracing of the effects of the built-in assumptions is vital if an understanding of the underlying processes is to emerge.

Finally, it is a relatively straightforward matter to extend these concepts to deal with several regions or districts simultaneously. Indeed it is possible to build more sophisticated population accounting models which, by making the explicit treatment of spatial flows of population between areas as well as their natural change, permit more comprehensive analysis and prediction (Rees and Wilson, 1977; Rees, 1979).

We should now consider a simple 'relational' model situation, for example, between population and household estimation. Housing policy is likely only to be successful if it is closely related to need, but an understanding of this need is complex and will involve the interaction of demographic, social and economic considerations (Blincoe, 1979). An important part of the urban planners' task will be to make estimates of the way in which households will be born, age and die, within their various sub-markets (Holm *et al.*, 1978).

People form households[14] in a variety of ways, for example, in student groups, as couples, as families with children, as families whose children have left home, as elderly couples, as single persons, including those widowed and divorced, and so on. Over a lifetime, an individual may go through the process of forming several such households. The problem of prediction is clearly a dynamic one, in that household structure is constantly changing.[15] The dwelling stock is also constantly changing through construction, demolition and adaption, and this makes it difficult to study and to predict both 'supply and demand' characteristics. The situation is also spatially dynamic as various types of households move from place to place through migration. There is also the problem of latent households to be faced.

Any prediction of dwelling demand needs to recognize that there will be people who, arguably, *need* to live as a separate household in their own dwelling but who are obliged to live as part of another household. The most common examples include newly married couples living with one set of parents, and young single persons who may be potential households but who are constrained by lack of suitable accommodation and/or by finance to live as part of another household. The two established approaches to household prediction are through an analysis of family type and 'headship' analysis. The former deduces an 'ideal' distribution of dwelling types to cater for population as it develops through its life cycle. The approach is well suited to the local level where it can be based upon detailed, individual household survey data, which can reveal the distribution of expanding, stationary and declining households in terms of their membership. These needs can be translated into crude estimates of potential housing demand, though residential inertia and the estimation of migration behaviour relative to the changing availability of accommodation is a difficult area. Time series data at this level are rarely available which makes any prediction of apparent trends particularly hazardous.

At the simplest aggregate level, the numbers of households of various types predicted in a given area can be calculated as a function of the age, sex and marital status structure of the population. Strictly, we should distinguish between *private* individual households, and *non-private* households – namely people living collectively in institutions, schools, hospitals, barracks and so on.[16] For the private sector, the population are normally dis-aggregated into groups that have different *headship rates*. A headship rate is defined as the probability of a person in a particular age, sex and marital status group being (or becoming) a head of a household. By extension, through making estimates of household structure and size for these groups, the 'non-head of household numbers' can be estimated. This can be summarized as $H_q = P_{asm}h$ where H represents the total potential households of type q in a given area; P is a given sector of the population in age group a, sex s, marital status m; and where h is a headship rate for household type q appropriate to that sector of the population. In practice, a breakdown of the population typically into thirty or more such groups is used (Hollis *et al.*, 1976).

On the urban scale, the necessary data to calculate headship rates are obtained from the Census of Population, though relating marital status to age may require estimation. However, at sub-urban level a 'small area' problem will arise in that the estimation of headship rates from census data will be subject to considerable sampling error,[17] and it is normally necessary to make assumptions as to how 'typical' a local area is of some larger area, such as a town or region. It is then necessary to project forward the headship rates, taking into account likely social trends that may be revealed by the data (Allnutt et al., 1970). Once suitable headship rates have been obtained for a given area, and estimates made as to how these may be expected to change, it is a straightforward matter to explore the possible effects of changes in the age and sex composition of the population, for example, through the use of a cohort survival model. This will produce a range of estimates of household structure and formation, which in turn, must be converted into housing type 'demands' having regard to average income levels, propensity of persons in the region to rent or buy particular types of dwellings, and so on. Also, given the necessary assumptions about suitable standards of density and layout related to price, estimates of land demand for new construction can also be made. This process will, however, also require an assessment of the trends in dwelling conversion, the potential capacity for conversion, say from houses to flats, and the probable patterns of improvement and demolition.

One vital factor has yet to be mentioned. The methods used so far do not cope with the problem of 'concealed' households (the latent demand), both from within the area, *and* from without. It will be intuitively clear that the success or otherwise of housing programmes, particularly the private sector, will directly affect the mobility of a population. It is unrealistic to assume, therefore, that an area is isolated, and this suggests the need to approach household prediction by taking into account a much broader range of social and economic criteria which arguably will contribute to the movements of population. Such relationships can be examined through regression analysis with household size as the dependent variable and a number of 'indicators' as the independent variables. The South Hampshire Study (Caulfield, 1970), for example, found that useful predictions of average household size, the percentage of 1–2 person households, 3–5 person households and large (6 or more person) households could be made using readily obtained Census data for the independent variables (figure 6.3).

The study found, for example, that large households were found to be associated with a high proportion of young people, a higher than average fertility rate and low levels of car ownership. Small households were associated with a high percentage of the elderly, low fertility and low car ownership. Medium-sized households were characterized by relative affluence related to larger than average dwellings, exclusive use of household amenities[18] and higher levels of car ownership. One advantage offered by the use of Census data is that limited time series analysis is

Figure 6.3 Regression coefficients relating household size to selected socio-economic data

Independent variables	Regression coefficients			
	Average household size	% 1–2 person households	% 3–5 person households	% 6 + person households
— Population aged less than 5	−4.91	+2.99	−2.72	−0.28
% Population aged 5–14	+9.47	−2.75	+1.88	+0.87
% Population aged 60 or more	−1.16	+0.48	−0.97	+0.06
Ratio of females to males	−0.14	+0.14	+0.18	+0.04
Ratio of children under 5 to females aged 15–44	+2.37	−1.03	+0.84	+0.19
Ratio of children under 15 to females 15–44	−0.86	+0.42	−0.37	−0.05
% SEG 'A'	+2.12	+0.02	−0.42	+0.39
% SEG 'B'	+0.65	+0.51	−0.93	+0.41
Ratio of economically active females 15–64 to single females 15 +	−0.08	+0.03	−0.04	+0.006
Ratio of economically active married females to married females 15 +	−0.55	+0.21	−0.19	+0.02
Ratio of economically active population 15–24 to total population 15–24	+0.64	−0.16	+0.12	+0.04
Ratio of economically active males 15–64 to all males 15–64	−1.03	+0.003	+0.16	−0.16
Constant	+2.82	+0.13	+0.99	−0.13
% Explanation	80	84	66	52

From Caulfield (1970: 222) (SEG: socio-economic group).

possible, where the definition of a variable has remained unchanged over a number of Censuses.

Economic activity

Urban planners are interested in economic activity, not simply because of the need to allocate land for industrial and commercial developments and provide a suitable infrastructure such as roads, water supply, but because of the consequential demands which are affected by economic activity, such as employment growth and decline, housing demand, household formation, income levels, car ownership, migration patterns. Economic Activity rates (Harris and Taylor, 1978), which represent the proportion of a population who are economically active, are crude indices and, in order to understand the local economic system, appropriate models are those which, like population models, can be manipulated in order to conduct experiments and make predictions. However, no locality is economically isolated. For example, people may work in one region and live in another, a region may have a 'branch' industry whose economic activity is dependent upon economic activity elsewhere. Building even a simple model of an economy is fraught with difficulties and yet an understanding of its processes is clearly vital to urban planning and policy making.

The most common modelling approach is to identify *sectors* in the economy. One way is to recognize that economic activity essentially involves producing and consuming goods and services. The local economy is divided up into units (people or industries) who *produce*, using the factors of production (land, labour, capital and entrepreneurial skill) and those who *consume*, again either as individuals purchasing goods and services or as 'producers' requiring inputs to their production, such as semi-finished products, and so on. A second is to split the economy into industrial activity or employment-based sectors, such as agriculture, manufacturing, distribution, financial services and so on.

The overall measure of a region's economic activity, its regional product, can be calculated in one of two ways. One is to add up the 'value-added' contribution of all business and government activity in the region, that is, by focusing upon *production*. It involves measuring the quantity of goods and services provided over a period of time (often a year) by everyone engaged in economic activity in the region.[19] An alternative is to focus upon *consumption* by calculating the earnings of all the factors of production, such as wages, profits, interest and rent. These two measurements, however, will not be the same, because, for a given product it is unlikely that its economic 'worth' has been wholly achieved within the region. For example, raw material may have been brought in from another region, that is, a regional *import*. Allowance must be made for this. Further, some of the income 'spent' in the region will have been 'earned' elsewhere by people living and working in different regions. Indeed, a whole range of regional *transfers* will occur including taxation, investment of capital in other regions, and financial transfers between central government and local government. A brief explanation can be offered drawing upon the notation of Krueckeberg and Silvers (1974).

A sectoring approach will minimally require the identification of four sectors – *consumption, investment, government* and the *transfers*, and can be summarized as $R \equiv C + I + G + X - M$[20] where R is the regional economic product; C represents consumption (the economic value of what is consumed in the region); I represents what is invested in the region;[21] G represents the value of purchases made by Government; X represents the value of purchases which are exported (transferred) out of the region; and M represents the value of the purchases imported (transferred) into the region. The value of economic activity within the four main sectors can then be made explicit as $R = (C - M_C) + (I - M_I) + (G - M_G) + (X - M_X)$ which, in effect, has disaggregated the *import* component for the respective sectors. The first term now represents the true amount of regional income which is earned by the production and sale of goods in the consumption sector *within* the region because it subtracts the apparent contribution of the imports. In fact, each of the terms in brackets now represents the contribution of each sector to the *regional income*. This is conventionally denoted Y, and is defined as $Y \equiv Y_C + Y_I + Y_G + Y_X$ where Y_C represents income earned in the consumption sector; Y_I in the investment sector; Y_G in the government sector; and Y_X in the export sector. Each of these was represented earlier and can now be summarised as: $Y_C \equiv C - M_C$; $Y_I \equiv I - M_I$; $Y_G \equiv G - M_G$; $Y_X \equiv X - M_X$. These are the fundamental building concepts of regional and urban economic analysis and can be extended. For example, the government sector can be split into local and non-local government; local government is then included with consumption because, generally, the demands placed upon its services are closely geared to income and population levels *within* the region. This leaves 'non-local government' income to be regarded as a 'transfer' from outside the region. It is also possible to merge the investment and consumption sectors so that the regional product is then determined as $R \equiv (C - M_C) + (X - M_X)$ and the regional income as $Y \equiv Y_C + Y_X$. So far we have treated consumption and production as implicitly covering all industrial and commercial activity. To be of practical use, it will be necessary to further 'sector' the system so that an accounting approach is possible in which estimates of each industrial and commercial sectors' change can be made, but also bearing in mind the economic dependencies between them. This will clearly be complex, since some economic activity will be heavily 'export' type, such as manufacturing or agriculture in which the regional products are distributed widely to other regions, whereas other sectors, such as retailing and service activities will be mainly oriented to serving the regions' own population and hence its consumption sector. Two difficulties immediately arise, one being measurement and the other being that industrial and commercial activity changes over time in the extent to which it serves local or more general markets.

A useful indicator which can help in understanding this situation is the so-called *location quotient*. This is a relative index which compares the proportion of production contributed by an industrial sector (say manufacturing) in a given region, to the proportion of production contributed by that sector nationally. An index greater than one, implies that the region is exporting some of its commodity and *vice versa*. This index requires assumptions about the homogeneity of demand for the products of this sector among regions and, in *income* terms, it is not always very meaningful. However, it can also be calculated in *employment* terms and this is useful to urban planners in providing estimates of employment change in a region. The location quotient then identifies whether or not the region of interest has a higher or lower proportion of its employees in a given sector than nationally. The fortunes of that sector are then of greater or lesser interest to the local planners depending upon the level of the index.

The concept can be put into notation as $\dfrac{R_i}{R} \Big/ \dfrac{E_i}{E}$, where R_i is the employment in the region in a given sector, and R is all employment in the region. This ratio is compared with E_i which is the employment in that sector nationally over E representing all employment nationally. It is also useful to distinguish between employment which results directly from consumption in a region and that which results from the 'export' economic activity of the region. This can be summarized as $R = \hat{R}_C + \hat{R}_X$, in which R represents the employment in a region, $\hat{R}_C$ represents the best estimate ($\hat{}$) of employment in the consumption sector and $\hat{R}_X$ represents the best estimate of employment derived from the exporting activities of the region. As the consumption function is likely to be some calculable function of population change and real income change, we can use this concept, referred to as 'economic base', to build a simple model for both prediction and forecasting.

A further basic concept in economic analysis is the multiplier. The use of this concept assumes that the consumption sector of the economy is the most amenable to prediction, so that consumption *in* a region will be some predictable function of the incomes earned by people living in the region. Broadly, economic theory allows income only to be either consumed or saved; the latter includes spending which is not immediately consumed, such as 'investing' in a house or buying raw materials for future use. Consumption within a region can then usefully be thought of as some (linear) function of income in the region. In notation, $C = \alpha Y$, where the coefficient α represents the share of regional income which is 'consumed'. We know that some of this consumption will involve imports (goods and services) into the region, M_C, and we must assume that their consumption in our region remains as a constant proportion, β, of consumption overall. We can then write $M_C = \beta C$. Earlier, we noted that income earned in the consumption of goods and services *in* the region minus those which were 'imported' is $Y_C = C - M_C$.

Substitute the expressions for consumption C, and imported consumption M_C, and we obtain $Y_C = \beta Y - \beta \alpha Y$ or, more conveniently, $Y_C = \beta(1 - \alpha)Y$. This means that income earned in the consumption sector of a region is assumed to be proportionate to the level of income in the region. This expression can now be inserted into the calculation of the regional income overall Y, which, for the simple two sector model used earlier, was $Y \equiv Y_C + Y_X$. We obtain $Y \equiv \beta(1 - \alpha)Y + Y_X$ and, by re-arrangement, this can be more readily used as

$$Y = \left(\frac{1}{1 - \beta(1 - \alpha)} \right) Y_X$$

It is the term inside the brackets which is known as the multiplier.

To use the multiplier it is first necessary to be able to estimate the values of the two coefficients reliably from empirical data. It is then necessary to be able to assume that this multiplier function will remain constant over the period that we wish to predict. Then, providing that an estimate *can* be made of a possible increase in the regional export income (that is, the sector which produces goods and services surplus to the requirements of the region) the multiplier concept can be used to obtain an estimate of the resulting increase in regional economic activity overall.[22] By extension, the model can calculate the effect of a direct increase in basic jobs (an example is given in Appendix 5) though, whilst there are good theoretical reasons for using the economic base concept as a forecasting model, in practice, a number of difficulties will be met. The first is that the model assumes a constant ratio of regional income to employment, which is only likely to hold in the short term due to technological change and capital substitution for jobs. Also wage costs will fluctuate over time and affect the relationship between incomes and jobs (Isard, 1969). In practice, it is usual to break down the model into industrial and commercial sectors and estimate changes for each sector, though there is always a danger in simply extrapolating past trends into the future (Leigh, 1970).

This further idea of sectoring, by increasing the disaggregation of the units of production can best be illustrated by reference to one form, namely, *input–output analysis*. Here, the main requirement is to translate changes in the estimated regional product into their implications for each of the employment sectors, and thereby make a prediction of likely employment change in each sector possible (figure 6.4). Such a requirement needs to take into account the way in which any given change in sectoral economic activity will work its way through the economic system *as a whole*. As the sectoral activities are not independent of each other we need a framework which takes this into account.

The most relevant form of input–output analysis for urban planners is to predict the occupational composition of the regional employment labour sectors, through estimating the output levels of those sectors given an overall estimate of regional performance (Morrison and Smith, 1976). However, assumptions also have to be made, as already discussed, as to whether or not certain sectors will grow faster than others so affecting the occupational composition of employment. Analysis of trends may prove to be an inadequate guide for this.

The basic procedures involved in an input–output analysis are illustrated in Appendix 5. The main operational task is to estimate the multipliers which indicate how much of a change in each industrial and commercial sector will result from an overall change in demand which itself will be due to changes in consumption, export and investment. An important feature of input–output analysis is that it stresses the inter-industry relationships within the modelled economy. It may be helpful to think of the analysis as attempting to answer the question –

if an estimate can be made for the overall demand for goods and services in an economy at a given moment in time, what levels of output will be required to meet this demand and also take into account the productive activities that are required to create these goods and services? (Masser, 1972:69).

As far as urban planners are concerned these 'productive activities' will

Figure 6.4 Typical industrial and service sectors in Input–output Analysis

Sector number and description	Minimum list headings included (SIC 1968)*
1 Food and drink	211–216, 218, 219, 229, 231, 232, 239
2 Chemicals and allied industries	221, 271–273, 275–279
3 Metal manufacture	321–323
4 Mechanical engineering	331, 332, 336, 337, 339, 341, 342, 349
5 Electrical engineering	361, 363–369
6 Motor vehicles	380, 381
7 Metal goods not elsewhere specified	391–394, 396, 399
8 Clothing	441–446, 449
9 Bricks, fireclay, and refractory goods, etc.	461, 469
10 Timber and miscellaneous wood manufacturers	471, 474, 475, 479
11 Paper, printing, and publishing	481, 485, 486, 489
12 Other manufacturing	491–496, 499
13 Construction	500
14 Gas and electricity	601, 602
15 Transport	701–707, 709
16 Communication	708
17 Distributive trades	810–812, 820, 821, 831, 832
18 Miscellaneous services	860–866, 871, 873, 876, 879, 881–889, 892–895, 899
19 Public administration	872, 874, 901, 906
20 Households	—

* SIC = Standard Industrial Classification.
Source: Smith and Morrison (1974: 18).

include the allocation of land for industrial and commercial activity, estimating the consequent numbers of jobs likely to be required in the sectors and so on. It must be noted, however, that this task, never easy even in a situation of economic growth, is more difficult in the face of economic re-structuring, technical change and labour displacement from traditional employment (Massey and Meegan, 1978).

It will often be necessary to produce employment estimates from the accounting values produced through an input–output analysis. This can be done by introducing an 'employment by sector' segment (or vector) into the model in which is represented the number of jobs likely to be associated with a given, say £'000 worth of gross output for each industry. The result will be an estimate of jobs, though with rapid technical change it is not easy to make the necessary assumptions to do this very accurately. An alternative is to proceed more indirectly by attempting to quantify the effect upon local *income* of a given increase in output in particular sectors; in effect, calculating a local sector income multiplier.

In practice, a large number of refinements are used by economists and planners, and detailed explanations are provided by Smith and Morrison (1974), Morrison and Smith (1976) and De Kanter and Morrison (1978). Enough will now have been said to show that the economic base and input–output approaches provide an important basis for making predictions about economic activity, though, as always, the necessary assumptions about how well the simplified model will reproduce the real-world situation must be fully acknowledged in interpreting any results. Some further limitations should also be noted. The method requires that externally derived estimates of final demand are available for each industrial sector, and the accuracy of these estimates will govern the validity of the whole process. The method also assumes that, as wages and spending are embedded in the model, the propensity to dispose of income remains constant although this is unlikely to hold over a longer period of time. The coefficients which represent the interactions are also calculated at one point in time and these will change with changing technology, which means that over time the dependency between the sectors will change. There is also the problem, at a local scale, of getting good enough data, which means that the approach is generally more applicable at a regional level.

Finally, in this section, we should briefly mention some extensions to the method which can enhance the quality of the analysis and lead to better predictions. A useful concept is *sharing*. The simplest form that this can take is to make the assumption that if a local region is able to maintain intact its relative advantages as a supplier, then, as the economy develops, the exporting region's share in supplying this growth will remain constant. An extension of this idea is the *shift and share* approach in which an analysis is undertaken of the extent to which the economic sectors in a region have grown or declined at rates different to other regions or national levels (Randall, 1973). Attempts to verify hypotheses posed in those terms can lead to an explanation of why this has occurred.

The shift and share approach requires that sectoral economic data are available for an historical period. The first task is to calculate the region's output for each industry that would have occurred if that regional industry had grown at the same rate as the national output. Subtracting this from what did occur gives a measure known as the industry's *shift*. Usually, this is further sub-categorized into *proportionality* shift (or 'composition effect'), which is the shift due to the difference between the total natural growth rate and the industry's natural growth rate, and a second part called the *differential* shift (or 'growth effect'), which is the difference between the industry's regional growth rate and its national growth rate. The latter is the more important for urban planning purposes since it represents the performance of the sector in the region, and an increase means that that sector finds the region an agreeable place to be. On the basis of such findings, and given good estimates of growth or change overall, it is possible to make predictions of future regional shares of economic activity by sectors. Some literature is cited at the end of this chapter.

One further promising area of research which builds upon the basic input–output model is that of the *commodity–activity framework*[23] and extends the analytic approach more generally to the 'urban system'. An 'activity' is any human, social or economic task undertaken for a particular purpose. Thus, industrial activity, retailing, local government, or the consumption of household goods are all activities. Activities, in turn, use resources such as land and buildings, labour and other material goods and services. These are the *material* objects in the system and can be characterized as commodities. In general, all the commodities (except natural resources such as land) will have been produced by activities in the system. Thus, houses are produced by construction activities, retail goods by factories and so on (Broadbent and Jaffe, 1975). Knowledge of these activities and commodities within an urban system enables a conceptual model to be built rather in the form of input–output transactions which can reproduce the main interactions or flows and which, in turn, can lead to the quantification of these relationships. The method is capable of a high level of disaggregation, both by sectors, such as for industry and commerce, and also spatially, typically into a multi-regional framework. The application of the theory to the urban context is clearly set out in Barras and Broadbent (1975) together with a case study.

Activity interaction

A useful area of activity interaction with which to introduce some basic principles is that of population migration. There are many causal and interactive links between migration and other social and economic phenomena though study is not easy.[24] Migration of population is not an end in itself. It arises, in a very real sense, from disparity in opportunity; migration can be broadly thought of as a mechanism for equating supply and demand in terms of individual opportunity. This means that the strongest relationship to be studied and estimated is the link between migration and employment opportunity (or lack of it), though other reasons give rise to migration (such as retirement, family factors and so on). As migration arguably occurs in response to economic and social circumstances, and since planners' policies and plans deliberately intervene in and change those circumstances,[25] migration will be affected by the relative success or failure of policy. It may therefore be an important indicator.

Because of the close link with policy there is a considerable opportunity for circular reasoning and self-justifying research findings. This needs to be guarded against in any research in the field. A variety of approaches have been used to study migration (Willis, 1974). For example, the history of industrialization has shown that economic and technological development requires a mobility of manpower. This relationship has provided one focus of attention by economists. A second approach, favoured by sociologists has focused upon the motivations and behaviour of individuals in respect of their migrations. A third approach by geographers has focused upon the spatial patterns in migration related to aspects of social, economic and environmental change. All migration research, however, faces two common difficulties. The first concerns data. In Britain, the absence of an official register of household movements (as in the Netherlands) means that official data is limited to the population Census. This provides data at a *household* level in terms of identifying changes of residence during the year previous to the Census and the five year period previous to the Census.[26] Such data, however, provides little in the way of explanation, for example it says nothing about duration of residence, frequency of moves, neither does it adequately deal with households who have had several migratory moves (Rees, 1977). A second difficulty is that officially, migration is, in effect, defined in terms of movement across administrative local authority boundaries which means that any analysis of trends may be seriously affected by the varying sizes and shapes of the administrative areas themselves (Willis, 1972b).

It may be helpful at this stage to identify the main motivational aspects that affect migration. These can be summarized under four headings (Willis, 1974) – Family life cycle; social mobility; inter-generational and career mobility; residential environment mobility (due to changing characteristics of a neighbourhood) and finally, social and locality participation. The life cycle will usually include the stages of household formation, marriage, a pre-children stage, child-bearing and rearing, post-children, widowhood and household dissolution. In the main, studies have focused upon identifying such stages and relating them to the age structures of a population, and to the accommodation (housing stock) demand and availability. Migration associated with the family cycle is not simply a function of the stages of that cycle, but will be affected by such factors as housing-type suitability as the family grows and declines, employment and family income, and personal preferences about residential location (including the perceived status of residential areas), extended family links and so on. In general, there is an observed, greater tendency for migration to take place among people with higher social and economic status. Age is also an important factor in that the age period 19–24 is one of high residential mobility among many young people, and the period 35–45 is a common range of upward social mobility. It also follows, due to the relationship between occupational mobility and age, that persons who do not move in the 25–44 age range will normally continue to remain in one location.

Propensity to move will, however, also be modified by the strength of social and locality participation in a given area. This is made up of the various forces – family and friends, location preference, education levels, aspirations and so on – which may inhibit or encourage a move away from a known environment.[27] A great deal of sociological work has focused upon an examination of migrational motivation through what is referred to as the 'ecological concept' (Wolpert, 1966). This essentially refers to the perceptions by which an *individual* assesses his place in the present environment compared to his possible future environments. The perceived difference between them, it is argued, directly affects his propensity to move, and it is clear that the ability to perceive and react to such relative advantage differs markedly between the various economic and social groups and strata within a population. The frequency of migratory movement and duration of residence in any one area are closely related. This feature is useful for prediction in that the probability of a person or household migrating from an area decreases as the length of residence in the area increases. Persons who have moved recently are the most likely to move again in the future and this means that, in effect, migration as a phenomena is not independent of previous mobility experience. This suggests that a form of stochastic approach (Chapter 2) is appropriate to predict such behaviour, though it is clear that the probability of migration varies enormously between occupations, social groups and between regions. While increased residence in an area appears to *decrease* the probability of that household or person will move outside the area, the principle does not appear to hold for further *dwelling* moves within an area (Willis, 1974). In this case the probability of a further move can increase, until some two or three years has elapsed when the probability of a further move will decline.

Given the deficiencies of official data, it will be clear that there is an urgent need for longitudinal study of migrant and non-migrant behaviour in a population at the local level in order to explain the relationship between migration and factors such as housing history, career patterns, values and aspirations, social mobility though an individual's lifetime (Willis, 1974). Data relating to duration-of-residence and frequency-of-movement is a most central need and has the advantage of emphasizing the migrant, rather than the area, as the unit of study. As yet, it is not possible to refer to work which may directly assist the planner's need to forecast, conditionally, migration movements at an individual level. The potential approach is clearly set out by Price (1959) who has expressed the probability of an individual moving from one area to another, *first*, as a function of the way in which an individual person perceives a preference for one residential area to another, and *secondly*, as a function of the interactions between an individual's characteristics and the characteristics of his own (present) location, and the other possible areas to which he might move. This can be summarized as

$$P = f(A) + f(B) + f[(A)(B)],$$

where the function $f(A)$ summarizes the individual's proclivity to migrate; $f(B)$ is the preference function that he has for the destination area in contrast to his present (origin) area; and $f[(A)(B)]$ represents the *interaction* upon the individual in this situation; particularly the empathy between the individual's personal characteristics and the characteristics of his present and possible future locations. The operationalization of such theory, however, represents a longer-term objective. More immediately, we can illustrate two useful research approaches to migration analysis for planners. The first is an 'econometric' approach in which migration is regarded as the *dependent* variable, and is influenced by a variety of demographic, social and economic forces or factors. This approach has been widely applied in urban analysis (Willis, 1972a).

By means of developing a system of simultaneous equations, the effects of the various, hypothesized 'causal' factors on migration can be conditionally explored. But also, we have already suggested that migration itself needs to be treated as an independent variable as well, and this interaction between cause and effect, suggests that *a priori*, it is appropriate to specify a model of urban development which takes into account the interactions between the various 'causal' factors. Willis (1974) also suggests that the approach is appropriate because of the limitations of official data which preclude any extensive measurement of the influence of the various factors on each other. Regression techniques can be used to estimate the influence of given variables upon migration without their detailed cross-classification, and can provide a means of testing hypotheses about which factors are most strongly associated with the migration, either singly or in combination. There is also the advantage that migration, as a phenomenon, is frequently 'lagged' over time with respect to its causal influences and a 'lagged' linear model is highly applicable in such a situation. There are, however, some methodological problems which must be noted.

Figure 6.5 Regression of migration and economic, social and demographic variables

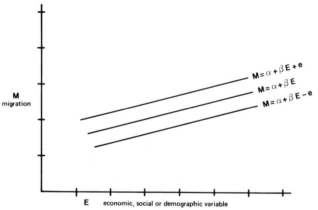

The approach in general can be summarized as figure 6.5. M represents gross migration flow and E represents a selected variable of some economic, social or demographic phenomena; α will be a constant and the regression coefficient, β, represents the propensity to migrate; e will represent the appropriate error influences and will give rise to a set of confidence limits surrounding the best linear fit, $M = \alpha + \beta E$. The general problems associated with the application of the linear model will apply and will include the difficulties arising from joint influences among independent variables, the dangers of spurious correlation and multi-collinearity. As far as possible any correlation between the independent (explanatory) variables must be avoided by careful selection and mutually exclusive definition.[28] Two particular methodological problems should be noted. One, (Greenwood, 1973, 1975) concerns the fact that a number of studies which have attempted to explain migration by means of a single-equation, regression model have found 'wrong' signs or non-significant coefficients on variables that, *a priori*, might have been thought to play a crucial role in the potential migrant's decision concerning his destination. The most troublesome are variables relating to income levels, income growth, and unemployment rates. One possible explanation for such results is that the coefficient estimates possess *simultaneous-equations bias*. This has been particularly marked in those studies that employ some measure of cumulative life-time migration, since migration that has occurred over a long period of time is especially likely to have influenced the various independent variables used. The problem (Willis, 1974) is that some spatial autocorrelation will be present which means that the error term, e, cannot be assumed to be independent of the independent variable(s). It also means that ordinary least-squares estimation is not fully efficient. This situation is highly likely in migration prediction for, when the error and the independent variable terms are correlated, some of the effect of the error is wrongly attributed to the independent variable. For example, this may occur when the non-economic attractiveness of an area (such as social attractiveness or a pleasant residential environment) is correlated with the dependent (say economic) variable for a region like the South-East of England. This variable might, for example, relate to higher wage rates. If regions with high incomes also have high in-migration due to other reasons, while unattractive regions have lower incomes and other non-economic indicators, then a regression of the economic variables on migration will produce a biased estimate for the coefficient β. To overcome this, the concept of an *instrumental* variable can be used, defined in such a way as to be uncorrelated with e but *correlated* with the independent variable (Willis, 1974). It will be clear that correlation between error and the independent variable(s) is most likely to occur when the equation to be estimated is part of a whole system of such simultaneous equations, for it can be hypothesized that migration is a function of many socio-economic variables, and these variables themselves will be a function of the migration.

The problem of autocorrelation and the use of an instrumental variable can be made clear by a simple example. We can state a simple migration estimation (as before) as

$$M = \alpha + \beta W + e,$$

in which M represents migration and W represents some single (say, economic) variable to which the migration is hypothetically related. The slope coefficient, β, of course represents the propensity to migrate, and e is assumed to be independent. The independent variable, given that it may have a reciprocal relationship with M, we define as $W = M + I$ in which I represents an instrumental variable, exogenously determined, that is outside the system. In effect it represents the influences other than W on the migration M. It will be helpful to consider the consequent regression estimation problem in the form of figure 6.6 which describes the relationship between migration M and the economic variable W, with e the error term. The observed combination of migration M and the economic variable W will fall within the band around the migration functions $M = \alpha + \beta W$ according to whether the error, e, is zero, greater than zero or less than zero. Any combination of migration M and the economic variable W, however, must also satisfy the equation $W = M + I$, (or $M = W - I$). Assume that I has a range of values as shown in figure 6.6. Since combinations of migration and the economic variable W determining M, must satisfy both conditions, all observations of M and W will be within the parallelogram $P_1P_2P_3P_4$. An ordinary least squares regression on the sample of observations within $P_1P_2P_3P_4$ would fit a line $\hat{\alpha} + \hat{\beta}W$, and this clearly is a bad fit compared with $\alpha + \beta W$, resulting in a considerable upward bias. Increasing the sample size does not make any difference.

Figure 6.6 The migration function and scatter of points around it

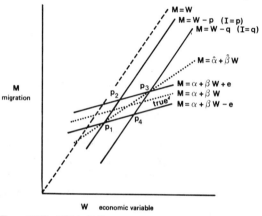

From Willis (1974: 131)

A consistent estimate of β can be obtained if an instrumental variable can be found which satisfies the two requirements already noted, but this will depend upon the quality of the empirical data available to the analyst.[29]

A useful study, in which the basic single parameter regression equation has been developed into a simultaneous system of equations, is that of Greenwood (1973, 1975) and an example taken from this work is reproduced in Appendix 6. This will make clear many of the principles already discussed. Another useful regression study which examines the directional components of a migration situation is Gleave (1973). One important outcome of such work is that, whereas migration is shown clearly to be a function of age, employment, unemployment, education, and so on, it is also clear that migration *influences*, for example, employment and unemployment levels over time. Also the in- and out-flows of population in an area will not be independent of each other. In other words, migration needs to be looked upon not simply as a consequence of change, but as an interactive element particularly in respect of its relationship with policy. This we discuss in Part 3 of the text.

One final point needs to be made. Like most migration analysis, the above example is cross-sectional and is therefore limited in the extent to which predictions over time of behaviour can be made. This is a limitation imposed by the data. The need for better longitudinal data in this area, and an explicit time series model for its analysis has long been argued.[30] But that possibility, other than for study at the local level, would appear to be a long way off. Migration is probably the single most important area where well-conducted local study would yield highly useful information to assist policy making.

Spatial interaction and allocation

We should now examine some attempts to introduce an explicit spatial dimension into models of urban activity. In theory, use of such models should allow prediction to take the form of hypothesized allocation of the various activities over space. This brings us close to the central concern of urban planning. A useful example with which to introduce basic concepts is that of shopping behaviour. We assume a situation in which the long-term success of a shopping location depends upon the trip-making accessibility of its location to the population that it serves, *relative* to the accessibility that the population might have to other centres that may be established by competitors. This can readily be recognized as a typical location problem in a free market situation. The example will also reveal inherent assumptions and limitations of the approach.

Both aggregate and disaggregate approaches are used to model spatial phenomena. The former, in which movement of people, say, are treated as collective flows to and from some facility, such as shopping or a recreation centre, has been the most widely developed and used by planners. The discussion following is based upon this concept and the principles of spatial modelling can be readily introduced. But more recent developments are beginning to suggest that a behavioural, disaggregated approach may become more widely applied. In this, the research focus is upon the individual and the model simulates the probabilities of an *individual* choosing to live in a certain location, or visit a particular facility and so on. The approach in other words requires an assessment of the utility function of an individual, that is, the 'worth' or value he puts upon a particular location for some purpose relative to the alternatives available to him. The concept of spatial opportunity (Chapter 3) is relevant here.

There are advantages in this approach. First, the underlying utility theory is well developed, and second, through survey and sampling methods that we have discussed (Chapter 5), household level data are gradually being acquired by planners. As yet the main area of development is in the field of transportation, particularly in modelling the choice of transport mode, though much of this work is somewhat peripheral to the main tasks of the urban planner, and cannot as yet be more generally applied. However, some emerging case study material is given in the Guide to Further Reading.

What is initially required is a concept which relates potential usage to the accessibility of a group of persons wanting to use some facility. The most frequently used (and mis-used concept) is that of the 'gravity model'[31] which essentially postulates that *increasing* distance to a facility whether it is a job, shop or entertainment is a *disincentive* to use that facility. Space, or distance is made explicit at the outset. Imagine a town, X, whose population can travel to a single shopping centre S, at distance d. As there are two distinct locations, namely the town and the shopping centre, we make these clear by the use of subscripts i and j respectively. This situation can now be formulated as a gravity model, to estimate the number of trips T, which will be made from i to j. We can write

$$T_{ij} = K \frac{X_i S_j}{d_{ij}^\alpha},$$

and in which K is a constant, and the coefficient α represents the degree to which the number of trips will diminish as distance between the town and shopping centre increases. This type of model has been widely used to explore the behaviour of people in their use of a variety of services and facilities.[32] To operate such a model, empirical data will be required, for example the size of town might be specified in terms of total population, or number of households, or purchasing power. Equally, the shopping centre might be defined in terms of floor space or number of retail outlets in the centre, or potential turnover.

In discussing how this model can be usefully applied to urban situations, the distinction between 'production' and 'attraction' needs to be recalled. In our simple example the 'producer' is the town ('producing' a number of journeys) and more obviously, the shopping centre is the 'attractor'. The relationship is as figure 6.7.

Figure 6.7 Relationship of trips or journeys, and distance

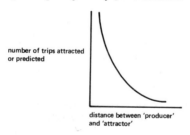

number of trips attracted
or predicted

distance between 'producer'
and 'attractor'

The simplest research application of the model is to a situation in which competition between attractors is present. Probably the best known example of this (and the earliest) is the so-called Reilly's Law of retail gravitation, which is useful to recall as it demonstrates an important concept. Reilly's hypothesis was that the shoppers living between towns, A and B, will be attracted to the towns according to their respective populations, P_A and P_B, and *inversely* with the square of the relative distance of the home of the shopper from the two towns, $(d_B/d_A)^2$. It is hypothesized that a potential shopper will visit the town with the strongest attraction computed as a function of size of centre and distance away. The main requirement then is to find the 'cutting point' between towns A and B, thus determining their serving hinterland. This cutting point will be given by

$$\left(\frac{P_A}{P_B}\right)\left(\frac{d_B}{d_A}\right)^2 = 1$$

and the most convenient form of applying this law is found by the rearrangement

$$d_A = \frac{d_{AB}}{1 + \sqrt{(P_B/P_A)}}.$$

This requires only that we know the 'sizes' of the towns, P_A, P_B, and the total distance between them. Assume the towns are $P_A = 4000$ households, $P_B = 16{,}000$ households and that they are 15 km apart, we find

$$d_A = \frac{15}{1 + \sqrt{(16{,}000/4000)}} = 5,$$

meaning that A's market boundary is 5 km away on the straight line joining A and B.

Although of limited practical use this example shows how, in principle, the gravity concept is useful in *allocating* activities, whether shopping, employment, residence or leisure between *competing* centres. The gravity concept, therefore, has given urban planners a basic idea upon which to build more sophisticated models of spatial activities which can be used to forecast a future urban situation and be tested by empirical observation. A further development was that of Hansen (1959) who postulated a basic spatial accessibility model in the form $X_i = \Sigma_j S_j f(c_{ij})$. X_i is the accessibility at zone i, $\Sigma_j S_j$ is the sum of the activities from other zones j, and $f(c_{ij})$ is a function representing the interaction between i and j. Typically, this will be in the form of some impedence to travel from j to i, such as distance, or as used commonly in the wide variety of transportation and accessibility models that have been built upon this principle, in terms of 'cost' (Weibull, 1976, Davidson, 1977). In an early application of spatial interaction principles, Zipf (1949) hypothesized that the amount of gross migration between two urban areas would be a function of the respective population sizes of the areas, modified by the distance (or intervening space) between the two areas so that increasing distance diminishes the propensity of people to move from one area to the other. Increased distance thus acts to increase the 'friction' against migration taking place. This can be expressed in notation as

$$M_{ij} = \frac{P_i P_j}{D_{ij}^{\alpha}},$$

where M_{ij} represents the gross flow of migrants from area i to area j, P_i and P_j are the respective population sizes of the two areas, and D_{ij} represents the distance between the two areas. The exponent α represents the mathematical form of the 'friction' at work. It will be realized that the idea of 'distance' as a disincentive or hindrance to migration is really a proxy for a variety of factors such as cost of migration, difficulty of journey, 'social' distance (that is how far j is *perceived* to be from i in terms of severed family ties, ease of visiting existing friends, etc.), and so on. Stouffer (1940) modified this concept, in effect denying the relevance of distance *per se*, and introducing the concept of 'intervening opportunities', which suggests that the number of persons who move a given distance is directly proportional to the number of opportunities (employment, for example) which they perceive at that distance, and inversely proportional to the number of intervening opportunities which compete to capture the migrant. The concepts, although widely applied, particularly in geographical analyses of migration, have somewhat been overtaken by methods built upon the so-called Lowry concept (Lowry, 1964) discussed shortly, notably by Rogers (1967) and Masser (1970).

The next step is to view the approach not just in terms of two centres, but many. For example, shoppers may have the choice of visiting a number of centres, all at differing distances (and costs of getting there) and with varying degrees of perceived attractiveness to the individual. Such a system can be represented in a matrix in which the cells represent the journeys (or trips, t) from a given producer, i (say, a household) to an attractor, j (a facility).

		Attractors, j			
		1	2	3	4
producers, i	1	—	t_{12}	t_{13}	t_{14}
	2	t_{21}	—	t_{23}	t_{24}
	3	t_{31}	t_{32}	—	t_{34}
	4	t_{41}	t_{42}	t_{43}	—

So far, we have not *constrained* the model. This can best be explained by noting that, in our example, increasing attractiveness of a centre will have the effect of increasing *ad infinitum* the number of journeys to it. Clearly, the ways in which consumers in a region spend their money on quantities of goods and services does *not* depend ultimately on the number of alternative shopping centres, but on their total disposable income. This means that we will want to specify a *maximum value* to the 'producer'. Typically, given a matrix representing all journeys, we can constrain the sum of all the t_{ij}s to the total possible number of trips that can be made. Let us represent this by T, so that

$$T = \Sigma t_{ij}$$

and this will be a *constraining* equation (see pp. 355–6).

A simple representation of a two-centre shopping situation can make these principles clear. Assume a situation of four residential areas, with their respective populations as shown in figure 6.8 (a). In one of these areas is a shopping centre, A, of a certain size, which at the moment serves all four zones and its average distance from each area is shown. Assume that it is

Figure 6.8 An application of the 'gravity' concept

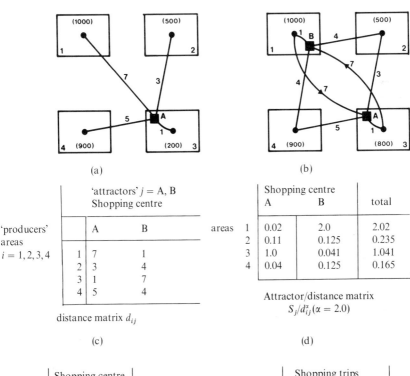

	'attractors' $j = A, B$ Shopping centre					Shopping centre		
						A	B	total
'producers' areas $i = 1,2,3,4$		A	B		areas 1	0.02	2.0	2.02
	1	7	1		2	0.11	0.125	0.235
	2	3	4		3	1.0	0.041	1.041
	3	1	7		4	0.04	0.125	0.165
	4	5	4					

distance matrix d_{ij}

(c)

Attractor/distance matrix
$S_j/d_{ij}^2 (\alpha = 2.0)$

(d)

		Shopping centre		total		residents	Shopping trips	
		A	B				A	B
areas	1	0.01	0.99	1.0		1000	10	990
	2	0.47	0.53	1.0		500	235	265
	3	0.96	0.04	1.0		800	768	32
	4	0.24	0.76	1.0		900	216	684
						3200	1229	1971

probability matrix

(e)

(f)

intended to develop a new centre in area one, B, which is intended to be twice the size of A (figure 6.8 (b)). By making certain assumptions, which of course would have to be tested, we can predict how the pattern of shopping trips might change.

It is convenient to summarize the data available about the inter-zonal distances in the form of a distance matrix (figure 6.8(c)). We assume first that the attractor/distance coefficient is $\alpha = 2$ as we used before, though empirical study might subsequently show this to have a different value. Secondly, we assume, for illustration, that the attractiveness of the centre is simply a function of its size so that the new centre B will be twice as attractive to a shopper as A. Clearly, this assumption would also need to be tested by empirical work. However, with the two assumptions made we can hypothesize the total attraction that the two centres will have for the residents of each area. The 'attractiveness score' for each centre, j, from each origin area, i, will be found from S_j/d_{ij}^z where S_j represents the 'size' of the centre ($S_A = 1, S_B = 2$), and d_{ij} the distance from each area, i, to a given centre, j. The *sum* of this attraction over all possible shopping trips is obtained by

$$\sum_{j=1}^{n} \frac{S_j}{d_{ij}^z}.$$

The calculations for centre A will be

$$\frac{1}{7^2} + \frac{1}{3^2} + \frac{1}{1^2} + \frac{1}{5^2} = 0.020 + 0.111 + 1.0 + 0.040 = 1.171,$$

and for Centre B

$$\frac{2}{1^2} + \frac{2}{4^2} + \frac{2}{7^2} + \frac{2}{4^2} = 2.0 + 0.125 + 0.041 + 0.125 = 2.291$$

These interaction values can usefully be summarized as the S_j/d_{ij} matrix shown in figure 6.8 (d). By summing the row and dividing each entry the values may be converted to probabilities showing that, for example, for area 2, 47 persons in every 100 would go to centre A, and 53 in every 100 would go to centre B. Given that it is assumed that the *total* number of trips which can be made by the residents of each area is known, we can readily apply these probabilities to estimating the way in which the total number of trips would be divided up between the two competing centres. This can be seen in figures 6.8 (e) and (f).

It will be clear that this process is simply imposing some realistic constraints onto the simple gravity concept. Careful scrutiny of the contents of figure 6.8 will suggest that the whole operation can be summarized by a single expression[33] namely

$$T_{ij} = O_i \left(\frac{S_j}{d_{ij}^z} \middle/ \sum_{j=1}^{n} \frac{S_j}{d_{ij}^z} \right)$$

in which T_{ij} is the sum of all the trips which take place, O_i represents the number of total trips which can be allocated to the two centres and the term following represents the *proportion* of those trips which can be allocated to each centre, according to the relative attraction of one centre (the numerator), compared to the overall attraction to *all* centres within the system (the denominator). In essence we have described a *production-constrained* model in which a finite limit has been put upon the number of possible inputs, that is the 'trips-to-shop' as a function of the number of residents. No limit, however, has been imposed on the number of shoppers who could be *allocated* to any one attractor (centre) and if the model were posed in an extreme form all shoppers could in theory be allocated to one centre.

This discussion will have suggested that there are a number of useful constraints which can be built into such a model. There are four possibilities all of which in various ways ensure internal consistency within the model between the estimated allocation of the trips and the external (or given) data which is being allocated. The four possibilities are (i) an unconstrained model; (ii) a production-constrained model (as we have used above); (iii) an attraction-constrained model, in which a given facility is only allowed to attract so many trips but from an unconstrained pool of potential trips; and (iv) the most commonly applied type in which both production and attraction are constrained. An example of the latter is reproduced as Appendix 7 which will make clear the basic principles.

Some general points must be made about the empirically determined coefficients. The fundamental assumption underlying the method is that the effect of distance to people's travel behaviour is inverse to the power α, and this value must be determined through study of the real world. There is, however, a mathematical difficulty with a simple exponent which is that as the distance between i and j becomes smaller and approaches zero, the number of trips that the model will predict approaches infinity. This is clearly unrealistic and an improvement is to use a negative exponent as the distance function in which the term d_{ij}^z is replaced by e_{ij}^{zd} and where e is the mathematical constant 2.718. This effectively introduces a fixed zero point to the function, which is made clear by a comparison of the two forms in figure 6.9.[34] In the original form the estimating equation

$$T_{ij} = K \frac{S_j}{d_{ij}^\alpha},$$

more commonly written $T_{ij} = K S_j d_{ij}^{-\alpha}$, now becomes $T_{ij} = K S_j e^{-\alpha d_{ij}}$.

The gravity concept predicts trips from i to j by taking only three variables as independent, the total number of trips from i, the size of centre j, and the distance from i to j. It will be intuitively obvious that this represents a gross oversimplification. The number of trips made from one place to another will normally depend not upon the number of trips *that it is possible* for a group of people to make, but how many they feel it worthwhile to make and how much it costs relative to that worth and so

Figure 6.9 Two functions relating trips to distance

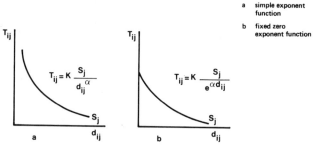

From Krueckeberg and Silvers (1974: 310)

on. At best the 'distance' concept is only a crude approximation. For example, in making a shopping journey use of a car will affect the propensity of an individual to make certain kinds of trips, and this factor will not be constant between areas. Ideally, then, the coefficients need to be calibrated individually for each 'producer'. Additional variables can also be introduced to represent factors such as *per capita* income, age of persons, purchasing tastes and so on. These coefficients will normally be obtained through a regression analysis of the topic from empirical data. It is frequently the case that separate calculations are done for various sub-groups in the population such as men and women, or different age groups, for each will have a different propensity to make trips and will differ in their access to a mode of transport.

As far as the 'attractors' are concerned we assumed that shopping centre size was the sole factor influencing people's preference. Clearly, this will also be a gross oversimplification and a whole range of parameters can be introduced here, including an index for the types and quality of shops, turnover or age of shopping centre, and so on. Frequently, it will be more realistic to express the 'distance' factor not in terms of linear distance as such, but in terms of travel cost or journey or some combination of these factors.

There is a general problem which must be noted. The more coefficients that are built in and the greater the degree of disaggregation, the greater the difficulty there will be in obtaining adequate data to validly calibrate the model, that is, to calculate plausible coefficients. In particular, as it becomes necessary to draw upon less and less satisfactory data, the degrees of freedom associated with the coefficients will decrease and hence their statistical significance. It follows that the predictive ability of the model will also fall, and some careful judgement is required on the part of the researcher to obtain both valid and useful results.

It will be clear that modelling a situation in this way for a complex system of interaction requires large amounts of data. Ideally, each 'flow' needs to be known or estimated and this is an important practical limitation for there will often be missing cells of data in the matrix. Whilst there are various estimating methods such as entropy maximizing which can be used to 'fill out' missing values, additional error is inevitably introduced into the model. This is one reason why aggregate approaches are limited and future research emphasis may be placed upon a more detailed analysis of individual behaviour as we noted earlier.

In the analysis of shopping behaviour an alternative perspective is that of central place theory (Parry Lewis and Bridges, 1975). This essentially postulates that for a given commodity there exists a level of demand below which it will not be offered for sale. Dealers in commodities with a high threshold level of demand will locate in a few centres with large trade areas, whilst businesses offering goods with a low threshold demand level will locate in many more centres with small trade areas. The result is a stepped hierarchy of trading centres, and studies using central place theory usually start by identifying a ranking system for the shopping facilities. The fundamental assumptions are that people will continue to walk to the shops for certain 'everyday' items, and that there will always be a need for a central shopping area where people can compare goods by looking at a wide choice. However, changes in retailing methods and growing congestion in town centres, are beginning to throw some doubt on these assumptions (Guy, 1980). Some kind of hierarchy certainly exists, but may not remain always in the same form.

The model we have described is essentially a distribution model, that is one which allocates, or models behaviour within a system according to assumptions and hypothetical constraints. Common uses of the gravity concept deal not only with transportation topics such as journey-to-work, or shopping or leisure, but the whole field of residential location as well. A guide to a variety of applications for further study is given at the end of this chapter. It should also be clear that the use of such models are essentially research tools. The model is a device for attempting to summarize by its coefficients, a complex real-world situation in simplified quantitative terms. Providing the researcher has focused upon the important issues in a situation, the model will allow him to search for and explain regularities in the system and this may lead to the development of theory and understanding.

The 'models' that have been discussed so far, both simple and relational (i.e. econometric) can help the planner to an understanding of the urban system, and this will help to predict the consequences of policies. It will also be clear that these models are partial. They relate to one substantive issue, as for example the population models, or they relate two such issues in some functional relationship, and/or can take on an explicit spatial form. These simple models are both effective and efficient for analysis and making predictions providing that valid data are available and that the necessary assumptions can be regarded as plausible. They serve a useful research function, but their application to the broader concepts of urban system study is limited by their partiality. It is an attractive possibility to attempt to build more complex models or simulations of the urban system by linking together these partial concepts. There are advantages and problems in so doing.

Urban systems modelling

Two general rules have been followed to develop more complex models of the urban system. The first has been by extending the spatial scope of more simple models, mainly by introducing more 'zones' or distinct areas into the model. These, frequently found in the transportation, and to some extent the population migration field, have revealed the difficulties all too clearly. First, the amount of interaction within the model increases as the square of the number of zones used as the model base. For example, a model of 140 zones (say of a typical urban area) involves 22,500 basic interactions. Further disaggregation, by types of journey, sub-groups of people, etc. enormously add to the volume of computing. There are, more seriously, other problems. Data are often deficient and limited in both quantity and quality. Increased complexity in the model, will mean that error effects from the data may not only be difficult to trace and therefore produce unknown effects on the results, but make the whole process unreliable. There are then serious difficulties in expanding the zonal basis of any modelled system without high quality data, considerable computing power and sufficient guiding theory to overcome these problems. Urban modelling has hardly reached this state of affairs.

The second, and currently more fashionable approach, is to attempt to couple together the partial or sub-models into more complex but more realistic arrangements. Better control can be exercised by following this route and a step-by-step development of theory is possible. Two such types of coupling should be distinguished (Batty, 1976c).

The first is when a series of allocation models are linked together, a situation often referred to as *loosely coupled*. Here, the partial models are simply arranged in some sequence, with a simple link between them. The second situation is where the models are *strongly coupled*, which means that the generation of activities is used as the device to link the partial models. In both situations the output or prediction from one sub-model, say dealing with population, or employment is used to provide input to another sub-model, say dealing with household formation or residential allocation, but it is the nature of the *link* between them that is different. Strongly coupled models are frequently explicitly spatial, and are controlled by strongly specified allocation constraints. The way in which this concept has been developed can best be illustrated by reference to the most widely applied example. This can also usefully introduce some derivatives of the method.

The model conceptualized by Lowry (1963, 1964, 1968) and so-named, is a good example of a *composite* model and blends the concept of the constrained gravity model and the export base multiplier, both of which we have discussed. In essence, the model is an approach to the estimation of future land requirements by making a fundamental distinction between activities which *serve* a region's population, for example through manufacturing, and *local* activities which are demanded by the population, such as shopping provision, recreation areas and so on. The main assumption underlying the approach is that estimates are made for the serving activities first, from which can be derived a whole chain of estimates about the demands which will follow. For the basic Lowry model there will be three main components representing activity sectors; (i) a basic sector which is defined as non-local (that is, exporting) and which is, in locational terms independent of local market forces; (ii) a household sector comprising residential population whose location is to be strongly influenced by the location of the basic sector job opportunities, and (iii) a retail (or more generally) a service sector (which may comprise both public and private sector agencies within it) which primarily exists to serve the resident population and is therefore locationally closely tied to it. Broadly, these sectors correspond to industrial, residential and service land uses, and in the operation of the model the sector activities are translated into land use demand estimates by means of *land-use/activity* ratios. It will be clear that these latter must be pre-determined by empirical study of real urban situations and modified in the light of assumptions as to how they are likely to change over time.

The starting point for the simulation is that a good estimate of basic employment is available for all the defined zones within a region, and that appropriate activity rates are known. From this data, estimates of the total population (or households) from the economic base are made, who then require to be 'serviced'. The model assigns the estimates of population (or households) to zones according to the distribution of export type jobs, though it is worth offering the reminder that location of the basic industry is independent of the location of the residential areas. This is a point of criticism of the model. It is clearly necessary to put constraints on the number of households who can be allocated to any one zone, so that, for example a maximum density constraint is not violated. Such a 'capacity' must be pre-specified for each zone. The *local* employment generated by this allocation is then calculated for each zone.

Several points must be noted. The first is that the estimated 'service' population (and their households) will themselves need 'servicing' so that further 'service' jobs are required, *et seq.*, but with diminishing increments. Second, as this service sector requires to be allocated to live in the area, already (hypothetically) occupied by the base sector households, and given the maximum density or capacity constraints, it becomes necessary to modify the initial allocations of residential population to 'provide room' for the service sector. This process cycles interactively until a stable situation is reached. Third, the service employment is often disaggregated into sub-sectors, for example, neighbourhood, local or district, and urban or metropolitan, allowing each to be represented by a different activity rate. A further refinement is that a minimum size constraint is placed upon the service sub-sectors, so that small centres of service sector employment cannot arise, until a certain threshold is reached.

As Batty (1976c) makes clear, once the allocations of the various activities are made in accordance with the predetermined constraints, the model also tests the predicted distribution of population against the distribution used to compute potentials to find out whether the two distributions are coincident. Lowry (1963) argues that it is necessary to secure consistency between these distributions because the model uses distributions of population and employment to calculate the potentials which indirectly affect the predicted location of these same variables. Consistency is secured by feeding back into the model predicted population and employment and reiterating the whole allocation procedure until the distributions input to the model are coincident with the outputs. It will be realized that interactive, allocative and adjustment processes are involved, and these can be usefully summarized as figure 6.10.

It remains to offer an introductory explanation as to how these processes may be formulated in principle using the notation that was introduced earlier. The basic 'attraction-constrained' gravity model is used to initially find the residential distribution of the basic labour force as

$$T_{ij} = B_j D_j W_i d_{ij}^{-\alpha},$$

where

$$B_j = 1/\Sigma_i W_i d_{ij}^{-\alpha} \quad \text{and} \quad \Sigma_i T_{ij} = D_j.$$

The term T_{ij} refers to the number of trips which are made by the residents of zone i to work in zone j; D_j is the total number of jobs in zone j; W_i represents the attractiveness of zone i as a residential location to members of the labour force and as before d_{ij} is the 'distance' between zones i and j, subject to the function α. If it is now recalled that the process is an iterative one, it will be clear that the term D_j, (the number of jobs in zone j) initially will represent *all* basic employment, but as the model successively allocates service employment at each iteration, it will represent some blend of basic and service employment. At each iteration, each addition of service employment will become progressively smaller until stability is reached.

It is a relatively simple matter to calculate the total number of resident workers allocated to each zone, R_i, by summing the total distribution of trips, so that $R_i = \Sigma_j T_{ij}$. From this an estimate of resident population can be obtained by the use of an *activity rate*, X_i. This is a ratio between the total population of an area and the proportion who are in employment. Total population P_i will be given by $O_i = R_i (1/X_i)$. In a similar way the number of households can be estimated.

Given now that the residential population is known for each zone, i, the distribution of the service trips can be calculated by the use of the production constrained model, in the form

$$T_{ij} = A_i O_i W_j d_{ij}^{-\alpha},$$

Figure 6.10 Generalized flow chart of the Lowry model

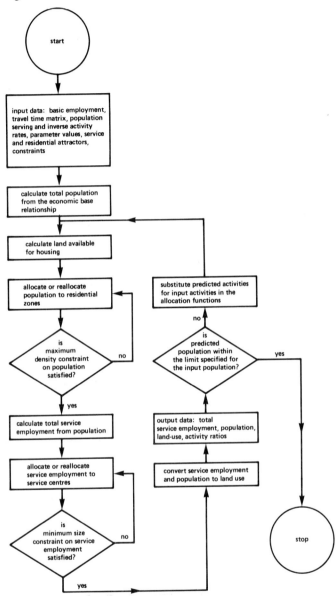

From Batty (1976c: 61)

where $A_i = 1/\Sigma_j W_j d_{ij}^{-\alpha}$ and $\Sigma_j T_{ij} = O_i$. Here, T_{ij} represents the number of service trips made by residents in zone i to services in zone j: O_i represents the residential population of each zone i; W_j is a measure of the attractiveness of zone j as a service centre; $d_{ij}^{-\alpha}$ is as already explained.

In exactly the same way as before, the total number of service trips made to a given zone, S_j, can be found by adding up the total number of trips to that zone, so that $S_j = \Sigma_i T_{ij}$ and this can be converted to the amount of service employment SE_j, by the use of a population service ratio X'_j; which expresses service employment as a proportion of the total population $SE_j = S_j X'_j$. This concludes the first iteration (cycle) of the calculations and the allocation process continues by re-entering the estimate of service employment, SE_j, back into the starting equation

$$T_{ij} = B_j D_j W_i d_{ij}^{-\alpha},$$

where D_j (initially the number of basic jobs) is replaced by successive calculations of the service employment which, in addition, is allocated to each zone. Eventually, after several such iterations, the system reaches a state of stable output values, which can be evaluated for consistency with the input data, and the calibration of the model. A careful attempt by the reader to follow through this notation will make clear the principles upon which the model is based, and will serve as a basis upon which more detailed literature can be understood.[35]

The basic concept outlined above is clearly an oversimplified representation of the real world, but a large number of refinements and developments have followed which allow more complex urban situations to be modelled. It also follows that this range of developments allows the analyst to choose a level and type of model specification which is appropriate both to his problem and his available data.

The approach also rests upon the assumption that the economic base concept and subsequent allocation of derived activity do, in reality, represent a plausible explanation of urban spatial structure. Clearly, this is a matter for debate.

The operational derivatives of the Lowry approach have been succinctly described by A. G. Wilson (1974) and Batty (1976c), in both the American and British contexts, and brief comment can be made on the more important concepts to be exploited. Two early developments (Crecine, 1964, 1968) were to dis-aggregate the population into different socio/economic groups, and secondly to allow for some 'time-lag' in the way the interactions operate in the model. It will be intuitively obvious that, in the real world, all manner of time lags will occur and these, once identified, can be accommodated by the model. Further developments have replaced the crude estimates of population and employment potential by more 'realistic' factors such as land rent costs, transportation costs, and measures of access to facilities such as schools.[36]

It is important to note a theoretical development by Garin (1966). Briefly, this work utilized a 'production-constrained' version of the gravity model in conjunction with the economic base concept. As Batty (1976c) shows, this effectively strengthens the coupling between allocation and activity generation. In simple terms, the model starts by finding the residential location of a given distribution of workers in basic sector employment, and then finds the population associated with this employment by application of an (inverse) activity rate. The first increment of service employment is derived from this basic population using a population-serving ratio, and this employment is then allocated to service centres. These workers in turn require residential locations and this leads to a further increment of population and to a further increment of service employment and so on. Eventually, a point is reached where further increments are insignificant. Although this process does not treat land uses explicitly, this can be done by applying simple land-use/activity ratios as discussed earlier.

Practical applications of the Garin concept have led to the development of urban systems models which explicitly treat not only the spatial allocation of activities but also the 'space stock' into which the activities have to be fitted. The most convenient way to represent this stock is by measurements of the floorspace required by the various activities. These developments, then, are attempting to reproduce the 'supply' side of the urban land market into the model. Certain main features should be noted. Within the allocation zones of the earlier models, a sub-model is used to allocate the 'stock' in terms of floorspaces within these zones. Then, these available 'stocks' are used to constrain the demand for space by the different activities to be allocated, so that in effect, as allocated demand 'fills up' the zones, the floorspace capacity is used up, and any excess demand must be allocated elsewhere, that is to other zones. Examples of this approach are to be found in work by March et al., (1971) and Echenique et al., (1969a, 1969b).

Many developments[37] on these themes have been developed by practicing planners over the last few years and, as a detailed review is beyond the scope of this text, a guide to this literature is given at the end of this chapter. It may be helpful however to point out that, in general, the application of activity allocation type models for predictive purposes has been mainly at the sub-regional scale or in dealing with more complex metropolitan systems, and has been particularly characteristic of practice in America. British experience, which has been more concerned with independent towns and cities, has focused more heavily upon the 'stocks-activity' approach to spatial predictive modelling and this will be made clear by reference to the selected examples cited in the bibliography.

The models referred to dealing with spatial allocation are essentially *non-optimizing*. That is, they do not seek to find an optimal (or 'best') answer to a problem posed so as to maximize or minimize some specified objective function. There is, however, a large body of urban modelling theory and practice which is concerned with seeking solutions to urban problems in an optimizing mode. In general, this makes use of mathematical (linear or non-linear) programming. Many examples will be found in the field of transportation planning, where for example, a problem can be posed to allocate a distribution of journey trips within an urban system so as to minimize overall transport costs (see, for example, Hadley 1962). The approach has been extended to a housing situation by Herbert and Stevens

(1960), and by Harris (1972), who allocated persons to housing or housing areas by maximizing their aggregate rent-paying ability. A further spatial application is that of allocating population and employment to zones in a regional system by maximizing a general welfare function over a number of economic criteria (Ben-Shahar et al., 1969). We have already referred in Chapters 2 and 3 to systematic plan generation and evaluation models which essentially operate in this 'optimizing' mode, (see Harris, 1976), including the recent work in multi-objective programming (Nijkamp, 1980).

As Harris (1976) has pointed out, trends in systematic urban planning or design methods based upon modelling approaches have stemmed from two principal sources. One has been the descriptive, systems models, which rapidly developed in the 1960s, particularly in transportation work, and which assumed, fundamentally, the relevance of a system wide view of urban affairs (Forrester, 1969). The other source has been the work of urban economists, developed from the founding theories of Alonso (1964) and Wingo (1961). This essentially combines traditional economic location theory and models of economic growth. In both cases, however, the building of *prescriptive* models has been problematical, not least because of the difficulty already noted concerning the problem of defining optimizing criteria (Chapter 3).

For the present, application of mathematical programming in the form of decision-optimizing methods for plan design are necessarily limited to well-bounded, discrete problems, and particularly those associated with urban facility location (Harris, 1976, 1978). Clearly, for larger-scale, more complex system-wide considerations, especially given plural and conflicting objectives, and where there will be much uncertainty, the planner must necessarily rely upon more holistic and less precise design and plan-making methods. But further, even where the uncertainty can be reduced to manageable levels, there remains the difficulty of specifying an objective design. Progress towards the greater use of mathematical programming in plan making, needs to address the question of values, the normative stance of the planner, and the need to integrate 'soft' (less precise) forms of data into the planning paradigm. Whilst this will continue to involve the traditional planning goals of efficiency and equity, the emphasis in the role of design and decision methods must shift to an exploration of their interdependence. Recent work in this area which sets out the potential of such systematic methods and evaluates alternative applications is by Harris and Wilson (1978) and a broad-ranging view of methodology and its implications for the planning paradigm is given in Harris (1978).

In conclusion, we believe it to be important to stress the use of modelling in planning in a *conditional* sense, for it then becomes possible to blend the highly assumptive trend-reinforcing tendencies of the use of models of the urban system, with the need for more normative considerations, of judgement about desired patterns of land-use and development, a point that we developed in Chapter 1. It is still the case that the best articulated view of this need is that of Chapin (1965).[38] Modelling, then, is primarily a research tool for developing insights and understanding of complex urban processes. Yet, clearly, once a system can be plausibly reproduced in a model form it is tempting to extend that model into a forecasting mode and to make use of it in the generation of plans and policies. This raises many philosophical and methodological issues that should be addressed within a policy context and to this we now turn.

Notes

1   See Bracken (1978) for a review of these forms.
2   Or 'decrement' if the population is falling.
3   The 'base' data for population analysis and prediction is normally taken from the decennial Census. 'Census' population or 'enumerated' population refers to the actual population resident in an area at the time of the Census. Many urban planning authorities prefer to use the estimate of home population, published annually by Government (OPCS) which refers to the population of an area after certain 'short-term' migrants such as students, members of the armed forces, etc. are re-allocated to their more permanent place of residence.
4   Examples in the literature frequently convert an exponential form to a linear form by a logarithmic transformation. This enables the more complex exponential arithmetic to be simplified and the reader should become familiar with this manipulation.
5   Also referred to as an 'asymptotic' form.
6   We cannot discuss these in detail though readers may care to note that the general form is given by $P_{t+n} = K_a b^n$ using the earlier notation. Examples will readily be found in Isard (1969) and Pressat (1972, 1978).
7   It is, in fact, alarming that so many urban population 'forecasts' are made by extrapolation from just the two most recent Censuses.
8   Also referred to as 'composite' methods.
9   More generally referred to as a 'cohort-survival' model.
10 It will be realized that each cohort calculation is, in effect, a simple, independently calculated linear equation. There is ample literature to guide the analyst or planner in the use of this model and a large number of computer-based versions are available (see Baxter and Williams, 1978; Bracken, 1976).
11 The net residual approach to net migration analysis is widely used (Siegal and Hamilton, 1952; Hamilton, 1966, 1967; Craig, 1970). The approach is sometimes referred to as the 'demographic' approach to migration estimation. Referring back, our earlier population composition expression was

$$P_{t+n} = P_t + B_n - D_n + M_n.$$

It will be clear that if an *historical* period is considered, then P_{t+n} (end of period), P_t (beginning of period), B_n (births) and D_n (deaths) will all be known. Any residual in the equation must be due to M_n, i.e. net migration over the period. This is the product of the gross in- and out-flows. If each cohort is treated independently, disaggregate net data can be obtained. This analysis is frequently used by planners to make estimates of the age *structure* changes taking place in a local population, where, for example, younger persons are leaving to seek employment and elderly persons are moving in, say, for retirement. The calculation of age and sex disaggregated net migration data, however, requires good estimates of disaggregated natural change which in turn is dependent upon the quality of the *local* survival and to a lesser extent, fertility data. Estimation of population change at the local level often means moving away from the census as a data base to sources such as the electoral register, household composition data, school records and health record data (Baxter and Williams, 1978). Population analysis at this level also frequently involves making estimates of migration not as an independent phenomenon, but rather by recognizing that migration usually takes place for a reason, such as to seek employment, or a better house, or for family reasons.

12   The model requires calibration for birth and death rates for each age group. These can be generated by the model or, more frequently, obtained from official data. The calculation of appropriate *group* vital rates is complex, but see Bracken (1976) and SDD (1975a). Normally, group rates can only usually be calculated from published data at *national* levels, and must therefore be modified in order to represent regional or more local variations in mortality and fertility. This is achieved by pre-multiplying the vital rates for mortality and fertility by so-called Area Comparability Factors.

13   As a result, the cohort survival mode in its 'forecasting' role is probably the most widely mis-used model and can be misleading if used unqualified to 'drive' other forecasts such as for employment or housing needs (see Chapter 9).

14   One difficulty which must be noted is that the definition of 'household' is not very precise and some allowance has to be made for this. The Census of population 1971 definition for a *private* household is 'any group of persons, whether related or not, who live together and benefit from a common housekeeping; or any person living alone who is responsible for providing his or her own meals'.

15   Evidence for this is obtained by means of 'indicators' such as the fall in average household size in Britain from 3.99 persons in 1921 to 2.89 in 1971; average age of marriage; increasing longevity; family formation pattern relative to age of mother; social attitudes towards co-habitation, increase in single person households, and so on.

16   This distinction is fundamental to most censuses and household data are normally published separately for the two sectors. Change in the non-private sector is fairly readily predicted from any planned change in the number of institutions themselves.

17   Particularly data relating to family size and marital status.

18   Census variables relating to household amenities include hot and cold water supply, inside w.c. and fixed bath. These variables are widely used as 'indicators' of housing quality (Chapter 8).

19   There are a number of measurement problems – some people for example have two jobs (one of which they may not officially disclose), or do work which is not officially recorded. The regional product has also to be estimated in money terms which has to be adjusted for changes in the value of money. It is then referred to as a regional product in *real terms*.

20   The expression $\equiv$ means 'is defined so as to equal'.

21   It is important to make clear that investment not only means purchasing equipment and so on, but any spending which is not consumed during the period of study, for example, building a house.

22   The reason, briefly, why it works is that an increase in production to earn regional export income will first directly increase regional income and, in turn,

increase regional consumption, typically through the spending of wages on goods and services. As the receiver of this income will in turn also spend his 'income' on further goods and services the effect is 'multiplied'. Eventually, the situation stabilizes when saving and import *leakages* cause the income flow cycle to slow down and eventually reach stability.

23 The underlying theory is drawn from economic analysis – see Koopmans (1951) and Makower (1965).

24 As already noted, there are frequently serious deficiencies in available data, and difficulties of definition. A working approach is to define migration broadly in terms of residential movement by individuals or households which incurs a break in community ties though clearly this is difficult to define adequately (Willis, 1974) and a minimum distance approach is often used as a crude proxy for this (Lee, 1966).

25 Government itself has a considerable influence here requiring migration through, for example, its decentralization policies of employment to less prosperous regions; through specific financial assistance to declining areas; assistance with removal of key workers through industrial locational policies; and through direct involvement with multi-national companies in major projects.

26 These issues represent real areas of deficiency in current knowledge about migration. Several studies have attempted to explain the clear deficiency in such data that the 'one year' migration data bears comparatively little proportional relationship to the 'five year' data. It is *not* the case that the one year data times five, roughly corresponds to the five year data, and this is usually explained partly by the incidence of unrecorded multiple moves in the five year period, and the better ability of persons to record more recent 'one year' movements. For economy the 'five year' question has not been used in the 1981 census.

27 This has been the subject of extensive sociological investigation. For example, see Young and Willmott (1957), Wolpert (1965).

28 A good example of compliance with such principles can be found in the work of Willis (1972c) in a study of migration in north-east England.

29 There is also a widely used alternative, through the use of two- or three-stage, or indirect least-squares estimation (see Christ (1966) or Wonnacott and Wonnacott (1970) for an explanation). In this approach, W is regressed on a variable *not* correlated with e, such as I, providing the required unbiased estimate for β.

30 See, for example, Rees and Rees (1977), and an extensive review by Gleave and Cordey-Hayes (1977).

31 The observation that human phenomena involved an interaction over space that could be explained by Newtonian physics is attributed to Zipf (1949) and Stewart (1942, 1947). Newton's Law states that the gravitational force of attraction between two masses is a function of the product of the masses themselves and inversely proportional to the distance between them. A variety of simple and more complex models of the urban spatial world have been developed by applying this principle. Newton's law is summarized as

$$F = K \frac{M_a M_b}{d^2},$$

where F is the attractive force, M_a and M_b are the two masses and d is the distance that separates them. K is a constant.

32   The principle can also be readily applied in the study of the movement of people themselves, that is, residential migration (see later in the chapter).

33   The derivation of this form, from the earlier notation is well described in A. G. Wilson (1974) or Krueckeberg and Silvers (1974)—see also pp 355–6.

34   See Krueckeberg and Silvers (1974: 309/10) for further explanation on this point.

35   Thus equipped, the reader will find the numerical example of Masser (1972) helpful, and is then recommended to the more advanced treatment by Batty (1976c).

36   See Crecine (1969).

37   One further concept that we cannot discuss in detail is that of 'entropy' and its application to urban systems modelling (see Ayeni, 1979).

38   Revised as Chapin and Kaiser (1979).

☐ GUIDE TO FURTHER READING

(Full references are given in the Bibliography.)

4 Research theory and designs

There is at present no single, comprehensive text to be recommended as 'next' reading by the serious student seeking guidance on research design in the urban field. There are, of course, the well established texts in the broad areas of theory and methodology drawn upon in this text. These will provide relevant, in-depth, further reading, though the urban analyst will require to synthesize much of this material to the particular circumstances of his investigation.

Harvey (1969) *Explanation in Geography* (particularly Chapters 1–6) will be found to be extremely helpful in guiding the student towards a fuller understanding of the theory of social research, much of it of direct relevance to the urban context. On the epistemology of the social sciences we refer readers to Brodbeck (1968) *Readings in the Philosophy of the Social Sciences* and Kuhn (1962) *The Structure of Scientific Revolutions*. On the application of scientific methods, Braithwaite (1960) *Scientific Explanation* is a standard text. More particularly geared to the methodologies of social science are texts by Kaplan (1964) *The Conduct of Inquiry* and Ackoff (1953) *The Design of Social Research*. On the operationalization of social research designs, Blalock (1970) *An Introduction to Social Research*, Campbell and Stanley (1966) *Experimental and Quasi-experimental Designs for Research* and Blalock and Blalock (1968) *Methodology in Social Research* are suggested. An introductory, practical text for the systematic construction of research designs is Meyers and Grossen (1978) *Behavioural Research: Theory, Procedure and Design*. A standard work in the conduct of field research is Schatzman and Strauss (1973) *Field Research: Strategies for a Natural Society*.

5 Research concepts and operations

On the operationalization of social research design there is an extensive literature. We particularly recommend Hoinville and Jowell (1978) *Survey Research Practice* as an excellent introductory text which also includes an extensive bibliography. The broad nature of the conduct of social research is discussed in Glaser and Strauss (1967) *The Discovery of Grounded Theory* and a good introduction to the behavioural approach is that of McKennell (1974) *Surveying Attitude Structures: A discussion of principles and procedures*. Burton and Cherry (1969) *Social Research Techniques for Planners* remains the only general treatment to date aimed at the urban practitioner.

On specific methodologies and procedures the following are recommended. On sampling methods Kish (1965) *Survey Sampling* and Yates (1960) *Sampling Methods for Censuses and Surveys* are standard works. Barnett (1974) *Elements of Sampling Theory* or Sudman (1976) *Applied Sampling* are good practical texts. On the use of geographical bases in sampling see Herbert and Evans (1974) *Urban Sub-areas as Sampling Frameworks for Social Survey*, and Herbert and Johnston (1976) *Spatial Processes and Form*, which contains case studies in several relevant aspects of spatial methodology. On the subject of sampling frames readers will find Pickett (1974) *Sources of Official Data* a valuable contribution particularly on the use of electoral registers as sampling frames, as well as Gray (1970) *The Electoral Register: practical information for use when drawing samples* and Gray and Gee (1967) *Electoral Registration for Parliamentary Elections*. On response error in sampling see Gray and Gee (1972) 1966 *Sample Census of England and Wales* and the more general problem of non-response in survey work in Moser and Kalton (1971) *Survey Methods in Social Investigation*. The subject of interviewing is dealt with comprehensively by Hyman (1975) *Interviewing in Social Research*, with a great deal of practical information given in Atkinson (1968) *A Handbook for Interviewers*. This latter also deals with a broad range of matters relating to field work organization. Oppenheim (1968) *Questionnaire Design and Attitude Measurement* is a widely used text, and Cannell *et al.* (1971) *Working Papers on Survey Research in Poverty Areas* provides insights into the practical problems of conducting interviews and particularly the problems of 'interviewer–respondent' relationships. The conduct of mail questionnaires is discussed fully in Berdie and Anderson (1974). *Questionnaires: design and use* while the analysis of attitude measures and scaling is described in Hoinville and Jowell (1978) *op. cit.* An excellent case study which provides numerous examples of question design and wording, questionnaire layout and answer coding is SSRC (1980) *Users Manual: Quality of Life Survey*.

On the subject of the use of official data sources see Benjamin (1970) *The Population Census* and the papers in the Methodological Series on the Social Survey Division of the OPCS. Atkinson (1968) *op. cit.* is also a good guide to definitions and classifications for official data. Other guidance in the use of census data is given in Hakim (1978) *Census Confidentiality, Micro-data and Census Analysis*. The introductory report to the General Household Survey – OPCS (1973) and the various Census of Population reports and commentaries also provide guides to the use of such data. Some 'user-orientated' comments upon the proposed content of the 1981 Census will be found in Black (1978) *The 1981 Census: A Local Authority Viewpoint*.

Only a brief guide to statistical texts can be given. We suggest Blalock (1972b) *Social Statistics* as a standard text and Johnston (1978) *Multivariate Statistical Analysis in Geography* as an excellent treatment of multi-variate methods in an applied context. A recent text that may well have considerable appeal for the student in an applied field such as Urban planning is Irvine *et al.* (1979) *Demystifying Social Statistics*. Those readers who have sufficient self-discipline will find problem-solving approaches such as Kohout (1974) *Statistics for Social Scientists: A Co-ordinated Learning System* and Chiswick and Chiswick (1975) *Statistics and Econometrics* particularly helpful. Of the many texts specializing in the analysis of social data, Schuessler (1971) *Analysing Social Data* is recommended. These texts all contain full bibliographies to more specialized areas of statistical methodology. Two useful primers in more specialized statistical methods are Ostrom (1978) *Time Series Analysis* and Glenn (1977) *Cohort Analysis*, both geared to the needs of social scientists. An excellent introduction to mathematical operations relevant to planners is Wilson and Kirby (1975) *Mathematics for Geographers and Planners*.

The application of systematic methods in urban analysis is given comprehensive treatment in Catanese (1972) *Scientific Methods of Urban Analysis*, Krueckeburg and Silvers (1974) *Urban Planning Analysis: Methods and Models* and Papageorgiou (1976) *Mathematical Land-Use Theory*. An introductory treatment of computing methods in planning is Baxter (1976) *Computer and Statistical Techniques for Planners*. An introduction to graphical techniques for presenting data is Everitt (1978) *Graphical Techniques for Multivariate Data*. A number of valuable essays in American urban analysis with an emphasis upon quantitative study will be found in Bernstein and Mellon (1978) *Selected Readings in Quantitative Urban Analysis*, particularly dealing with urban labour markets, housing and transportation. Case study information in the British context will be found in *Labour Force Surveys* (1971–79), biennially, and the *Directory of Local Authority Surveys*, 1978 (Department of the Environment, 1979a). Practical, official survey problems and advice to overcome them are also discussed in the *Family Expenditure Survey* (OPCS) and *National Dwelling and Housing Survey* (Department of the Environment, 1978b).

Recent applications which reveal methodological insights using regression and related techniques include Fogarty (1977) *Predicting Neighbourhood Decline within a large Central City: An Application of Discriminant Analysis*, and Bennett and Tan (1979) *Allocation of the UK Rate Support Grant by the use of Methods of Optimal Control*. Research in the perception of urban issues is reviewed in Hourihan (1979a, b) *The Evaluation of Urban Neighbourhoods*.

6   Urban simulation and prediction

This is an area where the reader is well served with texts that range from introductory to advanced. At the introductory level Reif (1973) *Models in Urban and Regional Planning* and Masser (1972) *Analytical Models for Urban and Regional Planning* are confidently recommended. A general overview of the more recent developments in modelling is Foot (1978) *Mathematical Modelling in Land-Use Planning*. A more comprehensive treatment is Chapin and Kaiser (1979) *Urban Land-Use Planning*. For those who wish to pursue their reading in a research orientation then Batty (1976c) *Urban Modelling* is an advanced text. For a critical review of the use of models in practice, which will provide many significant insights, see Massey (1974) *Models and Theories in Planning*.

For a broader discussion of the role of modelling in urban study see a review by Bracken (1978) *Simulation: Methodology for Urban Study* which covers research, design and pedagogic aspects of recent work, and Ayeni (1979) *Concepts and Techniques in Urban Analysis* is a recent introduction to a broad range of modelling aspects to the study of the urban system.

Much of the impetus to the development of urban models came during the period from 1968 to about 1974. This period was one when a number of sub-regional strategies were prepared (Coventry-Warwickshire-Solihull; Nottinghamshire-Derbyshire Studies) and the first wave of Structure Plans were under way. Most subsequent developments have built upon this work. It is relevant therefore to use this material as a useful introduction to case study reading. Generally, the urban models have fallen either under the 'Activity–Allocation' or 'Stocks–Activities' headings. The former tend to have been developed at the sub-regional or metropolitan scale, whereas the latter are more appropriate at the town scale. For a discussion of the problems of modelling complex systems and a step-by-step approach see Batty and March (1976) *The Method of Residues in Urban Modelling*. A more philosophical review is Batty (1978a) *Paradoxes of Science in Public Policy*.

Cripps and Foot (1969) in a study of Bedfordshire, and Batty (1969) in a study of Central and North East Lancashire were pioneering works using the Garin model. The same approach is well-described in the *Nottingham-Derbyshire sub-regional study* (1969). The *South Hampshire* strategy used an activity allocation model (Caulfield and Rhodes, 1971) with population disaggregation by socio-economic groups.

In contrast, the Stock-Activity approach has been pioneered by studies for Stevenage and Milton Keynes (Echenique *et al.*, 1972) and for Cambridge (Booth, 1970a, b). Two of the most thoroughly worked urban case studies in model form are those of Barras *et al.* (1971) *An Operational Urban Development Model of Cheshire*, and Barras (1975) *A Spatial Interaction Model of Cleveland*. The implications of a declining economy and the effect on the use of planning methods is discussed in Batey (1978) *Factors Affecting the Choice of Strategic Planning Methodology in a Stagnating Metropolitan Region: A Case Study of Greater Manchester*.

At the macro level, two good case studies are that of Burdekin and Marshall (1973) *The Calibration, Potential Development and Limitations of the Forrester Model* and Turner (1974) *The Design of an Urban Growth Model for Strategic Land-Use Transportation Studies*. Some comparative case studies in the application of models to urban analysis are to be found in Bourne (1975) *Urban Systems: Strategies for Regulation*. A valuable recent review is Nijkamp (1979b) *Gravity and Entropy Models: The State of the Art*, and a case study in the application of the Lowry model is Van Est (1979) *The Lowry Model Revised to Fit a Dutch Region*. A clear explanation of the concept of entropy in planning models is Webber (1976) *The Meaning of Entropy Maximizing Models*.

The theme of spatial opportunity as a modelling approach to urban facility accessibility has been recently reviewed by Breheny (1978) *The Measurement of Spatial Opportunity in Strategic Planning*. A wide-ranging review and good bibliography in the broad field of spatial modelling is Griffith and Jones (1980) *Explorations into the Relationship between Spatial Structure and Spatial Interaction*. The following notes suggest further reading and case studies in the more specific, substantive fields of urban analysis.

Population and migration

Many published reports of Structure Planning Authorities contain useful accounts of basic methods for analysis of population change and forecasting. Particularly recommended are those of Tyne and Wear (1976) or Merseyside (1980). An excellent introductory review and explanation of methods will be found in Scottish Development Department (1975b) Planning Advice Notes Series. Those wishing to make population forecasts in planning are recommended to Baxter and Williams (1978) *Population and Uncertainty at the Local Scale*, and Campbell (1976) *Local Population Projections*. General discussions about the problems associated with demographic data and its use are Brass (1974) *Demographic data and Prediction of National and Regional Population Trends*, and Benjamin (1974) *The Collection and Handling of Demographic Data now and in the Future*. See also the Journal, *Population Trends* (OPCS). Research has focused mainly upon migration – both as a social and a spatial phenomenon, the latter dominant in the analytical literature. The following selected references will guide the reader into the various themes within the subject, and these references contain ample bibliographies to more extensive literature.

An excellent review of the broad range of spatial modelling of migration (including gravity, spatial interaction, intervening opportunities, econometric and probabilistic models) is Stillwell (1975a) *Models of Inter-regional Migration: A Review*. Useful papers on the data problem for migration analysis are Ogilvy (1979) *Inter-Regional Migration since 1971: An appraisal of data from two sources – Labour Force Surveys and the National Health Central Register* and Rees (1977) *The Measurement of Migration from Census Data and Other Sources*; and a more methodological viewpoint particularly concerning the use of entropy-maximizing methods to 'fill out' areas of data deficiency is given in Chilton and Poet (1973) *An Entropy Maximizing Approach to the Recovery of Detailed Migration Patterns from Aggregate Census Data*.

Two references which deal with analysis of migration from a life cycle perspective are Bracken (1976) *Estimation and Cluster Analysis of Net Age Migration Profiles for Urban Areas in England and Wales* and Rogers *et al.* (1978) *Model Migration Schedules and their Applications*. In addition to the work of Greenwood referred to in the text, Gleave (1973) *A Simulation of the Relationship Between the Directional Components of Migration* examines an analysis of gross migration flows into and out of regions and the relationship of these flows. This is a good reference in regression techniques applied to the population field.

Case studies that will provide practical insights, in addition to those already noted in Chapter 6 are, Masser and Brown (1974) *Hierarchical Aggregation Procedures for Interaction Data* which sets out a spatial interaction approach to population movement on Merseyside; Hyman and Gleave (1977) *A Reasonable Theory of Migration*, a case study in the use of gravity and other methods of analysis applied to Manchester; and two widely referenced case studies by Stillwell (1975b) *Inter-County Net Migration in England and Wales*, and (1977) *Some Historical Tests of Spatial Interaction Models for Inter-Area Migration*.

At the behavioural level, case study insights will be obtained from Rees (1977) *The Non-Movers of the Upper Afan*; and Rees (1978) *Population and Industrial Decline in the South Wales Coalfield*. Most recent research concerns attempts to build more complex urban models linking, for example, input–output analysis, 'Lowry' or 'Garin–Lowry' models and cohort survival models. A good example is Gordon and Ledent (1980) *Modelling the Dynamics of a System of Metropolitan Areas: A Demo-economic Approach*.

Some references on the policy-making difficulties which arise from relative lack of knowledge about migration and related matters such as employment, are Madden and Batey (1980) *Achieving Consistency in Demographic-economic forecasting*, Bracken and Hume (1981) *Key Activity Forecasting in Structure Plans*.

Employment

There is ample literature available to introduce the student to the operationalization of the various economic methods of analysis discussed. The reader is referred to Edwards and Gordon (1970) *The Application of Input–Output Methods to Regional Forecasting: the British Experience*, and Hewings (1971) *Regional Input–Output Methods in the UK: Some Problems and Prospects for the use of Non-Survey techniques*. Case studies include De Kanter and Morrison (1978) *The Merseyside Input–Output Study and its Application in Structure Planning*; Morrison and Smith (1976) *Input–Output Methods in Urban and Regional Planning: A Practical Guide*. As an example of input–output analysis at the local scale Blake and McDowall

(1967) *A Local Input–Output Table* is recommended, which is a case study of St Andrews. Recent work in regional multipliers is discussed in Ledent (1978) *Regional Multiplier Analysis: A Demometric Approach*, while more general recommended reading to link the methods discussed in this text to theories of regional economic analysis is Richardson (1972) *Input–Output and Regional Economics*.

A widely quoted guide to shift-share analysis is Randall (1973) *Shift-Share Analysis as a Guide to the Employment Performance of West Central Scotland*; while readers who wish to study worked examples in greater detail are referred to Grampian Regional Council (1978a) *Shift and Share Methods of Employment Analysis and Projection*.

The application of the Garin–Lowry model and some derivatives are set out in Foot (1973) *A Comparison of some Land Use Allocation–Interaction Models* and Schinnar (1978) *Invariant Distributional Regularities of Non-Basic Spatial Activity Allocations: The Garin-Lowry model revisited*, whilst Moor (1973) *Economic Activity and Employment Forecasts: An Assessment of their Utility in Planning*, offers a review of economic activity analysis in the Strategic Planning Context. See also Palmer (1975) *Planning and Forecasting Employment and Economic Development in Structure Planning*. A good example of Local Authority analysis of its economy is that of Tyne and Wear County Council, Report of Survey–Note 2: *Economy*. A multi-regional example of economic analysis is provided by Paelinck (1973) *Multi-Regional Economic Policy based on Attraction Analysis*. On the subject of the interaction between migration and the labour market see Korte (1978) *Inter-Relationships Between Migration, the Labour Market and Housing Need: A Case Study of Kreis Unna*.

A good example of the application of regression techniques in urban economic analysis is Cameron *et al.* (1974) *The Determinants of Urban Manufacturing Location: A Simple Model*. An alternative methodological approach is illustrated by Firn and Latham (1977) *The Prediction of the Inter-Urban Distribution of Manufacturing Employment: A Markov Analysis of the Clydeside Conurbation*. Other relevant case studies that will repay reading include Dicken and Lloyd (1978) *Manufacturing Industry in the Inner City: A Case Study of Greater Manchester*; Cameron and Firn (1975) *Towards an Understanding of Intra-Metropolitan Location and Manufacturing: The Glasgow Case*; and Dicken (1976) *The Multiplant Business Enterprise and Geographical Space: Some Issues in the Study of External Control and Regional Development*.

On the emerging methodology of commodity–activity analysis there is a range of literature. The founding theory is comprehensively examined in Makower (1965) *Activity Analysis and the Theory of Economic Equilibrium*, and developments in Britain have been successively described by Broadbent (1970) *An Activity Analysis Framework for Urban Planning*; Broadbent (1975) *Activity Analysis of Spatial Allocation Models*; Barras and Broadbent (1975) *A Framework for Structure Plan Analysis*; Booth and Palmer (1976) *The Activity-Commodity Framework and Its Application in Strategic Sectoral and Spatial Analysis*; Barras (1978a) *A Resource Allocation Framework for Strategic Planning*.

The subject of economic activity rates for estimating the potential number of economically active persons in a population is reviewed by Harris and Taylor (1978) *The Service Sector: Its changing role as a Source of Employment*. Official data in respect of Great Britain are obtainable from the *Department of Employment Gazette*. Forecasts in activity rates are also officially published – see for example *Department of Employment Gazette* (April, 1974). A review of employment forecasting and associated problems in Structure Planning is Ashby (1976) *Employment Forecasting: Techniques and Problems in Structure Planning.*

Housing

Two papers to which the reader is confidently referred as critical discussions of the role of modelling in housing analysis are Boddy (1974) *Models of Housing Market Processes and Residential Location: A Critical Review Towards a Methodological Standpoint*, and Bourne (1976) *Housing Supply and Housing Market Behaviour in Residential Development.* A paper discussing household location preferences and migration is Adams and Gilder (1976) *Household Location and Intra-Urban Migration.* Case studies of the effects of tenure on household movement is contained in Murie (1974) *Eligibility Constraints on the Movement of Households Between Tenures*, and the question of modelling the movement of households through an analysis of their 'chain' effects is examined in Watson (1974) *Housing Chains and Filtering: Some Wider Effects of the New Building Programme.*

At the broader level of spatial residential modelling Baxter and Williams (1973) *Theoretical and Practical Issues Involved in the Disaggregation of Residential Models* is recommended, while the relationship of residential location and the operation of the housing market is treated in Senior (1974) *Disaggregated Residential Location Models, Housing Market Models and Duality.* A good case study in the allocation of new residential growth is that of Bather (1973) *A Linear Land-Use Allocation Model of New Residential Growth.* The concepts of combining models and a good bibliography will be found in Los (1979) *Combined Residential Location and Transportation Models.*

A guide and case study to household analysis and projection is Hollis *et al.* (1976) *Population and Household Projections for London: 1976.* The policy implications are discussed in Grey (1978) *The Policy Implications of Housing Forecasts.* On the subject of surveying housing needs see Hedges (1974) *Surveying Housing Needs: An Account of the 1972 Westminster Housing Survey.* Sources of information are well documented in Connolly (1979) *Housing: Sources of Information on Housing.* Other work which discusses policy implications is Grant *et al.* (1976) *Local Housing Needs and Strategies*, Blincoe (1979) *Analytical Models for Planning Housing Provision: A Critical Assessment of Current Practice*, while housing and migration inter-relationships are discussed in Johnson *et al.* (1974) *Housing and Migration of Labour in England and Wales.*

Further references on this topic are Plessis-Fraissard (1976) *Households: A Review of Definitions, Trends and Forecasting*; Hetherington (1973) *A Consideration of a Household-Based Projection Model for Greater London*, and more theoretic, the paper by Pickvance (1974) *Life Cycle, Housing Tenure and Residential Mobility.* Other work in the field of modelling the operation of the urban housing market which will be helpful to the student includes Doling (1973) *A Two-Stage Model of Tenure Choice in the Housing Market*; Jones *et al.* (1978) *A Two-Stage Model of Tenure Mobility*; Watson (1976) *Vacancy Chains, Filtering and the Public Sector*; and Ball and Kirwan (1977) *Accessibility and Supply Constraints in Urban Housing Markets.*

Retailing

A good specialist introduction to the relationship of urban planning and retailing is Guy (1980) *Retail Location and Retail Planning in Britain.* A wide-ranging paper which reviews the theory of modelling in shopping studies plus case studies is Brady *et al.* (1975) *Issues of Retail Location in Structure Planning and Associated Modelling Methodologies*. Case studies are Patricios (1975) *Shopping Models: Consumer Environmental Perception in Spatial Choice Behaviour for Convenience Good Shopping*; Roe (1974) *An Appraisal of Shopping Models* which includes case studies of 13 geographical locations; Parry Lewis and Bridges (1975) *Some New Approaches to Shopping Models with Particular Reference to Cambridge* – this example contains a model with a split function for local/non-local goods; and, at the macro level, Barnes (1974) *Hypermarket Prediction in Western Europe*.

A more advanced text edited by Jansen *et al.* (1979) *New Developments in Modelling Travel Demand and Urban Systems: Some Results of recent Dutch Research* contains several well-conducted case studies. The contributions by Richards, (1979) *A Disaggregate Shopping Model: Some Retrospective Thoughts*, and Verster *et al. The Effects of the Location of a Peripheral Self-Service Store* will repay careful study.

Recent work and a case study in aggregate spatial modelling of shopping behaviour is Batty (1978b) *Reilly's Challenge: New Laws of Retail Gravitation Which Define Systems of Central Places*. Other recent references to work in the field of facility location are Coelho and Wilson (1976) *The Optimum Location and Size of Shopping Centres*; Leonardi (1978) *Optimum Facility Location by Accessibility Maximising*; Leonardi (1979) *A Mathematical Programme Framework for the Optimal Location of Spatially Interacting Activities: Theory and Algorithms*, and Hay and Johnston (1979) *Search and the Choice of Shopping Centre: Two Models of Variability in Destination Selection*. A relevant case study which provides methodological insights is Black and Conroy (1977) *Accessibility Measures and the Social Evaluation of Urban Structure*.

Transportation

Finally, it has been a deliberate decision to exclude from this discussion a consideration of the whole area of transportation analysis and modelling. There are, of course, many parallel developments between the transportation and urban planning fields in the use of methodologies, particularly in respect of travel patterns, demand estimation and forecasting. For those who wish to extend their reading into this field the introductory texts by Hutchinson (1974) *Principles of Urban Transport Systems Planning*, Nash (1976) *Public Versus Private Transport* and Starkie (1973) *Transportation Planning and Public Policy*, are recommended and will efficiently guide the student to further reading.

On the behavioural side of transportation study, Bruzelius (1979) *The Value of Travel Time, Theory and Measurement* and Hensher and Stopher (1979) *Behavioural Travel Modelling* are recommended, with O'Farrell and Markham (1975) *The Journey to Work: A Behavioural Analysis* as a case study. Both provide insights into methodological issues. Bovy and Jansen (1979) *Travel Times for Disaggregate Travel Demand Modelling: A Discussion and New Travel Time Model* includes case study material, and many useful examples of contemporary work in the field of analytical methods applied to the transportation field are contained in Jansen *et al.* (1979) *New Developments in Modelling Travel Demand and Urban Systems*. A specialized case study is Thomas (1977) *An Interpretation of the Journey-to-Work on Merseyside using Entropy-Maximising Methods*.

☐ PART THREE

METHODS FOR
URBAN POLICY ANALYSIS

□ INTRODUCTION

In the first part of the text, it was made clear how the practice of urban planning, in responding to apparent deficiencies during the 1960s, made a fundamental distinction between strategic and local planning instruments. At the strategic level, the appropriate instrument was the Structure Plan, and at the local level a variety of types of Local Plans and Programmes were suggested.[1] Essentially, local plans are designed to guide development and, hence, should be the main instruments whereby the strategy is implemented. Effective implementation then requires that a clear and functional relationship is established between the different levels of planning instruments.[2]

An essential feature of the restructuring of the land-use planning system in 1968 was that the Structure Plan assumed an essential 'policy form', in contrast to the land use 'plan form' of the earlier Development Plans[3] and this has had important implications in the implementation of plans.[4] The earlier (1947/1962 style) Development Plans were largely assumed to be self-fulfilling, because of their essential physical (land-use) form and effective development control could substantially bring about their objectives.[5] In contrast, the broader policies of Structure Plans require a more explicit programme of implementation, partly through the preparation of local plans and *their* implementation (including the development control process), but also through a wide range of promotional, advocacy activities and the allocation of public spending resources.

It has become increasingly important for policy makers to know of the effects that the various policies and programmes bring about, particularly so that decisions about the use of limited resources can be made wisely, and that policies can be kept 'under review' to remain relevant to changing circumstances. It is a very real current concern (Broadbent, 1979) that the development and use of planning methodology should help to 'close the gap' between the preparation of plans and the powers of implementation so that plans, policies and powers are more directly harnessed to the achievement of planning aims.

The changes in the land-use planning system have raised many complex issues which the traditional approach to plan making tended to obscure. But, further, the last ten years or so has seen a remarkable growth in the number of agencies, organizations and statutory and non-statutory bodies who are involved in the implementation of urban planning policy. Some of these, like the local authorities have a direct political accountability to their elected members. Others, including Development Boards, statutory under-takers (water, electricity and gas) and so on are not so directly accountable. Given the importance of 'implementation' to effective policy making, the co-ordination and co-operation of these various bodies has become a vital matter. An understanding of inter-organizational relationship has become important to the proper understanding of the nature of urban policy.

The three chapters that follow are structured in a similar arrangement to Part 2. There, the broad sequence explained the nature and principles of social research, then the operations and concepts that had particular relevance for urban planners, and finally, how resulting data and information could be used to derive a systematic knowledge about urban affairs. Now, in turning our attention to the nature of policy we deal first (Chapter 7) with underlying theory in the field of policy analysis and explain its principles; second, in Chapter 8, we set out a range of methods that are relevant to urban policy study and discuss their practical application; and third, in Chapter 9, we discuss the implications of a policy orientation to the urban planning process with particular reference to methods for evaluation, monitoring and forecasting. Broadly, the relevance of adopting a *policy analytical* approach to these areas will be argued. As before, this part of the text also includes guides to further reading and case studies. Finally, the text concludes with a brief discussion of some broader implications when the urban planning process is viewed in policy terms.

It should be made clear that the structuring of the text into 'urban research methods' and 'urban policy analysis' does not imply that the latter is not a valid research area. Indeed, the following chapters will show how policy research builds upon many of the more classical research concepts that have already been described. But, equally, moving into policy research requires additional concepts and adaption to methods. Also, given the more limited history of public policy analysis, it is not to be expected that there is a great deal of established theory to guide the analyst, though the *relevance* of policy analysis and its usefulness to society and its problems has received extensive treatment (Rivlin, 1973; Pollitt *et al.*, 1979).

One final point should be made in introduction. The phrase 'policy analysis' has become popular in urban planning literature (as elsewhere) in recent years. Whilst the need for planners to understand and analyse the nature of, and effect of their policies is widely acknowledged, the phrase has been used very freely. Indeed, it can embrace almost any kind of analysis which, however indirectly, has some bearing upon policy. This is an unhappy state of affairs and extends the concept beyond its guiding body of theory. For example, the justification for the use of urban planning models (such as we described in Chapter 6) is often linked to an apparent intention to 'analyse policy'. However, a glance at some of the literature in this field shows that the true policy content of such analysis is often minimal, and indeed obscure. Policy analysis should have an explicit and direct focus upon the making, implementation and evaluation of policies, and their effects. In short, the phrase 'policy analysis' needs to be rescued from the methodological 'catch-all' state into which it seems to be drifting. It is intended that the structuring of this text will serve as a reminder of this point. As to the 'proper' role and scope of policy analysis in our field, it is intended that the following chapters will make a position clear.

In practice, too, there is evidence of a great deal of muddled thinking on this point. For example, some planning authorities are beginning to develop ways in which the impacts of policies, programmes and plans may be assessed. Others, it would seem, see monitoring as the mere acquisition of traditional data (on population change, employment, housing, transportation and so on) but without much attempt to distinguish effects that are due to policy from those that are not. We will suggest that an ability to make this distinction is the most important methodological challenge that planners face and for which a clear understanding of the potentials of policy analytical methods are crucial.

Notes

1   The Planning Advisory Group (1965) envisaged a limited number of local plan types: *viz Action Area Plans*; *District Plans*; *Town Plans and Village Plans.*
2   Reference has already been made in Part 1 to the sequence of official reports and documents that guided the restructuring of the planning system from 1965 onwards.
3   This can be readily seen even from a cursory reading of any of the Structure Plans cited at the end of Part 1.
4   Current government advice suggests three specific functions for the Structure Plan. These are:
    (a) To state and justify the county planning authority's policies and general proposals for the development and other use of land in the area concerned.
    (b) To interpret national and regional policies in terms of physical and environmental planning for the area concerned.
    (c) To provide a framework for local plans, which then, in turn, provide more definitive guidance for development and development control (Department of the Environment, 1979c).
5   The apparent virtues of the 1947 style of plan making, linking a clear spatial plan to effective development of central decisions have long been debated in the light of the changes made by the 1968 legislation which distinguished Structure Plans and Local Plans. See, for example, the comments of Bor (1974), Regan (1978) and Boynton (1979).

□ 7
POLICY STUDY:
CONCEPTS AND PROBLEMS

On the nature of policy

We must first attempt to elucidate the most important theoretical
dimensions and concepts which underlie an approach to policy analysis
within the urban planning field. It will then be possible to suggest and
explain the development of policy classifications within the field that will be
an essential first step in any analysis. But, as with the definitions of the
terms 'planning' in Part 1 of the text, and 'research' in Part 2, no simple
definition of 'policy' is possible.

It will be intuitively clear that there is usually a distinction between what
is intended to happen by someone in a given situation and what actually
does happen. At the broadest level, the concept of policy must embrace
both the intention of achievement and the outcome of a particular
intention. Any attempt to 'analyse' a policy situation must begin by
recognizing these components. If the outcome of a policy intention is
different in some way from the intentions of the policy maker and
implementers, then they are not the only influences in the situation. Indeed,
it is probable that theirs will not be the major influence and this raises
immediately a question as to the amount of 'control' that a policy maker is
able to exercise over the situation that he faces.

This degree of control will clearly vary considerably in different
circumstances, even when the policy maker is operating in a well-defined
statutory context. Land-use planning exercises a great deal of its control for
example, through the regulation of new development. The incidence of new
development over time, and in different locations, then, is an important
variable in the amount of control that urban policy makers can exercise. To
exercise control in a situation where little new development is being carried
out requires different forms of intervention, for example, through control
over direct public sector investment and other inducements and influences.
We will later comment upon the multiplicity of agencies and organizations
that are concerned in the implementation of urban planning policy. It is
frequently the case that the degree of control that the planner can exercise is
not only modified by political considerations, but the extent to which public
authorities can command the support and resources of other organizations.
These may well have conflicting motives and priorities.

In discussing the nature of policy, it will be useful to distinguish at the
outset between the forces of inertia and reaction. Inertia concerns the extent

to which a system or a situation is resistant to the changes imposed on it through the attempt to implement policies. The concept of reaction recognizes that human subjects of a policy will respond to that policy in positive, and frequently unpredictable ways. Thus, the 'system' may avoid the intentions of the policy maker or react in ways which may not only reduce the intended effect, but give rise to a whole range of unanticipated outcomes. It is fundamental to public policy analysis to expect that policy will produce unintended effects that may extend into all kinds of areas beyond the intentions of policy makers and which may reveal themselves only over quite long periods of time.

It is useful to distinguish three broad levels at which analysis of policy can be made. First, we can consider the *intentions* of the planner or policy maker.[1] These intentions may or may not be expressed as explicit or public objectives, and much may remain covert particularly in a strongly political situation, where there may be a considerable degree of bargaining among the actors. Second, we can attempt to study the actual *behaviour* of the policy maker in deciding upon and effecting a decision. For example, it is possible to study what he does in influencing others, what he says as recorded in statements or minutes and what he writes as set down in policy documents, Written Statements and reports. Third, it is possible to focus upon what actually *happens* (or does not happen) as a result of a given policy being implemented over a period of time. Policy can be thus thought of essentially in terms of 'goals, means and consequences'. This is, however, not a universal view. Ranney (1968), for example, considers policy more narrowly, as a matter of 'declaration of intent', and this corresponds to the everyday use of the term. To 'have a policy' is thus the equivalent of 'to have an intention to do something'. There is considerable philosophical debate on this point, some writers considering that policy consists only of the intended course of action, whereas others embrace the actual behaviour involved in implementing the intentions.[2] It is, however, generally agreed that the definition of policy lies somewhere between the intentions of individuals on particular decisions on the one hand and general social movements on the other. In other words, the concept of public policy implies both a plurality of actors and an explicit intention. We suggest that readers will find the advice of Heclo (1972) sound, in suggesting that, for serious study, it should be recognized that while policy is in its nature basically a purposive activity, a statement of purpose does not itself constitute the sum of a policy, and does not therefore *by itself* provide an adequate basis for empirical analysis.

This suggests that effective policy analysis needs to be broad in scope and that it should concern itself, on the one hand, with the circumstances under which a particular policy emerges and as to what has informed, motivated and influenced the decision maker. On the other hand, analysis must also consider the logical outcomes and consequences of having attempted to implement a particular policy. This distinction we return to later, but can usefully note that it suggests a starting point for an analytical framework.

While it will be clear that what is intended will frequently differ from what happens, some less obvious differences can also be subject to analysis. For example, as between what a policy maker *intends* to happen (his ideal position) and what he, more realistically perhaps, *expects* to happen. Equally, there may well be differences to measure between what happens as a result of a policy, and as to how this is perceived by various actors or groups affected by the policy. These differences, which are sometimes referred to as 'tensions',[3] provide a useful starting point for the study of the implementation of policy (Smith, 1973). Each 'difference' can be thought of as a kind of error effect and summarized as figure 7.1.

Figure 7.1 Policy implementation 'tension' matrix

Policy *outcomes*	Ideal	Actual	Perceived	Expected
Ideal	—	1	2	3
Actual		—	4	5
Perceived			—	6
Expected				—

After Smith (1973: 206)

In summary, the differences concern (1) discrepancy between what is ideal and what is actually achieved, (2) discrepancy between what is ideal and what is perceived, (3) discrepancy between what is ideal and what is expected, (4) discrepancy between what is achieved and what is perceived, (5) discrepancy between what is achieved and expected, and (6) discrepancy between what is expected and what is perceived. It may be readily appreciated that any attempt to systematically analyse a typical policy situation in these terms will not only be complex, but will need to draw upon a wide range of research methodology.

We noted earlier, in Part 1, how the last fifteen years or so have been characterized by a much increased public awareness of the extent and influence of public policy making over the lives of individuals. The statutory requirement built into the 1971 Town and Country Planning Act[4] for there to be a degree of 'public participation' in the preparation of structure and local plans reflects this movement. In the light of this growing awareness, it is hardly surprising that interest in public policy analysis in many spheres has grown rapidly and stimulated the analysis of public policy as a systematic area of study. Moreover, the need for effective analysis to inform the 'learning process' is now widely seen as an essential part of the search for more effective and publicly acceptable plans and policies in many fields. One indicator of this growing interest has been a rapid development of specialized literature dealing with public policy studies, particularly, for example, in defence, welfare, education, transportation and housing (Wildavsky, 1969). Though as yet there has been relatively little systematic work in the more general field of urban planning, and this may well be due to the breadth and complexity of planning policy making, there is nevertheless some established, though by no means unified theory, upon which urban policy analysis can develop.

What, then, is policy analysis and what can it offer to the urban planner? At a very general level, policy analysis can be defined as any type of analysis that generates and presents information in such a way as to improve the basis upon which public policy makers can decide what they should or should not do in a given situation (Quade, 1975). As will be made clear in this and the following chapter, there is a wide range of methods that are useful and which can bring a degree of systematization to policy study. This does not, however, necessarily imply a quantitative approach. Indeed, of all kinds of analysis, policy study has to deal with situations that are 'soft-edged'; where the problems are often difficult to define; where objectives are poorly perceived and with inherent conflict of values and opinions; where any number of 'solutions' may offer partial remedies and where there is likely to be 'trading-off' or bargaining in the implementation of a policy so that the behaviour of the participants may be difficult to predict.

Given the complexity of the urban system, any effective analysis of urban policy making and its implementation needs to be broadly based and to cover a wide range of traditional, discrete, but interlocking policy areas, such as housing, transportation, public sector finance, and so on. It is vitally important that any approach to the analysis of policies in these fields, either of policy formulation or implementation, should not be inhibited by the constraints of these traditional sectors. In other words, the conceptualized framework within which policy analytic designs should be created, must be cross-disciplinary and hence will draw upon political, economic and social theory, as well as the more narrow theory base of land use and spatial distributions. These requirements will emerge as a recurrent theme in the following discussions.

Two further introductory points should be made (Heclo, 1972). The first, briefly noted already, is that policies, like any decisions, can consist of something *not* being done. This can happen for a variety of reasons. For example, delaying a decision is a common tactic among policy makers, sometimes for quite explicit reasons such as lack of commitment to a project, financial limitations or uncertainty about its true value both to the potential recipients in terms of benefits and to the policy makers in terms of prestige. Non-decision making can also take more subtle forms. For example, postponing a decision about a controversial matter can be useful in 'defusing' a highly charged political situation. Neglect of an issue which might 'solve itself' or otherwise go away is commonplace, and delaying a decision which might be detrimental to a politician's chances of re-election is yet another example. A more complex situation can arise when several projects are competing for limited resources. Here, decision makers will seek the right tactical combination of programmes for both resource and political reasons.[5] Much of the motivation and behaviour associated with these situations may well be covert, but once identified can be made the subject of a systematic analysis.

An important extension to this thinking is the whole concept of 'negative externalities'. It is often the case in urban planning, that a decision to do something (or not, as the case may be) will affect the *costs* of some other potential action. For example, a traffic scheme may re-route heavy traffic in front of people's homes, but policy makers may not wish to face subsequent demands for the re-housing of these people, double-glazing or some other ameliorative measure. Given the chain-like situations which arise in almost every aspect of environmental policy making, such situations are widespread. The policy maker's dilemma is to establish his 'cutting-point' – how far into this chain of causal events he is prepared to admit reponsibility, if at all, following his initial policy action. There are of course a wide range of legal and procedural measures specifically designed to limit this chain of responsibility.[6] But in such a situation, the attention of the policy analyst may not be wholly welcomed by the policy maker. Analysis, if it is to contribute effectively to the development of theory must essentially look beyond the artificial limitations of administrative or legal arrangement. They are, after all, only artifacts, and cases can and should be argued for different 'cutting levels' of responsibility both from 'efficiency' and 'social justice' points of view.

The second point is an observation that has been widely noted both in policy analysis generally and in the study of urban policy. It is that of the limited analysis that has been undertaken, most of it has focused upon *inputs*. Some of the reasons for this we will make clear, but it is a fact that interest in the whole nature of policy has centred essentially on policy *making*, and debate about the attendant political and administrative system. In contrast, to a considerable extent, analysis has neglected the outputs and achievements of the policy process. Even the 'systems' revolution in planning thinking, noted earlier, which ought to have enabled planners to focus their attention onto the relationship between the plan and policy-making process and what it actually achieved, in practice, failed to do so. It is relevant to note in passing that both the urban statutory process and indeed the education of planners have been heavily oriented to the generation of plans and policies which, once effected through the political decision-making process, tend to fall into the background of planners' consciousness, at least until some new 'crisis' situation may resurrect interest. Even when this happens there is a tendency to treat the situation as a *de novo* state of affairs with little systematic attempt to relate the situation explicitly to the effect of, or lack of previous policies.[7]

Though there are some difficult technical and political problems to be faced in achieving this, the greater obstacle would appear to lay in the psychology of planning. The 'learning experience' may be uncomfortable, and politically or professionally embarrassing. Previous policies may be shown to have been misguided, based upon false assumptions or poorly chosen evidence. In short, they may have contained all manner of inadequacies. They may also have been formulated with small regard for real world issues or problems, but for more narrow, political and professional advantage.

It has been widely observed (Dror, 1976; Wildavsky, 1979) that the more governments and local governments attempt to ameliorate problems, the larger the difficulties seem to become. As Dror comments,

governments share both feelings of inadequacy and a tendency towards political crises. These result from tensions between contradicting tendencies. Governments are expected to deliver more and more under difficult conditions, while the capacities of government improve only very slowly, if at all. (p. 33)

Sub-themes within this statement are clearly exemplified by the urban situation. Governments, at both central and local levels, are faced with increased rates of technical, economic and social change, which constitute an essentially turbulent policy environment. Given the desire for clear, long-term policies to guide the development of the physical infrastructure, and the continuous pressure for adaption to accommodate this turbulent environment, it is clear that plans and programmes for the physical environment face a contradiction. They need to be both *rigid* enough to ensure consistency of development, and yet *flexible* enough to be able to adapt to and accommodate these changing circumstances. It can be suggested that the failure of the statutory land-use planning system to cope with these contradictory demands has a great deal to do with the lack of understanding by planners generally of the nature of, and the implementation of policy. This particularly concerns what should be realistically *expected* in any public policy field as opposed to an idealized position, and how events will be perceived differently by different people. There is also the important variable concerning the extent to which implementational powers are, in fact, used. No amount of refinement at the plan and policy making stage can make up for weak and ineffective implementation and this we discuss shortly.

At a different level, one important reason why analysis of policy, both of inputs and outcomes, is so vital relates to the very pace of both social and technical change and the difficulties that this seems to create for policy makers. In many fields, there is increasing unease that policies seem always to be overtaken by events. 'Circumstances change before policies have had time to work' is a frequently heard comment by decision makers. Certainly, the idea that circumstances will 'wait' for policies is a delusion, but it can be shown, particularly through policy analysis, that much change, (and notably at the local level) is in fact a *reaction* to previous policy intervention. So, as Wildavsky (1979) makes clear, the more government and local government intervene through public policies, the more each programme 'bumps into others'. The inevitable consequence is that 'more and more policy is about coping with the consequences of past policies and less and less about [autonomous] events in society.... The more we do [as planners]...the more there is to do.' There are two implications that we should note. The first is that such a situation is powerful in sustaining a body of professional attitudes and opinions, though a further discussion of the merits and dismerits of this are beyond this text.[8] The second implication, and for us an important one, is that in order to understand this situation it is vital to study this 'policy–policy' relationship. Faced with the situation in which some new policy is believed to be needed, we suggest that the traditional tendency of planners to begin by re-examining the real world context through empirical surveys, data and information, models, pre-dictions and forecasts – the validity of which in an applied field depends upon making assumptions about how policy does (or does not) work – is somewhat misplaced. More usefully, it can be argued, planners could begin by trying to understand why new policy is needed and what it is about an old policy that is not effective. This requires a focus on the use of both statutory and persuasive powers, resources, the extent of influence, degree of political commitment, and so on. It is *then* appropriate to relate this knowledge to the environment that the policy seeks to change, to assess the degree of intervention needed, and the most appropriate form for that intervention. Predictions, forecasts and targets can follow in the light of knowledge about the idealized and expected outcomes of the policy. We return to this theme in a later discussion of the role of monitoring and forecasting within the planning process (Chapter 9).

The increasing pace of change, particularly that of technology and the economy, poses a further direct challenge to the traditional *modus operandi* of the planner. As Quade (1975) has observed, in the past when events moved more slowly, the corrective effects of experience and professional competence played a larger role than today. Through trial and error, and political bargaining, it was possible for public officials to take account of the slower evolution of technical and economic forces. In short, the future was inherently more predictable. Increasing pace of change, coupled with the growing pressure we noted earlier on the part of the public for a 'say' in urban affairs, means that urban problems are seen to be that much more complex and that so called 'expert opinion', which has traditionally been the cornerstone of urban plans and policies, will increasingly be shown *to be opinion*, however informed. Coupled with the fundamental difficulty of defining goals and objectives for action, as we have already discussed, it becomes increasingly difficult to make a 'right decision'. Thus, we cannot solve problems because we (increasingly) find ourselves unable to define what will constitute the solution.

It can be argued that a more realistic mode of operation is to accept the notion that plan and policies do not lead to permanent solutions, but rather that we should accept the idea of permanent problems, that may be superseded, but cannot be solved (Wildavsky, 1979). The role of plan and policies is then more modest, namely to attempt to ameliorate one problem, and thereby transform a situation, without, as far as possible, creating a more difficult problem. As we discuss later, this view has some important implications for the role of evaluation methodology in planning, but first, and before discussing the vital role of policy analysis to this view, we ought to consider a framework for examining the context within which urban policy must operate.

Political, judicial and professional contexts

It is a theme of this chapter that policy cannot be effectively analysed, much less explained, outside an understanding of the context into which it is born and in which it is expected to operate. How can this context best be described? A starting point is to observe that public sector planning systems comprise political, judicial and professional components (Regan, 1978).[9] In practice, they exhibit some blend of these components, though generally, one of the components tends to dominate. It will be helpful to examine briefly the characteristics of these components, drawing upon Regan's analysis. Professional activity within the planning system is characterized by two features. One is a concern for technicality, and the other for rationality. As we have already discussed, the former implies that the issues are to a large extent capable of assessment only by people who have particular skills and expertise which is obtained through specialized training. The latter implies the applicability of an essentially rational approach, through the identification of goals and objectives, a high level of information, an objective analysis of courses of action and the selection of an appropriate strategy. In order to cope with changing circumstances, unpredicted events and so on, some kind of 'feedback' through on-going monitoring is required. Posed in these terms urban planning is similar in its operations to any other recognizable professional activity, such as engineering. As we have begun to suggest there are serious weaknesses in applying this model to a public policy field, though there is no doubt that the professionalization of town planning over the past fifty years or so has sought to move planners firmly into this 'technical' position. As Regan suggests, land-use systems can certainly be given a professional emphasis and, in such systems, there is a tendency for the opinions of expert planners to be decisive and for the preferred strategy to be as comprehensive as possible. In general, 'the professional' role will push the system towards skill and technique and the attachment of great importance by planners to the justification of advice by various kinds of technical analysis.

A second perspective is to view the urban planning system as a judicial system. Such a view also has two essential features. One, is the existence of a body of rules or relatively objective standards, and the second is an agreed process for the determination of disputes by reference to those rules or standards. The basic characteristic then is the acknowledgement of conflict between individuals, or between an individual and 'the public interest'. The main requirement of the planning system is to be able to arbitrate, and there are advantages and disadvantages in such a model. First, a judicial system is capable of displaying openness, consistency, equality and predictability, and from a 'user' perspective these would appear to be desirable features, providing that the system also minimally imposes upon the action of the individual 'user'. However, the judicial approach with its emphasis upon rules and standards can produce rigidity. Given, as already noted, that land-use planning is, in practice, attempting to regulate a system of constant change, excessive adherence to formal rules means inflexibility and increasing tensions within and around the system. Equally, it is clear from experience that a strongly adjudicating procedure can become cumbersome, and subject to high costs and long delays. Much of the pressure to change the 1947 Development Plan system arose from such concerns (Bor, 1974).

A third perspective on the planning system is to view it explicitly as a political system, though this view is by no means as clear as the two already noted. According to Regan, at its broadest, a political system concerns the institutions and processes under which a state, or locality, is governed. There are clearly many contrasts world-wide in political systems and their relationship to urban planning. In Britain, in a broadly liberal democracy, the mainspring for change is that of public opinion coupled with the 'ideological' positions of alternative governments. Looking at the planning system from these views reveals clearly the strong contradictions between political and professional components. For example advocating a more pragmatic, adaptive position, nearer to the shifting and compromising stance of day-to-day politics brings problems of consistency, and difficulties in maintaining a long-term view. Analysis of decision making then becomes more problematical.

Figure 7.2 Judicial, political and professional components in a planning system

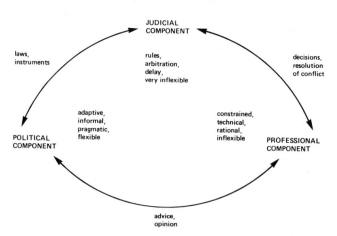

The model, which is summarized as figure 7.2 is useful as an analytical framework in two respects.[10] First, in a historical mode, it is informative in tracing the recent development of Statutory Town and Country planning and to suggest reasons why inherent tensions within the planning process

arise over time. According to our earlier view these tensions and the adjustments made by the 'system' to cope with them, will have a considerable impact upon the way in which policy is generated and will need to be explained in an analysis.

From the 1909 Act[11] to 1948, land-use planning was largely 'judicial' in its nature. This reflected the public health ancestry of planning legislation in terms of rigid rules about the use of urban land (for example, as in the 1932 Act).[12] This undoubtedly produced an inflexible system, with a poor ability to adapt to changing circumstance. Moreover, minimal 'political' influence and modest 'professional' inputs meant little pressure for adaption. The post-Second World War reforms brought about a dramatic shift in emphasis.[13] The effect of establishing Local Planning Authorities with wide powers was to give a massive injection of comprehensive professionalism exercised through the production of Development Plans and through the control of development in accordance with those plans. 'Expert advice' became the corner stone. The 'judicial' role in this system, though continued, became relatively less important and focused upon arbitration over the conflicts between the individual and the public interest, as for example through Development Plan public inquiries, and planning appeals. The period from 1945 to the mid-1960s was also characterized by a small and covert political element, though there were exceptional arguments in the 1950s, particularly concerning compensation and betterment. In general, there was minimal participation, little attempt to involve the polity in decision making, and a total reliance upon the representativeness of elected members. The result was minimal politicization of planning issues.

Reasons for the reforms of the late 1960s, were discussed in Chapter 1, and post-1968, these brought about a marked shift in the position of statutory land-use planning within its political, judicial and professional contexts. Until those changes, Town and Country planning had been dominated by either a judicial framework or a professional framework with the turning point in 1947. Regan's (1978) analysis suggests that domination of a system by a single component generally produces a stable, though inflexible situation, but one that can contain its inherent tensions. Post-1968 more dramatic changes occurred, notably that with increased attention focused on the political dimension, the inherent tensions within the system became more sharply revealed, whatever the intrinsic merit of a move towards a greater political contribution. Not only did this embrace a greater degree of public 'participation', but more important for this discussion, it involved an explicit move towards *policy* as an instrument rather than a total reliance upon a development plan capable of strict judicial interpretation.

One conclusion of Regan's argument is that any public policy field which tries to reconcile a significant role for the three traditions (professional, political and judicial) in a stable relationship will face immense difficulty. In short, these traditions have antithetical tendencies, and hence pull in different directions, and the planning system, in trying to embrace these diverse and mutually contradictory elements is faced with irreconcilable tensions. This has important implications for the way that the planning system is operated,[14] but also means that these tensions will be focused directly on to the policy content.

The judicial system, including administrative procedures, rules and standards is inherently inflexible, and indeed, this is one of its operational virtues. Clearly, however, any administrative and judicial system must be capable of being changed to meet new circumstances through legislation and other statutory instruments. The professional system is relatively inflexible, not because that is seen necessarily as a virtue, but because of inertia of the traditions, skills and attitudes of those who operate it. However, recent experience has shown that the responsiveness of professionals to changing circumstances is faster than that of administrators, whose main concern is the consistency of the statutory system. Over time, then, frustration by professionals over the rigidity of the administrative system is inevitable. But the conflicts between the judicial and professional traditions on the one hand and the political tradition on the other is potentially more dramatic. The latter's virtue is of extreme flexibility, even pragmatism, which conflicts badly with the professional's belief in his ability to take a 'long-term view' and the judicial quest for consistency and equity. It is clear that lawyers currently view the policies and expressions of the Structure Plan as being 'flexible' to the point of deliberate vagueness in attempting to ensure 'something in it for everybody' (Boynton, 1979), a view shared by many administrators and not a few professional planners.

Several polarizations can be seen in this analysis which relate directly to the concept of policy flexibility. First, there is the long-term/short-term issue posed by professional and political conflict. Second, but on the same axis, the 'positivism' and search for proof and reasoned justification of the expert, against the 'normativism' and susceptibility to public opinion of the politician. On the professional/judicial axis there will be tension as the inflexibility of legal and administrative procedures confronts professionals being pushed by political pressures to modify their policies in an adaptive way. Finally, there will be tensions between political and judicial contexts in that new legislation invariably imposes changing demands upon judicial judgements, and politicians are themselves frequently frustrated by administrative difficulties in implementing radical reforms through their policies. The policy environment then will be one of constant tension and adjustment. In land-use planning terms, however, one feature dominates these conflicts. It is that land-use planning, uniquely among public policy fields (such as education and social services) is highly statutory, and it is this feature upon which the limited discussion on the subject of policy flexibility has focused (Eddison, 1971; Bor, 1974; Smart, 1977). Yet the statutory framework mainly specifies the form and content of the policy instrument, that is the Structure Plan, and requires the approval by central government of local policies. The statutory framework does not prescribe in detail any way in which the policies shall be implemented and it is already clear that there can be considerable variation, both in policy intention as revealed by approved documents, and in the outcomes of adaptive implementation

Implementation

The mere availability of statutory planning powers does not by itself ensure the effective implementation of any policy. Indeed, it takes far more than the formulation of an apparent answer to any public problem on paper to achieve a useful outcome. As Quade (1975) shows, there are additional tasks, including communicating the policy to those involved and convincing them that it is a valid approach; setting down the legal and statutory boundaries, and securing and allocating the necessary resources. Moreover, as the financing, implementation and management of urban plans and programmes rest with a large number of central and local government agencies and a wide range of other statutory and *ad hoc* bodies there is a *major* communication problem. Moreover, urban plans and policies need to relate to a wide range of other policy documents and co-ordination with their intentions also poses a major challenge. Figures 7.3 and 7.4 draw upon recent research and reveal the organizational richness[15] of both the implementing and policy-making environment.

It is widely acknowledged that implementation is about organizations and their motivation (Williams, 1971).[16] At the most basic level, implementation means motivating or persuading people to behave in accordance with a policy, but this is neither readily achieved, nor predictable. A 'rational' response on the part of an individual who is subject to a policy, for example, cannot be assumed. People may well choose not to forgo immediate personal gain or pleasure, even though a longer-term social or even personal benefit may clearly accrue to them. Moreover, any attempt to implement a policy which involves a more efficient allocation of resources will invariably imply a re-allocation, even if only in terms of the opportunity costs of the options forgone (Quade, 1975). The result is that even when public policy making is successful in its implementation, it is almost certain to suffer public criticism.

In the urban field, the complexities of the numerous agencies involved, the variations in their resource bases and their control powers, and the complexity of the formal and informal negotiations that surround both the preparation and implementation of policies, makes it a difficult task to assess the link between a particular policy and a particular outcome. In short, how much of an observed effect is due to having a policy at all? In some cases, particularly where the level of control is high (as for example the statutory planning control over advertisements) the link may be measurable, even self-evident. Otherwise, it may be obscure, though we will suggest means whereby such policy analysis *can* be conducted.

At a simple level, implementation can be defined as 'the process of

Figure 7.3 Influential implementation agencies for Structure Plan policies

---

Employment:

EEC:—European Regional Fund, European Social Fund, European Coal and Steel Community. Department of Employment. Manpower Services Commission. Welsh Office Land Department. National Economic Development Office. New Town Development Corporations. Development Commission; Welsh Development Agency: Scottish Development Agency. Confederation of Small Industry in Rural Areas; Highlands and Islands Development Board. Development Board for Rural Wales. Land Authority for Wales. Development Corporation of Wales. English Industrial Estates Corporation. Small Firms Information Services. British Steel Corporation: Land Ltd. Nationalised Industries. Private concerns.

Housing:

Housing Associations. Co-operative Housing Agency. National Building Agency. Housebuilders Association (NFBTE). Private Developers. Landlords and Tenants Associations.

Transportation:

British Transport and Docks (Port Authorities). British Airport Authority. British Waterways Board. Municipal Bus Operators. Inland Waterways Amenity Advisory Council. British Rail Board. Civil Aviation Authority. Confederation of Independent Bus Operators; National Bus Company. National Freight Corporation, Freight Transport Association, Road Haulage Association. Inland Waterways Association. Aerodrome Owners Association.

Conservation/countryside and leisure/recreation:

National Park Planning Boards. British Tourist Authority; Regional Tourist Boards. Arts Council. Forestry Commission. Sports Council; National Playing Fields Association. Nature Conservancy Council. Countryside Commission. Civic Trust. National Trust. National Farmers Union; Farmers Union of Wales. County Landowners Association. Timber Growers Association. Ramblers Association; Camping and Caravan Clubs of GB and Ireland. Council for Protection of Rural England/Wales; Commons Preservation Society; Friends of the Earth Ltd.

Others:

Ministry of Agriculture, Forestry and Fisheries. Department of Energy. Welsh Office Transport and Highways Division. Water Authorities. Area Health Authorities. Postal and Telecommunications Boards. Historical Buildings Council; Ancient Monuments Society; Council for British Architecture.

From Bracken (1980a: 11)

interaction between the setting of goals and actions geared to achieving them' (Pressman and Wildavsky, 1973). Clearly, implementation is about some kind of link between what is intended and the outcome but, as Jenkins (1978) argues, such definitions are almost certainly over-simplistic, for they pay little attention to the *dynamics* of the implementation process, or, in other words, to the interaction between ends and means. Thus:

Figure 7.4 Non-statutory plans and programmes

Title	Administrative area	Progress	Time scale (years)	Review date	Type of approval
(a)					
Area management	Sub-district	Experimental	3	—	District
Community land programme	District/county		5/10	Annual	DOE
Corporate planning	County	In operation	3/5	Annual	District/county
Highway programmes	National	In operation	10/15	Annual	DOT
Housing investment programmes	District	From 1978-9	3/5	Annual	DOE
Inner city programmes	District	From 1978-9	3/5		
National parks plans	National parks/districts	In operation	5/10	5	Park Planning Board
Recreation strategies	Regional sport and recreation councils	From 1977-8	10/5	3/5	Regional, etc. councils
Regional strategies	Regional	Most regions in England and Wales	10/15	3/5	DOE
Rural action	Small areas/counties	In operation	5/10	—	Development Commission
Transport policies and programmes	County	From 1975	3/5	Annual	DOT
Water plans	Regional water authorities	From 1976	5	Annual	DOE
Waste disposal plans	County	Not yet in operation	5/10	—	DOE
(b)					
Public Expenditure Survey–Treasury	National	From 1961	3/5	Annual	Cabinet
EEC regional development plans	Regions (DOI)	Yet to commence	3/5	Annual	EEC Commission
Employment service plans	Employment service areas (18)	From 1976	3/5	Annual	Manpower Services Commission
Health Service plans	District, areas, region	From 1977	3 & 10/15	Annual	Next higher tier
Regional industrial strategy	Regions (DOI)	Experiment for 1 year	3/5	—	DOI
Regional tourist plans	Regional tourist board	In operation	10/15	Annual	Regional Tourist Board
Scottish financial plans	Districts, regions	From 1977	5	Annual	Scottish Office
Joint care plans	Counties and area health authorities	From 1978	—	Annual	Counties & Area Health Authority
Personal social service plans	Counties	From 1978-9	3/5	Annual	DHSS
Training service plans	Training services areas (7)	From 1976	3/5	Annual	Manpower Services Commission
Scottish regional reports	Scottish regions	From 1978	—	—	Scottish Office

(a) Under supervision of Department of Environment (DOE) and Department of Transport (DOT)

(b) Under other central government departments

   DOI: Department of Industry

After Broadbent (1979: 4–5)

To define implementation rigorously may be difficult, yet taken in its general sense of action programmes and activities to achieve objectives, the problems and issues surrounding implementation emerge from every corner of political life (p. 205).

The more that is learned of the difference between what is specified as being intended through planning policy making (for example as set down in written statements and other policy documents), and what is achieved, the more clearly demonstrated is the gulf which frequently exists between policy making on the one hand and effective implementation on the other.

This raises a large number of questions that policy analysts have begun to attempt to answer. For example, why is it that policies so often fail to achieve what they say they want to achieve? Why are policies so apparently susceptible to changing circumstances? Why is implementation frequently discussed, but, it would seem, infrequently analysed? Is this latter point due to a weakness of methodology or of concept? Does the difficulty lie in the specification of the *ends* of a given programme of action, or does the difficulty lie in making effective use of the *means*? Would we get better results from the planning system by trying to make superior plans or by trying to achieve superior implementation of existing plans and policies? These are fundamental questions about any system of planning. In discussing some of these questions, Jenkins (1978) makes the significant observation that while all policy deals in some way with conflicting interests, it appears that getting agreement on the *ends* of a programme is in fact the easier part and that more often than not, it is in the allocation of *means* that the real conflicts may arise which can jeopardize the programme of action. For example, conflicting participants, whether policy makers or subjects, may well oppose the means advocated by others. Moreover, they may see little to be gained by making any move towards direct action themselves. The overall result can be that many policies never mobilize sufficient support at any one time to make effective progress towards their aims.

The problem is compounded by the multiplicity of actors and organizations. Each works within its own system of constraints, a feature clearly revealed by Pressman and Wildavsky's (1973) classic analysis of the Economic Development Administration's (USA) employment project in Oakland. This exemplified the problem that numerous actors and agencies each working to its own time scale, and with its own sense of priorities, will tend to create all kinds of difficulties in the way of the actions of others, not necessarily because of deliberately sought conflict, but because preference over the use of means will be inconsistent. A consequence is that the situation can rapidly create an 'organizational problem' beyond the experience and/or ability of the principal actors. The result is that a long sequence of negotiations and approvals may be needed among the different groups and agencies, and even a small step forward in implementation can become fraught with organizational problems, and these become increasingly concerned with means and not ends. It is then, the maintenance of a consistent view of implementation that poses the real design problem for a programme of action. This also poses some major problems for research into policy making, because implementation tends to become a 'one off' activity, in which plan and programmes are treated as isolated events. This considerably inhibits the development of systematic knowledge and theory about the implementation process.

The value of Pressman's and Waldavsky's analysis to us is that it shows that the process of public policy implementation is essentially a series of continual and inter-related decisions involving a multiplicity of actors, none of whom have any marked degree of control over the whole situation. Implementation then can never become the 'discrete' task that designing, or generating a plan or programme documents can be, and the essential internalization of learning through experience is that much more difficult to achieve. Not surprisingly, there is a notable lack of literature about the policy implementation process in most applied fields.

Some common features of these comments and the present state of Structure Planning are clear. First, as we have discussed, urban plan and policy making is a complex process, not simply because of an elaborate statutory requirement for consultations and public debate, but because planners see their policies as reaching into so many facets of urban life. Second, there is a wide range of opinion and value judgement about almost every aspect of a strategic policy. Third, for traditional reasons, many urban plan makers have assumed that plans were largely self-implementing through development control mechanisms. This particular weakness has taken a long time to reveal itself, and it is a quite recent phenomenon that plan makers are beginning to realize that the essential learning process about urban affairs (which ought to inform the preparation of policies) can only really be effective against a background of experience in the implementational arena of urban policy.

Before moving on to discuss the methods by which policy analysis can be conducted through classification and systematic research, a word of caution must be introduced. It is not to be expected that policy analysis will be able to serve the development of theory in the field of public policy making and implementation in the same way that other types of analysis have served the development of theory (Greenburg *et al.*, 1977). Policy analysis is an activity very much in its intellectual infancy, and there is by no means agreement that a general theory of policy implementation can be evolved (Jenkins, 1978). Some writers, Lowi (1970, 1972) for example, argue optimistically that policy content and outcomes (even though different to intentions) *are* capable of being treated systematically to the extent that general explicative statements can be made. Others, including Greenburg *et al.* (1977) are less certain, particularly those who view implementation as an inherently localized and responsive phenomenon, for which uniqueness is dominant and therefore about which few general statements or rules can be formulated. This debate is far from resolved. There is, however, more general agreement about what needs to be studied in order to find out if systematic theory can develop. The question to be answered is essentially whether policy (as a phenomenon) is fundamentally different in its nature to the other phenomena that we study. This, it will be recognized, is an exactly analogous argument to that posed earlier in the general discussion of the nature of social science.

As Jenkins (1978) comments, it would seem from case studies in public policy implementation, that local perspectives of policy impact often differ sharply from those of the higher level policy making agency. Even more crucial is the further observation that these local perspectives are also influential in the way that local organizations are receptive or not to a particular policy. This suggests that it is necessary to study both the policy development and implementation environments in order to understand why policies come about and the effects that they may have (Heclo, 1974). Study of implementation processes ought to reveal variations in the way that a given policy will be carried out, depending upon the *local* circumstances, and systematic knowledge gathered here ought to lead to useful theory.

Policy analytic frameworks

There have been numerous attempts to classify the relevant categories of variables that comprise any policy implementation process. A useful context for the later discussion of relevant methodology can be obtained by considering the essential features of this work. First, a clear model is that of Smith (1973), in which there are four broad components: (i) the idealized policy; (ii) the implementing organization; (iii) the target group; and (iv) the policy environment. Each of these components should be briefly examined. First, the idealized policy. For analytical purposes it is possible to identify four clear criteria. First, there is the *formal policy*. This can be defined as the formal decision statement, law or programme that the agency, authority, or government is attempting to implement. Essentially, this refers to the form that the policy takes, in contrast to the *type of policy*. This, (the second criterion), can be usefully treated under three headings:

(a)   Policies may be complex or simple in their nature, or it may be more appropriate to distinguish between broader non-incremental policies and small-scale incremental ones.

(b)   Policies can be categorized as 'organizational' or 'non-organizational'. The former requires the establishment of an organization or at least some modification to an existing organization. The latter type depend upon action being taken outside the formal organizational context.

(c)   Policies can be classified as distributive, re-distributive regulatory, self-regulatory or emotive-symbolic.

The third criterion for the analysis of idealized policy relates to the nature of the *policy programme* by which the policy will be implemented. Here again, Smith's classification identifies three headings:

(a)   The intensity of support, which refers to the degree to which a particular agency and its actors is committed to the implementation of the policy.

(b) The source of the policy, which might vary from an essentially technical or professional origin to an explicit political gesture.

(c) The scope of the programme for implementation, referring to the possibility that a policy might be general in its effects or, in contrast, intended to focus upon a small geographic or topic area or group of subjects.

Fourth, there is the important matter of the *image of the policy*. An essential part of analysis must be to attempt to assess the impact that the policy invokes on the society. Clearly, the perceptions of those affected by the policy will be influential in formulating their attitudes, and there will develop some kind of reactive effect between implementers and recipients.

The second broad component for analysis is that of the implementing agency or organization responsible for putting the policy into effect. Here, Smith's typology suggests three important criteria to guide analysis. First, there is the point that an understanding of the organization structure (for example its stability) and the qualifications and commitment of its personnel who must implement the policy, is essential. An administrative organization in a state of internal change, and/or the presence of uncommitted personnel clearly reduces the capacity for effective implementation. Second, it is important to consider the leadership of the administration and the effectiveness of influential officers and elected members in motivating successful implementation and command of resources. The third criterion under this heading refers to the capacity of the organization to meet the objectives of programme implementation, for example, in committing resources, evaluating progress, and making sensitive adjustments to maintain a continuity of operations.

The third broad component is the *target (or subject) group* which is defined as those who will be affected by the policy and who are thus, in effect, required to adopt a new behaviour pattern. There are both collective and individual considerations here, among which the most important can be identified as:

(a) The degree of organization (or institutionalization) of the subject group which will considerably affect the extent to which they may collectively oppose, modify or even evade the policy makers' intentions.

(b) The extent of leadership among the target group which will be an important variable in aligning individuals against (or conceivably in favour of) a policy.

(c) The prior policy experience of the subject group.

There is considerable evidence from the activities of many pressure and lobby groups, that the cumulative experience has important effects upon the ways in which they respond to new policies, and this is notable in the fields of transportation and housing. Analysis of the responses which subjects make when confronted by new policy can reveal much about their possible compliance, indifference or opposition to policies, and hence be useful in explaining the further reaction of policy members and implementers.

Finally, at the broad level there is the matter that we have already discussed to some degree, namely the *policy environment*, that is, the whole context out of which policy has emerged, including the political, judicial and professional components. Similar policies will not produce similar outcomes where differing cultural, social, political or economic conditions prevail, and in order to explain policy, knowledge of the contexts in which it has been formulated is vital.

The relationship of policy to its context is the focus of Lowi's (1970, 1972) framework. This suggests that analysis of public policy should *focus* upon the central issue concerning the properties of political relationships. Starting from the position that policy is essentially a behavioural matter, that is it seeks to encourage some change in behaviour to occur, the central issue to emerge from analysis will be the matter of *coercion*. Lowi's approach is to develop a classification distinguishing four types of policy for which degrees of coercion and political activity can be used as constructs. These policy types are identified as distributive, regulative, re-distributive and con- stituent. Lowi's (1970, 1972) work suggests that these can be usefully defined as shown in figure 7.5. This has been annotated to illustrate how the typology can relate to the urban context and will serve to make clear the definitions of the policy types.

Figure 7.5 Types of coercion, policy and political activity

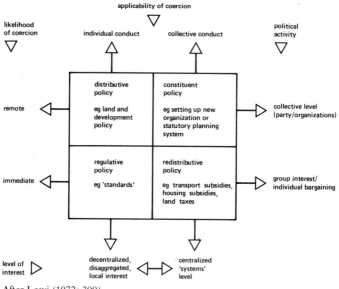

After Lowi (1972: 300)

Finally, in this section, the essentially operational view of policy study is well illustrated by the work of Van Meter and Van Horn (1975). They suggest the invocation of a framework which focuses upon policy as it is implemented into the local environment, and hence is perceived by the subjects within that environment. The key concepts in their analysis are 'change, control and compliance'. First, change. As already noted the purpose of policy is to bring about a different set of circumstances or events from that which would otherwise be. The first area of inquiry then is to examine questions not only about the nature of that change, such as the objectives of the policy and its implementational operations, but to ask questions about the *limitations* to achieving change that will be met in attempting to impose the policy. A highly relevant area for study here is the degree of resistance to change of the organizations involved. Second, and clearly related, is the matter of control, which as noted earlier is a *key* issue in any implementation. Here, a relevant question is 'to what extent can a policy be imposed upon the subject groups? Thirdly, there is again the matter of compliance. No subject group is entirely passive in the event of having a policy imposed upon them. Here, policy analysis can attempt to assess not merely the degree of compliance, but also to define at which point or level some reaction will be mobilized and which may dramatically modify the policy environment. Clearly, this may take an explicit political form and may involve other types of direct action by subjects that will influence policy makers.

Van Meter and Van Horn's analysis, then, attempts to construct an overall model for the implementation process. In effect they postulate that the relationship between policy making and its implementation is subject to a number of independent variables defined as:

1   the policy standards and objectives
2   the policy resources
3   the characteristics of the implementing agency
4   the degree of inter-organizational communication and enforcement activities
5   the disposition of the implementers
6   the prevailing economic, social and political conditions, generally known as the policy environment

These variables are all amenable to analysis in some form, though it is important to note that, as is so common in social situations, they will not be independent of each other, a point to be borne very much in mind in drawing inferences from empirical information.

A useful distinction made in the analysis is that the study of policy implementation seeks only to measure and explain what Van Meter and Van Horn (1975) refer to as programme performance, namely the degree to which *anticipated* outcomes are actually achieved, rather than to face the much more difficult task of attempting to trace and measure the diverging effects of the ultimate performance of a policy. As they argue, a policy may be implemented effectively, but if it is ill conceived, or because the problem has 'moved on', it may still fail to have a significant interest. Hence, successful programme performance may be a necessary, but not a sufficient condition, for the attainment of positive ultimate outcomes.

In the earlier discussion of research methodology it was pointed out that the researcher needs to be well aware of the potential jeopardizing factors which will create difficulties in the conduct of analysis. The same treatment can be given to policy study. For example, Greenburg et al. (1977) have discussed these factors under four headings as being the most problematical for the policy analyst.

The first is that the policy process takes place over an extended time scale, and this gives rise to two types of problem. As we have already discussed, the implementation process is a multi-stage affair with many decision points and this means that there are inevitably considerable problems in deciding which particular events and decisions are the most important for analysis. The second type of problem arises from a 'learning effect'.[17] Over time, the values held by the participants in the implementation will change, indeed they will be modified by the very involvement in the implementation. The researcher cannot, therefore, expect an initial set of opinions, values or attitudes to be held consistently throughout the process.

The second heading is that a given policy outcome is, in itself, a complex phenomenon, and may have several equally important aspects. The researcher needs to be aware that a narrow focus of attention onto one particular aspect of a policy effect can produce a very unbalanced analysis of the impact of the policy on its environment. Thirdly, analysis of policy making and implementation is complicated by the presence of a large number of participants, and there is considerable danger for analysis in oversimplifying the diversity of their attitudes, opinions and influences in the formulation of policy. Finally, Greenburg et al. (1977) point out that public policy as a research focus is complex because the process cannot be readily described by simple additive concepts and models.

Public policy is almost never a single, discrete, unitary phenomenon. Indeed the appeal of public policy study as a focus of intellectual endeavour lies precisely in its richness; the complexity of the unit of analysis simply and appropriately reflects the fact that an action of government is rarely meaningful if conceived of as a discrete, disembodied event and that the impacts of a single government action on society are not understood properly if taken in isolation from one another. (p. 1533).

Policy then must be expected to reflect the complexity, the arguments, debates and conflicts which went into its formulation and the 'chains of reciprocal interaction'[18] among the sequence of events that is implementation (Jenkins, 1978). But this complexity ought not to prohibit attempts at systematic study. As Greenburg et al. argue, so long as it is accounted for and confronted directly, so long as hypotheses are sufficiently precise, theoretical statements can be advanced and tested which will adequately and usefully represent reality.[19]

The potential contribution of policy analysis can now be summarized. First, theory formulation. A systematic attempt to study policy is an important way to reduce the complexity of a policy situation to manageable proportions so that understanding may follow; though this 'reduction' process will involve making and testing assumptions about the world of policy and its implementation, and requires judgement about what are the important and non-important issues and outcomes. Fundamentally, it is a subjective process, and subjective judgement will dominate the outcome of the analysis. As Wildavsky (1979) points out, whatever analysis shows that a policy has achieved can only be judged in value terms, that is, as to whether what has been achieved is better or worse than doing something else. It cannot be judged for example in terms of 'true' or 'false' which could be verified by some objective tests. In such a situation – each problem faced and each policy offered by way of amelioration will tend to appear to be unique, and it is this apparent uniqueness which inhibits the development of theory. The major contribution of policy analysis is to enable common and general theories to be identified. It is, then, as much a means of searching for regularities as the more classical forms of research discussed earlier.

Second, policy analysis is important in identifying and clarifying those areas and issues about which information exists and where it is inadequate (Quade, 1975). Earlier, we noted how an important question faced by any decision maker related to the selection of information which he could and should use in formulating proposals and policies. In order to counter-balance a purely subjective approach on the part of policy makers, a clear understanding of the role and potential of information in serving the policy making process is vital, and this we will further discuss in Chapter 9.

Policy classification

We conclude this chapter by a review of recent research by Bracken (1980) which has developed a classification for structure plan policy content from a detailed analysis of six Structure Plan Written Statements[20] and some four hundred policies. Given the paucity of previous work in developing planning policy classifications, an essentially empirical approach had to be employed by means of which the classification could emerge by searching for regularities in the 'data'. An immediate problem to be faced by any such attempt to develop a classification lies in making the choice of the case studies to be used. The conflict to be faced is between the desire to keep the sample as small and therefore as manageable as possible, bearing in mind that verbal statements cannot be as readily manipulated as numerical data, and on the other hand the need to choose a representative sample in order that generalization is possible. Here is a good example of the importance of the need to draw upon previous work, and the need to make such choice an explicit and carefully considered matter. Drawing upon other published reviews (Drake et al., 1975; Barras and Broadbent, 1979) a selection of plans were made according to clear criteria, which, a priori, it was argued were most relevant. In effect, the problem faced is typically that of any researcher attempting to develop a classification in a situation when complete knowledge of the universal set (i.e., the generalized field) cannot be known (Sneath and Sokal, 1973).

The selection criteria then made explicit the need to cover as much divergence as possible in the policy types which might result from the potentially different 'policy environments' of the Structure Plan authorities. The most important criterion was the necessity of obtaining a good blend between 'shire' and 'metropolitan' counties, so as to embrace the contrasts of urban and rural situations. Also, previous research (Barras and Broadbent, 1979; Drake *et al.*, 1975; Bracken and Hume, 1979c) had shown that, for a variety of reasons, Structure Plans possess their own discernible style or emphasis in terms of policy content. Thus, an attempt was made in the research to include a variety of different and self-evident document types. This included an example of a mainly restrictive/control-oriented document (East Sussex), and a notably promotional/advocacy style document (Greater Manchester) and so on. Additionally, a range of ages among the plans chosen was also believed to be a useful criterion to meet, in order to take cognizance of the possible effects upon content of the various circulars and other advice[21] emanating from central government over the period. As a result, the plans studied range from 1973 to 1979 and reflect not only the effects of formal advice but also the 'learning' effect of planners 'in the task' of producing the later examples of plan. *A priori* it might be expected that later policies would become more sensitive, particularly in their wording and explicitness in facing political issues.

Having made a selection of documents, the problem next faced is that of organizing the daunting number of policies that the documents provide, in short how to cope with a mass of verbal data. As a starting point, it was decided to examine the policies that were specifically concerned with the topic areas of conservation, countryside, recreation and leisure. The reasoning was that, *a priori*, it was believed that the proposals under these headings would be broadly similar in all areas, thereby allowing the analysis to identify the various ways in which common policies might be articulated. This would provide useful experience in the study of more complex written policy statements. This proved to be a useful procedure and from this experience, the typology was extended to cover other substantive areas of employment, housing and transportation policies. In sum, these topics cover the most important aspects of structure plan preparation and are recognized as the 'key areas' upon which the local planning authorities should concentrate their strategies for development.[22]

The actual policy classifying procedure consisted of a progressive extraction of the policies for each of the topic areas in the document. At each step, the policies were 'grouped' according to their apparent similarity in nature, scope and purpose. This 'typecasting' often revolved around the identification of policies dealing with either the same type of issue or problem, and/or having a similar objective. For example, some policies are aimed specifically at giving guidance on deciding planning applications to carry out development; some are concerned with setting standards of design or physical layout, and so on. Another useful technique used in the task was that of singling out key words or phrases in the policy statements, such as '...land will be made available...' (for a particular use). In effect a form of content analysis was employed.

In actually deriving the policy typology for such a procedure, it was recognized as necessary to strike a balance in the way that the policy types were to be described. Whilst it was important in producing an exhaustive typology to ensure that it did not contain too many categories, thereby reducing its descriptive power, the ever-present danger of modifying the meaning of policies by overlooking nuances in the wording in order to 'fit' the policies to the typology had to be guarded against. It was therefore not surprising that a small number of policies failed to fit even the broadest of the grouping categories, and these were left as residuals.

The typology which resulted from this work is summarized as figure 7.6 and can be briefly explained. Four broad criteria eventually emerged as a suitable basis for classification. Criterion A, as its title suggests, is intended to distinguish the broad orientation of policy intention. At the simplest level, which will suffice for many analytical purposes, the criterion can be posed as a strict dichotomy of A(1) where a policy is seen as having a 'control', 'negative' orientation towards development, as opposed to A(2) where the orientation is to 'promote' and encourage development. A further refinement is also to distinguish a category of policy which is both promotional in its immediate purpose, but which at a broader level has the objective of 'controlling'. An example would include a policy to provide, say, a country park, where the objective may be to remove recreation pressure from an established park (a National park) or an area of Outstanding Natural Beauty.

Figure 7.6 A categorization of Structure Plan policy types

A *Broad policy purpose*
    1   Protection of existing environment
    2   Development of new environment

B *Implementation agency*
  (I) Operations
      1   County council
      2   District council
      3   Quango (quasi-autonomous governmental organization)
      4   Other organization
  (II) Resources
      1   None
      2   Resources available from:
          a central government
          b county council
          c district council
          d quango
          e other organization
      3   Bids for resources from $B(II)_2$ made by Structure Plan authority/council
      4   Statement of support for bid by other organization (i.e. other than Structure Plan authority)

C *Specific nature of policy*
  1   Guidance on treatment of planning applications for particular development
        or changes of use
        a encouragement – 'like to see'
        b permissive – 'will be allowed'
        c restrictive/control; with exceptions allowed
        d restrictive/control
        e 'other factors to be taken in consideration'
  2   Standards to be applied from:
        a regulations
        b recommendations by other agencies
  3   Statement with a commitment to ensure the availability of land for a
        particular use
  4   Statement pertaining to the phasing/programming of specific developments
  5   Statement pertaining to the locational specificity of development:
        a whole plan area
        b unspecified unique locations in the area
        c specified locations in area (choice of)
        d specific unique location(s) in area
  6   Statement offering a commitment to aid and encourage the development or
        maintenance of a particular type of land use and/or service
  7   Statement recognizing commitments (particularly in relation to past
        planning permissions and development plans)
  8   Statement pertaining to organizational/administrative aims (e.g. to establish
        particular operational and consultative machinery)
  9   Statement giving guidance or making recommendations for consideration
        in other policy documents (local plans, subject plans, etc.)
  10   Statement suggesting changes in central government approach in relation
        to strategy or resource allocation (type or amount)

D *Residuals*
  1   Policy devoted to creating or maintaining communications networks
  2   Statement pertaining to the provision of a very specific facility or service,
        e.g. bus lane
  3   Statement pertaining to the segregation of conflicting uses or improvement
        of the environment
  4   Monitoring intention

From Bracken (1980a: 8)

The criterion at B recognizes the fact that whilst Structure Plans set out
the policies that the authority considers should shape the future strategic
use of land in their area, many matters influencing implementation are
wholly or partly the executive responsibility of agencies other than the
planning authority. This is recognized explicitly in many planning
documents for example,

While the County Council can plan its own activities so as to support and
implement Structure Plan aims and policies, their achievement depends on
consistent action being taken by other agencies as well. In this way, the cumulative

effect of individual decisions by different agencies can have the greatest possible effects on the county's major problems. (Tyne and Wear Structure Plan, 1979: 139)

The main agencies involved in plan implementation were noted in figure 7.3. In Section B of the typology a distinction is made between those agencies involved in the actual carrying out of the policy (operations) and those agencies involved with either providing and/or controlling the resources necessary to implement a particular policy. Some policies require few, if any, resources,[23] relying, for example, upon statutory powers, while others may require the bringing together a complex of agencies in order to provide and channel the necessary resources of both material and manpower. For example, central government directly provides much of the finance for the implementation of housing policies, yet District Councils are responsible for the allocation and control of that spending. Transportation resources are a matter which bring counties and central government together in this way, through the Transport Policies and Plans, themselves a contributory influence to the Structure Plan.

The third criterion, C, distinguishes among the specific purposes of the policies particularly as to its function as stated by the planning authority. The headings under this section will be mainly self-explanatory as will the residual matters shown at D.

The application of this framework and its utility as a first step in developing a policy analytic capability for Structure Plan analysis has been discussed by Bracken (1980a). It is argued that such a framework is an essential pre-requisite to any systematic understanding of the policy content of plans and one which can provide an essential objective focus against which the durability, performance and success of policies can be assessed. Even at the descriptive level, such classification is vital to cope with the diversity and range of the content of contemporary land use plans.

Finally, one must note a limitation of the approach which the earlier discussions in this chapter will have suggested. A study of policy documents, even when coupled to a study of supporting evidence and technical appendices, (such as Reports of Survey or Topic Reports), does not reveal the entirety of the policy maker's intentions. Policy documents are tactical documents, and their content reflects this role in the policy maker's eyes. A further study of policy intention can come only from document study *coupled with* studies of the environment out of which policy has emerged *and* knowledge of attitudes and perceptions among the policy makers themselves. This we make clear in the next chapter.

Notes

1 It has already been made clear in earlier discussion about the nature of the planning process, that it is frequently convenient to treat the 'planners' and 'decision makers' (i.e. elected members) as operating a single role.

2 See for example Rose (1969), Etzioni (1968) and Lasswell and Kaplan (1950).

3 See for example Zollschan (1967).

4   The Town and Country Planning Act, 1971, (section 8[1]) requires that:

> When preparing a structure plan for their area and before finally determining its content for submission to the Secretary of State, the local planning authority shall take such steps as will in their opinion secure:
>   (a) that adequate publicity is given in their area to the report of the survey under section 6 of this Act and to the matters which they propose to include in the plan;
>   (b) that persons who may be expected to desire an opportunity of making representations to the authority with respect to those matters are made aware that they are entitled to an opportunity of doing so; and
>   (c) that such persons are given an adequate opportunity of making such representations; and the authority shall consider any representations made to them within the prescribed period.

This requirement has been considerably developed by subsequent regulations and circulars.

5   So that the decision to proceed or not with one programme may well have more to do with bargaining over several such programmes rather than the inherent merits of any one programme.

6   A corner stone of planning legislation dating from the 1909 Town and Country Planning Act, is that refusal to allow an individual the right to develop his land does not qualify him (except in very particular and rare circumstances) to claim compensation for not being able to do so. In effect, then, the Legislation limits the consequences of a particular action by the public body.

7   In moving to the new style 'post-1968' planning system, local authorities made very little attempt to document the need for their new planning policies in the light of their experience of earlier plan and policy implementation. The Scottish Development Department, however, made clear the importance of continuity of policies from the 'old' to the 'new' system and as a result several Scottish Regional authorities produced reviews of present 'old' style policies and how they could be related to the needs of, and the style of, Structure Plans. For example, see Grampian Regional Council (1976).

8   There is however a considerable body of theory on the theme of the self-perpetuation of professionalism and bureaucracy (see Merton, 1968).

9   An earlier framework by Levin (1972) postulates an analysis also based on three dimensions, namely administrative, technical and political processes.

10   In some respects this 'three-focus' framework accords with the contrasting 'rational/comprehensive' and 'incremental' conceptualizations of the planning process that we noted earlier. Generally, the professional/technical focus has been identified with 'comprehensiveness' and the political focus with 'incrementalism', although hybrid possibilities exist.

11   Town Planning, etc. Act 1909.

12   Town Planning Act, 1932.

13   The legislative framework was mainly created by the Town and Country Planning Acts of 1943 and 1947, the New Towns Act, 1946, Distribution of Industry Act, 1945, and National Parks Act of 1949.

14   Though a discussion of the administrative implications is beyond this text.

15   These figures reveal the situation as at Spring 1980. Clearly, any such list can rapidly become overtaken by events.

16   Jenkins' (1978) argument goes further and suggests that implementation is a highly normative activity, which essentially involves a struggle for control, in effect, a multi-faceted attempt by agencies and organizations to control their

own environments by manipulating the environments of others. Concepts of
control and compliance are therefore highly relevant as foci of study.

17 See the discussion of the learning effect in social research in Chapter 5.
18 The idea of incremental change is itself a complex concept. See, for example,
    Dempster and Wildavsky (1979).
19 Greenburg's *et al.*, (1977) paper goes on to discuss in some detail the
    formulation of hypotheses within this framework.
20 These plans are East Sussex County Structure Plan – East Sussex C.C. (1975),
    Herefordshire County Structure Plan Written Statement (Hereford, C.C., 1974);
    Greater Manchester Structure Plan Draft Written Statement – GMC (1978);
    Merseyside Structure Plan Written Statement–Merseyside C.C. (1979); Teesside
    Borough Council (1973); and Warwickshire County Structure Plan –
    Warwickshire C.C. (1973).
21 Including the informal Structure Plans Notes of the Department of the
    Environment.
22 Whilst government advice in Circular 98/74 (Department of the Environment,
    1974b) stressed that the 'key' areas should be employment, Housing and
    Transportation, it is a widespread experience that countryside/conservation has
    been perceived by the public as an equally vital area. The effect of public
    participation exercises has frequently meant the elevation of this as a 'key issue'
    (see Bracken and Hume, 1980).
23 Excepting that is, the cost of public servants and their organizations necessary
    to 'operate' the statutory planning system.

POLICY ANALYSIS:
MODES AND METHODS

Methods and underlying theory

In Part 2 of the text, which dealt with the more traditional areas and methods of urban research, it was noted that while the choice of methods and research designs is an important 'decision area' for the researcher to face, a *prior* level of justification concerned the purpose of the research. In turning from the conduct of research into substantive matters (such as urban systems, population and employment change, or mobility, and so on) to research into policy making and policy implementation, the questions to be answered in deciding what to do, rather than the subsidiary question of how to do it, are even more crucial. As we will discuss, the methodological problems cannot be treated independently of the theoretical and ideological positions from which the researcher proceeds.

In this chapter, a range of available methods is discussed with which the urban researcher can conduct a study of policy, but it will be implicit that analysis of policy raises many philosophical questions about the normative stance of the analyst and hence the extent to which any policy directed research can be regarded as objective. Whilst it will be useful to explain the underlying theory, concepts, methods and their application, the presence of these more philosophical issues must be borne in mind. Reference to them will certainly be encountered by the student in further reading of the cited literature. It will already be clear that research into policy will involve going beyond the more traditional confines of the research methods appropriate to the analysis of the substantive concerns of a subject. Although the principles of policy research build upon the traditional experimental and non-experimental approaches that have already been discussed, an explicit concern with policy will usually involve four additional areas (Quade, 1975).

First, it will mean involvement in various ways with the policy-making and decision-making body *in person*. This 'executive bureaucracy' will include professional planners and administrators and politicians. Matters of co-operation and questions of confidence will immediately arise and these will demand methods of approach to research that we have not yet introduced. Second, there will necessarily be a direct involvement in some way with the subjects, that is, the recipients or clients, of the policy. We have already discussed how, in an urban planning context, the various client groups in society will have conflicting aims and attitudes to the intentions of planners and policy makers. Any attempt to analyse policy must deal directly with the benefits and disbenefits of policy as perceived and experienced by these groups.

Third, in that any practical concern with policy must relate not only to the intention to do something but also with its implementation, policy analysis must concern the extent to which policy statements and their intentions can in fact be implemented without those intentions being violated. A further requirement is that there needs to be some attempt to understand how the policies being studied are, or have been, constrained or modified by the institutions and their personnel who are involved either as 'implementers' or 'recipients' of the policies. This feature is often problematical because the effects of public policies frequently 'spill over' into areas that are not immediately obvious at the time a given policy is envisaged.[1]

Policy analysis will involve a wide range of methods. Therein lies its uniqueness, being fundamentally a hybrid research activity, though this brings some difficult theoretical and methodological problems. Wildavsky (1979) has summarized the repertory of methods in the following terms. The policy analyst will need to draw upon qualitative political theory for refining the 'normative picture of where we want to go'; quantitative modelling for systematizing knowledge about means and ends, and the probable consequences of taking action through policies; micro-economic theory for examining and understanding the effect of limited resources upon policies; and macro-organization theory for understanding the processes of policy implementation and the need to be able to explain the 'learning experience' of making and implementing policy.

As will shortly be made clear, in facing this disparate task, two main methodological themes will be involved. Policy analysis in any field will involve the use of *case studies* in order to examine a policy situation in depth, and *comparative analysis* which only can lead to theorizing beyond the single unique event. This has been made clear by Newton and Sharpe (1977) who argue that effective policy analysis can be achieved by a complementary blending of comparative analysis and case studies,

despite their undoubted refinement, case studies can tell us little if we do not know how they fit into the broader picture; similarly the comparative approach, for all its value in identifying the broader contours and general patterns of the system, cannot provide a comprehensive account of the policy process and its outcomes. (p. 62)

Whilst it is widely acknowledged that policy analysis will proceed by drawing upon a broad range of methods, from descriptive case study to quantitative analysis, it is still very much in its infancy, and systematic frameworks for discussing and explaining the constituent methods are not well refined, much less their proper integration. It is not to be expected that anything like the degree of certainty can apply over the choice of methods as with research designs already discussed.

A useful starting point in a discussion of the methodology of policy analysis is to identify the main dimensions by which analysis can be conceptualized (Nagel, 1977). The first dimension that can be identified is that policy studies relate to public (or collective) decisions and policies, as opposed to those of individuals. This means that the field of policy study is inherently complex, with multiple and conflicting objectives and an inherent 'policy dynamic' so that almost every action can be relied upon to produce a reaction. As already discussed, not only will there be disagreement over 'ends', but also most likely over 'means' as well. By implication, it means that public policy analysis, in tracing the evolution and the impact of policy, will necessarily move more across many traditional subject and policy field boundaries.

A second dimension is to distinguish between policy causes and policy effects. Analysis of policy causes, the 'why' and 'how' of policy making, will relate *inter alia* to social norms and attitudes to urban affairs; to the environmental contexts within which planners and politicians operate; to individual and collective self-interest, motivations about a problem or issue, or urban crisis; to reaction to other policies, and so on. In other words, to a whole range of beliefs, intentions and actions by public, planners and politicians. Essentially, this kind of policy research will attempt to explain why policies in a certain area have been developed in the way that they did, and why they have taken a particular form. Clearly, a detailed knowledge of the statutes and administrative systems within which the policy emerges and has to operate is an important consideration. Statutory and administrative systems are however not static. Policy emerges into an environment which is already being influenced not only by existing policies, but also within an administrative context which is in a constant state of being manipulated. Any analysis of policy will need to come to terms with these influences.

Analysis of the effects of policy will have to embrace both changes to the environment and behavioural and attitudinal change on the part of individuals and groups in society. Thus, matters both of impact, coercion and compliance need to be considered. These can be further classified into intended and un-intended effects, short-term and long-term effects and so on. An additional distinction can be made between the direct effects upon the recipients of policy and the retrospective or 'learning effects' upon the policy makers and implementers.

Yet a third dimension in the development of a general framework for policy analysis is to focus attention onto the methodological development of the various research designs that are appropriate. Broadly, these seek to test the validity of various, hypothesized cause and effect relationships by the application of as systematic an approach as the topic of study will allow. Given the purpose of this text, it is appropriate to focus mainly on these methodological frameworks rather than to extend the discussion of the philosophical justifications.

Some broad guidelines to guide the use and development of methods can be set down (after Roos, 1977). These are:

1   Strategies for the selection of events (policies), variables (both causal and effectual), and their treatment must be set down.
2   As far as possible, standardization of the specification of research designs should be adopted.
3   As 'time series' collection of data and information is extremely important, the early identification of emerging policy deemed to be worthy of study is vital, as is:
4   The need to 'build-in' to policy programmes the facility to analyse systematically the impact of policy.
5   Following points 3 and 4, it is clear that a commitment to continuity of research (particularly data collection) is vital and should not be subjected to inconsistencies that 'political crisis' type responses often bring.
6   That large-scale, multiple objective projects (and these are common in the urban field) raise some difficult problems in management terms and these particularly affect the specification of priorities *within the policy programme* that makes an efficient research design difficult to construct.
7   That full and comprehensive documentation during the conduct of the analysis is vital.
8   That, where possible, a quasi-experimental approach should be adopted, particularly in that 'control' will be a difficult concept to apply, but that useful comparisons can be achieved by the use of matched pairs of locations, and finally:
9   That in making inferences in policy research, there will be a need to integrate findings both from research into policy-making processes and into the substantive contexts and impacts of that policy making.

In facing this complex situation in the use of methods, it is appropriate first to make clear the quantitative distinction. As Nagel (1977) has summarized, 'non-quantitative' policy research methods will include (a) journalistic descriptions of incidents of policy formulation or implementation, (b) philosophical analysis of sets of normative values and ultimate social causes, (c) historical descriptions of previous attempts to deal with various policy problems, (d) anthropological or ethnographic studies dealing with the handling of policy problems in particular cultural, political and professional situations, (e) legal analysis of the statutes, regulations and conventions which are part of the context for a particular public policy field. As noted earlier such descriptive modes are commonly used at an early stage in the formulation of hypotheses and these methods also have an important role in providing frameworks in which quantitative analysis can be set. However, for most areas of policy study, the data will not be readily quantified, and a different focus of attention applies.

Whilst all research attempts to develop some theoretical explanations and hence to overcome the problem posed by the uniqueness of events and the difficulty of generalizing, the use of non-numerical data, such as the analysis of verbatim statements will make the task of the policy researcher different in its nature. This has important implications in the use of analytical methods and it will also mean that the success of an analysis will need to be evaluated in different terms.

Some analysis of policy can involve a degree of quantification and, here, the use of the more classical forms of research design is relevant. Two types of application can be distinguished (Nagel, 1977). One type involves inductive statistical analysis. This proceeds from an analysis of empirical data about a situation to induce a knowledge of relationships between selected variables by the use of standard methods including cross-tabulation, analysis of variance and linear regression. Normally, such an analysis will be enhanced by the consistent collection of data over time. Such analysis can be set in an explicit experimental or quasi-experimental mode and extended into the area of policy study. For example, the approach can sometimes be used by working with an experimental group that has been subjected to a new policy (or an alleged policy cause), and a control group of some kind which has not, in order to determine the effects of the policy or the policy cause. Of course, the application of quasi-experimental approaches in policy studies cannot approach the degree of problem isolation or measurement precision that one can expect in a non-policy situation, though useful inferences can be made.

It is important to note that the analysis of policy can take several forms. In the simplest application, the policy implementation represents the independent variable and the various outcomes, provided that they can be adequately differentiated, are the dependent variables. But, alternatively, it may be of interest to attempt to analyse why a policy has arisen in one area and not in another. Why for example has one council with a housing problem chosen to formulate a policy for the amelioration of that problem, when another council with a very similar problem has not? The policy is now the dependent variable, and the independent variables may well include, the perceived severity of the problem (this might be defined in terms of indicators of the amount of homelessness or quality of the housing stock), the political structure, resources availability, and so on. These factors will be variously capable of quantification and sometimes only in binary form, that is as influence present *or not*, political structure changed significantly at election *or not*, and so on. This type of analysis frequently takes the form of examining situations in which some influence X precedes a particular situation Y and this may allow a causal relationship to be inferred. Care must however be taken to exclude the common types of alternative explanation (Chapter 4), where X merely co-varies with Y or where there are complicating, indirect influences between X and Y.

A further similarity with the more traditional research areas can also be noted. Policy analysis can be undertaken both directly (and most commonly) via empirical study, or alternatively via simulation. Both approaches broadly involve a before-and-after treatment. Either the situation is studied in order to explain why the policy has emerged in whatever form, or the situation is studied in order to explain the effect that the policy may have had. In the empirical approach the real-world situation is studied. Clearly, the success of the investigation will depend upon the degree of 'control' over the research situation that can be exercised. In so doing certain practical problems must be faced. For example, in order to explain the 'emergence' of policy, anticipation may well be required, for retrospective measurement creates an additional uncertainty, particularly in dealing with 'soft' data. For example, asking a person his attitude to, and perceptions of a problem in retrospect will give rise to the difficulties of 'recall' and the effect of subsequent learning. There will most likely be problems of post-rationalization to be faced as well if the person is an active participant in the policy process.

In contrast, in tracing policy effects, alternative types of problem arise. First, there is the problem of time lag. Even where the effects of policy can be clearly ascertained, the exact moment in time when measurement should best be made can never be precisely known. Many urban policies have effects over long periods of time and these effects become increasingly indistinguishable from other policy and non-policy effects. Secondly, policy effects are influenced by the degree of acquiescence, or compliance, of the subject groups towards the policy, and over time they will react in various ways to it. It then becomes problematical to define the 'primary' influence of a policy against these consequential effects.

In contrast, the policy situation can be replicated for study in a simulation model such as a 'role play' exercise. Here, the complexities of the real world can be controlled by making plausible simplifying assumptions, but the outcomes in terms of an understanding of the situation will be heavily influenced and certainly limited by the extent to which the model is an adequate representation of the real world. Also, the performance of the actors will be influenced by the fact that the context for the study is a simulation. There are, however, some useful possibilities for the use of simulation in policy studies and these have been discussed by Bracken (1978).

It was noted earlier, in the discussion of traditional research designs, that research could be conceptualized both as a communicative or as a problem-solving process, and this is equally relevant to research into policy. For example, linking this distinction to the further distinction between quantitative (hard data) and qualitative (soft data) approaches, we can offer a simple conceptual framework to set out the methodologies for urban policy analysis (figure 8.1).

This suggests that the two most important dimensions in setting out a policy analysis framework are, firstly, that relating to the degree of quantification that is possible, and secondly, the placing of emphasis upon either the analysis of the policy-making process and its environment, or the policy-effectuation process and its outcomes. These dimensions are then capable of sub-division into problem-solving and communicative approaches. Though it does not relate exactly, it may be helpful to deal with this distinction in terms of what are widely referred to as 'programmatic' and 'case study' modes of policy analysis (Olson, 1970). The former

Figure 8.1 A basic 'methods' framework for policy analysis

| | | information base | |
		non-quantitative (soft)	quantitative (hard)
policy making process and contexts	ps	descriptive analysis	operations research, cost benefit analysis, programmatic analysis
	c	decision theory, operational game theory	
policy content, impacts and outcomes	ps	social policy outcomes, indicators, impact analysis	controlled experiment quasi-experimental applications, output studies
	c	analysis of power/influence, content analysis (eg of minutes and documents)	

ps — problem solving mode

c — communicative mode

concerns analysis of policy through an evaluation of the particular programme components and choices that fall within a policy area and upon which action could be taken. This can be described in problem-solving terms, each programme of action being designed to 'solve' a particular problem. The latter mode we discuss shortly.

'Programmatic' methods have been drawn principally from the fields of economics and operations research. Essentially, the data and their analysis is organized around making comparisons between the alternative courses of action (policies) which can be postulated as having the potential, when implemented, or reaching some objective or set of objectives, (Olson, 1969). We noted earlier how, in the urban field, such 'rational' approaches have been treated under three headings – *systems analysis*, which require some knowledge of how the formulation of objectives can be influenced by intervention into the system under control; *economic* methods, such as cost–benefit analysis, which essentially concern the analysis of situations in which there are competing means to utilize a given set of resources: and *operations research* in which objectives are more precisely specified and objective choice can be made as to the most appropriate tactical course to follow to achieve a given end.

Essentially, these approaches all involve processes of optimization in which the various outcomes of alternative courses of action can be compared in terms of some 'criterion of desirability', so that the best of the attainable outcomes can be reached. Quite apart from the ultimate problem of determining the objectives, most applications of these methods in urban planning have foundered on the problem of sectoral optimization,[2] namely, that in attempting to optimize *part* of a complex system, the system-wide (or aggregate) situation might be made worse. Thus, an 'optimal' solution to a traffic congestion problem – build a new road – might produce all kinds of external effects, which 'in sum' may yield net disbenefit in terms of overall welfare.

In practice, ambitious attempts to apply systems and cost–benefit analyses have almost universally failed to provide prescriptive answers when applied to social fields (Heclo, 1972). Two areas of literature reveal this most clearly. One concerns the history of PPBS[3] (Plan Programme and Budgeting System) which reached an extensive development in the late 1960s in the USA and to a lesser extent in the UK in the early 1970s. PPBS was devised to extend programming methods of systematic analysis to the entire budget of an agency, government department or local authority. Essentially, it involves both a re-organization of the agency, and its operations in terms of goals, which can be optimized via an identified, and agreed objective function. The difficulties encountered have been summarized by the terms 'comprehensiveness, comparability and certainty' (Heclo, 1972). First comprehensiveness. While, as we have already discussed, benefits and costs of a particular programme are inherently difficult to measure and quantify, it is even more difficult to be sure that the entirety of a particular situation is adequately represented in a particular analysis. Further, as standards do not exist for making the various costs and benefits commensurate, programmatic approaches fail to cope with competing objectives. Finally, as there is so much uncertainty in public policy situations, there is simply insufficient data, knowledge and understanding of policy implementation and its causal effects to predict with certainty the outcome of any decision choice. It is also clear, particularly with PPBS, that political influences both on the part of decision makers and their subjects, have tended to be regarded as 'minor, troublesome' influences and even as externalities to be assumed as irrelevant. In short, the inherent political dynamic and 'mobilization of bias' which surrounds policy has been largely ignored. There is a considerable literature on this theme (Wildavsky, 1969; Heclo, 1972), and in the British context the attempt to analyse 'programmatically' the third London Airport decisions make exemplary reading (Self, 1970). This study revealed most clearly, the tendency for such methods to focus upon the most easily measured variables and to neglect broader and 'softer-edged' considerations.

In general, then, there are severe limitations in the approach, *both* in terms of guiding decision making and as a theoretical base from which policy making can be explained. However, at a more limited level, the need to make explicit the choice processes in policy formulation is a helpful feature in analysis, as is the need to make clear in some way the opportunity costs which inevitably arise in any area of public policy (Olson, 1970).

In contrast, the 'communicative' mode of policy analysis focuses, not upon the attempt to improve the efficiency of choice in a particular situation, but rather to attempt to explain why a particular choice has been made. This can then lead to an understanding of both process and context. In this mode, it will be clear that rather different kinds of information are required. This more holistic approach begins, not with an analysis of some 'desired' objective, but rather with a consideration of the organization of the agency, what it does through its operations and policies, and proceeds to analyse the functions that it performs, as a basis for developing an understanding of its policies.[4]

An immediate limitation to be faced in this approach is that policy effects are invariably broader than the rather arbitrary divisions into which administrative organizations are structured. It is important, then, not to allow such structures to dominate the research framework, and this may be a powerful reason why any objective analysis of policy needs to be externalized from the personnel of a given policy unit, who may well have narrow, sectoral interests in maintaining the structure of their organization.[5] This is particularly necessary in public sector policy making where the effective judgement of the 'worth' of a particular department's policy, often needs to be judged in terms of how well (or badly) they complement the efforts of other units in the hierarchy, that is, both within and between governmental organizations (Olson, 1970).

The essence of the approach has been summarized by Schon (1971).

Where we cannot establish controls we form judgements...about what has happened or what has led to particular effects, by noting processes *internal* to what is happening. It is possible to watch one thing grow out of another. It is possible...to observe how actions have precipitated a new state of the system. As the observer moves from situation to situation he develops more or less explicit *models* of 'situation-action-and-effect'. These become the bases of...projective models...in the sense of being conceptual pictures or descriptions which relate characteristics of action, situation and outcome. They are 'projective' in the sense of being projected on to the next situation, always as a perspective on that situation and always subject to transformation through contact with that situation. (p. 233)

The approach is essentially based upon maximizing the learning experience to be derived from the incremental, sequential and repetitive attempts to ameliorate a given problem (Wildavsky, 1964).[6] This is clearly sympathetic to the view that policy emerges not as a matter of deliberative, rational choice, but rather through reaction to circumstances, one notable influence on which will be the existence of previous policies. Clearly, *any* analytic framework, which seeks to impose an arbitrary stationary view onto such a process (either to make decisions or to analyse their effects) is likely to result in misleading oversimplification. What is required, then, is a form of analysis which can 'follow events'. In this light we need to take a closer look at the case study approach.

Case study

Case study is an approach to analysis well suited to the needs of policy analysis, though its potential is limited by the 'one-off' manner in which it is commonly used. This serves only a limited learning role, and does not usually make a contribution to the development of theory. What is required is the development of systematic frameworks *within which* to set the case study approach that will allow a more general contribution to knowledge about urban policy.

In setting down the principles by which case study can be applied as a research method, it is essential to point out that a case study approach to policy analysis is not inherently un-scientific or non-theoretic. As Heclo (1972) points out, the common belief that case studies are an inadequate research method stems from the fact that many researchers assume that the development of theory will somehow emerge automatically from case study narrative. The earlier discussion of research methods will have shown why this cannot be. The problem, then, is not the case study technique itself but rather the ability of the researcher to build a context for the use of case study techniques that takes him beyond mere description. The most important point (Heclo, 1974) is that, as the case study approach is intended, ultimately, to explicate some phenomenon or situation, it should be designed within a theoretical context as indeed with other research approaches. As with other research designs, case studies make use of selected data and information to test deductions from theoretical hypotheses.

Essentially, the case study approach is characterized by an attempt to unfold the 'pathology'[7] of a situation from the assembly and study of a suitable number of 'cases'. These are selected or, where possible, manipulated to be similar in what are judged to be important respects. It is vital that these 'important respects' are well understood by the researcher and are capable of clear definition and expression. As we discussed earlier, reviews of literature, wide-ranging discussion, and experience, are all essential means whereby the researcher can reach this position.

In the conduct of case studies, a variety of research methods may be employed. Broadly, these will include analysis of the content of historical and contemporary documents, participant interviews with policy makers and subjects, analysis through sample surveys of attitudes, opinions and behaviour, and analysis of changes within the environmental circumstances that surround the policy formulation or implementation. In some cases, a study of documentary evidence only may suffice, such as written policy statements, minutes of meetings, and so on. Content analysis can be used to search for key words and phrases and these can provide a useful framework to cope with the diversity of policy material (Holsti, 1969).

However, a study of documents will be constrained by the extent to which the researcher believes that the documents reveal the full policy intentions.[8] For example, urban Structure Plans vary considerably in their policy content and treatment. Relevant questions are – to what extent does this variation represent real differences in policy intention, as against merely representing a different style of language or presentation? And, to what extent are policy makers prepared to make their policy document overt expressions of their policies? For reasons of wanting to avoid criticism or blame, or simply to leave room for later manoeuvre or bargaining, policy makers may prefer to leave certain aspects as covert and implicit. Normally, a case study of documentary evidence alone will pose as many questions as it will answer, and the analyst will want to approach policy makers and subject groups directly through interview work. Whilst appropriate methods for the conduct of such interview surveys have already been discussed (Chapter 5), asking questions about policy raises some unique methodological problems. Before facing these in detail, some points of principle should be established.

In making inferences from the findings of case study, the greatest uncertainty is that of external validity (Chapter 4). It will frequently be the case in policy analysis that the subject area will be poorly defined and this means that generalizing from the 'sample' of the case study will be difficult. In other words, as Heclo (1972) asks, 'a case of what?' How should one define and represent the subject studied to show what it is representative of? Fundamentally, as we have already discussed, the answer can only lie in reaching a sufficient level of definition and description in terms that are widely acknowledged. But there is a practical principle which can help (Heclo, 1972). The problem becomes less severe when the *inter-case* variability is minimized. The more similar the selected case studies are in terms of the attributes selected as the focus of the study, the more valid any generalization. A general requirement of case study research design, then, is to minimize this variability for what are believed to be the most critical elements of the study.

A coherent conceptual framework is essential in this situation and, in our context, could focus, for example, upon clearly defined problems or issues in urban policy making.[9] A clear framework is also essential because we are dealing with a 'dynamic' environment subject to both policy and autonomous forces. These will disturb any protracted, longitudinal type study of policy so that the researcher needs to maintain a clear overview in order to assess the degree of disturbance caused by any one effect. This is why, in policy study, it is important not only to examine the way in which particular variables vary over time but, in order to explain those variations, it is necessary to examine *the varying contexts* in which those changes are occurring. This will be vital in determining what is unique or general about the policy relationships.

The problem of external validity is, of course, not unique to policy research and there are no easy answers. The main points are to suggest a thorough research design; to draw fully upon accumulated knowledge; to be aware of pitfalls and 'jeopardizing influences', and to be cautious in making inferences. A further problem is, however, unique to policy study and concerns the need to study *non-decisions*. Pioneer work by Nagel (1961) revealed how the study of non-decisions was both a necessary and possible area for study. Earlier, we noted how policy could be defined not only in terms of 'intention' but, additionally, in terms of 'action'. Clearly, policy effects also occur through decisions *avoided*.

As Bachrach and Baratz (1970) summarize, the researcher's problem is one of asking how it is possible to obtain evidence through case studies in situations where the overt exercise of political power does *not* embrace all decision making and where conscious decisions do *not* embrace all of policy making. Nagel's work showed that through research into both policy contexts and policy-making processes, a reasoned analysis of both decisions and non-decisions is possible. Practically, the problem has to be faced at two levels.

We have already noted how policy is formulated as part of a continuous process of deliberate actions and reactions to a situation. In such a situation, there will be many influential relationships, for example, between planners, politicians and public. Some of these will be covert and well-documented in minutes of meetings, press reports on public meetings, transcripts of 'participation' discussions, and so on. Others will be covert and many will be extremely subtle, even devious. These relationships may be stimulated into an observable form (as a discussion or protest, a petition and so on) by some event. Often, the 'event' will be the threat to implement a policy, and hence these relationships become amenable to study and explanation.

The researcher clearly has a more difficult problem when no conflict and debate can be readily identified and for which no documentary evidence exists. A typical example is where a less advantaged group in society acquiesces to the prevailing consensus of the decision makers, although it cannot be empirically determined whether the consensus is 'genuine' or has been enforced through a non-decision (Bachrach and Baratz, 1970). A useful approach to this problem is, however, to assume that *over time* acquiescent groups and their points of view may well emerge in some form and therefore be observable to an analyst who is prepared to take a longer-term view of the policy context and is prepared to broaden his information base beyond readily available documentation. It is a widely accepted principle in policy analysis, both for this and other reasons that we will discuss, that the longer-term view *must* prevail (Newton and Sharpe, 1977). This has implications for the 'monitoring' of policy within the planning process (Chapter 9).

The main technical issues in the conduct of policy research through case study should now be discussed. First, it should be noted that policy research invariably involves a 'political' dimension. For example, policy makers may be unwilling to answer directly even a properly posed question for several reasons. They may feel that the researchers' findings will expose weaknesses in their policy arguments or even in their knowledge. They may feel that the research is giving help to critics or political adversaries or, by revealing future intentions, will foreclose future options which the policy makers may wish to keep open. They may be disinclined to help the researcher if they feel his inquiry is abstract or vague, of no 'practical relevance', or too time consuming with no clear benefit to the persons or groups approached.

Any researcher in these situations will need to carefully nurture a relationship with his subject groups. It is really a matter of confidence and a wise policy researcher, if he wishes to obtain such insights, will take a great deal of trouble to explain the purposes and nature of his research, to stress the benefits that may accrue to the subject groups from the analysis, and in the course of time, to fulfil any obligations by way of making available his findings. Of course, where the researcher starts from an *explicitly* political position in policy research, he must expect variations in the extent to which those responsible for policy will co-operate.

Second, policy research will involve a wide range of data. For example, it may involve the use of quantitative measures (such as performance indicators, evaluated costs and benefits and so on – see later), but mostly will rely upon 'verbal data'. Clearly, systematic study is made that much more difficult though the principles of measurement (Chapter 5) will still apply. Concepts, issues and terms will need to be defined as unambiguously as possible, in order to permit communication and questioning. Various types of scaling may be used to bring a degree of order to the data, of which nominal and ordinal scales are particularly relevant.

Both deductive and inductive forms of inference can be used in the analysis of case studies and, as in other types of research, will involve analysis at different 'levels'.[10] For example, at an initial stage only very general inferences may be made from a limited number of cases, probably involving a large number of unverified assumptions. However, the task of specifying those assumptions and identifying the 'most important' criteria enables the researcher to redefine his case material, add new cases, and refine the parameters of his research design. In this step-by-step way, he will sharpen the focus of his analysis to the point where some tentative theory may emerge.

Case studies have traditionally been used by researchers in many fields to obtain an initial 'feel' for their subject, that is, as an exploratory research tool.[11] However, policy analysts have been concerned to develop the approach itself into a more rigorous design. This has revealed the potential of a more systematic approach to case study analysis and the design criteria by which it can be achieved. The most influential work has concerned the developing field of community studies and particularly that which has attempted to elucidate the distribution of power through an examination of actual decision-making processes within the political system (Banfield, 1961; Dahl, 1961). Dahl's study, in particular, revealed the potential of using case studies to identify 'key community decisions, not so much for their own intrinsic interest, but as observable phenomena relevant to the broad question of the exercise of community power'.[12] Such work has revealed the vital role of the political context in explaining choice in policy formulation and the structure and extent of 'local power and influence' in policy making. It has also clearly revealed the contribution to understanding that can be achieved by setting a case study approach into a more rigorous research context.

A further influential piece of work by Bauer *et al.*, (1963) should also be noted. This revealed how changes in economic and political environments were themselves partially due to reactions of powerful groups in society to *previous* policies and *their* effects. In other words, it became clear that a case study approach was capable of revealing that policy was not simply a dependent variable, the outcome of a process of making deliberate choice, but rather that policy itself is a dynamic, independent variable which stimulates reaction and hence influences future policy making (Heclo, 1972). It is thus clear why, in setting down the principles for case study research designs, it is vital to bear in mind that policy can only be 'explained' by an analysis of the erstwhile policy environment within which policy makers and planners operate.

Given that policy itself must be seen as both a dependent and independent variable, it becomes all the more important to use the case study approach to 'follow events' and isolate as far as possible the chain-like effects of action and reaction. It is frequently argued that it is precisely in this role that the case study approach is highly appropriate having the ability to 'move with the reality of events'. However, it is also a criticism that most case studies appear to be unnecessarily static by failing to focus attention onto how events move and change. That is, they tend not to be designed to study the transformations within the system that they address. As Heclo (1972) points out, popular decision-making analyses typically tend to stop at the point of decision rather than to attempt to explain the decision sequences which properly constitute policy. The barrier appears to be conceptual rather than technical in attempting to infer the general dynamics of policy making from charting the interactions of just one policy event. The policy process is, thus, too frequently treated as a series of instantaneous states, each state derived from the previous one and having implications for the next. Clearly, any analysis which cuts across this situation at a moment in time cannot hope to adequately explain the continuity of the process, and the 'structuring' implicit in such a research design will impose its own limitations on the breadth of perspective obtained.

A better approach made clear in Bauer's *et al.* (1963) work, is to undertake longitudinal case study in which the policy is treated explicitly as a strand of events through time. Thus, the policy case study can be envisaged, not in terms of a 'plurality of juxtaposed units', but as a *series* of successive differentiations in a moving, but always incomplete process. By relating events to their contexts, the case study technique can identify the essential transformations that have taken place. Policy and plan making, is thus seen as a *inherently* continuous and adaptive process. It must also be recognized that the transformations will take place even without an explicit policy formulation stage. Indeed, transformations will often take place in spite of policy formulation, and analysis may well reveal the partiality of the influence that an explicit attempt to formulate policy may have in a given situation. We return to this theme in Chapter 9.

In summary, we conclude that there are three principles to be observed. The first is that any policy analysis must begin from the identification of key policy variables which are to be the focus of the study. The second is that their relative importance within decision making and policy effectuation processes needs to be assessed and understood. And thirdly, the patterns of interaction over time that surround the policy-making and effectuation processes need to be clearly identified and assessed.

Analysis of policies and events

It is a recurrent theme in this text that better decision making about urban affairs, depends not so much upon the refinement and sophistication of complex and prescriptive techniques but, rather, upon broadening the base and enhancing the analytical power of descriptive methods in order that planners and policy makers can be better informed, and more aware of the consequences of their actions. Such analysis will inevitably be partial, not only because it is infeasible to consider *all* decision alternatives and their consequences in a given situation, but also because of the impossibility of rationally considering all the opportunity costs involved. In other words there will always exist a large number of possible ways in which finite resources might be expended, and any of these may be equally appropriate given the problem of resolving competing and conflicting aims and causes of action, and the inherent uncertainty of the future (Lindblom, 1959b). 'Complete analysis' is therefore out of the question and, as widely observed, decision makers in practice 'muddle through' by a mixture of habit, intuition, experience and pragmatism, and whatever 'incomplete analysis' of a situation they believe is useful and relevant as an aid to their decision making (Vaupel, 1974). How can such a situation be studied?

We suggest four broad headings. At the most immediate level, policy analysis can focus upon the actual *behaviour* of individual decision makers and their advisers. Relevant questions are: what are their motives? what is the interplay among the representative factions in a committee or council? and so on. Secondly, we can focus upon the broader *motivations* of the policy makers. Why are they motivated to produce a given policy? What is it about the real world in conjunction with the 'internal' policy environment that has given rise to particular policy outcome? Third, we can focus upon the *expectations* of policy makers, in their attempts to transform one situation (as they perceive it) into another by means of their policies. Fourth, we can attempt to understand the *inter-active effects*. These will begin to inform the policy maker as to whether or not he has done a sensible thing and if unexpected and unwanted effects are occurring. In short, is the policy a success?

This simple framework can provide a useful starting point to examine relevant methods for analysis.

Drawing upon Vaupel's examples, we can readily envisage a simple, public policy decision-making situation. The decision process will often comprise three stages of resolution:

1   A possible decision alternative is considered and on the basis of some intuitive judgement, it is assigned some very approximate value, that is, it is 'evaluated'.

2   Another possible decision alternative is compared with the first, and an intuitive estimate is made as to whether it is better or worse than the first alternative.

3   If the second seems better, it is chosen; if worse, the first alternative is chosen, and so on.

In practice, most decisions are made by this kind of reasoning, which typically, is likely to be seen by an individual decision maker in terms such as:

I can probably get Plan A through the council, but Plan B will be more controversial, as it is more ambitious. I think the chances of getting Plan B through are less likely. However, I prefer Plan B to Plan A: It will be better for my reputation and it will be a bold step in the re-development of the city. However, the council members will have an eye on re-elections and may not want to commit themselves to an expensive measure. But there would be personal prestige for them if they could be persuaded to adopt Plan B. If I submit Plan B and they turn it down, I think I will appear forward-looking and bold, and they will appear over-cautious. That would not be too bad for me, but if I submit Plan A, and they turn that down, that will be the worst outcome for me. I don't think that is very likely because they will want to be seen to be in support of doing something in this situation. I think that's important for my own reputation as well. So the adoption of Plan A will not be so bad. I will press for Plan A.

It will be readily appreciated that such a process of reasoning is commonplace, and the essential comparative judgement rests upon the interpretation of terms such as 'probably', 'less likely', and the evaluation of the alternative outcomes as 'better' or 'worse' and 'not so bad'. The reasoning can of course be extended. For example, other alternatives could be added, such as another option, Plan C, or submission of both A and B, or a modification to say, B, involving a general commitment with detailed consideration in three months' time, and so on. The reasoning could be extended to make a more detailed assessment as to how the council members individually might react to Plan A, or Plan B, what interplay there might be between factions on the council which might affect the probability of their supporting one plan as against the other. Further, the reasoning might be extended to consider the attitude of the council members to the various groups of citizens who might be affected by the plans and so on. Such an approach to analysis suggests how a decision situation can be 'decomposed' into constituent parts and this will bring additional information to bear.

The advantages of analysing and treating policy decision processes formally has long been argued,[13] though in practice there are important limitations. In part, these relate to the plurality and complexity of the problem situation and the public accountability of urban policy making. But also, there is the practical problem of information. The question is: How much information about options, their merits and dismerits can be realistically communicated among decision makers and synthesized into real decision situations? As Levin (1976) has discussed, this is a crucial question, for attempts to systematically set out complex decision processes in a verbal non-quantitative way rapidly meet the clumsiness and imprecision of language as an effective medium and this seriously limits the number of options that can be effectively considered.[14]

Yet, as discussed earlier, attempts to quantify the process through such methods as strategic choice, or mathematical programming demand an unrealistic simplification and require a level of knowledge, particularly of trends and the dynamic and interactive effects between variables, that our present data sources cannot hope to provide. But further, most programmatic methods have to assume the equal relevance and implementability of the various options over time. To do otherwise would require a detailed analysis of previous policy making, and its effects. Even then, it might be difficult to anticipate how even a similar policy would behave in the future. We would argue that urban planners, for example, know too little at present about urban policy implementation to be able to make estimates about the durability and robustness of their policies in a way that allows such 'programmatic' approaches to make a useful contribution to policy making.

Although these methods have yet to prove their usefulness as urban decision-making aids, they are valuable in the analysis of policy processes. This can be illustrated by further reference to the concept of the 'decision-tree'[15] (Chapter 2). Applying the earlier example (after Vaupel) it will be clear that each distinguishable policy option and its anticipated outcome can, in theory, be explicitly represented. Then assuming availability, two types of quantitative information can be superimposed. One relates to the probability of achieving an outcome, the other to the relative degree of 'satisfaction' associated with each outcome. For the former, the planner may assess that the 'quite good' prospect of the council adopting his Plan A amounts to a 90% probability, whereas the prospect of their accepting Plan B is only, say, 30%. In appraising the satisfaction, or 'utility', of the respective plans no clear objective scale will exist. A useful technique however, is to assign the value of 0 to the 'worst' envisaged outcome and the value of 1 to the 'best' envisaged outcome. Intermediate outcomes are assigned values relative to this scale. How should these values be determined? A commonly applied yardstick is that an intermediate value, say 0.7, implies that the satisfaction from a particular outcome is roughly equated with the level of satisfaction that would be associated with the chance of 70% certainty of the best outcome being achieved. The worst

Figure 8.2 Principles of decision analysis

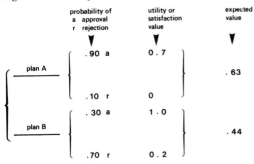

From Vaupel (1974: 50)

outcome, that is, submit Plan A and have it failed, is given the value 0, whereas the 'better' rejection policy, from the planner's point of view, is to have Plan B rejected, assessed as 0.2.

These, admittedly highly subjective, assessments of probability and utility, can be used to calculate an 'expected value' of each outcome (figure 8.2). Given that the expectation of any outcome is a matter of both its probable occurrence, and the perceived utility associated with it, the model can be posed as theoretically justified.

The 'expected value' for Plan A will be

$$90\% \times 0.7 + 10\% \times 0 = 0.63$$

and for Plan B

$$30\% \times 1.0 + 70\% \times 0.2 = 0.44$$

which 'confirms' the decision to present Plan A. It is also clear that, assuming the assessments of the probability of the outcomes is correct, that the presentation of Plan A is better until the utility value associated with Plan B rises to 0.5. For a rejected plan it is unlikely that 'personal' credit for having conceived an 'ambitious and bold' plan which was not adopted could in any way equate with a 50% chance of having a plan adopted. Our concern is not however with using such a decision tree approach 'to make the right decision', for the uncertainties and subjectivity involved may bring no advantage over a more intuitive approach. Indeed, as we discussed in Chapter 2, there are dangers in attempting such a decision-making approach in a social field because of the options which are necessarily excluded by the formal structure of the approach.

However, as far as the *analysis* of policy is concerned the approach can offer certain advantages as an analytic framework. First, the task of setting out the decision tree, even if incomplete, is a useful way of visualizing a complex situation. In itself, this can be helpful in setting out more detailed research designs, whether those designs will involve attempts to quantify the process or rely for analysis upon narrative and verbal description.

Second, attempts to attach quantitative probabilities to policy outcomes and utilities can often help to clarify the evaluation process in policy making. This is really a matter of communication. For example, a phrase such as 'a 90% chance...' conveys more information than an expression such as 'it is probable...' and will facilitate debate. Third, the invocation of such a framework can help the policy maker identify the weak areas of analysis, where further information would be useful and/or where concepts are at their most subjective. For example, tracing a decision through a framework such as we have illustrated might reveal that analysis of the past voting records of members of the council would have provided useful insights into attitudes towards the current plan, or, perhaps, that incomplete information as to the costs and benefits of the plans was instrumental in causing the council to be more cautious in reaching a decision than the planner had anticipated in his original assessment of a probable outcome.

An important consideration which can be studied through an extension of decision theory concerns the extent and amount of analysis which it is necessary to undertake in order to arrive at an informed position so that public policy decisions can be made. Put simply, the point is when do we have enough information to make a decision? This is no easy matter, for while it can readily be argued that decision-makers face most public policy decisions with incomplete and inadequate information, it is not easy to argue the case for further investigation and analysis when the contribution that will be made towards a better decision can only be guessed. But clearly, some kind of judgement is required as to the 'worth' of analysis against the time and cost involved and urgency of the decision. One general rule can be easily stated, namely that decision makers should be deliberate up to the point where likely benefits from improving the plan or policy are just worth the time and effort of the additional inputs (Rawls, 1971, 1973). In Vaupel's (1974) terms, it means that decision makers should continue to systematically treat a decision problem only as long as the expected costs of further analysis are less than the expected benefits. As this is difficult to assess in public policy making, an alternative focus is provided by the analytical framework we have described, in that the expected benefits depend upon two factors. The first suggests that it is important to know if the analysis will suggest a significantly different decision and secondly, that the potential difference between the 'expected utility', of one decision as against another is sufficiently important to warrant the extra analysis.[16]

Conscious and deliberate use of this rule will often be helpful to a decision maker in deciding whether it is worthwhile considering an additional course of action; or undertaking a research programme for further information; or even trying to define the estimates of outcome or expected utility by some additional work. Even if such an approach to analysis is not used in a quantitative manner, a degree of systemization can be obtained through its logic which will enhance the quality of a reasoned treatment.

Moreover, the approach leads to a further useful concept, that of sensitivity analysis. At its simplest, this involves making an estimate, or calculating where possible, by how much it is necessary to violate any of the assumptions and assessments in a decision-making situation to cause a *different* policy option to be preferred. As Vaupel (1974) comments, knowledge of the sensitivity of a particular policy decision to a change in the probability or utility values can be particularly helpful in deciding whether or not to explore the possibility of alternative policy options. For example, if the outcomes of a particular policy can only broadly be anticipated, there may be little point in trying to refine the quality of that particular decision. More reliance, then, needs to be placed upon assessing the policy action over time to make sure that the 'option' is still relevant to circumstances as they unfold.

In moving away from an analysis of decision-making *per se* to a broader analysis of the whole policy environment in order to explain the emergence and nature of policy, it will be helpful to recall the research principles discussed in Chapter 4. Whilst the purpose of all research design is to bring a systematized approach to study, a focus upon policy brings additional difficulties. The policy analyst's main problem is to attempt to draw upon the logic and systematic power of traditional research designs, while confronting the problem that only a much lower degree of quantification will be possible in the policy field because of the presence of values and value systems.

In particular, we noted the value of quasi-experimental designs in which emphasis is placed upon obtaining data and information from an extended series of observations (Campbell and Stanley, 1966; Campbell, 1972) to offset the difficulties of applying truer experimental or non-experimental designs. The use of the interrupted time-series design is particularly useful in enabling a research strategy to be formulated which can enable hypotheses about policy to be tested, though some simplifying assumptions will almost certainly be necessary. The most important of these will concern the probable presence of several independent variables. This requires that the analyst makes some judgements as to their relative importance, in order that he can focus his research onto a limited number of variables and events. It is also important that he is aware that these independent variables and events may well interact in complex ways. However, this is not unique to policy research. What is unique is that the analyst will need to make a clear distinction between policy and non-policy effects (J. O. Wilson, 1974). This is not easy, for effective analysis requires, above all, a thorough grasp of the whole policy context, and it is unlikely that such understanding can come from any single piece of research. Accumulated knowledge and research experience in the field will be vital for the researcher to develop a necessary breadth of knowledge. Then, at least, he should be aware of the non-policy events which *may* jeopardize the drawing of inferences from his analysis.

The analytical power of a quasi-experimental design rests upon presuming a sharp cutting point between the 'before' and 'after' situation

(Roos, 1973; Roos, L. L., 1975).[17] The problem in applying any such study to a policy situation is that policy-related changes may take effect only slowly or indeed with a considerable time lag. Traditional statistical, time-series methods of analysis do not cope very well with these situations,[18] but as L. L. Roos (1975) shows, the analyst can take two practical steps which can help. The first, is that generally, the *more* 'before' and 'after' observations that *can* be made, the more likely the analyst is to be able to identify particular policy effects. Second, the shorter the interval between the collection of the last 'before' observation and the first 'after' observation, the greater the chance of eliminating rival hypotheses that there are other policy effects which can explain the observed change. It will be clear that it is the 'historical' and 'maturation' effects (Chapter 4) which are liable to cause the greatest difficulty, particularly since they may give rise to non-policy effects simultaneously with the implementation of the policy.

A further help in dealing with these effects in policy research is to use a 'multiple replication' design. This attempts to measure some policy impact at different locations, say, in several cities. Any similarities observed over time may be more plausibly attributed to the impact of the policy, for other non-related causal events and effects are less likely to be identically present and therefore equally influential at each location. Such an approach is, however, only applicable where policy is applied simultaneously over a number of 'independent' geographical locations, though many policies of central government relating to land, housing, inner-city areas and so on will fall into this category.

The essential operational requirement of a quasi-experimental approach, then, is that a large number of observations can be made over a period of time. This brings some specific problems, that we should note. First, any extended study of policy effects requires that a clear and constant view is held as to the nature of the policy being studied. The difficulty here is, that for political reasons, different policy areas become more or less fashionable from time to time. As a result there may be reluctance to continue to monitor and collect data about a policy issue that is no longer thought so important, even though it may become more important again in the future. Second, an interrupted time-series analysis of policy (whether of its emergence or its impacts) necessarily involves some 'before' observations. In order to achieve this, and establish the pre-policy context, the research needs to anticipate the introduction of policy, perhaps by a considerable period of time. Again, the resource question needs to be faced. It will require persuasive argument that if policy makers genuinely wish to learn of the effects of policy, so as, for example to assess the wisdom of spending resources in a certain way, then a systematic study from an early point in time is clearly vital. In practice, policy often arises in response to quite short-term crises which makes its anticipation difficult. The urban planner, however, faces somewhat fewer difficulties in this respect than researchers in other public policy fields, such as health or education, for his main areas of policy concern long-enduring problems of land allocation, housing, employment and so on which exhibit characteristics that extend over considerable periods of time. And, perhaps more importantly, the continuing statutory requirement to produce urban plans and programmes means that at least planners ought to be able to argue consistently for long-term, 'policy-based' approaches to analysis in order to better inform future plan making. Some practical implications of this are discussed in the next chapter.

In the simplest application of the interrupted time-series approach, information is obtained which focuses upon a single dependent variable, such as the rate of land development. Examination of the trend in this rate over time may reveal the influence of a particular policy. If the 'before' and 'after' observations do reveal significant differences, then the hypothesis that there is no difference can be rejected and it may be inferred that the policy has had some influence.[19] We have so far included the possibility of analysing both the emergence of policy, and its effects by such a design. It may now be helpful to state this distinction more formally (after Roos, 1977).

The conventional approach to a time-series research design presumes that some event, E (such as the implementation of a policy) is seen as affecting a variable, V, and this effect is measured over time and compared to the pre-policy situation. This mode of policy research can therefore be described as 'variable-causing' ($E \rightarrow V$). In practice, most systematic policy research has been done using this framework, which builds directly upon the concepts of the experimental research designs. However, in the analysis of policy an alternative mode is feasible using the same longitudinal design. Here, it is hypothesized that some change in an independent variable causes the event, namely the emergence of the policy. This can be called the 'event-causing' mode ($V \rightarrow E$). In fact, a great deal of historical analysis is implicitly carried out in this mode, typically where a lengthy record of change, involving many factors (or variables) is scanned in order to seek explanations of some event. Typically, we might ask: what circumstances gave rise to the Planning Advisory Group's redesign of the planning system in the 1960's? or what are the circumstances that led up to the introduction of New Town policies, or Inner City programmes, or Housing or Transportation programmes, and so on? The essential feature of this mode is that the whole context out of which the policy has emerged is explored.[20]

One important reason for making this distinction is that it provides useful guidance in the identification and structuring of information. In particular, it will make explicit the way in which the various types of data and information have to be synthesized. In the 'event-causing' mode the design focuses not so much upon the interruptions in a series of observations, but rather upon such factors as:

1 the *level* of variables which precedes the policy event
2 the *rate of change* in these variables, and/or
3 the changes in their *inter-relationships*

A distinction must be drawn between the *levels* of measurement among such variables and *rates of change*.

Figure 8.3 Variables as predictors of events

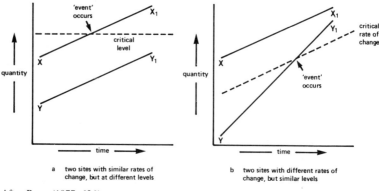

a two sites with similar rates of
    change, but at different levels

b two sites with different rates of
    change, but similar levels

After Roos (1977: 626)

In figure 8.3 two geographical locations are assumed in which public policy response to some phenomenon is being considered, such as unemployment or poor housing. The incidence (or level) of this phenomenon differs, that is, it is 'worse' in town X than town Y. Next assume that policy makers have a notional threshold or critical level at which they will be provoked, no doubt for a variety of reasons, to take action by initiating some ameliorative policy. It can readily be seen (a) that whilst towns X and Y may experience similar *rates* of increase in a given variable, the differing *levels* account for policy reaction in one and not the other. In contrast, (b) the towns may experience similar *levels*, say as revealed by a survey, but here the event-causing factor is hypothesized as being a critical rate of change.[21] Policy makers in town Y may be provoked into ameliorative action, not by the 'level' of the problem, but rather by the rate of change. This will probably be perceived as a deterioration in some situation, such as an increase in the housing waiting list, or numbers unemployed, or say, a pressure lobby from the building industry to release more land. Research, in this mode, seeks to explain *why* the more gradual deterioration to a higher level may not have provoked a policy reaction in one location, whereas a sudden change even at a 'less worse level' may provoke a response in another.

This distinction will enable many familiar policy situations to be conceptualized. Two final points need to be borne in mind. First, in making any inferences from such a design, data from several locations are most desirable. In general, the greater the number of locations that can be studied, the more likely the researcher will be able to identify the critical values for level and rate of change. Under these circumstances any explanation offered on the behaviour of policy makers is more likely to be right. Ideally, such data are required both from sites where the policy event has occurred and where it has not though this clearly may be difficult to anticipate. Second, as always, the possibility of jeopardizing factors must be noted. A general problem (Campbell, 1969) is that unmeasured, independent variables may be present in the analysis and it is possible that they have not been revealed by exploratory study.[22] Here, we must rest upon the assumption that *important* variables *are likely* to be revealed by careful and conscientious exploratory study, extensive reading of related, prior research and a thorough grasp of the situation context.

A more difficult problem will be coping with the so-called 'intervening variables' (Roos, 1977). The most troublesome of these will be 'public opinion' which is an important catalyst in many policy situations. When mobilized, it acts as an intervening variable and affects the thresholds at which policy makers will react (or choose to avoid reacting) to a given situation. As Roos points out, without some attempt to measure this effect the *post facto* 'explanatory' argument will be very weak. This will be a particular problem where a variable itself may not have changed very much, but public opinion has, possibly for emotive reasons. For example, levels of traffic on a road may increase only marginally, but one independent event, such as an accident, may lead to quite dramatic changes in public opinion and hence influence policy makers. The use of attitude measurement (Chapter 5) and participant interviews are important ways in which a systematic attempt may be made to record changes in levels of opinion, though the researcher must guard against the presence of post-rationalization in posing historical questions in such a situation.

Other jeopardizing factors, which deserve brief mention, relate to the possibility of the presence of cyclical changes. These make it difficult to distinguish between the level of a variable and its changing (rising or falling) characteristics as the predominant causal influence.[23] Finally, in a situation where there are several influential variables and the researcher has successfully identified them as being important, there can be the complication that it may be some combination of the influences that has triggered the specific policy response.

Indicators

One area of firmly established methodology in the analysis of policies, particularly of outputs and outcomes, is that of 'indicators'. The remainder of this chapter is devoted to an outline explanation of their principles. In making use of indicators, urban planners can draw upon the considerable experience of a wide range of social sciences, and it is widely argued that the development of meaningful and informative indicators is central to the development of a policy analytic capability on the part of planners.

The development of indicators owes much to the attempts to assess and evaluate the various outcomes of welfare and employment programmes in the USA during the 1960s (Bauer, 1966). Development work in the UK has been more recent, but a notable advance was made by the publication of the first volume of Social Trends in 1970,[24] when the idea of using informative indicators of social conditions received official sanction. There has also been a rapid development of the use of various indicators of economic performance.

The use of indicators arises in two ways (Cazes, 1972). One is as part of the quest for systematic knowledge about society and the second is to learn of the effects of various policy interventions on society. In practice, the use of indicators lies very much at the intersection of these themes, for they are effective both in the study of policy formulation (that is, in the analysis of the environment out of which policy emerges) and in assessing the impacts of policy as it is implemented. The need for 'indicators' arose primarily from realizations of the inadequacies of published, official data. As already noted, much official data serves a wide variety of purposes and, because of the need to provide a consistent, standardized record over time, such data cannot (and indeed ought not) be too readily varied to suit changing circumstances. There is, then, an inevitable conflict between the data normally available and what particular analysts would like to see. The concept of an 'indicator' is to use, refine or manipulate data from one form into another to bring it into a more meaningful focus for a particular purpose.[25]

Three points need to be emphasized. First, indicators tend to be 'one-off' and whilst useful in policy study cannot stand alone as data (Carlisle, 1972). Rather, they are valuable in *conjunction* with ordered, systematic statistics as for example from a Census. While indicators are helpful in making the most of traditional sources, they must essentially be regarded as a complementary methodology. In practice, their use lies between illustrating official data on the one hand, and the drawing of local inferences on the other. Second, indicators are notably *non-neutral*, for they are defined and used by the analyst in a way which reflects *his* judgement as to what is useful and relevant to 'explain' a situation. Indeed, as Olson (1969) has shown, the selection of a (social) indicator, means, in effect, that an explicit decision about a purpose of a (social) policy has been made, and that changes in the indicator can measure the extent to which that purpose is being achieved. Third, as with all measures (Chapter 5) there is the important problem to be faced of establishing the empirical counterpart of the indicator, so that it is capable of being interpreted.

Providing these conditions are met, indicators help us in three specific ways (Carlisle, 1972). First, they can be used in a descriptive mode to produce more complete and precise answers to many socially relevant questions. For example, how adequate is the housing stock? A relevant indicator here might be constructed in the form of an index, from data on housing condition, dwelling size and household composition. The construction of such an indicator is often the starting point of an information system. Essentially, these indicators attempt to describe a phenomenon that cannot be measured directly, but about which useful data can be constructed. Such indicators will, however, be very specific to a particular task and therefore have only a limited application. Indeed, there may be dangers in attempting its use in situations for which it was not designed.

Second, indicators can be used to directly answer 'policy-oriented' questions. For example, how well does public transport serve a local population? Indicators are useful here because policies, as we have noted, are often set down in very general terms. Yet those policies will have effects upon the lives of individuals, and policy-oriented indicators that relate to these effects are useful in making the inferential link between broad policy implementation and its localized effects. Whilst indicators cannot provide normative information (as to what *ought* to be done in a situation) policy-related indicators are valuable in shedding light upon the essentially dynamic environment in which policy intervenes. The essential design requirement is that each policy intention should have associated with it a clearly defined indicator, or set of indicators, which are capable of revealing discrete information about the performance of that policy. This, too, has important implications for policy monitoring.

Third, indicators have a useful role to play as diagnostic instruments. They can be devised in such a way as to reveal and communicate the emergence of problems. These might include imminent shortages of land, changes in public opinion, deterioration of the quality of housing stock, rising traffic congestion and so on. In this mode, the analyst will need first to broadly anticipate the event he wishes to diagnose, define a suitable indicator and relate this to data which will be available. Again the implications for monitoring and information systems will be clear.

Some cautionary points also need to be made. In the design of indicators there is a common tendency to substitute measures of some physical phenomenon for social measures. For example, data about the physical condition of residential buildings may indicate something about the quality of the building stock in an area, but they are not *per se* measures of living conditions. Equally, measures of unemployment by 'head of household' unemployment data may give a misleading measure of household income levels for, clearly, other members of the family may be in work.

Like so much in social research there is no single, generally accepted definition of an indicator. A widely acceptable definition might be

a defined concept which is capable of measurement and is regarded as being relevant in providing information about some aspect of a social system or its operations.

But as Rose (1972) points out, it is important to remember that indicators are essentially measures of concepts, not 'facts'. They can therefore only have significance by virtue of reference to a larger body of ideas. Essentially, they must take their references from current social economic and political theories about the content of the world and what the researcher and policy maker believes to be worth studying.

The definition and meaning of an indicator will be unique to the situation that the researcher faces but, providing certain conditions can be met, an indicator can have a more general utility (that is, produce information in which others can have confidence). These conditions can usefully be set down as guiding principles in the specification of an indicator (after Carlisle, 1972). First, an indicator must be defined explicitly in the context of the system about which it is to inform, both as to its composition and as to the way in which it can be used. Second, an indicator should relate to the essential 'dynamic', or change within a system, and this will most commonly by expressed in terms of progress towards (or away from) some social objective, however implicit. Finally, to be meaningful, an indicator needs to relate explicitly to the policy intentions of the policy maker or planner. Overall, his main operational consideration will be to select a sufficient number and type of indicators to be useful for a particular study, but not to use so many that he becomes swamped with information. Again, careful judgement about what is important and un-important in a given situation is vital.

An example will make these principles clear. In the case of Housing Action Area Studies (Department of the Environment, 1975b) it was recommended that planners should use just five census-type indicators as a first sieve in identifying a short list of areas for special attention and action. In order to identify 'Housing Action Areas' and 'Priority Neighbourhoods' (that is, areas of housing stress) the following household indicators were recommended:

   (i) Proportion of households without exclusive use of (i.e., share or lack) all basic amenities (bath or shower, inside w.c., hot water tap).

  (ii) Proportion of households lacking individual amenities such as baths, w.c.'s, hot water.

 (iii) Proportion of households sharing amenities such as baths, w.c.'s, hot water.

 (iv) Proportion of households overcrowded – in terms of more than 1.5 persons per room, or some other appropriate standard.

  (v) Proportion of households in privately rented accommodation.

It was also recommended that this list could well be complemented by a house condition survey of the entire area concerned, and this can be expressed in the form of an indicator.

The following general advice makes clear how the indicators were to be used:

In addressing the use of indicators for the identification of potential General Improvement Areas (G.I.A.s) defined as areas which offer scope for creating a better environment and which contain stable communities largely free from housing stress: districts with a preponderance of privately rented houses, especially furnished dwellings, will tend to be unsuitable for G.I.A. treatment which relies predominantly on voluntary action on the part of the owners. (Department of the Environment, 1975c: para. 18)

As a result, it was recommended that authorities should look first at areas which, according to the indicators, contain:

medium proportions or number of households or persons who lack amenities; fairly high proportion or numbers who live in owner-occupied accommodation; and fairly low proportions of households or persons who (i) have amenities, (ii) are overcrowded and (iii) live in privately rented accommodation.

In this way indicators have been widely used in the initial identification of potential housing action areas. Refinements, including the combining of indicators with weighting and scaling by means of indicator scores in the form of indices are commonly used to extend the methodology (O'Dell and Parker, 1977). A guide to further reading on this subject follows at the end of Chapter 9.

Notes

1 There is a yet further dimension of *comparative* policy analysis which can concern how a variety of policy problems are treated in different nations, cultures and political systems though a discussion is beyond the scope of this text.

2 There is an unfortunate conflict of terminology in the literature here. This problem is sometimes referred to as 'sub-optimization', a term which also refers to the 'near' achievement of a particular strategy as an aim (i.e. satisficing).

3 Though a good explanation of the theory and methodology of PPBS will repay reading. See, for example, Krueckeburg and Silvers (1974).

4 The approach is also referred to as 'structuralist/functionist' analysis, though there is considerable, unresolved philosophical debate about the functionalism and dysfunctionalism of organizations, that is beyond the scope of this text. See Olson (1970). Broadly, an organization is considered to be functional if its operations are conducive to the survival, expansion or well being of the society or system of intervention of which it is a part. It is dysfunctional if it tends to prevent the same.

5 This can be seen for example in the current changes affecting Local Authority Planning Departments. There are strong advantages in seeing a research and monitoring function as a level above narrow, departmental responsibilities and interests. See Chapter 9.

6 This is a view of the political system as a self-modifying communications network, capable of learning and innovation (see, for example, earlier work by Lindblom (1965) and Deutsch (1966)).

7 The case study concept had its origins in clinical studies.

8 Analysis of strategic land-use planning documents is also complicated by the variable role given to the Report of Survey. Some authorities have included a great deal of supporting evidence in the Written Statement itself, while others have relied upon the Report of Survey and Topic Reports to communicate this evidence.

9 The 'dimensions' shown in figure 1.4 are some possible examples.

10 These can be likened to the earlier discussion of 'filters' (Chapters 1 and 5).

11 And therefore to be seen merely as a useful way of setting up more traditional experimental or non-experimental research designs.

12 There is a considerable literature on the exercise of community power and 'local' influence in policy making. See, for example, Merton (1968) as a standard work, and case studies by Bachrach and Baratz (1970), Crenson (1971) and Roos (1974). Case studies in Britain are dealt with in Newton (1976) and Jenkins (1978).

13 See, for example, Raiffa (1968) or Schlaifer (1969) on the trend towards systematic policy making in the late 1960s in the USA.

14   Decision makers may, of course, *prefer* this situation simply because it *does* limit the number of options that can be considered.

15   The approach has been well developed in the field of management, though there are important differences between public and private sectors. The 'managerial' aspects are extensively reviewed and explained in Wagner (1975) or Stoner (1978).

16   This can be put in notation. If the probability is p and the difference in the expected utility values is d, then the expected benefits of the analysis equal $p \times d$. If the cost of the analysis is c, then the net benefits of analysis will be $p \times d - c$. Thus, a decision maker should begin or continue to analyse a decision problem as long as the decision maker believes that $pd > c$. Because deciding how to decide is itself a decision problem the $pd > c$ rule can also be derived by doing a decision analysis. Basically, the decision maker faces two alternatives – no further analysis and further analysis. The first decision means the adoption of the decision which is currently thought best. Let the expected value of this outcome be designated by v. The second decision has two possible outcomes; either that the decision maker reaches a better decision or the decision maker does not reach a better decision (i.e. does not change his or her mind about what to do). If p is the probability that the decision maker will reach a better decision, if d is the expected difference between the value of this better decision and the old decision (which has a value of v) and if c is the expected cost of further analysis, then further analysis should be chosen if $p(v + d - c) + (1 - p) \ (v - c) > v$ which reduces to $pd - c > 0$ or equivalently, $pd > c$ (Vaupel, 1974).

It is of interest to note that the simplified form of the $pd > c$ rule is the rule of thumb known as satisficing (Simon, 1957). A decision maker who 'satisfices' is in effect making the judgement that once a satisfactory course of action has been uncovered, the probability of finding a significantly better course of action is so low that the cost of further analysis is not worthwhile.

17   Some writers express this situation by suggesting the quasi-experimental approach essentially means looking for a 'burst of variance' in the measurement of a possibly causal variable (Roos, 1975).

18   In contrast, where a *large number* of time-series measurements have been obtained, the methods of Box and Jenkins (1976) and Glass *et al.*, (1973) are highly applicable though policy study will rarely fulfil the rigorous requirements.

19   A variety of ways of formulating this design are available and a variety of statistical methods have been proposed for analysis—see for example Caporaso (1973), or Campbell and Cook (1976).

20   Both frameworks are however using the same causal model – that is of assuming the precedence of an independent variable in order to make a causal inference.

21   It should be noted that the conventional regression analysis of level, that is, of the *intercept*, and of rate of change, that is, *slope*, is equally applicable in this mode.

22   It is of course always *possible*, though perhaps unlikely, that a completely unrelated variable may have 'caused the event' by some accidental association. A good research design can also seek to eliminate this risk by attention to detail in hypothesizing the independent variables, and by drawing as widely as possible upon available information. Time to prepare thoroughly is thus a vital requirement of the researcher.

23 As Roos (1977) points out, this can also be a problem if 'new' data points are relatively close to the slope generated by 'older' data. Level and slope cannot then be separated. The argument revolves around a 'slope of a particular magnitude extended over a given length of time'; level is obviously affected by these 'growth rate' considerations. Examination of the 'residuals' (Appendix 1), however, provides clues as to the importance of the absolute level – that is beyond that expected from the 'growth rate'.

24 *Social Trends* (HMSO, London).

25 Through, for example, correlation between variables, composite variables, scores or ratios or proportions, etc. Two points must be noted: (i) the ever-present danger of inferring simple relationships in complex situation needs to be guarded against, and (ii) when data are combined, the effects of combining the 'errors' of both sources needs to be carefully observed.

□ 9
POLICY AND PLANNING: SOME METHODOLOGICAL IMPLICATIONS

In this final chapter, we examine the implications of a policy-based view of urban planning for the development of planning methodology. This will raise broader issues that concern the conceptualization of urban planning as a continuous adaptive process, and this we comment upon in the conclusion to the text.

Traditional thinking, based on the rational/comprehensive view of the planning process essentially sees the plan or policy document as the output of a technical and deliberative process. Our discussion of implementation will have revealed the inadequacies of this model in a public policy field. However, we will suggest that if strategic urban planning is viewed as a 'policy process' then considerable benefits accrue. Not least, that the view explicitly demands the integration of activities that the traditional process treats at worst as distinct, and at best in a crude form of linear dependence. Fundamentally, we suggest this integration involves three components. The first is that of *activities* in which planners engage in order to intervene in the urban system. The second is the *policies* that communicate these activities and often, though by no means invariably, guide the activities. Third, there are the *outputs* or consequences of these activities, which in turn will influence the revision of the policies.

Regarding urban planning as a policy process, reveals an over-riding feature. It is that planners and elected members (as with any 'managers') will manipulate and operate the system so as to influence its performance to the way that they want it to work. Viewed from this (policy implementational) standpoint the essential components in order to explain this manipulation are *commitment* and *powers*. These we should briefly examine.

Commitment has been identified by Hickling et al. (1979) as a key factor in any policy process: 'the primary output of a continuous process is a continuously evolving body of commitment to policies and action' (p. 50). Commitment is then clearly a factor which should be assessed in policy analysis. It is also important to note that there appears to be a natural decay about commitment to policies. For example, politicians may find it difficult to maintain commitment to a policy given the pragmatism of political life and the need to be seen to be making short-term achievements. For professional planners, long-term commitment may give rise to frustrations over conflicts and tensions *vis-à-vis* other implementation agencies, such as government departments, other local authority departments as well as the private sector. Making long-term decisions about land use in periods of severe financial restraint is another factor which may affect commitment. There is also the major jeopardizing factor of political change at both central and local levels which will conflict in terms of commitment with the longer-term view of professional planners.

Second, there is the matter of the powers available to decision makers to intervene in the urban system. These are neither constant over time as governments make adjustments, nor indeed, are they consistently *used* by planning authorities. While, traditionally, urban planning has been founded upon Town and Country Planning Legislation (as now under the 1971 Act) and to some extent under Public Health and Housing Legislation, there has been a recent tendency for this power base to broaden. This includes powers under Transportation Legislation and, notably, the Local Government Act (1972). Some Local Authorities have promoted their own enabling legislation to carry through a particular planning task.[1] It has been widely noted (Barras, 1978b; Barras and Broadbent, 1979; Bracken and Hume, 1981) that in the preparation of their Structure Plans, local planning authorities have not made as explicit as might have been expected, the necessary 'power base' upon which the successful implementation of policies would depend.[2] In part, this observation reflects the traditional view of plans as being more or less 'self-implementing' through the Town and Country Planning Acts. Yet the powers of authorities to deal with the 'key policy issues' as recommended[3] to local planning authorities (namely employment, housing and transportation) as the basis of the Structure Plan, are widely distributed among the various statutes.

Faced with this situation, it is perhaps not surprising that so many Structure Plan policies are little more than bland hopes based upon broad assumptions about the influence that the authority can exercise. Latterly, there is evidence of a recognition of the weakness of this situation, and examples can be cited where explicit attempts have been made to relate the policy statements of plans to the powers that are available to assist in implementation. A good example is that of Tyne and Wear Structure Plan (1979), and it is relevant to quote some examples from the part of the plan dealing with economic development (ED).

Policy ED1: New economic development and employment should be given high priority but a balance should be maintained between the regeneration of the older industrial areas of the County and the development of new industrial land.

The County Council, the District Councils, and the Department of Industry all carry out programmes of economic development measures. In co-operation with the other agencies concerned, the County Council will monitor the level and distribution of economic development activity and give a high priority to its rolling programme of economic development measures, which it will seek to use to secure this balance. The measures could include the acquisition and preparation of land, the development of advance factory space, the improvement of transport facilities and the environment in older industrial areas, and the provision of selective financial assistance under the Tyne and Wear Act and the Inner Urban Areas Act.

Policy ED10: A wide range of new opportunities for economic activity should be created both in inner areas and elsewhere by:
  (i) The assembly and preparation of industrial land (including environmental improvement and reclamation of derelict land where necessary).
  (ii) The development of advance factories and workshop units;
  (iii) The provision of suitable access to the main highway network.

Within the inner areas the implementation of this policy is likely to require substantial intervention and investment by public authorities, particularly in the fields of land purchase and assembly, clearance of dereliction and obsolete services, levelling and re-instatement of the bearing quality of land, provision of main services and access, and the encouragement of development through the provision of loans and grants. This is because the costs of development in such areas are generally abnormally high as a result of past neglect and previous uses. Without the injection of public funds such areas would remain undeveloped, unused and unsightly. The assembly and preparation of large-scale new sites for industry is also likely to require action from public bodies in order to assemble land and provide main services and road and rail access. The District Councils and the Department of Industry (through the English Industrial Estates Corporation – EIEC), as well as the County Council have powers and responsibilities in this field. The County Council will consult with these other public agencies about their economic development programmes in the preparation of its own Economic Development Programme, particularly District Councils, EIEC, and Statutory Undertakers, in order to ensure that duplication is avoided, that the activities of the County Council and others are complementary, and that experience is shared.

Minimal attention to the analysis of past and present policies, in the preparation of plans reveals the lack of commitment among urban plan-makers to the concept of planning as an on-going managerial activity. We suggest that there is now an urgent need to broaden an understanding of policy implementation and assess its effectiveness. Failure to do so will certainly mean that policies will not be adapted effectively to changing circumstances. Without such knowledge, there is no way of knowing whether building in a degree of flexibility into policies, will in fact, be likely to produce the degree of flexibility upon implementation. And further, unless the mechanics of implementation are more fully understood, including the use made of powers, resources, influence and the need to maintain commitment, it is equally unlikely that policy will be managed effectively whether it is intended to be flexible or not.

Analysis of such situations requires a broad framework within which methods can be set. Page (1978) has postulated one such analytical framework which makes clear the need to study *structure, process* and *outcomes*. In this model 'Structure' refers to the statutory and non-statutory arrangements which shape the nature of central and local government and constrain policy-making behaviour. 'Process' refers to the activity of planning as affected by inter-governmental relationships, and 'outcomes' refer to the effects of the policies as they are implemented. The main contribution of such models of planning activity has been to make clear, not only the need to study outcomes, but also organizational structure and actor behaviour in the operation of the system.

Although the statutory context for urban planning is clearly defined, it is subject to change through political pressures and professional opinion. There is also considerable latitude for planners and politicians to operate within it and, in effect, to 'adapt' the system continuously from within. For example, they may choose to make use of certain powers and not others, or interpret situations more narrowly or broadly. A recent IOR (1978) report, in a discussion of the concept of the Scottish Regional Reports[4] as effective and adaptive policy vehicles, makes clear how an analysis which focuses on policies can reveal the behaviour of the actors in the way that they operate and adapt a planning system.

First, there is the need to identify the continuous process of *re-appreciation* of the local area by the actors, and in what ways they perceive people to be affected by the policies. Second, there is the need to analyse the process of *policy development*, much of which takes place within the framework of particular committees and departments within an authority. This process of adjustment will be influenced mainly by the need to adjust to levels of financial and other resources, and may be subject to political change. Third, there is the need to analyse the process of *inter-organizational* adjustment, given, as we have already seen, the large number of agencies which are involved in the process. Such analysis will need to observe a whole range of formal and informal channels through which planners and politicians make the process work.

It will now be clear that the vital contribution of a policy analytic approach is to reveal how policy emerges out of the whole context within which the actors operate. Clearly, urban planning *can* be viewed as such a policy process, for if this were not so, then strategic land use planning would suffer major discontinuities while planners deliberated about the preparation of their plans. It must be recalled that since 1947 most local planning authorities have undertaken just two major exercises in strategic land-use plan making (the earlier 1947-style Development Plans and more recent Structure Plans) though day-to-day decision making and implementation has been a far more continuous activity. However, it must also be stated that day-to-day decision making, if it is not to lead to longer-term inefficiencies and conflict, needs to be set in some kind of guiding context. Viewing the planning process as essentially a matter of continuous implementation of policy and adaption, places plans, policy documents and programmes firmly in the role of 'means' and not 'ends'. These are, in effect, the means of temporarily encapsulating the most important aspects of a situation. Their purpose is to facilitate communication and reflection: the measurement of achievement; the predicting of possible outcomes and consequences; co-ordination and the setting of future guidelines.

The question then arises as to how the 'technical' operations such as evaluation, monitoring and forecasting can best be developed to enhance such a policy process. Traditional thinking suggests that the most appropriate way in which to improve co-ordination between 'the plan' and 'the policy process' in an uncertain world, is by constantly trying to improve the quality of the plan by refining the use of analytical, forecasting and evaluative methods so as to better anticipate the future and select options which lead towards it. The conventional wisdom of a plan maker has found this approach attractive as it accords to the planner a clear, technical role, and in the use of methods a clear and self-evident sequence of operations – formulate ends; analyse; forecast or predict; derive options; evaluate alternatives; implement chosen policy; monitor in order to review and so on. In the light of our discussions, the weaknesses of the approach will be apparent, notably that the process of plan making, and the use of its attendant methodologies are artificially divorced from the policy process which they ought to inform. Whilst it is possible to postulate an idealized planning system in which these technical operations can serve the formulation of policy within a statutory planning programme, maintaining such a role in a dynamic policy environment has proved to be a difficult matter.

If urban land-use planning, at the strategic level, is regarded as a policy process, then, we would argue, a more realistic use of 'key' methods becomes available. First, it is no longer necessary to restrict the use of methods in a linear dependence. It can be suggested that the use of these methods needs to be related, not to each other (so that what can be readily forecast becomes the criterion for what should be monitored, or what can be evaluated becomes the criterion for deciding what should be forecast, and so on), but to the continuous policy process, as one policy situation is transformed into another. As already made clear, this transformation will happen whether an explicit plan is prepared or not, and the objective of preparing the plan in *parallel* to this transformation is that debate about further consequences may be more informed, that expectations can be spelled out, that data and analysis can be employed where they are judged to be relevant to 'explain' the transformation and so on. It is our firm view that the planners facing the need to enhance the quality of policy formulation, need to adopt such a stance in the use of methods. We discuss the more detailed implications in the following sections.

Evaluation

Evaluation can be regarded as the corner stone of attempting to improve the quality of planning activity and policies, and will involve making explicit value judgements about the worth of particular policies. As already noted, in that policy outcomes cannot be judged independently of the process and procedures by means of which the policy was formulated, it is a necessary part of the learning process to examine both the process and the outcome. It is relevant to ask not only 'has the policy achieved what was intended?' and (so that assessment is not seen simply as a means of steering events back towards a pre-determined goal) 'is the resulting situation preferable to what was intended?', but *also* to assess the role and performance of the system in reaching the new state of affairs.[5] Evaluation then should not only lead to the discovery of better policies and programmes to accomplish existing objectives, but directly to alteration of the objectives themselves and review of the performance of the system of implementation (Wildavsky, 1972). In broadening the scope of evaluation, however, a number of problems arise, not least, as Hickling et al. (1979) suggest, that there is little point in investing time and effort in developing a fuller understanding of the policy implementation process and assessing its contribution unless, ultimately, this is likely to lead to an increase in the confidence of decision makers in facing future decisions. In other words, it is necessary to have some clear idea of how increased knowledge is likely to lead to better decisions, and this requires relating the knowledge to the policy-making environment within which the various agencies operate. In Wildavsky's (1979) terms, evaluation is fundamentally about 'linking knowledge and understanding with power' in order to achieve what is believed to be worth pursuing.

One of the inherent weaknesses of current urban planning practice is that the question of 'who does the evaluating' is rarely directly faced. For example, there is considerable evidence that where evaluation methods have been employed by planners within the plan-making process, the range of options considered has been far from embracing the widest range of feasible alternatives that could have been considered in a given situation. There would appear to be advantages in freeing the use of evaluation methodology from the immediate processes of refining policy formulation into the broader perspective of performance assessment. And though it is clearly desirable that planners' professional skills and judgement are used in measuring and assessing policy performance, the additional insights of independent inquiry are also highly desirable. Although this would undoubtedly involve higher costs, the sharper perspective of independent judgement we would judge to be vital in order that policy can be developed in a way that is relevant to the perceived aims and needs of client groups. It is, then, important that evaluation should be a 'public activity' which can provide evidence and inform a wide-ranging debate about policies and outcomes, which in turn can influence decision makers. Independent assessment, through inquiry and the employment of the various research means that we have discussed, such as case study and attitude survey, are the effective means whereby the value that the community (whether as individuals or groups) places upon particular policy can be assessed.

Before setting down some criteria for this broader role, a general difficulty must be noted. Evaluation methods are a means to answering vital questions about the effects and the worth of policies. But, as Jenkins (1978) points out, this learning process is two-sided. It certainly can lead to better future policy, but evaluation will also exposure failures, reveal misjudged decisions, and weakness in present policy. It may well reveal implementation as a sometimes stumbling, pragmatic and illogical process as decision makers and implementers seek to match limited resources to aims and needs, and modify policy intentions to cope with shifting circumstances.

Yet, it should be realized that the link between implementation and evaluation is conceptually extremely strong. Indeed of all the methodologies that can be related to the activity of planning (forecasting, monitoring, and so on), it is evaluation which is the most difficult to distinguish conceptually from the implementation process itself (Jenkins, 1978). Essentially, this is because the act of policy implementation is itself a learning activity and hence will inform the actor not only about what his policy is doing, but will also cause him to reflect upon how achievement differs from expectations (as revealed by the 'tensions' (Chapter 7)) and will inevitably cause him to question the wisdom of one approach to the amelioration of a problem as compared to another.

Making a stronger link between policy implementation and evaluation activity by planners has several important implications. First, and arguably the most important, is that the *emphasis* of evaluation shifts from the 'evaluate in order to act mode' (that is seeing evaluation as a means simply of making explicit choice over selected, potential policy alternatives) to the 'evaluate in order to learn' mode. In this, evaluation is closely related to the management tasks of continuous policy adaption and review. This activity will be revealed by analysis of decision processes and the documentation surrounding the debates of that process. In this context, the role of the plan or policy document itself may not be very important. As Hickling *et al.* (1979) comment:

Published plans are to be seen as only one form of output, among many other tangible and intangible products, from a process in which many kinds of activity are intertwined – activities of monitoring, policy review, issue identification, work scheduling and day-to-day operation. (p. iii)

Keeping in mind the distinction made earlier as to the importance of evaluating both 'process and outcome', we can suggest the components upon which evaluation activity can be focused within a policy context. They are: (i) change; (ii) control; (iii) compliance, and (iv) commitment. Assuming for the moment that relevant information is available their importance for policy evaluation can be briefly discussed.

As we have already noted, the effects of policy implementation in a given urban situation will occasionally be dramatic, but more commonly will be partial, and may indeed be quite marginal. (This has some important implications for forecasting as we shortly discuss.) Evaluation of policy requires, at minimum, that a clear knowledge is obtained about changes in the urban environment and the ways in which particular policies can and have related to those changes.[6] The second component is that of control, and there are two related concerns that evaluation must address. First, any attempt to assess policy must relate the outcomes to the degree of control and powers that have been employed to effect the policy. Under this heading we must include the development and use of resources which, in themselves, are a form of power. We noted earlier how there is evidence that

later Structure Plans are making much more clear the relationship between
the policies and the powers to effect the intentions as planners come to
terms with the demands of implementation. Effective evaluation, then,
requires that the functions and operations of the power base are
understood. The second point is that the propensity of planners and their
authorities to use available powers varies. Indeed this variable, which will
reflect enthusiasm about policies, political commitment, practicability and
the expectations of results, can account for notable variations in the
performance of agencies and their programmes, even though apparently
endowed with the same or similar powers. Case studies, and attitude
surveys are important means of studying these variations.

Matters of change and control have featured in our earlier discussions,
but the questions of compliance and commitment related to evaluation we
should treat rather more fully. In any assessment of urban policy, the degree
of compliance on the part of the public and among implementing agencies
is an important variable. Consider a policy to exercise development
restraint in an area. How effective is such a policy? Is a would-be developer
persuaded to develop elsewhere by such a policy, or does he continue to
exert pressure in expectation of eventually being allowed to do so? In other
words, is the 'consumer's' reaction one of acceptance and the searching for
alternatives, or a greater resolve to achieve his original intention? Many
similar situations can be readily envisaged.

At a broader level, we have already noted how the Structure Plan does
not influence development necessarily directly, but is implemented through
a wide variety of other instruments (Local Plans, Water Development
Plans, Housing Plans, Transportation Plans, and so on) many of which are
operated by semi-autonomous agencies. The question then arises, what is
the degree of compliance on the part of these other agencies in their
attitudes towards the strategic land-use plan? While the Structure Plan is
the formal, publically accountable vehicle which should inform and guide
the various development programmes, this is not always so and an
important matter to assess is the extent to which the form and content of
the Plan *does* assist in the co-ordination of investment and development
activities. This is, however, no easy task given the complexity of the inter-
organizational linkages that influence the implementation of land-use
policy. Evaluating the degree of compliance can provide useful insights into
the effectiveness of organizational arrangements and use of powers. It can
be argued that a good plan is one which *in its implementation* can inspire
confidence on the part of investors, establish public credibility and the
compliance of the agencies who are instrumental in its implementation.

An important further question that evaluation can address is as to how
the Structure Plan can be used (and if necessary complemented by other
and less formal arrangements to secure development) to *co-ordinate* such
complex activity. Hickling *et al.* (1979) suggest that this can best be faced by
recognizing four main dimensions, each of which can be posed as an
evaluative need:

(i)   to assess progress in improving current decisions, relating to issues of present concern;

(ii) to assess progress in developing working relationships which are of future value to all concerned;

(iii) to assess progress in adaptation to wider systems to support future co-ordination; and

(iv) to assess progress in encouraging continuous deployment and growth of co-ordinative skills within continuous processes of strategic decision making. (p. 41)

As with all evaluation exercises it is necessary to establish the criteria by which assessment can be made. Drawing upon Hickling's work these four headings can be discussed in turn. First, there is the matter of attempting to improve the quality of current decisions. Hickling *et al.* suggests that this is largely a matter of confidence. A useful approach to evaluation might be to attempt to answer the following questions:

Are we avoiding mistakes (in implementation) that might otherwise have been made? Are we making more informed judgements about the use of real resources by reducing risks, of investing the wrong amount of resources in the wrong place at the wrong time? Are we cutting down the element of surprise as to what other people are intending to do? (p. 42)

It will be clear that such questions can be readily posed in terms of localized investment decisions, say, relating to the construction of a sewerage system, or road or housing scheme. However, for reasons that we have discussed, obtaining realistic measures in order to evaluate broader economic risks, say, are more problematical, and assessing the 'political risks' involved in public policy can be daunting. Also we must be aware that the implementation of policy itself will be an important independent variable in bringing about further reaction. This suggests that it may be preferable to face the matter of confidence directly rather than to attempt to refine the measurement of factors that are inherently immeasurable because of their dynamic and 'social' nature. Hickling *et al.* therefore suggest that the evaluative criteria should not be posed in terms of such measurements, but rather in terms of broader questions relating to more normative criteria. These will include commitment and also judgements about the utility of particular policies and the contribution that stated policies can make to a programme of implementation.

In attempting to improve the quality of future decisions, the attainment of co-ordination between implementing agencies will be a key factor. Here an evaluative question might be posed differently, for example,

it is felt that any gain in confidence (say, from the carrying out of surveys, or analysis) will be sufficient to justify the necessary resources, in respect of this co-ordinating activity, given that *each* agency involved in the implementation process is likely to view the value of a policy or programme in its own terms. (p. 43)

Viewed from this perspective, no single evaluative criterion can be established. It is then more relevant to know whether or not the degree of

effort required to achieve some co-ordinated approach has in ,
contributed to more effective implementation as seen by those who woulɯ.
have to provide the additional effort and resources to achieve it.[7]

There is currently much concern both by planners and 'users' as to how
the credibility of plans can be sustained over time (Boynton, 1979). For a
plan, to be effective, needs to provide clear, consistent and firm guidance,
yet it needs to be adaptable to changing circumstances. It needs to be seen
as publicly accountable, which implies a degree of consultation and
participation which is not only time-consuming but often appears to be an
inefficient means of informing the decision-making process. This can also
reduce flexibility by foreclosing options. To achieve a set of policies to
display flexibility where that is judged to be a virtue, and firm guidance
where that is to be achieved, is the major test of urban policy making. The
essential point we make here is that a plan's success or otherwise in this
respect relates directly to its credibility and hence is likely to be reflected in
the degree of compliance experienced in implementation. These are
then important considerations for evaluation.

The fourth heading, commitment, also refers to the actions of individuals
in the implementing of plans, but is a feature which may only indirectly
relate to the quality of the plan itself. The research implication is that, in
order to evaluate the role of policy, we must study the way in which
individuals behave within their respective agencies. Here we recognize that,
in a continuous policy process, individuals are continuously seeking to
make commitments in a pragmatic way, by responding to economic and
political circumstances and uncertainty about the implementation of policy
and its likely outcomes.

As Hickling *et al.* comment, the role for evaluation is to attempt to
answer such questions as whether there are general principles or precepts of
a managerial nature which can clarify the relevant options that face a
decision maker (where that is appropriate and believed to be useful) and
reveal more clearly the likely consequences of a commitment to a given
policy or programme of action. Evaluation of the co-ordinative activity of
individuals (and their organizations) within the planning process, ought to
lead to an understanding, not only of its contribution to the effective
management of urban planning processes, but also towards a more
conscious employment of management skills, and review of the Structure
Plan. Whilst the resolution of the mutual dependency of agencies and actors
must, to some extent, depend upon the existence of a clear policy, and
mechanisms for the formal exchange of information and consultations, it is
probably even more dependent upon the willingness or commitment of the
actors to 'make the system work'. For it is only at this level that the
inevitable inefficiencies of statutory and managerial processes will either be
raised to obstacles or reduced to minor hindrances which can be readily
overcome (Jowell, 1977).

Following a detailed case study on this theme, Hickling *et al.* (1979) came
to the conclusion that:

m of co-ordinating initiatives seen in practice involved negotiation of
ments across organizational boundaries, and others called for formal
mmitment within the initiating organization alone, *others could be*
informally by individuals in the way they handled their personal
s with others or in the way they contributed to informal group
emphasis added)

... ... course of the case studies it was found that all these levels of
initiative could be mutually re-inforcing in achieving the effective
implementation of policy. In order to make judgements about the success
and failure of actors' behaviour, it was found that several levels of
evaluation were called for, namely:

(i)   To assess success or failure in dealing confidently with current issues.
(ii) To assess success or failure in building up mutual understanding as a
      basis for more effective co-ordination on future issues.
(iii) To assess success or failure in making the Development Plan system
      a more effective vehicle for the development of co-ordinating
      practice.
(iv) To assess success or failure in moving towards continuity in the
      application of co-ordinative skill on which must depend the smooth
      management and implementation of policy and thus the effective use
      of resources by public authorities and private enterprises alike.

This discussion will have revealed the major implications of broadening
the concept of evaluation to embrace both the outcomes of policy and the
process out of which it emerges. Whilst, any systematic approach to policy
evaluation ought to help organizations and individuals engaged in the
process to better understand the problems that they face, commitment from
individuals is vital to achieve any positive policy outcome. But equally, lack
of *relevant* information is a serious handicap, and with this in mind we turn
to consider the question of monitoring.

Monitoring

The traditional view of monitoring within the planning process (Chapter 3)
is that of a 'control' in which the outcomes of the planning and
development processes are observed, for example by 'indicators' such as
population change, house building starts, changes in residential densities,
traffic flows, and so on. These changes are then related to the intentions of
the plan with the explicit intention of finding out in what areas and in what
directions implementation and/or policies might need to be changed in
order to bring the plan back 'on target'.[8] But, as Floyd (1978) comments,
this approach can only be relevant to situations in which all the
uncertainties surrounding the choices of alternative planning strategies
could be eliminated at the survey stage: where a complete understanding of
their implications could be acquired during analysis; and where no major
change would occur in the plans and in their environment during
implementation.

In planning policy terms, these assumptions can never be met and we should usefully reconsider the concept of monitoring within the planning process. It is a serious concern that the development of relevant and effective monitoring has not received the attention, for example, that has been given to forecasting by planners.[9] Yet it is a vital concept to any adaptive process (Haynes, 1974), but must not be seen as the mere gathering of data. This is hardly likely to reveal much of direct benefit to making any assessment of policy effectiveness, unless the monitoring is closely coupled to the policy implementation activity itself. Many of the traditional monitoring indicators used by planners, such as population and even employment change, have proved quite inadequate as meaningful measures, because they neither reveal the effects of policy implementation quickly or uniquely enough. It has therefore proved quite impossible to distinguish policy effects from other autonomous components of change. With this in mind, we suggest some guidelines to ensure that monitoring develops as a full and relevant methodology *within* the planning process.

A widely subscribed starting point is to establish a clearer perspective on the proper role and operation of monitoring activity (Haynes, 1974; Floyd, 1978; Wenban-Smith, 1979). Primarily, monitoring must be the means to a continuous assessment of the relevance and contribution of plans and policies to unfolding and dynamic problems and issues. It must, then, be a dynamic activity in itself, capable of adjustment to what is believed to be worth knowing about the performance of policies. In this role, it is not sufficient that monitoring should focus only upon changing circumstances and trends but, additionally, that it should be the means to relate such knowledge to the practical implementation of policies. Monitoring then, should be capable of revealing not only the extent to which policies are, in fact, contributing to the resolution of strategic issues, but also as to whether changing values, unforeseen problems and even new opportunities, are suggesting the need to modify policies or to put forward new ones.[10]

It will become clear that we are suggesting that monitoring must not be conceptualized as a detached technical exercise, though the collection of *relevant* data and information may well be organized as technical tasks.[11] Rather monitoring must be seen at the very focus of the coupling between technical and political activity in the planning process. There are fundamental questions to be faced about what should be monitored, and in what form, which can only be answered at a political level in order that relevant data are obtained.[12] Initially, it may well be that the most relevant data about a policy outcome may not be readily expressed in a quantitative form. For example, it may be desirable to know whether or not a policy exercising restraint over the allocation of residential land can in fact be implemented, given that such a policy may require co-ordinated action by different agencies.[13] Equally, it may be highly relevant to know of the reactions of those upon whom the policy is to be imposed and the extent to which they may comply. Vital information about such matters can be obtained in 'soft data' form long before any effects of the policy reveal themselves through measures such as rates of house building and population change.

In the design of monitoring operations, it is important to note the extent to which agencies other than the local planning authority are active in the policy environment. Normally, many other agencies' policies will be at work, including central government's regional policies, water and transport agencies, and other local government departments in the fields of housing, education and social services. Effective policy monitoring will need to keep abreast of the activities of these agencies, *their* policies and changes, and most importantly, the effectiveness with which they are implemented.

If monitoring activity is to serve the refinement of decisions about the validity and relevance of policies, or cast light upon the assumptions which underpin those policy decisions, then monitoring itself needs to concern equally implementation and outcome. For example, it may be found that some policies cannot be implemented. In other cases a 'problem' may 'move on' so that the policy is no longer relevant, or conflicting opinions about priorities and use of resources among differing agencies (whose effective co-operation is required to implement a policy) may thwart implementation. Attempting to monitor outcomes only may never reveal anything of significance. On the other hand, monitoring the behaviour of those engaged in implementation may reveal a great deal, particularly the need for change in working practices which can help to keep a policy effective, even though the policy itself and its objectives may remain unchanged. Monitoring, then, needs to be broadly conceived, closely coupled to implementation and adaptive in itself.

Experience of a large number of planning authorities who are embarking on monitoring exercises has already revealed some serious weaknesses. Many existing planning policies have been couched in forms which prevent, or at least inhibit, accurate and valid monitoring. Several points should be noted. First, there is again the matter of the use of powers. We noted earlier that the past ten years or so had been characterized by a diversity in the number of planning instruments available to local authorities and a broadening of interventional powers under a growing body of legislation. In order to assess the effective use made of these powers and instruments it is necessary for the authority to have made clear in its policies how the various powers were to be used. Many planning policies are so bland as to give little indication as to how powers, let alone resources are to be used.

Second, arising from the same point, making any quantitative assessment of achievement is difficult. A policy which sets targets, say for housing development, or the release of land, is clearly more monitorable in its progress than one which merely offers a bland commitment to a 'continued programme of development'. There is, however, a conflict which must be recognized. Precise policies, while more readily monitored, may not be favoured by an authority. There are two reasons. The first is because they may 'indirectly' set targets which can become norms in making development control decisions. Second, they can deprive authorities of the ability to revise their policies by subtle changes in implementation without having to draw attention publicly to the 'target' implications of the change. In short, the need for clearly monitored policies may well conflict with the desire of an authority to retain sufficient flexibility by a more covert approach to policy wording.

This suggests that a clear understanding of the nature and underlying meaning of policy statements is vital to a proper appreciation of monitoring possibilities (Bracken, 1980a). A useful distinction can be made between policies that set limits upon some expected outcomes (assuming successful implementation) and policies which more directly attempt to prescribe the way in which a choice of action should be made (Friend, 1977). As Floyd (1978) shows, many of the policies of structure plans belong to the objective or 'target' type and in effect they are designed not to secure some precise implementation, but rather to set a context for subsequent decisions. For these, effective monitoring is problematical. More positive, prescriptive policies, which are clearer in their implications, ought to be capable of more precise assessment. Floyd (1978) gives examples of forms that this type of policy can take:

(i)   policies can indicate an appropriate response to a particular situation (for example, in permitting a development application of a particular kind);
(ii) policies can outline the factors which are to be taken into account in taking a development decision;
(iii) policies can set discretionary limits to the range of options from which a choice of subsequent action can be made; and
(iv) policies can formulate more precisely the way in which choice of action should be taken according to external circumstances.

Yet a further useful distinction can be made between the monitoring of an authority's own decisions and investment and the extent to which other agencies (both private and public) have conformed to the policies advocated by the authority. As Floyd points out, there are several practical problems to be faced which relate to our earlier discussion about the commitment of organizations towards policies and their assessment. For example, an authority is quite unlikely to support any monitoring programme which will reveal its own failure to meet a stated policy commitment. Equally, an organization may be keen to be seen to conform with the policies of another agency (including central government) where that is a necessary part of political bargaining. There can be other such effects too. For example, failure of an agency to conform with the policy of a planning authority, as revealed by its monitoring may well result in increased tension in inter-organizational relationships. Ultimately, failure of one agency to conform to the policies of another may give rise to a demand for increased powers by one to exercise greater control over the other.

It was noted earlier that the facility with which a particular policy can be monitored depends upon the way that it has been phrased. A policy which includes a quantitative specification or target – 'to build so many houses by

1986', etc. – can be readily monitored in its progress. However, rarely will the path of policy achievement be smooth and it then becomes highly relevant to ask a whole set of related questions about a particular policy performance. Again Floyd (1978) has provided some guidance and suggested the type of questions that are relevant:

(i)   Is the incidence of the type of development to which the policy refers changing in some measurable way?

(ii) How much difficulty is being experienced by implementers in securing compliance with the policy intention?

(iii) Are there difficulties being experienced which can be attributed to changing autonomous circumstances since the policy was formulated?

(iv) Are conflicts emerging between policy intentions that were not foreseen?

(v)   Does the scope and content of the policy being considered need revision?

It is crucial to effective policy monitoring that such questions should be *regularly* addressed to the policy options and statements of a plan, and it will be clear that the blending of numerical data on performance obtained via surveys etc, and 'softer' information through broader research methods, will be vital. The latter will reveal changing attitudes and perceptions among professional and lay actors involved in the process, and public response as revealed by local discussion, and as reported by lobbying, letters, press comment and so on. Essentially, then, monitoring will involve the handling of information in a variety of 'hard' and 'soft' forms, for which general classifying and ordering procedures have already been discussed (Chapter 5). In the development of monitoring systems for strategic land use planning, four main headings have been suggested as a classifying framework, which effectively summarize the holistic approach (SDD, 1979). These relate to the main purposes of monitoring, as:

(i)   The need to demonstrate progress in the application of Structure Plan policies and proposals. For example, a proposal to develop a certain amount of land would require continual monitoring to check whether the threshold had been reached which would 'trigger' the need to review development control policies.

Examples of the type of information which it is appropriate to collect in informing this area are development control decisions, records of rates of development and records of land availability.

(ii) The need to test the effectiveness of policies in relation to key issues and objectives. For example, a periodic check of housing development would be required to see if the community's need for dwellings had been met.

Relevant data here will include information on local authority capital programmes, transportation and housing plans, progress on local plan preparation, housing returns, records of rates of development or progress in specified projects, records of land availability, and regular information from service departments.

(iii) The need to test the relevance of the Structure Plan policies and proposals in the light of change. For example, the passage of time may reveal the need to adjust policies in relation to objectives affected by political or social changes.

Examples of information about political change are: central government circulars; new legislation, policy and organizational changes in the public or private sector. Understanding of changes will be obtained from programmes and reports of other agencies; records of planning applications not in accordance with structure plan policy; reports dealing with resources for implementation, and so on. Public reaction to policies and events can be assessed through national and local press, and the results of publicity and consultative procedures.

Finally:

(iv) The need to test the assumptions that led to the definition of the key issues and main objectives of the Structure Plan. For example, the specification of industrial land requirements could depend on an assumption about the trend in, say, structural change in industrial employment, or more generally in industrial investment.

Examples of information about political change are: central government General's) estimates of population and projections, reviews of forecasts for housing demand and supply, employment data and so on. Also the various censuses of population, employment and (retail) distribution.

Clearly, the type of information which will be used by differing authorities in reviewing plans and policies will vary, but we should note the limitations of aggregate data for effective monitoring. Data relating to population, employment and housing, for example, are often difficult to relate to policy implementation at the local level. Attributing change to a policy effect is often problematical, not only because the policy is unlikely to reveal its effects uniquely through a given element of data, but because much 'official' data are published infrequently (as with a census), and therefore only report on a situation with a considerable lapse of time. Moreover, some official data, for example the mid-year population estimates, are not objective in the sense of census data, but are themselves estimates which reflect the *expected* effects of various government and local government policies, notably the release of residential land. There is a considerable, and recognized, risk of circular reasoning in such estimates. Also, given that the policy changes which local planners might wish to observe are unlikely to be revealed by such data over periods of time up to say five years, such aggregate data are limited in the extent to which they can usefully inform a policy monitoring process.

We suggest that a more appropriate basis for monitoring lies in the rigorous collating of information relating to *local* development processes. A good example might be the conduct of local studies of floorspace in relation to workers in different kinds of industry and commerce. Such data can be obtained directly from development approval records for new development, but much change occurs within the urban system which does not fall under the heading of new development. These can be typified by changes in occupational densities. Here, planners must rely upon carefully focused local study in areas where such change is believed to be well represented. Such data are vital if planners are to effectively monitor and understand the *dynamic* nature of the inter-relationships and hence better understand the complexity of links between policy and non-policy effects.

A closely related matter is the way in which information, however obtained, will be *used* by planners and policy makers. Data and information, whether derived from official sources, from local empirical studies, as subjective indicators, or 'hard' information, can be used in a variety of ways, that is, in more than one theoretical context. Fundamentally, it is a matter of judgement as to how much significance should be attached to it (Sheldon and Freeman, 1970; Rose, 1972). In designing and operating a monitoring system it is vital that there should be awareness of the ways in which the data and information are to be used. We can usefully draw attention to a classification by Rose (1972) which will provide some guiding principles.

The first point is to note that policy makers are essentially eclectic, that is, they will utilize and draw upon many different kinds of information, which they will regard or discard according to their needs. As has been widely experienced in urban planning, policy makers rarely see anything particularly special about 'hard', numerical data; indeed they are often suspicious of it. Essentially, the policy maker needs information which *he* can understand, though this is not to be taken as a reason for limiting its scope. Rather, it means that information needs to be clearly related to the concepts with which the policy maker is familiar (which means policies) and which he can relate readily to the necessary judgements that he has to make. Beyond this, he will tend to disregard information, however valid in itself. In the design of monitoring activity, it is relevant to ask if it is possible to explain why policy makers may accept the validity of some information and indicators, and reject others.[14] Or why some initiate and sanction surveys and others do not do so in very similar circumstances. Perceptions of relevance are clearly important and these can be interpreted as 'costs' in obtaining and processing the data. Rose (1972) suggests that there are four such cost factors which offer an explanation.

First, there is the *true cost* of obtaining data and information. In urban planning, the majority of data are traditionally obtained from national surveys (e.g. censuses) and paid for by central government. For a local authority these data are 'cheap' even if special 'small area' tabulations are required. The main local cost lies in the need for skilled manpower to undertake analysis and provide selected information. As already noted, much of these data are very general relative to the policy needs of planning authorities.[15] But, in extending the quality and scope of the 'local' data base, the real cost of data becomes increasingly apparent. Local policy makers may well need to be persuaded of the necessity to make available the necessary resources and this will be affected by the second factor.

This is termed the *cost in value* conflict. Any information which (even potentially) is in conflict with a policy maker's established views and values will tend not to be welcome. After all, to accept its relevance may well force him to alter the very premises by which he has justified a policy. In such a situation, the tendency of the policy maker will be to advocate a 'cheap' alternative, namely to deny the usefulness of information; or postpone a survey or even to misperceive the information. Two paradoxes arise. As such action will tend to defend the *status quo*, this may not be in the long-term interests of either the policy maker or the community. The researcher or planner has an important role to play in identifying the long-term implications. Second, there is a tendency for the most controversial matters to be starved of data (when more information might be extremely valuable) and, conversely, for data to be collected about the least controversial matters which may not serve any very useful purpose.

Third, there are the 'costs' of *action* which relate to the utility that policy makers assign to new information in that it may imply a disturbance of the *status quo*. Acquiring information which clearly indicates the need for new policy can all too readily lead to pressure for a commitment to expenditure which policy makers might not want to face. The fourth 'costs' are, in contrast, the costs of *inaction*. These typically arise when maintaining the *status quo* becomes increasingly difficult due to changing (usually deteriorating) conditions in some policy area. Impending political crises; new elections; a deterioration in an issue, such as housing; increased pressure group or lobby activity, may all provoke policy makers into a sudden request for 'new information'. When the costs of inaction become high relative to the costs of action, there is often a sudden and strong inducement on the part of the policy maker to 'do something'.

In summary, the argument is that it is reasonable to expect that policy makers will only sanction monitoring where the perceived utility of its data is greater than the costs that can be set against it.[16] This 'political' dimension poses a considerable challenge in the design of any monitoring and information service. Policy makers need to be made aware of the value of long-term, well-conducted study and in order that change can be understood. Above all this requires that a consistent view of events worthy of being monitored is held which should not be jeopardized by political expediency. Equally, any long-term system needs to be flexible enough to accommodate and make good use of data which will result from such expedient demands. While there is no easy resolution of this, a constant dialogue is necessary to establish both a long-term commitment to monitoring events that are believed to be worth monitoring, and efficient channels to ensure that relevant short-term data are communicated in which policy makers are likely to have particular confidence.

In practice, Rose (1972) suggests that the most effective way to ensure that data and information are used by policy makers is to link the utility of information to the costs of *inaction*.[17] While the utility of new information is sometimes difficult to assess, the costs of inaction can often be made quite explicit to policy makers through the monitoring process. Examples include a deterioration in housing availability; shortages of development land, or increasing traffic congestion. It is argued that such information tends to have powerful effects upon decision makers who are normally wary of any situation which will imply a lack of foresight and result in blame for incurring greater costs in the long run.

A final comment should be made concerning the organizational and reporting arrangements within an authority for its monitoring activity. Inevitably, in considering the most effective ways in which information can be made available to personnel within organizations, there are conflicting requirements. As Floyd (1978) points out,

there is a need to ensure that information flows – especially of intelligence – are facilitated by the organizational arrangements and that the information that is often found only in the heads of individuals can be brought to bear on issues and choices as they arise.

This is reflected in the attention given by many local authorities to the collaboration between different sections and includes the use of specialist teams to facilitate information flow.[18] However, any new organizational structures cut across traditional lines of communication which can inhibit the availability of information and intelligence within the system.[19]

Forecasting

In Part 1, comment was made as to the limitations of the presently used methods for forecasting within the urban planning process. These broadly treat the subject material in a sectoral way, producing estimates independently for population, housing, employment and transportation changes, though often loosely linking the sectors so that for example population estimates feed into employment or housing estimates. Sometimes, the coupling is reversed and population estimates are derived by incorporating housing and employment estimates. Further, refinement has occurred in which the sectoral estimates are more closely coupled and this can ensure a higher degree of internal consistency in the production of population, employment and household estimation for a given area (Madden, 1976; Cockhead, 1978; Breheny and Roberts, 1978, 1979).

While displaying distinguishing features, these approaches broadly fall within the traditional mode of planning forecasting, relying heavily upon published official data, and well-established sectoral estimating methodology, including the cohort-survival population model, activity rate and headship rate estimation, and so on. These approaches have proved themselves to be quick and cost-effective and readily understood. They also suffer disadvantages which become more critical as attention focuses upon the need to relate forecasts to the implementation and effectiveness of policy. In this section, we examine some important implications for the use of forecasting methods in planning which arise when the primacy of policy as the focus of planning activity is fully recognized. This will complement the earlier discussions of evaluation and monitoring.

There are, of course, inherent problems to be faced in *all* forecasting, which is an activity aiming, in effect, to continuously erode infinite uncertainty. Four particular disadvantages of conventional planning forecasts, however, can be readily identified. First, the forecasts start from a static sectoral base and attempt to predict the future of a dynamic system. They therefore involve considerable simplifying assumptions. For example, the inter-relationship between, say, housing, employment and migration, which clearly contributes to a large part of the dynamic of the local development process, is poorly understood and poorly resolved in making forecasts. Second, the quality of information available varies enormously as we have already noted, both between and *within* the various sectors. Information all too frequently reflects general, national needs rather than local sensitivities and, as a result, even sectoral forecasts contain all kinds of inadequacies due to the unbalanced nature of the data base. Local 'adjustments' are frequently incorporated by planners with scant empirical foundation. One might imagine that a priority in the planning process would be to assemble data and information in such a way that consistency could be attained. Yet it would seem that an inadequate overview of the proper role and nature of forecasting within the process has prevented this until quite recently.

Third, given the variation in the quality of the data base, and a lack of understanding of the sectoral linkages, there is no great evidence of an awareness of the effect of this variation on the robustness of the forecasts themselves. So that 'errors' resulting from one part of the forecasting exercise are frequently (and conveniently) obscured in subsequent use of the output in another part of the exercise. Fourthly, the development of conventional forecasting methods in urban planning has been heavily dominated by 'supply' considerations,[20] that is in respect of population 'supply' (people), labour 'supply' (workforce) and household 'supply' (households). In contrast, urban planners far more rarely make systematic attempts to forecast the 'demand' side of the equation. Reasons for this appear to be on two levels. First, the estimation of labour demand (job availability) and housing demand (provision of dwellings) requires a greater use of time and resources in order to undertake the necessary research and analysis, and moves planners away from the ready and cheap availability of official data. Second, and more fundamentally, it requires that planners develop a much clearer perspective upon the driving forces of the local development process to which, traditionally, they have adopted a passive role. It will be clear that failure to effectively encompass both sides of the equation within a forecasting exercise which purports to inform a policy-based activity will reveal its inadequacies all too quickly, as the assumptions upon which they are based are seen to be at variance with events.

An alterntive is that 'supply'-based estimates could be of greater value where they are linked to explicit, political advocacy statements of policy intention,[21] rather than their traditional use in an attempt to 'technically justify' a particular policy.

While much can be done to develop a better understanding of the linkages between the 'components of change' such as population, employment, household formation *and* the development of the local economy and its associated development process,[22] two outstanding issues remain unresolved. These, we would argue, are crucial to the development of improved forecasting for urban planners. Both have been raised already in earlier discussion. The first is how the degree of *control* that can be exercised by a planning authority over various types of real world change should be incorporated into the forecasting framework. The second, which follows, is how realistic assessments of policy implementation and success can be incorporated.

As De Jouvenal (1968) has pointed out, considering the future is always a combination of guesses and decisions in different mixtures according to the relationships between the phenomenon being considered and the actors' power to intervene. In some situations, planning may merely monitor and respond to a dynamic system *which itself* will set the pattern for the future. On the other hand, positive planning intervention, by restricting or promoting development, may enable a choice of futures to be offered. This has long been recognized as for example in Popper's (1972) distinction between *prophecy* – as a passive reaction to foreseeable events – and *prediction* – which seeks to grapple with future events. In Cross's (1972) terms this distinction is succinctly made in the terms 'reactive adaptation' and 'predictive control', and this can be readily related to our earlier discussion in Chapter 1 (figure 1.2) about the modes in which it is possible to conceive a planning system and the role of methodology within them.

We suggest that, to make effective the use of methods, planners need to hold a clear view as to the nature of the system that they operate within defined, particularly in terms of the degree of control that *can* be exercised. It is then possible to develop and use methods in a way that pays proper regard not only to events and policies, but the effects that each has on the other (Hoem, 1973). The need then to conceptualize forecasting and policy making as mutually complementary activities is vital, for each constrains the other.

Forecasting maintains a running representation, projected into the future of how things are going, and how, as assumptions they may be expected to go. The second [policy making] maintains a set of standards, projected into the future, which defines the state of affairs to be attained or maintained and defines a set of on-going actions designed to attain or maintain these states. (Vickers, 1974: 639)

 Thus, a vital distinction needs to be maintained between the monitoring of autonomous forces on the one hand and policy-based forecasting of activities on the other and a convenient terminology is to refer to the former as *projections* and the latter as *predictions*[23] (Breheny and Roberts, 1978). Study of many contemporary planning reports will reveal the extent to

Figure 9.1 A forecasting framework for planning

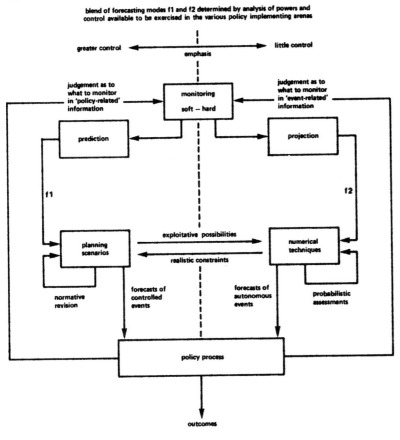

which this distinction is inadequately appreciated in practice (Mort, 1978). Figure 9.1 summarizes diagrammatically the principle that we advocate.[24]

We suggest that as a first step to enhance the quality of forecasting activity in urban planning, planning authorities should carefully and explicitly assess the extent of control that they can exercise over the development process (whether in terms of promotion or restraint). Research methods by which this might be achieved have already been discussed. Second, the effectiveness of this influence as empirically observed, needs to be related to the powers and influence that the authority has or can anticipate having in the future in order to produce forecasts. Forecasting of events should reflect the probability of success in using powers and the exercise of influence over events which will normally be only partially under direct or even indirect control.

A revised model which can guide the preparation of forecasts within the planning process can be postulated as follows:

(i)   The planning authority needs to truthfully and critically evaluate the powers which it has at its disposal.

(ii) It should undertake a programme of public participation geared to obtaining information on two matters: one is the identification of what are seen to be significant issues and problems in the area (rather as public participation is seen currently); but, further, participation, together with the views of elected members, should set the degree of intervention desired by the authority in tackling its perceived problems. This will be subject to the constraints of (i) above.

(iii) The authority should undertake analysis of its local economy and associated development processes. As we have noted, this is an area of great weakness in current practice (Barras, 1978b). The implications for forecasting were noted by Parry Lewis (1973) who makes the simple though fundamental point, that a great deal of traditional forecasting can be criticized in that it is not based upon any real understanding of the processes or the phenomenon that is the subject of the forecast. A suitable framework for such an analysis has been proposed by Barras and Broadbent (1979), onto which an authority could map its own classification of powers and its political resolve to intervene in the development process.[25]

(iv) From this analysis will come a clear perspective on the data and information needed to understand the nature of and effect of existing policies for intervention and the requirements to produce forecasts, which will recognize explicitly the extent of intervention that the authority wishes to employ.

Clearly, the balance between the forecasts produced on the assumptions of continuous trends and the modification of trends by the effective implementation of policies will depend upon the differing political wills of each authority. Under conditions of development pressure, and healthy levels of investment, it is clear that the strategic forecasts can be influenced more by the 'creative control' position of the authority. On the other hand, an authority faced with the prolonged run-down of traditional industries, and low growth prospects, rural depopulation and so on, needs to rely more upon forecasts of the 'predictive' type and for the authority to adopt a position of advocacy.

The important point is that the conceptual basis of this distinction is fully appreciated, and that an appropriate blend of methods is employed. This can clearly vary not only between circumstances but between the sectors within one plan or policy document, as well as, of course, over time. It is thus possible to envisage a different blend of forecasting approaches within one operation which might treat differently the forecasting of strong restraints over residential development from the active promotion of industrial development in an area where population had recently grown rapidly but jobs were limited. Such an area typically might be found currently on the fringe of a large conurbation.

In other words, it is not to be expected that a unitary approach to forecasting is necessary across the sectors of a plan for which the exercise of control might vary considerably. In principle, then, we are suggesting that, if the strategic planning forecasting is to mature into a policy-relevant exercise, it needs to move away from the position of regarding the local development process simply as a reality to which it must respond. Rather, such forecasting needs to be in terms of the policies to initiate change and the powers available to effect the policies.

But, further, strategic planning forecasting needs a new perspective because of the increased uncertainty surrounding the urban environment at the beginning of the 1980s. Planning will only remain a credible activity if it is seen to be capable of making more plausible forecasts of events than hitherto, and developing ways of quicker and more flexible responses to changing and unforeseeable circumstances, some of which, as we have seen, will be the unanticipated outcomes of present policies. In this light, the importance of a policy focus for the closer and more functional integration of evaluation, monitoring and forecasting becomes clear. In short, the revised paradigm needs to develop a coherent and consistent framework which gives a meaning to the role of these key operations. Without this, any re-arrangement of operations will amount to an unsystematized tinkering with the planning process.

Two main implications can be identified from this line of thinking (Bracken and Hume, 1981). First, the present use of planning techniques, particularly of evaluation, monitoring and forecasting, does not adequately accommodate a view of planning focused upon issues of control and power. Indeed the relationships which we argue need to be identified so as to inform the need for policy (and hence permit realistic forecasts) are not capable of clear analysis by conventional planning techniques and data. The main requirements are a shift in balance so that a much higher level of local information is incorporated to complement official data, and a shift from attempting an exclusively objective analysis of trends to a complementary analysis of the behaviour and performance of agencies and actors within the planning process at the local level.

This means that in making forecasts, planning should become more consciously eclectic in the sources from which it draws its experience, technique and indeed, inspiration. It can be suggested that in attempting to provide a pseudo-technical justification for policy, planners have neglected rich sources of experience in a broader but more selective data and information base. Two possibilities exist for the exercise of such selectivity. The traditional route lies in the identification of problems and issues, but without necessary regard to the potential for implementation. The alternative, is to proceed directly from a policy position on what are regarded as being the most crucial areas in the implementation of policies and where revision or modification may be appropriate.

Analysis then must take place at two levels. There will necessarily always be present an immediate technical level which will focus upon the on-going changes in the socio-economic and physical land-use systems. This, if well conducted, may lead to an understanding of underlying processes. To make useful forecasts, however, such analysis needs to be complemented, and guided by analysis at the policy level. Indeed, explanation of phenomena can only be achieved by an integration of these two levels of analysis.

A reading of Structure Plans will reveal how little explicit anticipation of the potential and problems of policy implementation is formally set down. Contingency or fallback positions, or alternative conditional positions which might be called into operation if unexpected events occur or if policy produces unanticipated outcomes, are rarely admitted. Clearly, better quality forecasts would enable a greater degree of anticipation of unexpected outcomes. Much public policy, and urban planning policy in particular appears muddled and based more upon hopes and wishful thinking rather than a realistic assessment of policy aims *and* achievements. Not surprisingly, evaluation is poor in these circumstances and informative monitoring is problematical. In general, it is clear that emphasis over the past ten years or so on plan making rather than policy review and updating has clouded the issue.

What guidelines, then, can be suggested by which planners can improve on this situation? Given a recognition that contemporary public policy is both partial, *and* also varies considerably between the sectors it addresses (housing, employment, etc.) and that policy analytic methods are available to study policy both before, during and after implementation, a set of guiding principles can be set down. Using De Jouvenal's (1967) insights, the key is for the authority to identify the *points of fulcrum* on which policies exert their influence to deflect the course of events. To identify these, an explicit conceptualization of the local development process is vital, linked to an assessment of the powers (including resources) available to make policies work, and an assessment of the political will of the authority to maintain a commitment to implementation. While it is not possible at this time to set down a complete prospectus for this development, reference to current work will help to explain the potential.

On the employment side, work by Bovaird (1978) shows how an assessment can be made of the effectiveness of local authority influence on employment trends and which can be developed into a coherent framework for the analysis of local authority intervention. The analytical approach focuses upon policies geared to the objective of increasing local income levels and job opportunities. The framework incorporates a number of segments (investments, wage levels, and so on) linked to hypotheses which, in turn, are related to the creation of income. Against this analysis Bovaird reviews the powers available to intervene in this sector for the creation and maintenance of employment, ranging from technical and financial advice, 'key worker' housing provision, investment subsidies and infrastructure provision. This form of analysis offers a clear and realistic framework within which planners can identify the 'point of function' by means of which they can direct the system. These, in turn, will provide key foci for forecasting exercises. It also means that a probabilistic view can be taken of the likely effect of intervention at each point of fulcrum, which opens up the possibility of a more probabilistic approach to forecasting (as we shortly discuss) and makes possible the incorporation into the forecast of judgements about the *degree* of control that is likely to be exercisable. This, for example, makes it possible to explicitly incorporate and anticipate political change (and hence changes in powers) into the forecasts.

Whilst the framework is elegant, it is at an early stage of development and is capable of refinement, notably by distinguishing the treatment of employment by sectors, or investment linkages, or multi-locational decision making and so on.

In the field of housing, there is evidence of a similar approach to analysis. For example, it is widely recognized that the determinants of migration vary with spatial scale (Cordey-Hayes and Gleave, 1974), so that housing opportunities are influential in short-distance migrating moves, while longer distance moves are stimulated by employment opportunities. But in the preparation of Structure Plans, it is clear that planners conceptualize the housing market and its operations in no clearer a manner than they do the local economy. Reliance upon aggregate past-trends data often reveals little of help in formulation of policy, and even less to understanding. It is clear that much of the uncertainty which makes policy making difficult derives from this lack of understanding. So, in addition to a policy-based model of the local authority influence on the local economy, there is a need for a similar model of public intervention in the housing market. It is not too optimistic to suggest that these 'key activity' policy-based analytical frameworks provide the possibility of a greatly enhanced capability to develop understanding of such variables as migration, journey to work patterns, household formation and so on.

A useful approach which can be cited in the housing field is that of Crofton and Webster (1974), indeed the following quotation is highly relevant to this whole discussion.

It is important to understand the ways in which the operation of the market prevents the realisation of policy objectives and causes policy changes to have unforeseen consequences. Not only do governments make exaggerated claims for the effectiveness of their policies and play down those processes whose existence is embarrassing for them, but there are also wide-spread failures of understanding among officials and professionals as well as politicians and the general public. (p. 839)

Their approach to analysis focuses upon the allocation of housing via an identification of the economic determinants of supply of, and demand for housing on the one hand, and an analysis of changing factors over time on the other.[26] The starting point of the analysis is a statement of broad aims regarding the future of housing in the local area, together with a consideration of standards of provision. New provision is estimated by reference to the capacity of the supply agencies and finance. Housing need is broken down into need groups defined by social and demographic criteria including price, size, location and flexibility of allocation. It is then possible to determine the ability of each group of population to obtain an acceptable standard by examining the restrictions on access to housing controlled by each supply agency (developers, local authority, housing associations, etc.). The aim is not to derive a precise quantification of need, but rather to identify *market processes* as a basis for future estimation, and the production of more realistic guidelines for policy.

As Blincoe (1979) has identified, there are a number of advantages, not least is the fact that, because the analysis takes place against a specific policy backcloth, it produces information relevant to the review of policy. Both examples, then, illustrate the frameworks which are policy-driven and therefore policy analytic. The specific analytical advantage which then occurs is that these frameworks are independent of any particular statistical technique, and their inherent assumptions (see earlier discussions). Indeed, their non-reliance upon high quality data to obtain useful insights into the policy process means that they are amenable to the incorporation of a wider range of methods than traditionally employed. These can be broader, more holistic and, above all, capable of allowing a blending of observation and judgement.

It remains to consider the implications of this thinking for the broader processes of forecasting and policy making. Three criticisms of traditional sectoral forecasting have to be faced. Forecasts have built into them values, beliefs and injustices of the *status quo* (Harvey, 1973) and can readily become self-fulfilling prophecies (Miles and Irvine, 1979), particularly where the technical and political assumptions about how social and economic systems operate are observed behind a smoke-screen of empirical verification.[27] Second, while the search for regularities within social systems is an important goal to develop understanding, those regularities themselves reflect hopes, desires and aspirations that are not independent of policy, either as perceived or anticipated. Third, traditional forecasting does not relate well to the requirement for public involvement in the planning process (Garner, 1979) both because uncertainty is difficult to communicate and because technical forecasts too readily become defensible positions for the professional actors.

The problems in 'technical' forecasting run deep. Enough will have been said in this discussion to illustrate that better forecasting will not be achieved simply through the addition of feedback loops or the 'technical' integration of forecast estimates. Nor will tighter rationality, or adding assumptions squeeze out the value bias and inherent subjectivity from technical forecasts. More relevant and better quality forecasts, coupled with more relevant evaluation and monitoring will come when the policies are recognized as the only possible integrative focus of the planning process and the activities of planners.

Notes

1   For example the Tyne and Wear Act (1976) or the South Glamorgan Act (1975).
2   The same argument is true of the failure to make clear how resources would be used in the implementation of policies.
3   We noted earlier the role of circular 98/74 (Department of the Environment, 1974b).
4   It is important to note in this context the developments in Scotland where the broader, more corporate approach to land use planning and related matters is expressed in a *Regional Report*. Many have argued the virtues of such a non-statutory policy document to complement the rather rigid instrument of the Structure Plan. The Scottish Development Department have also published broad, *National Planning Guidelines*. For reviews and comment on the innovations see Diamond (1979), McDonald (1977), Lothian Regional Council (1975), and Wilkinson and Howat (1977). The development of policy planning units within the local government (regional) structure in Scotland is discussed in Midwinter (1978).
5   This will, for example, take the role of evaluation well beyond government advice to planning authorities, namely that evaluation should relate to just four criteria:
    (i)   the effectiveness of policies to meet aims
    (ii) the resources consumed
    (iii) the incidence or distributional effects
    (iv) the degree of certainty that could be attached to any particular option
6   We have already discussed a wide range of research methods that are relevant, including conventional quantitative methods, case study, use of indicators, impact study and so on.
7   This 'collective' view of evaluating implementation can also be applied at the level of the individual planner or elected member. The question becomes one of trying to find out if the experience of co-ordinating and implementing a policy does help to build a clearer understanding of the contexts in which other actors work, in their various institutions, subject to *their* accountabilities, and *their* attitudes and perceptions of problems, risks and opportunities.
8   Though, as always with indicators, the identification of the critical thresholds at which change becomes significant is a problem and involves some difficult value judgements. As we noted in Chapter 8, the level of change at which policy makers may be provoked into action on some issue (normally a deteriorating situation) will vary widely.
9   We suggest that there is a clear link between the considerable attention given to plan generation and forecasting, and the relative neglect of implementation and monitoring.
10 This view, and following comments are based upon a discussion note of the Scottish Development Department (1979), which reported on a joint SDD/Scottish Regional Authorities working party on Structure Plan monitoring.
11 Indeed, many of the research methods such as surveys and sampling designs that have been discussed earlier are highly relevant.
12 It is always important to bear in mind the highly selective way in which policy makers will use data and information.

13 This is a developing theme in the literature on monitoring and implementation. See for example Wedgewood-Oppenheim et al. (1975).

14 It may, as Rose (1972) points out, be simply congruity or incongruity with ideological aims that makes one person see a particular meaning in a body of data and someone else decline to accept its validity. However, an important feature of the use of indicators is that they *are* capable of direct interpretation in ways that are meaningful to policy makers.

15 Whilst this remains largely true, there has been a growing awareness throughout the 1970s of the problem. Many consultations now take place between government departments and users (notably local government and other public agencies) and there are extensive consultations with user groups in the preparation, for example, of the population census (see Black, 1978). The problem remains that scope and coverage of official data is limited and the needs of users inevitably diverse and conflicting.

16 This utility/cost concept can be described in notation so that the information will be used if:

$$U_i > C_o + C_c + C_v + C_a - C_{ia}$$

where U represents the utility and the subscripts to the costs represent original data cost, local data cost, cost in value, costs of action and cost of inaction respectively. Such a statement is valuable in making clear as how these variables must be weighted in addressing the utility of policy related information.

17 This argument can also be expressed in a similar notation as above, *viz.* that new information will be called for where

$$U_i + C_{ia} > C_o + C_c + C_v + C_a$$

18 Some local authorities (e.g. Kent CC) have found a commitment to a fixed time cycle of urban plan and policy monitoring helpful. Three or four year cycles are being adopted.

19 There is a growing literature on the organization problems of handling data and intelligence within complex organizations. See, for example, White (1974), McLoughlin (1975), and Hambleton (1978).

20 Careful note should be made of this preferred use of the terms 'supply' and 'demand'. We refer to the estimation of population (people), employment need (workforce) and housing need (households) etc. as the *supply* component. *Demand*, as labour demand for example, refers to the requirements of employers for workforce (i.e. job availability) and housing *demand* refers to the provision of dwellings. Readers must be warned that there is a great deal of ambiguity in the literature concerning expressions such as 'job supply' and 'job demand'.

21 Which takes its justification from a political stance supported by 'softer' forms of data and information.

22 Current research in this direction is noted later, and in further reading cited at the end of this chapter.

23 Though this is not consistent with our definition of the term as used earlier.

24 The methodology known as *cross-impact analysis* which attempts to relate trends and events within a single, holistic forecasting framework may well be capable of development into the urban policy field. Policies are thus treated as 'events' on a moving pattern of trends upon which they have some, but always partial influence. On the theory and application of cross-impact analysis see Enzer (1970), Dalkey (1972), Eden (1977) and the critique of Kelly (1976).

25 This could, for example, lead to the development of a 'non-spatial' key diagram, which would set out the scope and extent of the local authorities' intention to intervene in the development process, both by restraint over development and/or its promotion, by making sites available and bargaining with the private sector, etc.

26 Their analysis is then a rejection of the 'balance sheet' approach to assessing housing provision as for example conducted through a conventional 'housing needs' study.

27 A good example is in the field of transportation: 'It is by no means improbable that state provision of an ever-increasing network of motorways, rather than for example, the maintenance and improvement of rail transport, is one of the main factors contributing to an expansion of car ownership' (Miles and Irvine, 1979).

☐ GUIDE TO FURTHER READING

(Full references are given in the Bibliography.)

7 Policy study: concepts and problems

On the theory and relevance of policy study, Rivlin (1971) *Systematic Thinking for Social Action*, (1973) *Social experiments: The Promise and the Problem* and (1974) *How Can Experiments Be More Useful* are a stimulating series of papers. See also Vickers (1970) *Value Systems and Social Process*. The Open University text by Pollitt *et al.* (1979) *Public Policy in Theory and Practice* is recommended as a good contemporary introduction to concepts. Jenkins (1978) *Policy Analysis* is also recommended. Both of these texts contain discussion of theory and case studies relevant to urban planning. A deeper treatment of concepts, and a text that will repay reading for the more inquiring student is Wildavsky (1979) *Speaking Truth Unto Power: The Art and Craft of Policy Analysis*. See also an earlier work of Coleman (1972) *Policy Research in the Social Sciences*. A recent text which contains both discussions of principles, methods and case studies is Bulmer, ed. (1978) *Social Policy Research*. The urban student is particularly recommended to the contributions of Donnison (1972) *Research for Policy*, and Bulmer (1978) *Social Science Research and Policy-Making in Britain*.

Many of the papers cited in the text will provide helpful discussions on aspects of theory and methodology in the field. Among journals, *Policy Studies*, the *American Political Science Review*, and *Policy and Politics* provide a rich source of material for the researching student. For example, the relationship of policy analysis and implementation has been reviewed in a special edition of *Policy Analysis* (ed. Williams, 1975). The journal *Public Policy* contains numerous papers in the field of policy analysis, particularly in the development of methodology and research designs.

Widely quoted texts dealing with the development of policy science are Ranney (1968) *Political Science and Public Policy*; Ranney (1969) *Planning and Politics in the Metropolis*; Sharkansky (1970) *Policy Analysis in Political Science*; Dye (1972) *Understanding Public Policy*; and Rein (1976) *Social Science and Public Policy*. The latter is a good introductory text for the student unfamiliar with the field.

Of particular relevance to the British reader will be the texts which deal with the development of an analytical approach to the study of local and central governmental processes. See for example Stewart (1973) *Management in Local Government*, and (1974) *The Responsive Local Authority*. Stewart and Greenwood (1974) *Corporate Planning in English and Local Government* and Eddison (1975) *Local Government: Management and Corporate Planning* deal with the movement towards a greater corporateness in the management of local affairs. At central government level, see Self (1975) *Econocrats and the Policy Process*, Smith (1976) *Policy Making in British Government* and Keeling (1972) *Management in Government*. On the trend towards a greater policy orientation in urban planning see Solesbury (1974) *Policy in Urban Planning*.

318

For those who require guidance on further reading in the general field of policy analysis the excellent bibliography of Jenkins (1978) *Policy Analysis* is recommended. For further reading in the field of the politics of urban planning see Simmie (1974) *Citizens in Conflict: A Sociology of Town Planning* and case studies of Elkin (1974) *Politics and Land Use Planning: the London Experience*, and Blowers (1980) *The Limits of Power: The Politics of Local Planning Policy*.

8   Policy analysis: modes and methods

Heclo's (1972) *Policy Analysis* is particularly valuable for urban planning for his argument is to stress the model by which policy emerges as a learning process. This, in turn, depends upon multiple interaction, inter-organizational communication via complex networks and the diffusion of knowledge and ideas. The paper also draws attention to the many policy taxonomies that have developed as does Jenkins (1978) *op. cit.* A good set of readings in the broad development of policy analytic methods is Pavitt, ed. (1980) *Technical Innovation and British Economic Performance.* An example of applied work is Packer (1975) *Financing Health Care and Education: Consumer Units and Resource Allocation* and a great deal of practical material in the field of policy and programme evaluation will be found in Weiss (1972) *Evaluation Research: Methods of Assessing Program Effectiveness.*

In the field of policy impact study, Newton and Sharpe (1977) *Local Outputs Research: Some Reflections and Proposals* will guide the analyst, notably by stressing the importance of longitudinal study, and the problems of measurement of impacts. This work also relates to a local government context. A discussion of the problems of external and internal validity in policy analysis is Roos (1975) *Contrasting Social Experimentation with Retrospective Evaluation: A Health Care Perspective.* A systematic approach to decision analysis related to town expansion schemes is Levin (1972) *On Decisions and Decision Making*, and a more general text on the analysis of local decisions from an 'organic' viewpoint is Friend *et al.* (1974) *The Inter-corporate Dimension.* Further reading on the importance of inter-local authority operating practice to policy analysis is Brazier and Harris (1975) *Inter-Authority Planning* and Hickling *et al.* (1979) *The Development Plan System and Investment Programmes.* The latter comprises a series of case studies.

There is considerable literature on the general theme of the development of policy within strategic land-use planning. Students will find the following material useful in seeking an overview: Solesbury (1974) *Policy in Urban Planning*; Holman and Hamilton (1973/4) 'The British urban programme'; the White Paper – *Policy for the Inner City* Cmnd 6845 (1977); and the Birmingham Inner City Partnership (1977) *Initial Policy Paper.*

A wide-ranging review of methods using social indicators is Land and Spillerman (1974) *Social Indicator Models.* The policy application of indicators is thoroughly discussed in Shonfield and Shaw (1972) *Social Indicators and Social Policy.* Specific works in the urban context which will provide the student with practical guidance are Boyce (1970) *Towards a Framework for Defining and Applying Urban Indicators in Plan Making*; Knight (1974) *A Conceptual Background to the use of Social Indicators for the Identification of Areas of Urban Deprivation*; Craig and Driver (1972) *The Identification and Comparison of Small Areas of Adverse Social Conditions*; O'Dell and Parker (1977) *The Use of Census Data to Identify and Describe Housing Stress*; Holterman (1975) *Census Indicators of Urban Deprivation*; Department of the Environment (1975b) *The Use of Indicators for Area Action –*

Housing Act 1974; Flynn *et al.* (1972) *Social Malaise Research: A Study – Liverpool*; and Edwards (1975) *Social Indicators, Urban Deprivation and Positive Discrimination*.

A standard text on content analysis is Holsti (1969) *Content Analysis for the Social Sciences and Humanities*.

The following references deal with a selection of policy-related research which will be of particular interest to urban planners. Many of these will reveal the blending of more conventional research designs and those of policy analysis. Also, they will provide further bibliographical guidance for the reader into the more specialized areas of urban policy study.

The subject of policy initiatives in the local economy has received considerable treatment in the literature, much of which contains interesting methodological insights. See, for example, reviews by Bramley *et al.* (1979) *Local Economic Initiatives: A Review*; Robinson (1979) *Local Authority Economic Initiatives*; and assessments by Rogers and Smith (1977) *The Local Authority's Role in Economic Development: The Tyne and Wear Act*; and Wright (1978) *A Review of Available Local Authority Powers Relevant to Employment*.

The policy-related aspects of industrial location and employment are well illustrated in Cooper (1976) *Government Influence on Industrial Location*; Rose (1978) *Policy Co-ordination and Programming of Employment Measures by Local Authorities*; and a case study by Struthers and Williamson (1979) *Local Economic Development: Integrated Policy Planning and Implementation in Merseyside*.

Relevant material on the theme of relating housing policy to needs, are Grant *et al.* (1976) *Local Housing Needs and Strategies*, which includes local authority case studies; Department of the Environment (1979b) *The Assessment of Housing Requirements*; Niner (1975) *Local Authority Housing Policy and Practice*; and Niner (1976) *A Review of Approaches to Estimating Housing Needs*. Two related pieces of work are Doling (1976) *The Family Life Cycle and Housing Choice*; and Cebula (1974) *Local Government Policies and Migration*. A wide-ranging review is Cullingworth (1979b) *Essays on Housing Policy: The British Scene*.

In the field of shopping, a large number of policy impact studies have been carried out by means of a variety of methods, including 'diary studies', direct consumer observation, consumer interviews, etc. Many studies reveal clearly the problems and potential of case study approaches. Recommended examples are Bruce and Mann (1977) *The Brent Cross Shopping Centre Impact Study: Results of the First Diary Study of Household Shopping Trips*; Shepherd and Newby (1978) *The Brent Cross Regional Shopping Centre – Characteristics and Early effects*; and Malcolm and Aitken (1977) *The Impact of a Superstore: Fine Fare, St. Ninian's, Stirling*.

A good example of a local authority, policy-related, shopping study is that of Hertfordshire County Council (1977b) *South West Herts: Shopping Impact Study*. On the same theme, see also Guy (1976) *A Method of Examining and Evaluating the Impact of Major Retail Development Upon Existing Shops and their Users*. An extensive bibliography of case study and other analytical work in the field of retail planning is URPI (1980) *Retail Planning Methods: Bibliography*. Public policy study and office location is discussed in Alexander (1979) *Office Location and Public Policy*.

In the field of transportation there is a considerable literature, though a great deal of it does not deal in detail with the effects of local public policy *per se*. Research insights will be obtained into behavioural aspects and policy effects from Hillman *et al.* (1973) *Personal Mobility and Transport Policy*; Hillman *et al.* (1976) *Transport*

Realities and Planning. Two case studies that will repay reading are Mosely *et al.* (1976) *Rural Transport and Accessibility* and Hertfordshire County Council (1977a) *Public Transport for Rural Communities.*

9 Policy and planning: some methodological implications

There is an extensive literature on the broader, epistemological aspects of forecasting and policy relationships. In particular, we suggest readers consult Ascher (1978) *Forecasting: An Appraisal for Policy-makers and Planners.* This text includes an excellent discussion of forecasting concepts, and case studies in the fields of population, employment, energy and transportation. A further text in the same vein, though more general, is Armstrong (1978) *Long Range Forecasting.* In the local authority policy-making context, a good case study treatment is Eden (1977) *Modelling the Influence of Decision Makers on the Future.* There is a considerable literature in the field of forecasting in social contexts, of which Miles and Irvine (1979) *Social Forecasting: Predicting the Future or Making History?,* and an earlier paper by Freeman *et al.* (1972) *Progress and Problems in Social Forecasting* are recommended. Also, De Jouvenal (1968) *Notes on Social Forecasting* contains many insights that have contemporary relevance. A broad review of forecasting concepts is Emery (1968) *Concepts, Methods and Anticipation.*

On the subject of monitoring for development planning, Floyd *et al.* (1977) *Monitoring for Development Planning* is recommended for further reading and includes case studies. This work has also been published as a Department of the Environment Research Report, No. 23 (1977b). Two more general reviews are Haynes (1974) *Towards a Concept of Monitoring,* and Wedgewood–Oppenheim *et al.* (1975) *An Exploratory Study in Strategic Monitoring.* Practical reports of the development of monitoring systems that can be recommended are those of Tyne and Wear (1976) *Tyne and Wear Structure Plan: Reports of Survey*: and Cleveland County Council (1980) *County Structure Plans: Monitoring and Review.* A highly developed system for land use monitoring is that of Grampian Regional Council (1979) *Development Analysis Booklets,* while the need for and the potential of integrating 'hard' and 'soft' data is revealed by Merseyside County Council (1976) *Merseyside Industrial Monitor.* Bovaird (1978) *A Framework for the Monitoring and Evaluation of Local Employment Measures* makes clear the importance of the integration of these areas of methodology in planning. Case studies in the analysis of the local economy are those of Lloyd (1977) *Manufacturing Industry in the Inner City: A Case Study of Merseyside;* Dicken and Lloyd (1978) *Inner Metropolitan Industrial Change, Enterprise Structures and Policy Issues: Case Studies of Manchester and Merseyside;* and Lloyd and Mason (1978) *Manufacturing Industry in the Inner City: A Case Study of Greater Manchester.*

Developments in thinking about housing policy and the estimation of need are well revealed in papers by Blincoe (1979) *Analytical Methods for Planning Housing Provision: A Critical Assessment of Current Practice;* Crofton and Webster (1974) *Improving Housing Allocation;* Holm *et al.* (1978) *Policy-Oriented Housing Models: Some Tentative Applications;* with a broader review of the area by Murie (1976) *Estimating Housing Need: Technique or Mystique?* Official guidance will be found in Housing Services Advisory Group (1977) *The Assessment of Housing Requirements.*

The policy implications of demographic change are revealed by Buxton and Craven (1976) *Demographic Change and Social Policy: The Uncertain Future;* and the case study of Glasgow District Council (undated) *Glasgow: Implications of Population Changes to 1983.*

On the theme of achieving a higher degree of internal consistency within strategic planning forecasts, see Madden and Batey (1980) *Achieving Consistency in Demographic-Economic Forecasting* and a paper by Schinnar (1976) *A Multi-Dimensional Accounting Model for Demographic and Economic Planning Interactions*, which provides useful insights to the statistical aspects. Applications on this theme have been published by Madden (1976) *A Population, Employment, Housing Forecasting Framework for Merseyside*; Cockhead (1978) *Integrated Forecasting for Strategic and Resource Programming: The Approach Developed in the Grampian Region*; and Grampian Regional Council (1978b) *An Integrated Forecasting Methodology for Strategic Planning.*

Applied critiques on the integration of forecast components in planning are Hayton (1979) *An Appraisal of Forecasting Methodology and Integration in the Strathclyde Structure Plan* and Bracken and Hume (1981) *Key Activity Forecasting in Structure Plans: A Critique.*

□ A CONCLUDING COMMENT

Urban planning is a complex activity and, as practised, is influenced in various and sometimes conflicting ways by its administrative, political and technical contexts. From time to time the development of its theory has favoured a particular perspective and brought with it 'fashionable' attitudes in the use of methods. As we have seen, the 'rational-comprehensive' paradigm, associated with the development of 'systems thinking' has most recently given way to broader policy perspectives. Such a shift, as with those earlier, tends to be seen by many as offering an *alternative* basis upon which the activity of urban planning can be conceptualized and, hence, as a preferred position from which a general theory of urban planning activity may be advanced. In one sense, the development of the policy-based paradigm continues this theme in offering an alternative conceptual framework, though some advocates (Rondinelli, 1973; Rittel and Webber, 1973; Swain and Logan, 1975; for example) make clear the limitations, and indeed the contradictions, of attempting to explain by means of *any* unitary theory, an activity as diverse as that of urban planning. In the light of their comments, it seems improbable that any such theoretical position can be reached which would be so widely acceptable as to 'characterize' urban planning (at least at the strategic level) in the same way that other and maturer professional activities can be characterized. Some, of course, would argue that the adoption of any explicitly political stance is antithetical to the development of any corpus of professional ideals and concepts.

For the foreseeable future, this text propounded the view that urban planning activity needs to lie somewhere between mere technical determinism on the one hand, and unsystematized futureology on the other. This, however, is a broad canvas and implies both a blend of concepts and methods and the inevitability of conflicting views and attitudes about their relevance and use. The implicit, 'integrative' paradigm to blend values and facts, judgement and proof, intuition and certainty, individuality and consensus is, by its nature, not easily described. It seems clear that expert opinion will continue to be a *sine qua non* (Helmer, 1977) but, as we suggest, systematic study, research and analysis, *can* make matters more explicit, *can* lead to understanding and *can* enhance the quality of judgements about the urban past, present and future. The challenge to the student as future theorist and practitioner of the 'art and science' of urban planning, is to equip himself with a sufficient grasp of concepts, methodology and technique to be able to make informed decisions about their appropriateness to the issues and problems that he faces, in order to follow these decisions with reasoned and justified application.

☐ APPENDIX 1
STATISTICAL NOTES
AND CHECKLIST

A sound grasp of basic statistical methods will be essential for many areas of urban research and analysis. The following checklist will provide a brief guide to those concepts and principles which will be most commonly employed. It is intended that the reader can check his knowledge and understanding against these notes.

Urban analysis is normally undertaken in two stages. The first, *description*, concerns finding and measuring relationships among variables. The second stage is to establish *dependency*, that is, the extent to which change in one phenomenon (variable) leads to changes in another. This may lead to causal explanation and theory. Relevant statistical methods are classified under two headings – *descriptive* and *inferential*. The aim of the former is to succinctly and with *validity* provide unambiguous communication about some measured phenomenon. The latter concerns the making of generalized inferences, usually from a representative set of data (a sample), and hence will rely to a large extent upon probability theory in the form of statistical tests for *significance*. Where data are obtained by means of sampling it is vital that the concept of *sampling error* is understood, that the researcher is satisfied with the *reliability* of his data, and has full information about the scale of measurement (Chapter 5).

A further basic concept is that of 'comparison' in which the researcher delimits phenomena with significantly *similar* properties or conversely with significantly *different* properties. In both cases, the purpose of analysis is to express the comparison in a statistically valid and unambiguous way. When analysis is undertaken in respect of two variables and their data we have a *bi-variate* analysis; for more than two treated simultaneously, a *multi-variate* analysis. Recalling the distinction above between description and dependency, statistical methods can then be readily classified into

(i)   *measures of association* and
(ii)   *measures of dependency* for the bivariate case and
(iii) *measures of inter-relationship* and
(iv)   *inter-dependency* for the multivariate situation.

(i) The most important measure of association is that of *central tendency*. This comprises two components – an average value (i.e. arithmetic *mean*, *mode* or *median*), and an associated measure of *dispersion* which indicates how the data points (x_i) are scattered about the mean $(\bar{x})$. If the data are distributed symmetrically on each side of the average value, a *normal distribution* may be present, but if not then the distribution is referred to as *skewed*. Dispersion is measured in a number of ways, for example by calculating the range from lowest to highest score, or by an *Inter-Quartile Range*, which essentially represents the scatter across the most central 50% of the data points and thus is not distorted by possibly chance, extreme values which might be present in a set of data. A better measure however involves the concept of *mean deviation*, which calculates the average amount by which all data points differ from their mean value ($\bar{x}$). This is normally expressed as the variance (σ^2), which itself is specified in terms of a range above and below the mean by the standard deviation (σ), sometimes called the *Root mean square deviation*. The relationship between the standard deviation and the normal distribution is of particular importance in determining the probabilities of a particular occurrence in an analysis, and the variance is a key concept in the analysis of the statistical significance of relationships between variables. Simple comparisons between sets of data are sometimes made by a *relative* indication of mean value based upon the relationship of the mean and its standard deviation. This is known as the *coefficient of variation* ($CV = (\sigma/\bar{x})100\%$). A normal distribution of the data must be assumed.

A distinction must be clearly maintained between *continuous* and *grouped* data. The former includes measures such as distance or time, the latter a population divided into age groups. Where grouped data are manipulated it is vital that the *stated limits* and *widths* of the various groups as they are defined is understood and taken into account when measures of average and distribution are calculated.

In order to compare sets of data with different means and standard variations, the influence of their differing scales of measurement must be removed by *standardization*. This changes the value of the scores without changing the shape of their distribution about the mean. *Standardized data* have a mean ($\bar{x}$) of 0 and a standard deviation (σ) of 1. The standardized values, known as *Z-scores* are obtained as $Z = (x - \bar{x})/\sigma$. These scores have properties which make them particularly suitable for comparative analysis. The importance of a normal distribution of the data has already been noted (because certain statistical properties concerning significance follow) and standardized data can be converted into an approximate normal distribution by *normalizing*. In effect, normalizing involves stretching and shrinking the measurement scale and thereby removing the skewed properties of a distribution of data scores about their mean value.

The *normal distribution* is by far the most common probability distribution that the analyst will encounter but others should be mentioned. The normal distribution essentially describes the probability of a given measure exceeding some specified value (expressed in terms of standard deviation) with the essential assumption that this situation will occur under constant conditions over an *infinitely* long set of observations. The distribution can say nothing about which event of many may exceed a given value. The *Binomial and Poisson* distributions, however, can be used to indicate the *probability* that, of a given number of occurrences, a proportion will exceed some specified value. These distributions are important in an analysis of the probability of certain conditions occurring with a particular frequency. The Binomial distribution's characteristic is that it reflects the frequency or probability with which different possibilities are likely to occur, for any given percentage probability of the specified conditions and any given number of occurrences being considered. It is frequently the case that a value can only be ascribed to the probability of some occurrence (i.e. a road accident) and not to its 'non-occurrence'. In such situations, the binomial cannot be used because the total number of events (occurrence and non-occurrence) cannot be known. The Poisson concept, however, enables a distribution to be constructed based simply upon the average number of occurrences observed and their frequency. The distribution estimates the probability of 0, 1, 2, 3...events occurring during a period based upon the mathematical constant of exponential natural growth, *e*, which has a value of 2.71828.

The concept of *statistical significance* is of great importance. If an observed difference between two or more sets of data is found to be statistically significant then it means that it is *improbable* that such a difference could have occurred *by chance*. Tests for significance enable the analyst to assess, with validity, the probability that there is some *real* difference between the data, *or* that the difference is merely the result of unobserved influences at work in the process of observation and measurement. Methods of analysis will therefore normally involve *statistical procedures* used to compare and contrast the data, and *tests* which establish the validity of the measures obtained.

Tests for significance are divided into two broad categories, *parametric* and *non-parametric*. These are distinguished by the assumptions which must be met in their use, the former being the more demanding and, as a result, providing a more powerful (stringent) test. In brief, parametric tests require that sampled data are closely approximated to the normal distribution and that the variance of each set of sample values used in the analysis should be comparable – *homogeneity of variance*. Where sample size is large some relaxation can be permitted. Otherwise, non-parametric tests needs to be used, and can also be applied to a wider range of data including 'qualitative' data measured by nominal and ordinal scales (Chapter 5).

An important concept in carrying out tests for significance is the *Null Hypothesis*, which concerns the significance of the difference between what is observed (the sample) and the hypothesized value (the population) (Chapter 5). The Null Hypothesis (H_0) postulates that *unless* a significant measure of true difference in a population is achieved by sampling, then it is *not possible* to conclude that such a difference exists. Conversely, an *experimental (or research) hypothesis* (H_1) can be postulated which the analyst attempts to justify, which will state that a significant result *demonstrates* a real difference in the true population data. In practice, the

Null hypothesis is the more valuable for it has to be positively *disproved* before a significant result can be claimed.

Inferential statistics – (a) parametric methods: making inferences about measures of association between two variables or sets of data, is essentially a process of generalizing about the differences as observed through some sampling process. To make valid inferences, the analyst must be fully aware of the assumptions that underlie his chosen method. Where the assumptions for a *parametric* test can be met (above), the most straightforward approach is to use the *Standard Error of the Difference between Sample Means*. This indicates whether or not the observed difference between any two sample means is such that it is probable that a significant difference also exists between the two population true means. The difference is found as

$$S.E._{\text{diff}} = \sqrt{\frac{\sigma_a^2}{n_a} + \frac{\sigma_b^2}{n_b}}$$

The observed difference is then compared to this measure of error from both sample sources. At the 95% probability level, we would expect an observed value of twice the $S.E._{\text{diff}}$ on more than one occasion in twenty, etc., according to the properties of the normal distribution. The *t*-test statistic is used. It is important to note that the test requires that the samples are truly independent, which rules out the use of the test for a 'matched pair' research design, neither can the difference between 'before' and 'after' samples be tested. Refinement to this test is necessary where it cannot be assumed that the population variances are approximately equal.

A more complex, and more powerful test is the *Analysis of Variance*, which tests the measure of association between two or more variables by using the concept of 'between samples' and 'within samples' errors. The statistic used is, in fact, a variance ratio which has a known sampling distribution. The ratio is obtained by comparing the differences which may be observed *between* any two sample sets of data and the differences which may be observed *within* each sample. The importance of making this distinction is to determine whether or not it is the mere chance stratification of the data into the sample groups which accounts for the observed differences or errors. For example, if the 'between' difference is not *significantly* greater than the 'within' difference, then it is possible that the observed difference between the sample strata *may* be due to chance grouping. Any inferences made about the true differences between the samples and hence between their populations may be invalid. A *F*-statistic is used for the test, which requires that the sample or group populations should be approximately normally distributed, they should have equal variances, the sampling should be random and independent, and that the variables have been measured at least on the interval scale (Chapter 5). As before, some violations of the first two assumptions may not be too critical in practice.

(b) Non-parametric methods are appropriate to a wider range of situations, and can cope with non-normally distributed (skewed) data. Some of these methods are also applicable to *qualitative data*, i.e. data of nominal and most types of ordinal scaling. The most commonly applied test is the chi-square (χ^2) which, however, does require data in a particular form. This is too often overlooked in practice. The test determines whether the distribution of observed frequencies across categories or groups can be reasonably attributed to random fluctuations. This is done by finding out if these observed frequencies differ significantly from the frequencies which might be expected according to some assumed hypothesis. The data must then be in the form of frequencies of occurrence, and the 'expected' frequency *must* be clearly thought out otherwise it is not possible to interpret the results sensibly. The *strength* of a relationship between two variables can be tested by the related ϕ^2 (phi square) statistic. Finally, it must be noted that χ^2 *can* give significant results simply due to the use of a large sample and it is also adversely affected by a very small sample size. Other tests are available for these conditions, such as the Fisher Exact Probability Test.

The foregoing has only tested for the strength of an association. The concept of correlation is used to describe both the *strength and direction* of a bivariate relationship. It is applicable to ordinal, as well as the higher-order scales. The correlation coefficient is a *relative index of association*, and must be distinguished from regression, which is an absolute measure. Correlation is also a standardized measure which is independent of the scale of measurement and hence widely applicable to different measurement scales. There are two types of correlation measure. The *Rank Order Correlation Coefficient* (Spearman's ρ (rho)) is calculated from the rank order of items of data. *The Product Moment Correlation Coefficient* (Pearson's r) gives a superior measure but is subject to more stringent assumptions in its use. (It is, in fact, based upon the concept of variance and is therefore a parametric measure). Where doubt exists, the Spearman's coefficient is the 'safer' measure, though for computation reasons it is Pearson's coefficient which will be found on many pocket calculators. Both measures are used to assess the proportion of total variance explained by the relationship between any two variables. Thus a value of $r^2 = 0.65$ is interpreted as meaning that 65% of the variance in one variable is predictable from the variance of the other. Finally, mention should be made of the Mann–Whitney U-test, which is the non-parametric equivalent of the (one-way) Analysis of Variance (above) and is a very easy test to apply.

Most statistical tests can be extended to embrace two-way and three-way situations where more variables are involved.

(ii) Measures of dependency concern the question, 'assuming a relationship exists between two variables x and y, what change in y occurs as a result of a given change in x?' This functional relationship is expressed in notation as a linear regression $y = bx$, where b (the so called 'slope' or 'regression' coefficient) represents the function of y on x. The purpose of using linear regression can be usefully summarized as 'to determine the unique function which best expresses the relationship between variables in a linear form and therefore predicts as much as possible of the variation (variance) in a dependent variable (y), and in so doing minimizes the amount of unexplained variation'. This latter will be due to any one of a number of 'error' effects, the smaller the amount, the better the *goodness of fit*. The simplest measure for goodness of fit is the *Coefficient of Determination*

$$\text{C.D.} = 1 - S^2_{yx}/S^2_y$$

where S^2_{yx} is the residual *unexplained* variance of y on x, and S^2_y is the variance of the y scores about their mean. Thus, the coefficient shows the proportion of the variance of y, which is accounted for, or is explained by, the linear function and x. Thus, the remainder of the variation has to be attributed to a possible variety of error sources (Chapter 5).

The statistical significance of the regression coefficient, b, can be tested by calculating its *standard error*. The coefficient may then be tested against the *t-distribution* so as to show whether or not there is the probability that the variables *are* unrelated (i.e. independent of each other) and whether or not the apparent linear association is due to sampling error. If the observed value for t, obtained as the ratio of the regression coefficient to its standard error, exceeds the critical value from the *t*-distribution for a given confidence level, we may conclude that the data provides sufficient evidence that the two variables *are* linearly related. It is important to note that (unlike linear correlation) regression of x on y, and y on x will not normally produce an identical result. Regression is thus an *asymmetric* measure of association which is important in establishing the direction of a relationship, and possibly a causal structure. Linear regression requires a number of important assumptions to be met which should be fully understood particularly concerning the independence of the variables.

(iii) Social systems are complex and analysis can often be made more realistic by moving to a multi-variate situation. By increasing the number of variables to be handled simultaneously in an analysis, fewer simplifying assumptions have to be made. The analysis itself, however, will become more complex and the results may be more difficult to interpret. Multi-variate analysis will normally begin from a *source data matrix* which displays the inter-relationship between all the variables and their observations. As earlier, multi-variate analysis is concerned primarily with the variances and co-variances among the data, and the data can be standardized, etc. as already noted. Also the matrix can be partitioned into groups of variables which are regarded as *dependent* upon others which are regarded as *independent*. Among useful measures of *inter-relationship* among variables are *partial and multiple-correlation coefficients*. Here, the 'dependent' and 'independent' variables may be several in number. Analysis of inter-relationship can be thought of as falling into two stages. First, we can seek to explain how much of the observed variation in a dependent variable can be explained by the influence of the other *variables in combination* – which is multiple correlation; second, we can partition the influence of independent variables into their respective contributions 'controlling' for the effect of others, which is partial correlation. In both cases, the full assumptions of the linear correlation model ideally should be met. The most important concerns the need to define the 'independent variables' so that they are statistically unrelated to *each other* – if not, *multi-collinearity* will be present, which means that the respective contribution of each variable in 'explaining' a portion of the variation in the dependent variable becomes extremely difficult, and also that the exercise becomes very sensitive to any sampling errors in the data. Both multiple and partial correlation coefficients can be tested for significance, normally with the F-statistic. An extension of this type of analysis, is *factor analysis* which is a family of methods primarily concerned to identify and measure inter-relationships among variables *and* to identify possible sources of *inter-dependency*. Essentially, this involves a process of 'reduction' to find the extent to which observed variations among a group of variables may be accounted for by a smaller set of explanatory variables, called *factors* or *components*. These, however, are hypothetical and require considerable interpretation.

(iv) Finally we note the role of *multiple regression* as the most commonly used technique for measuring inter-dependency among variables. The simple linear model $y = a + bx$ is expanded in the form $y = a + b_1 x_1 + b_2 x_2 \ldots b_k x_k + e$, where several xs (independent variables) are employed to 'explain' the variations in y (dependent variable), subject also to an error component, e. Each x has its own associated regression coefficient, b. As in the bi-variate case the linear model is used to obtain a set of b coefficients which, together, provide a best 'goodness of fit' as a trend to the scatter of observed values. The multiple correlation coefficient can be used to measure this 'goodness of fit', in an analogous way to the simple linear model noted earlier. The resulting (multiple) *Coefficients of Determination* can be readily tested for significance by means of the t-test. Alternatively a more comprehensive test can be obtained by an *Analysis of Variance* of the model results, including residuals, and the use of the F-statistic probability distribution. In a *stepwise* regression the analyst introduces independent variables sequentially which enables him to make judgements about which are the more significant (and therefore useful) variables and which are not. As before stringent assumptions need to be met in the use of multiple regression with which the analyst should be familiar. Not the least of these is that the *underlying* relationships among the variables *are* (appropriately) linear. Where they are not, more complex forms of model may have to be used.

It is suggested that, at the least, the student should find the content of this note familiar. If not, some recommendations for reading are given in the guide at the end of part two of the text.

APPENDIX 2
ANALYSIS OF FOUR-VARIABLE NON-EXPERIMENTAL RESEARCH DESIGN

Assume a situation in which there is one dependent variable or subject, Y, and several independent variables, X_1, X_2,...X_n, and also that it is not possible to control for the influence of these separately as in an experimental situation.

Assume also that any attempt to manipulate one of the X variables would probably influence the other Xs as well as Y, in effect meaning that there are several dependent variables as well. To study this situation requires that we approach the problem in a way which allows, initially, *all* variables to be treated as dependent on each other, that is, a *simultaneous* approach. Using the earlier example,* we are now not assuming that migration is necessarily the dependent variable. It might for example be a *cause* of the rate of housebuilding through builders responding to demand. We therefore treat our supposed independent variable, Y, as an X-type variable for the moment. The principles can best be explained by means of some notation.

In general, we can state,

$$X_1 = a_1 \qquad\quad + b_{12}X_2 + b_{13}X_3 \ldots [+e_1]$$
$$X_2 = a_2 + b_{21}X_1 \qquad\quad + b_{23}X_3 \ldots [+e_2]$$
$$X_3 = a_3 + b_{31}X_1 + b_{32}X_2 \qquad\quad [+e_3]$$
$$\vdots \qquad \vdots \quad\; \vdots \qquad\; \vdots \qquad\qquad\quad \vdots$$
$$X_n = a_n + b_{n1}X_1 + b_{n2}X_2 + b_{n3}X_3 \ldots [+e_n]$$

Each X is defined, in turn, as dependent upon every other X, and an explicit error term for each equation is included. Ignoring for the moment the constant terms (as), our interest focuses on obtaining values for the weights (bs), which represent, numerically, *the extent of the influence of each* X *on the other* Xs. Each statement, is, in effect, an extended version of a simple regression. For example the relationship between X_1 and X_2 as represented by the following graph or table of data, can be summarized as:

*pp. 191 ff.

331

X_1	X_2
3	0
5	1
7	2
9	3

given data

$X_1 = 3 + 2X_2$

linear statement
(form: y=a+bx)

graph

It will at once be clear that such a system is complex even for a few variables, and the task of using the principles embedded in such a research framework will be greatly assisted by reducing the number of elements. We have stated a reciprocal system, that is, we have allowed each X to be affected by all other Xs *reciprocally*. Common sense suggests, however, that, in the social world, reciprocal causation is very rare, mainly because human actions always take place in a normally self-evident temporal order. Consider the following system of four mutually dependent variables, in algebraic and diagrammatic terms:

$$X_1 = a_1 \qquad\quad + b_{12}X_2 + b_{13}X_3 + b_{14}X_4 + e_1$$
$$X_2 = a_2 + b_{21}X_1 \qquad\quad + b_{23}X_3 + b_{24}X_4 + e_2$$
$$X_3 = a_3 + b_{31}X_1 + b_{32}X_2 \qquad\quad + b_{34}X_4 + e_3$$
$$X_4 = a_4 + b_{41}X_1 + b_{42}X_2 + b_{43}X_3 \qquad\quad + e_4$$

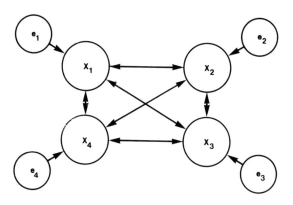

If non-reciprocity can be assumed, one half of this system is redundant. Thus, if X_1 is a cause of X_2, then b_{12} will have a non-zero value (representing the extent of the influence of X_1 on X_2), whereas the reciprocal, b_{21}, will be zero, and so on. Further simplification is possible, for if standardized measures are used the constants (as) can be omitted. This results in a much simpler set of expressions, namely:

$$X_1 = e_1$$
$$X_2 = b_{21}X_1 + e_2$$
$$X_3 = b_{31}X_1 + b_{32}X_2 + e_3$$
$$X_4 = b_{41}X_1 + b_{42}X_2 + b_{43}X_3 + e_4$$

and in which we have now assumed X_4 to be the *most dependent* variable. This 'ordering' of the variables is a matter of judgement from whatever general knowledge of the system that we possess. If this is not possible a more systematic approach is required in which each variable would need to be examined in alternative order.

The object of this structure is to attempt to isolate and measure the influence of, in turn, X_1 on X_2, X_2 on X_3, and so on. Apart from the first term, where there is only an error term to deal with, the influences on the respective variables will be partial, that is, X_3 is partially influenced by X_1 and partially by X_2 plus its own error effect (e_3). A statistical measure for such an influence is obtained by calculating a partial weight and this is written $b_{xy.z}$. The statements can now more correctly be shown as

$$X_1 = e_1$$
$$X_2 = b_{21} \quad X_1 + e_2$$
$$X_3 = b_{31.2} \quad X_1 + b_{32.1} \quad X_2 + e_3$$
$$X_4 = b_{41.23}X_1 + b_{42.13}X_2 + b_{43.12}X_3 + e_4$$

Consider variable X_3 for example. The first right-hand side b weight ($b_{31.2}$) now explicitly refers to the partial correlation between variables X_3 and X_1, when the influence of X_2 is controlled. In the second term, we have an explicit partial between X_3 and X_2 when the influence of X_1 is controlled, plus the associated error term as before. The same principle is applied to variable X_4 and any subsequent variables in a more complex system.

So, if we wish to *assume* that there is a minimal influence directly between, say, X_1 and X_3 in the system, we set the weight $b_{31.2}$ to zero, subject to a statistical assessment of any measurement errors. This device, of making assumptions about the influence of any selected independent variable, means that we have a systematic way in which the inter-relationships in a complex system can be examined, one step at a time. This gives a reasonably straightforward way of systematically examining a data set comprising several variables in a non-experimental mode.

At the simplest level, the main sequential influences at work in the hypothetical system ($X_1 \rightarrow X_2 \rightarrow X_3 \rightarrow X_4$) can be examined by solving the equations assuming that high quality data are available for the four variables. Ideally, this procedure requires that the data, if from a sampled source, are normally distributed and that the sampling is truly random.

☐ APPENDIX 3
DETERMINATION OF SAMPLE SIZE AND CONFIDENCE LIMITS

Note that we denote the sample standard deviation as s and reserve the symbol σ (sigma) for the population standard deviation (p. 166). Conventionally, lower-case symbols are used to denote the sample and capital symbols for the population. However, the capital sigma, Σ, has an alternative conventional use, namely, meaning the sum of.

Assume we are given the following:

Number of items, $n = 100$,   Sample mean, $\bar{x} = 50$,
Sample standard deviation, $s = 9$,   Population true mean $= \hat{\bar{X}}$,
Chosen confidence limit $= 95\%$ (Approximately $(95.45\%) = 2\sigma$),

$$\hat{\bar{X}} = \bar{x} \pm 2\left(\frac{s}{\sqrt{n}}\right) \rightarrow \hat{\bar{X}} = 50 \pm 2\frac{9}{\sqrt{100}} \rightarrow \hat{\bar{X}} = 50 \pm 1.8.$$

The true population mean lies between 48.2 and 51.8 with a confidence limit of approximately 95%. We cannot say anything about the true population standard deviation at this point, though the sample standard deviation can be used as an approximation.

If we wish to reduce the range of the estimate, that is, to express the true population values more closely, the confidence level of the estimate may be relaxed *or* the size of the sample increased. Thus, in the example, setting the confidence limit to approximately 86% (86.64% equates with 1.5 in the normal distribution) gives

$$\hat{\bar{X}} = \bar{x} \pm 1.5\left(\frac{s}{\sqrt{n}}\right) \rightarrow \hat{\bar{X}} = 50 \pm 1.5\frac{9}{\sqrt{100}} \rightarrow \hat{\bar{X}} = 50 \pm 1.35.$$

The new confidence limit gives a closer estimate of the true mean, though in practical terms this often leads to difficulties because reducing the confidence levels makes the interpretation of results more difficult. The alternative is to increase the size of the sample, n. Consider the same example, with a 95% confidence limit and the sample size doubled to 200,

$$\hat{\bar{X}} = \bar{x} \pm 2\left(\frac{s}{\sqrt{n}}\right) \rightarrow \hat{\bar{X}} = 50 \pm 2\frac{9}{\sqrt{200}} \rightarrow \hat{\bar{X}} = 50 \pm 1.27.$$

Now the range of the true population estimate has been reduced to lie between 48.73 and 51.27 and this represents a considerable improvement on the estimate from a sample of 100 items.

335

Adjustment for finite populations and small samples

An important measure in sampling is that of the true standard deviation of the population. The sample standard deviation is used as an estimator for this, and if a sample were exactly representative of a population then their standard deviations would be identical. In general, the larger the sample the closer these two values will become, and this suggests that some compensation is necessary where samples are small. The relationship between the sample standard deviation, s, and the estimate of the population standard deviation, $\hat{\sigma}$, is $\hat{\sigma} = s\sqrt{(n/n-1)}$. The expression $\sqrt{(n/n-1)}$ will be close to unity when n is large and for large samples the correction will be negligible, but for small samples it is important. We may now refer back to the calculation of the standard error of the mean and restate the formula more correctly as $\hat{X} = \bar{x} \pm \hat{\sigma}/\sqrt{n}$. A better way, however, is to introduce the correction directly into the calculation of the standard deviation as

$$\hat{\sigma} = \frac{\displaystyle\sum_{i=1}^{n} x_i^2}{n-1} - \left(\sum_{i=1}^{n} x_i\right)^2$$

It is worth noting that, if the sampling fraction (n/N) remains fairly small and the sample size is sufficiently large to keep the correction factor near to unity, the size of the population has virtually no effect on the standard error of the sample mean. Thus, a sample of 500 items from a population of 100,000 will give almost as close an estimate of the true population mean as a same-sized sample from a population only one-tenth of the size.

In the case of a small population, it is important to pay close attention to the *proportion* which the sample represents of the population, that is the sampling fraction. A useful correction for this may be constructed by $\sqrt{1 - n/N}$, which is used in the calculation of the standard error of the mean. This gives

$$s = \frac{\hat{\sigma}}{\sqrt{n}}[\sqrt{(1-n/N)}] \quad \text{or alternatively,} \quad s = \sqrt{\left[\frac{\hat{\sigma}^2}{n}(1-n/N)\right]}$$

There remains to consider the possibility that, in random sampling, the situation may arise in which it is possible only to obtain a *very* small sample of a population. With very small samples the probability values of the normal distribution cannot be assumed to apply, even though the population itself may be normally distributed, and there is increased risk of error. In these cases, a more stringent test must be applied, in which the so-called Students' t-distribution is substituted for the normal distribution.

Sample size for a binomial distribution: if it is decided that a standard error of $\pm 3\%$ is appropriate to an investigation (that is at the 95% level of probability an estimate of the true population value of $\pm 6\%$) *and* it is known that the sample population of $p\%$ is, say, 30, we may readily find n as

$$\text{s.e.} = \sqrt{\frac{p\%q\%}{n}} \quad \text{or} \quad n = \frac{p\%q\%}{\text{s.e.}^2} \rightarrow n = \frac{30 \times 70}{3^2} \rightarrow n = 233.$$

Alternative sample sizes for other confidence limits can be similarly determined. We must note, however, that *at least* an estimate for p (or q) is required *before* we can make this calculation. We are faced, however, with a problem, because it is the values for p and q which we will be seeking in our investigation, and we must initially either make an estimate for p (or q) or conduct a pilot study to provide an estimate of the sample proportions.

The greater the proportional difference between p and q, that is the smaller either term becomes, then the smaller the sample size necessary to maintain a given level of confidence. Where there is doubt as to the probable values for p and q, a conservative estimate is obtained by assuming $p = q = 50\%$. It may be helpful to consider this point with a table. Given the following combination of values for $P\%$ and $Q\%$, we can calculate $\sqrt{(PQ)}$, for a given sample size, as

$P\%$	0	10	20	30	40	50	60	70	80	90	100
$Q\%$	100	90	80	70	60	50	40	30	20	10	0
$\sqrt{(PQ)}$	0	30	40	46	49	50	49	46	40	30	0

and this shows how the value of $\sqrt{(PQ)}$ is at a maximum when P and Q are equal, that is, when the population is equally divided.

A simple example may make these principles clear. We assume that a land use survey is to be conducted in an urban area by sampling at random selected points. From a pilot trial of, say, 400 observations the following frequencies are obtained expressed in percentage terms:

Residential%	Industrial%	Commercial%	Open Space%
50	20	15	6

A 95% level of confidence is decided upon and the standard error of the estimate for each of the land-use categories is found by s.e. $= \sqrt{(p\%q\%/n)}$. $p\%$ represents the percentage observed in a given category and $q\%$ will be $100 - p\%$. Considering first the residential land category, we obtain s.e. $= 2\sqrt{(50 \times 50/400)} = \pm 5.0$. The estimate of true percentage of residential land is thus between 45.0 and 55.0 at the 95% confidence level. At the 97.5 confidence level we would obtain s.e. $= 3\sqrt{(50 \times 50/400)} = \pm 7.5$ which widens the limits of the estimate to between 42.5 and 57.5. We may decide that this gives us a sufficiently accurate estimate of the proportion of residential land and it follows that a sample size of 400 items is adequate. However, if we consider the estimate for 'Open Space' from the same pilot sample size we obtain, s.e. $= 2\sqrt{(6 \times 94/400)} = \pm 2.37$. At the 95% confidence level we find our estimate to lie between 3.63 and 8.37. We may well decide that this is too broad to be useful. To improve this we can either relax the confidence level, or increase n. The same procedure will readily show the minimum size of sample that will yield an estimate at a chosen confidence level. Increasing the sample size will also improve the quality of the estimate of all other land uses. It is now possible to evaluate the size of sample, and its cost, in terms of the chosen confidence level and tolerance, and select a sample size for the investigation proper. The percentage values in the example are readily convertible to absolute measures if the total area of the study is known.

If particular sample replies fall into more than two categories, the value for n may be modified. For example, responses to questions often take the form: yes, no, don't know, no reply. The latter two classes may be very small, and in these cases it will be preferable to replace n by n', so that $p+q = n'$. If it is expected that there will be an appreciable loss of replies to these 'other' categories, the initial sample size may be increased in order to maintain confidence levels. Alternatively, attention can be focused specifically onto one of the observed characteristics, say p, and q is then defined as including all other responses to the question.

Obtaining estimates from stratified random sampling

First, we discuss the estimates in respect of the strata themselves. This is quite straightforward, for each stratum may be regarded as a single random sample. The 'best estimate' of the stratum population standard deviation will be $\hat{\sigma}_h = s_h\sqrt{(n_h/n_h-1)}$ where s_h is the sample standard deviation, and the expression under the root sign the correction to estimate the population standard deviation. As small sample size is common in stratified sampling, the Students' t-distribution should be used to assess the limits of the population mean. In dealing with strata we are, by definition, using a *finite* population for which we should make the small population correction given by $(1-f)$ where f is the sampling fraction. This will compensate for the tendency of the sampling error to be over-estimated as the strata population decrease in size. The standard error of the mean for a stratum sample will be s.e. $\bar{x} = \sqrt{(\hat{\sigma}_h^2/n_h)(1-f)}$ and from this the limits of the strata true means can be found for selected probability levels, again according to the Students' t-distribution.

An estimate may also be made of the size of the stratum population (N_h), for in selecting stratified samples it is quite common for this to be unknown. To find this estimate, we will need to know the standard error of the stratum population. For this we recall that the sampling fraction (f) represents the proportion of sample size to stratum size. Its inverse is referred to as the *raising factor* (rf). If we take the estimate of the standard error of the sample mean for a given stratum, multiplying by n_h will give the standard error for the stratum sample total and further multiplying by the raising factor (rf) will give the estimate of stratum population. Thus,

$$\text{s.e. } X_h = (n_h)rf_h\sqrt{[\hat{\sigma}_h^2/n_h(1-f_h)]}$$

which may be arranged more conveniently as s.e. $X_h = rf_h\sqrt{[\sigma_h^2 n_h(1-f_h)]}$.

Given a constant sample fraction, the two estimates for the overall sample mean and the whole population total may be found as follows. The standard error of the overall sample mean is found by firstly taking the best estimate of the variance $\hat{\sigma}_h^2(1-f)$ (for a finite population) for each strata and weighting it by multiplying by the number of units in the sample for that stratum n_h. The result is summed over the number of strata (g) into which the whole population is divided, as $\sum_{j=1}^{g} (\hat{\sigma}^2 n(1-f))_j$. The standard error of the overall sample mean is found by dividing by the overall number of sample units, $\sum_{j=1}^{g} n_j$, and taking the square root, as

$$\text{s.e. } \bar{X} = \sqrt{\left(\sum_{j=1}^{g} (\hat{\sigma}^2 n(1-f))_j \middle/ \sum_{j=1}^{g} n_j \right)}.$$

The estimate of the overall population total, N, is obtained by using the raising factor as previously,

$$\text{s.e. } N = rf \sqrt{\left\{ \sum_{j=1}^{g} [\hat{\sigma}^2 n(1-f)]_j \right\}}.$$

There remains to consider the cases in which the sample fraction *varies* between the strata, in which f and rf will not be constant. The standard errors for each stratum may be calculated as above except that appropriate values for f will be used for *each* stratum. However, in order to estimate the overall sample mean, the constituent values must be weighted to take into account the variable sampling fraction. This can best be done by multiplying into the term $\Sigma[\hat{\sigma}n(1-f)]$ the square of the raising factor rf. It is necessary to take the square of this value as the term is, in effect, modifying the variance of the stratum sample values. The estimate of the overall sample mean will be then obtained by dividing the product by the estimated total size of the whole population, $\hat{N}$. This latter is obtained by taking the number of samples in each stratum, multiplying by the appropriate raising factor, and summing, as $\hat{N} = \sum_{j=1}^{g} (n_j rf_j)$ and the standard deviation for the overall mean will be given by

$$\hat{\sigma}\bar{N} = \sqrt{\left\{ \sum_{j=1}^{g} [\hat{\sigma}^2 n(1-f)(rf^2)]_j \middle/ \hat{N} \right\}}$$

Recalling again that the standard deviation is given in general by s.e. $= \dfrac{\hat{\sigma}}{\sqrt{n}}$, the expression can be divided by $\sqrt{N}$ to yield the standard error for the overall sample mean, as

$$\text{s.e. } \bar{X} = \sqrt{\left\{ \sum_{j=1}^{g} [\hat{\sigma}^2 n(1-f)(rf^2)]_j \right\}} \middle/ \hat{N}.$$

Readers who wish to follow the detail of this substitution may consider the following steps

$$\frac{\hat{\sigma}}{\sqrt{n}} \rightarrow \sqrt{[\Sigma\sigma^2 n(1-f)rf^2/\hat{N}]}/\sqrt{\hat{N}} \rightarrow \sqrt{[\Sigma\sigma^2 n(1-f)rf^2/\hat{N}/\hat{N}]}$$

$$\rightarrow \sqrt{[\Sigma\hat{\sigma}^2 n(1-f)rf^2/\hat{N}^2]} \rightarrow \sqrt{[\Sigma\hat{\sigma}^2 n(1-f)rf^2]}/\hat{N}.$$

SIMPLE MATRIX METHODS
APPLIED TO THE ANALYSIS
OF POPULATION CHANGE

Assume a given age-disaggregated section of a population, say, females, in five-year age groups. These groups will in effect be an array or (input) *vector* and can be represented as figure A4.1. In a simple survival model, a survival rate is separately applied to each of the groups in the array and thereby an estimate is obtained of the number of survivors expected at the end of the predicted period, n, and who will form groups n years older. The use of matrix methods allows such a series of operations to be performed as one. It requires that the complete array of survival factors is embedded in a so-called matrix operator which is pre-multiplied into the input vector, and will thereby produce an output vector of survivors.

Figure A4.1 Population vector of age groups

$$\underset{(n \times 1)}{\boldsymbol{p}} = \begin{bmatrix} p_1 \\ p_2 \\ p_3 \\ p_4 \\ \cdot \\ \cdot \\ p_n \end{bmatrix}$$

Figure A4.2 Survivorship matrix with survival coefficients

$$\underset{(n \times n)}{\boldsymbol{S}} = \begin{bmatrix} 0 & 0 & 0 & 0 & . & . & 0 \\ s_{21} & 0 & 0 & 0 & . & . & \cdot \\ 0 & s_{32} & 0 & 0 & . & . & \cdot \\ 0 & 0 & s_{43} & 0 & . & . & \cdot \\ \cdot & \cdot & \cdot & \cdot & \cdot & \cdot & \cdot \\ \cdot & \cdot & \cdot & \cdot & \cdot & \cdot & \cdot \\ 0 & 0 & . & . & . & s_{n,n-1} & 0 \end{bmatrix}$$

Consider the operator matrix shown in figure A4.2. Each value at s (s_{21}, s_{32} and so on) represents a survival rate for successive age groups as defined in the input vector, $\boldsymbol{p}$. Thus, s_{21} is the survival probability factor of the

341

youngest age group, p_1 and so on. It is fundamentally a part of the theory of matrix manipulation (and the reason why the method applies so elegantly to a *dynamic* topic such as a population) that, by placing the successive survival rates in the sub-diagonal of the matrix (that is the diagonal line immediately *below* the true diagonal), when the matrix and vector are multiplied out the resulting vector not only contains the number of survivors but they will be automatically aged forward by the time interval implicit in the data. It follows that by placing the survival values, *two* diagonals down from the true diagonal, the population is aged over *two* intervals and so on. But further, the necessary fertility rates can be built into the same matrix operator. Assume that in the population vector $\boldsymbol{p}$, p_1 represents females aged 0–4, p_2 ages 5–9, and so on. The group p_3 will be the first fertile group, for they will age (in a five-year forecast) to become almost the group 15–19 (p_4) at the end of the period. The fertility rates to be applied to this group (p_3) and the successive fertile age groups (p_3, p_4, $p_5 \ldots p_n$) can be simply entered in the appropriate positions in the *top row* of the matrix operator. On output, the number of births, aggregated over the fertile age groups of the mothers will appear in the p_1 position in the vector (figure A4.3).

Figure A4.3 Population vector pre-multiplied by survivorship and fertility matrix

$$\underset{(n \times n)}{\boldsymbol{S}} = \begin{bmatrix} 0 & 0 & f_{13} & f_{14} & \cdot & \cdot & 0 \\ s_{21} & 0 & 0 & 0 & \cdot & \cdot & 0 \\ 0 & s_{32} & 0 & 0 & \cdot & \cdot & 0 \\ 0 & 0 & s_{43} & 0 & \cdot & \cdot & 0 \\ \cdot & \cdot & & & & & \cdot \\ \cdot & \cdot & & & & & \cdot \\ 0 & 0 & 0 & 0 & 0 & s_{n,n-1} & 0 \end{bmatrix} \underset{\boldsymbol{p}^t}{\begin{bmatrix} p_1 \\ p_2 \\ p_3 \\ p_4 \\ \cdot \\ \cdot \\ p_n \end{bmatrix}} = \underset{\boldsymbol{p}^{(t+n)}}{\begin{bmatrix} p_1 \\ p_2 \\ p_3 \\ p_4 \\ \cdot \\ \cdot \\ p_n \end{bmatrix}}$$

(n represents time interval of projection)

A numerical example will make this process clear and can be checked by the reader familiar with matrix operations (figure A4.4). If it is assumed that the survival and fertility rates are unchanged for a further predicted period, the operator matrix is simply multiplied into the output vector to advance a further time interval. Alternatively, a *transition matrix*, containing data to alter the operator matrix of survival and fertility values can be prepared, and at each interval in the process the vital rates can be modified in accordance with a set of pre-determined assumptions which in turn can be verified by testing the results.

Figure A4.4 Numerical example of a population estimation by matrix methods

$$
\begin{bmatrix}
0 & 0.85 & 0.6 & 0 & 0 \\
0.95 & 0 & 0 & 0 & 0 \\
0 & 0.9 & 0 & 0 & 0 \\
0 & 0 & 0.85 & 0 & 0 \\
0 & 0 & 0 & 0.7 & 0 \\
0 & 0 & 0 & 0 & 0.5
\end{bmatrix}
\begin{bmatrix}
1500 \\ 1300 \\ 1000 \\ 900 \\ 750 \\ 600
\end{bmatrix}
=
\begin{bmatrix}
1705* \\ 1425 \\ 1170 \\ 850 \\ 630 \\ 375
\end{bmatrix}
\quad *(1105+600)
$$

$$S \qquad\qquad p^{(t)} \qquad p^{(t+n)}$$

In this example, given a sex-specified vector, the fertility probabilities would have to relate to the probability of a female birth occurring. A separate but similar calculation would be necessary to generate the first element in the male vector, so that the input vector for that calculation will be females, and the output must be transferred to the male survival exercise to provide the new male infants. It should also be noted that the fertility rate should be compensated to not just the number of 'live births' but the number of infants who may be expected actually to survive to form a new group aged 0–4 years. For further reading see the standard text by Rogers (1971) in the use of matrix methods in urban and regional analysis.

□ APPENDIX 5
INPUT – OUTPUT ANALYSIS:
AN INTRODUCTORY EXAMPLE

First an example can make clear the operation of the regional multiplier concept (pp. 187 ff.).

Suppose that, in a given region, 85% of income is spent on consumption, leaving 15% saved, and that 30% of all spending brings in 'imports' to the region. The coefficients are therefore $\beta = 0.85$ and $\alpha = 0.3$. The multiplier is

$$\frac{1}{1-0.85(1-0.3)} = \frac{1}{1-0.595} = 2.47$$

which means that, if through some direct economic activity in the region £100 worth of export sector earnings can be achieved, then the overall economic benefit within the region will amount to £100 times the multiplier, that is £247. It will now be clear that if we have good estimates about the region's economic performance by industrial sectors, which includes information about the 'export' component, and knowing the value of the multiplier coefficients from empirical study of the region, we can readily assess the likely impact within the region from new economic activity. This estimate can be made in terms of income, or in terms of jobs which will be a more meaningful calculation for the land use planner. Here, the employment attributable to base (or export) activity is denoted B, and the employment attributed to the non-basic (consumption) sector as N. Using the multiplier concept this latter will be a function of the size of the basic employment sector, so that, $N = (N/B)B$. The N/B ratio, called the 'base ratio' must also be assumed to be constant over time. Now, it can be readily seen that total regional employment, E, which is ultimately what we are interested in calculating, will by definition be the sum of these two employment sectors, that is, $E = N + B$.

Substituting the multiplier concept into this statement in order to estimate the *total* employment resulting from any increase (or decrease) in the employment in the base sector, gives $E = (N/B)B + B$ which can be rearranged more conveniently either as

$$E = \left(1 + \frac{N}{B}\right)B \quad \text{or} \quad E = \left(\frac{1}{1-(N/E)}\right)B,$$

the latter showing clearly the similarity with the regional income multiplier model.

Turning now to the input–output model we will assume a four-sector situation, say, with three industrial sectors and a household sector. The basis of an input–output analysis is a transactions table in which inter-sector economic activity is summarized (figure A5.1). The purchasing sectors are detailed across the top of the table and the producing (or selling) sectors are listed down the side. Each row of the table shows the value of the respective transactions between the sectors. Thus, Sector B purchased £250 of goods and services from Sector A, and so on. It will be readily appreciated that the system is similar to double-entry book-keeping, in which the output of a given sector is 'accounted' in terms of the inputs that this forms to other sectors. The household row entries consist of wages and salaries paid *to* households by the sectors, though in practice these entries will include other types of income such as dividends and interest, which means that the household 'row' entries do not directly represent the value of labour input to the system. The household column indicates the value of finished goods and services provided by each sector to households. The raw input row and final demand column represent the 'leakages' in the local economy respectively representing imports into and exports out of the region from and to other regions.

Figure A5.1 Input–output analysis: a transactions table

			Sectors			Final	Gross
Purchases		A	B	C	Households	demand	output
Sales							
Sectors {	A	0	250	150	80	200	680
	B	270	0	320	150	400	1140
	C	0	280	0	180	350	810
Households		160	60	140	0	350	710
Raw input		250	550	200	300	0	1300
Gross input		680	1140	810	710	1300	4640

Recalling the earlier discussion the basic input–output table will be largely self-explanatory. However it may help to make clear that, for example, sector B produced £1140 worth of products of which £400 worth was consumed by the final demand, £270 by sector A, £320 by sector C, and so on. The *inputs* required for this activity amounted to £550 from primary inputs, (energy, raw materials, etc.) and £250 from sector A, £280 from sector C and so on. Readers can readily trace similar interactions for the other sectors in the table.

Attention mainly focuses upon the interactions *between* the sectors because, when an increase in output is introduced into part of the system, they will govern the way in which that increase affects the rest of the system.

These interactions can be summarized by calculating some simple coefficients. For example, an output amounting to £680 in Sector A required an input from Sector B of £270 and the interaction coefficient will be $270/680 = 0.397$, and so on. The reader can check that the complete table of coefficients will be

		Sector			
	Purchases	A	B	C	Households
Sales					
Sector ⎰ A		0	0.219	0.185	0.113
⎱ B		0.397	0	0.395	0.211
C		0	0.246	0	0.254
Households		0.235	0.053	0.173	0

Recall that our main concern is with the inter-action and how, if we then increase a final demand for one or more sectors, we can *trace* through the inter-sector implications. The key parts to this calculation can be summarized as follows using the data from figure A5.1.

The final demand can be represented as a vector $\mathbf{d}$, the gross output by a vector $\mathbf{x}$, and the interdependencies among the sectors by the matrix of coefficients $\mathbf{A}$, that we have just described.

$$\mathbf{A} = \begin{bmatrix} 0 & 0.219 & 0.185 & 0.113 \\ 0.397 & 0 & 0.395 & 0.211 \\ 0 & 0.246 & 0 & 0.254 \\ 0.235 & 0.053 & 0.173 & 0 \end{bmatrix} \quad \mathbf{d} = \begin{bmatrix} 200 \\ 400 \\ 350 \\ 350 \end{bmatrix} \quad \mathbf{x} = \begin{bmatrix} 680 \\ 1140 \\ 810 \\ 710 \end{bmatrix}$$

These data represent a system which, from our input–output table, we know to be justified, that is it represents a feasible real-world situation. The whole idea of presenting the information in this form is that the effect of a change in one sector can be very readily calculated with all consequential effects *calculated simultaneously* by the use of simple matrix mathematics. (As was done earlier for population – Appendix 4.)

First, however, it is necessary to introduce a new mathematical concept. This may be made clear if we realize that in the system above the three elements, $\mathbf{A}$, $\mathbf{d}$ and $\mathbf{x}$ are, by definition, causally linked so that manipulating $\mathbf{d}$ by $\mathbf{A}$ will by definition yield $\mathbf{x}$. This, however, cannot be done directly and, for mathematical reasons, it is necessary to use the inverse matrix of $\mathbf{A}$. Recall that in ordinary arithmetic the inverse of a number is that which a number must be multiplied by to give a value of unity, so that the inverse of 4 is 0.25, then $4 \times 0.25 = 1$. If the inverse of the matrix $\mathbf{A}$ is calculated, then the pre-multiplication of the vector $\mathbf{d}$ by this inverse will yield the value in the gross output vector $\mathbf{x}$ simultaneously over all sectors. The inverse of $\mathbf{A}$ will be found to be

$$\mathbf{A'} = \begin{bmatrix} 1.237 & 0.398 & 0.444 & 0.337 \\ 0.672 & 1.363 & 0.759 & 0.556 \\ 0.260 & 0.395 & 1.280 & 0.438 \\ 0.371 & 0.234 & 0.366 & 1.184 \end{bmatrix}$$

The great advantage of matrix methods, which in effect operate *simultaneously* upon any number of related linear statements, such as the rows of the system in figure A5.1, is that the change in the system as a whole, as a result of a change in any one statement, can be readily seen. Given that we now know that the inverse matrix, $\mathbf{A'}$, contains the coefficients to reproduce *all* the interactions within the system simultaneously, we can find out exactly what effect, say, an increase of £200 final demand for sector A goods would achieve, simply by pre-multiplying a new vector $\mathbf{d'}$, by the inverse for the system. We obtain

$$\underset{\mathbf{A'}}{\begin{bmatrix} 1.237 & 0.398 & 0.444 & 0.337 \\ 0.672 & 1.363 & 0.759 & 0.556 \\ 0.260 & 0.395 & 1.280 & 0.438 \\ 0.371 & 0.234 & 0.366 & 1.184 \end{bmatrix}} \underset{\mathbf{d'}}{\begin{bmatrix} 200 \\ 0 \\ 0 \\ 0 \end{bmatrix}} = \underset{\mathbf{x'}}{\begin{bmatrix} 247 \\ 134 \\ 52 \\ 74 \end{bmatrix}}^{*}.$$

* Figures rounded to nearest integer

The application of matrix methods in this way is referred to as the 'Leontief Inverse' (Leontief, 1967). The calculations for inverting a matrix can readily be performed by computers. An application and case study will be found in Morrison and Smith (1976). The calculation can be readily checked as

$$\underset{\mathbf{A}\ matrix}{\begin{bmatrix} 1.0 & -0.219 & -0.185 & -0.113 \\ -0.397 & 1.0 & -0.395 & -0.211 \\ 0 & -0.246 & 1.0 & -0.254 \\ -0.235 & -0.053 & -0.173 & 1.0 \end{bmatrix}} \underset{\mathbf{B}\ inverse}{\begin{bmatrix} 1.237 & 0.398 & 0.444 & 0.337 \\ 0.672 & 1.363 & 0.759 & 0.556 \\ 0.260 & 0.395 & 1.280 & 0.438 \\ 0.371 & 0.234 & 0.366 & 1.184 \end{bmatrix}}$$

$$= \underset{\mathbf{AB}\ identity}{\begin{bmatrix} 1 & 0 & 0 & 0 \\ 0 & 1 & 0 & 0 \\ 0 & 0 & 1 & 0 \\ 0 & 0 & 0 & 1 \end{bmatrix}},$$

which is the matrix equivalent of multiplying an ordinary integer number by its inverse to yield one (i.e. $0.25 \times 4 = 1$).

The output vector, $\mathbf{x'}$, shows that the final result of this increase in demand for the goods and services of sector A, after *all* the multiplier interaction effects have worked their way throughout the system, would yield an overall increase of £247 (not £200) in sector A demand, £134 for sector B demand and so on. Summing these gives an overall total of £507 and therefore a crude production multiplier effect of $507/200 = 2.54$.

Equally, an increase of £200 in the final demand for the goods and services of sector B, gives

$$\underset{\mathbf{A}'}{\begin{bmatrix} 1.237 & 0.398 & 0.444 & 0.337 \\ 0.672 & 1.363 & 0.759 & 0.556 \\ 0.260 & 0.395 & 1.280 & 0.438 \\ 0.371 & 0.234 & 0.366 & 1.184 \end{bmatrix}} \underset{\mathbf{d}''}{\begin{bmatrix} 0 \\ 200 \\ 0 \\ 0 \end{bmatrix}} = \underset{\mathbf{x}''}{\begin{bmatrix} 80 \\ 273 \\ 79 \\ 47 \end{bmatrix}},$$

which is interpreted in the same way, given an overall production multiplier effect of $80 + 273 + 79 + 47 = 479/200 = 2.40$.

☐ APPENDIX 6
A REGRESSION APPROACH TO
MIGRATION ANALYSIS

The approach can be used in a number of forms. In Greenwood's (1973, 1975) work, for example, seven estimating equations for migration are used with seven jointly dependent variables. Five of the questions are structural and two are identities. The dependent variables include the number of labour force (CLF) (in Greenwood's original model, labour force relates specifically to the civilian labour force), out-migrants from the area (OM), the number of labour force inmigrants to the area (IM), income change in the area (ΔINC) (the symbol Δ, capital 'delta', is conventionally used to represent a change in a variable over a specified period of time), employment change in the area (ΔEMP), unemployment change in the area ($\Delta UNEMP$), labour force change (ΔCLF), and natural increase of the labour force ($NATINC$). The seven equations are as follows:

$$OM = f_1(IM, \Delta INC, \Delta EMP, \Delta UNEMP, \Delta INCb, UNRb, CLFb,$$
$$EDUb, AGEb', e_1)$$
$$IM = f_2(OM, \Delta INC, \Delta EMP, \Delta UNEMP, INCb, UNRb, CLFb,$$
$$e_2)$$
$$\Delta INC = f_3(OM, IM, \Delta EDU, \Delta GOVT, DEW, DNS, e_3)$$
$$\Delta EMP = f_4(OM, IM, NATINC, INCb, \Delta EDU, \Delta GOVT, DEW, DNS,$$
$$e_4)$$
$$\Delta UNEMP = f_5(OM, IM, NATINC, DEW, DNS, e_5)$$
$$\Delta CLF = EMP + UNEMP, \text{ and}$$
$$\Delta NATINC = CLF + OM - IM$$

where each of the variables is defined as follows.
Dependent variables: OM is the outmigration over the period from the base date, b, to the final date b'; IM is the gross immigration over the same period; ΔINC in the income change over the period; ΔEMP is the employment change; $\Delta UNEMP$ is the unemployment change; ΔCLF is the labour force change, in total, and $NATINC$ is the natural increase of the labour force.

The exogenous variables, that is those determined outside the system, are, $INCb$, the median income of persons residing in the area; $UNRb$, the rate of unemployment prevailing in the area at time, b; $CLFb$, the labour force at time b; $EDUb$, the median number of school years completed by persons 25 years old and over at time b; $AGEb'$, the median age of the population at time b'; ΔEDU the education change, that is the ratio of the median number of years of school completed by persons 25 years old and over at time b'

compared to time b; $\Delta GOVT$, the change in local government expenditure over the period; and DEW and DNS are regional dummy variables. The error terms are represented as e_i.

Specific features of this approach should be carefully noted. The most important is the use of two migration variables, one relating to *out*-migration and one to *in*-migration. This is in contrast to the more commonly used single variable relating to *net* migration. Studies have shown that the impact that migration has on both the sending and receiving localities depends significantly upon the characteristics of the movers themselves. The characteristics of the out- and in-migrants for any given locality will not be identical and may not even be similar. Moreover, the importance of certain variables in explaining *out-migration* is likely to be different from the importance of these same variables in explaining *in-migration*, and some variables that are relevant to explaining out-migration are not relevant to explaining in-migration. This latter group of variables for example, includes those that relate to the characteristics of the population from which the migrants are drawn. The use of two gross-migration variables allows for differences in the determinants and consequences of out- and in-migration to be estimated.

The structure of the equations can be readily traced by the reader. For example, out-migration is assumed to be a function of in-migration, income, the unemployment rate, employment, education and age structure, *and changes in* income, employment and unemployment. In-migration is hypothesized as a function of out-migration, income, unemployment and employment rates *and the change in* income, employment and unemployment. As we noted above, since a simultaneous equations model is used, ordinary least-squares is not an appropriate estimation technique and Greenwood used a three-stage, least-squares method to solve the equation, thereby avoiding the over-estimation bias illustrated in figure 6.6. A discussion of this is beyond this text, though Wonnacott and Wonnacott (1970) provide a detailed account, and computing programs are widely available.

Some results of Greenwood's investigation, using census data for 100 American metropolitan areas are summarized in figure A6.1.

Brief comment can be made upon these findings. In-migration of labour force members for example, causes a greater employment growth in the urban areas studied, in that a 1 per cent increase in in-migration induces a 0.232 per cent increase in employment change, and further, also induces greater income growth in these areas. Migration of labour force is influenced by the growth of employment opportunities, for a 1 per cent increase in change of employment results in a 2.843 per cent increase in in-migration. This suggests that the process of economic growth provides significant inducement to in-migration and is, in effect, acting as a multiplier influence. It is also clear that out-migration did not encourage greater income growth so that regional incomes were narrowed through migration, which as Willis (1974) points out is contrary to the hypothesis of neo-

Figure A6.1 Migration model esimates by three stage least-squares method

Independent variables	Equation for				
	OM	IM	ΔINC	ΔEMP	$\Delta UNEMP$
OM, β: t:		0·318 (3·290)	−0.023 (1·090)	−0.224 (3·229)	−0.399 (3·192)
IM	0·139 (0·880)		0·043 (2·220)	0·232 (3·945)	0·192 (1·965)
ΔINC	−1·247 (1·614)	2·166 (2·147)			
ΔEMP	0·165 (0·303)	2·843 (7·491)			
$\Delta UNEMP$	0·476 (1·225)	−0·598 (1·250)			
NATINC				−0·011 (0·624)	0·047 (1·689)
INCb	−0·545 (3·112)	0·212 (1·043)		−0·065 (0·345)	
UNRb	0·339 (1·876)	−0·439 (1·983)			
CLFb	0·791 (5·525)	−0·546 (5·477)			
EDUb	1·288 (3·474)				
AGEb'	−1·212 (5·201)				
ΔEDU			0·462 (3·364)	−0·715 (1·464)	
$\Delta GOVT$			0·033 (0·834)	0·071 (0·588)	
DEW			0·045 (2·669)	0·129 (2·513)	−0·104 (1·125)
DNS			−0·003 (0·212)	0·172 (3·005)	0·172 (2·305)
Constant, α	6·431 (5·059)	−3·427 (2·191)	0·117 (1·177)	0·689 (0·513)	2·064 (3·490)
ordinary least squares } R^2	0·96	0·93	0·46	0·72	0·20

(Logarithmic) regression coefficients and t-test ratios (in parentheses)
From Greenwood (1973:102)

classical economists that inter-regional out-migration would eventually restore regional equilibrium and obviate the need for further out-migration. It appears that out-migration depresses such growth, as well as depressing employment growth, for a 1 per cent increase in out-migration induced a −0.224 per cent change in income. Out-migration appears to relieve unemployment.

The positive and significant coefficient on EDUb in the out-migration equation and the negative and significant coefficient on AGEb' suggest that

APPENDIX 6

increased education levels encourage, while increased age levels discourage, out-migration. This is perhaps not surprising, but highly relevant is the positive and significant coefficient on OM in the in-migration equation, indicating that localities which experience relatively heavy out-migration also tend to experience relatively heavy in-migration. This result is interpreted as an indication that where out-migration tends to be relatively heavy, so does return migration. The point is confirmed by several pieces of analytical work in the British context (see, for example, Gleave, 1973; Hyman and Gleave, 1977). In general, these findings disprove the supposed 'simple' economic relationship between declining regions and out-migration, and prosperous regions and in-migration.

APPENDIX 7
EXAMPLE OF A DOUBLE-CONSTRAINED GRAVITY MODEL: RESIDENCE AND EMPLOYMENT

The double-constrained model can readily be explained by an example drawn from Masser's (1972) work. Consider the simple case of a model of three zones and 1000 residence-to-work trips (figure A7.1a). Each zone has an appropriate number of residents and jobs as shown. We also assume that the average distance that a person travels *within* a zone if he works in the same zone as he lives is 2 km and that the distance coefficient, α, is 2. In the attractor/producer matrix these entries will form the diagonal of the matrix, $i = j$ (see p. 200).

The first task is to calculate the total interaction in the system which will then enable the constant, K, to be found. The total interaction is found by entering the appropriate values for each pair of zones into the basic spatial interaction equation

$$t_{ij} = KO_iD_jd_{ij}^{-\alpha},$$

more readily calculated by

$$t_{ij} = KO_iD_j(1/d_{ij}^2),$$

where the trips from one 'producer', i, to one 'attractor' j, is given by the product of the numbers originating from the producer, O_i, multiplied by the numbers attracted to the destination, D_j, qualified as before by the distance function. Entering the numbers of people who live in zone 1, $(O_1 = 200)$ and work in zone 1 $(D_1 = 500)$, given $K = 1, d = 2$ and $\alpha = 2$, gives

$$1 \times 200 \times 500 \times 1/(2 \times 2) = 25{,}000.$$

Similarly, the apparent interaction between residents of zone 1 $(O_1 = 200)$ and work in zone 2 $(D_2 = 300)$ gives

$$1 \times 200 \times 300 \times 1/(3 \times 3) = 6667.$$

This process is repeated for all pairs of interactions in the system (nine calculations) and the result can be readily summarized as the interaction matrix figure A7.1(b). Summing row and column totals gives the total amount of interaction in the system, 126,889. However, this must be scaled to the level of the 'given' number of trips which we know are in the system, that is 1000.

Figure A7.1 Example of a double-constrained gravity model
(a) Given data

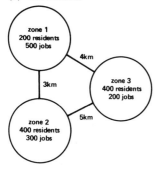

(b) Interaction matrix

	Zone	1	2	3	Total residents
Residents	1	25,000	6,667	2,500	34,167
	2	22,222	30,000	3,200	55,422
	3	12,500	4,800	20,000	37,300
Total jobs		59,722	41,467	25,700	126,889

(c) Trip distribution matrix

	Zone	1	2	3	Estimated residents
Residents	1	197	52	20	269
	2	175	236	25	436
	3	99	38	158	295
Estimated jobs		471	326	203	1000

(d) Row and column justified distribution matrix

	Zone	1	2	3	Total residents
Residents	1	154	36	10	200
	2	176	208	16	400
	3	169	57	174	400
Total jobs		500	300	200	1000*

From Masser (1972: 96–103)
*Columns contain rounding errors

The scaling constant, K, is therefore calculated as $1000/126889$ $= 0.007881$ and each cell in the matrix must be re-scaled by multiplying by this constant. The trip distribution matrix in figure A7.1(c) will be the result.

For the moment, the only constraint which has been applied to the system is the total number of work trips and inspection shows that inconsistency with the given data is present. This is not surprising for no zone-wise constraints have been imposed. For example, the model has predicted 269 residents and 471 jobs in zone 1 compared to the 200 and 500 given, respectively.

To ensure that the model correctly predicts for each zone, additional constraints must be imposed, by zones on both producers (residents) and attractors (jobs), that is a *double constraint*. This requires two separate sets of scaling factors which must be estimated for each zone. The simplest form in which this can be done is by adding the two scaling factors A_i (for the producers) and B_j (for the attractors) to the basic formula, which becomes

$$T_{ij} = A_i B_j O_i D_j d_{ij}^{-\alpha},$$

and where each scaling factor is defined by,

$$A_i = 1/\Sigma B_j D_j d_{ij}^{-\alpha},$$

$$B_j = 1/\Sigma A_i O_i d_{ij}^{-\alpha}.$$

It will be clear that each factor is partially defined in terms of the other factor and, this will mean that a convergence process will ensure the 'balance' of the system in accordance with the limiting values for residents and jobs in each zone. It is also necessary to constrain the overall number of 'producer' trips to the total number of residents in the system, and the overall number of 'attractor' trips to the total number of jobs in the system, so that

$$\sum_{i=1}^{n} t_{ij} = D_j \quad \text{and} \quad \sum_{j=1}^{n} t = O_i$$

respectively. Solving the system will require finding values for the two unknowns A and B, and it is initially necessary for these to be estimated. In fact, any initial value will do. Once this is done, the arbitrary value for either A or B is used in the basic formula, and this enables the other to be estimated. In turn this enables the first to be re-calculated and so on. After several iterations, stability will be achieved and no further change in these values will occur. The calculations involved are straightforward though space does not allow them to be set out here, (see Masser, 1972), and for larger systems computer programs are readily available (see Baxter, 1976). Once the stabilized values for these factors are found it is a simple matter to re-calculate the trip matrix for each zone using the basic, double-constrained formula

$$T_{ij} = A_i B_j O_i D_j d_{ij}^{-\alpha},$$

in which all the right-hand-side terms are now known.

The result will be the interaction matrix of trips from residence to work as shown in figure A7.1(d) and it will be noted now that the row and column totals do in fact accord with the data given for each zone. Examination of the cells then shows that the model predicts, for example, that, of the 200 residents in zone 1, 154 work in the same zone, 36 in zone 2 and 10 in zone 3, and so on.

For those readers unfamiliar with the term Σ (capital sigma) which means 'the sum of': it should be noted that this term is made more explicit by the notation $\sum_{j=1}^{n} S_j$, which means that all values for a data array (a series or a vector) S, numbering from 1 to n, are to be summed.

□ BIBLIOGRAPHY

Ackoff, R. L. (1953) *Design of Social Research*. University of Chicago Press.

Ackoff, R. L., Gupta, S. K. and Minas, J. S. (1962) *Scientific Method: Optimizing Applied Research Decisions*. New York, John Wiley & Sons.

Adams, J. S. and Gilder, K. A. (1976) Household location and intra-urban migration. In D. T. Herbert and R. J. Johnston (eds) *Spatial Processes and Form*, vol. 1, 159–92. London, John Wiley & Sons.

Alexander, C. (1964) *Notes on the Synthesis of Form*. Cambridge, Mass., Harvard University Press.

Alexander, C. (1965) The city is not a tree. *Architectural Forum*, April, 58–62 and May, 68–71.

Alexander, I. (1979) *Office Location and Public Policy*. London, Longman.

Allnutt, D. E., Cox, R. T. S. and Mullock, P. J. (1970) Projecting growth patterns in regions. In Ministry of Housing and Local Government/Welsh Office: *Statistics for Town and Country Planning*, Series III, *Population and Households*, no. 1, 33–70. London, HMSO.

Alonso, W. (1964) *Location and Land Use: Toward a General Theory of Land Rent*. Cambridge, Mass., Harvard University Press.

Amos, F. J. C. (ed.) (1973) Education for planning. *Progress in Planning*, 1 (1). Oxford, Pergamon Press.

Armstrong, J. S. (1978) *Long-Range Forecasting*. New York, John Wiley & Sons.

Arrow, K. J. (1964) Comment on 'A Strategy of decision'. *Political Science Quarterly*, 79, 584–8.

Ascher, W. (1978) *Forecasting: An Appraisal for Policy-Makers and Planners*. Baltimore, Johns Hopkins University Press.

Ashby, J. (1976) Employment forecasting: techniques and problems in Structure Planning. In *Policy Analysis for Urban and Regional Planning*, Seminar proceedings. London, PTRC.

Ashby, W. R. (1964) *An Introduction to Cybernetics*. London, Methuen.

Ashworth, W. (1954) *The Genesis of Modern British Town Planning*. London, Routledge & Kegan Paul.

Atkinson, J. (1968) *A Handbook for Interviewers*, Government Social Survey (M136). London, HMSO.

Ayeni, B. (1979) *Concepts and Techniques in Urban Analysis*. London, Croom Helm.

Bachrach, P. and Baratz, M. S. (1970) *Power and Poverty: Theory and Practice*. London, Oxford University Press.

Bains Report, The (1972) see Study Group on Local Authority Management Structures.

Ball, M. J. and Kirwan, R. M. (1977) Accessibility and supply constraints in urban housing markets. *Urban Studies*, 14, 11–33.

357

Banfield, E. C. (1961) *Political influence.* New York, The Free Press.

Barras, R. (1975) A spatial interaction model of Cleveland. Planning Research Applications Group (PRAG), *Technical Paper,* 11. London, Centre for Environmental Studies.

Barras, R. (1978a) A resource-allocation framework for strategic planning. *Town Planning Review,* 49 (2), 296–305.

Barras, R. (ed.) (1978b) Current issues in Structure Planning. *Policy Series,* 4. London, Centre for Environmental Studies.

Barras, R. and Broadbent, T. A. (1975) A framework for Structure Plan analysis. Planning Research Applications Group (PRAG), *Technical Paper,* 8. London, Centre for Environmental Studies.

Barras, R. and Broadbent, T. A. (1979) The analysis of English Structure Plans. *Urban Studies,* 16 (1), 1–18.

Barras, R., Broadbent, T. A., Cordey-Hayes, M., Massey, D. B., Robinson, K. and Willis, J. (1971) An operational urban development model of Cheshire. *Environment and planning,* 3, 109–242.

Barnes, K. (1976) Monitoring development plans. *The Planner,* 62 (7), 207–10.

Barnes, W. N. (1974) Hypermarket prediction in Western Europe. In *Retailing,* Seminar proceedings. London, PTRC.

Barnett, V. (1974) *Elements of Sampling Theory.* London, English Universities Press.

Batey, P. W. J. (1978) Factors affecting the choice of strategic planning methodology in a stagnating metropolitan area: a case study of Greater Manchester. Department of Civic Design, Liverpool, The University.

Batey, P. W. J. and Breheny, M. J. (1978a) Methods in strategic planning. Part I: a descriptive review. *Town Planning Review,* 49 (3), 259–73.

Batey, P. W. J. and Breheny, M. J. (1978b) Methods in strategic planning. Part II: a prescriptive review. *Town Planning Review,* 49 (4), 502–18.

Bather, N. J. (1973) A linear land-use allocation model of new-residential growth. In *Urban and Regional Models,* Seminar proceedings. London, PTRC.

Bather, N. J., Williams, C. M. and Sutton, A. (1975) Strategic choice in practice: the West Berkshire Structure Plan experience. *Geographical Papers,* 50. Department of Geography, Reading, The University.

Batty, M. (1969) The impact of a new town. *Journal of the Town Planning Institute,* 55, 428–35.

Batty, M. (1971) An approach to rational design. *Architectural Design,* 41, 436–39 and 498–507.

Batty, M. (1974a) Social power in plan generation. *Town Planning Review,* 45 (3), 291–310.

Batty, M. (1974b) Plan generation: design methods, based on sieve maps, potential surfaces, lattices and Markov chains. *Geographical Papers,* 25. Department of Geography, Reading, The University.

Batty, M. (1976a) A political theory of planning and design. *Geographical Papers,* 45. Department of Geography, Reading, The University.

Batty, M. (1976b) Models, methods and rationality in urban and regional planning: developments since 1960. *Area,* 8 (2), 93–7.

Batty, M. (1976c) *Urban Modelling: Algorithms, Calibrations, Predictions.* Cambridge University Press.

Batty, M. (1978a) Paradoxes of science in public policy: the baffling case of land use models. *Geographical Papers,* 69. Department of Geography, Reading, The University.

Batty, M. (1978b) Reilly's challenge: new laws of retail gravitation which define systems of central places. *Environment and Planning A*, 10, 185–219.

Batty, M. and March, L. (1976) The method of residues in urban modelling. *Environment and Planning A*, 8, 189–214.

Bauer, R. (ed.) (1966) *Social Indicators*. Cambridge, Mass., MIT Press.

Bauer, R., de Sola Pool, I. and Dexter, L. (1963) *American Business and Public Policy*. New York, Atherton Press.

Baxter, R. S. (1976) *Computer and Statistical Techniques for Planners*. London, Methuen.

Baxter, R. S. and Williams, I. N. (1973) Theoretical and practical issues involved in the disaggregation of residential models. In *Urban and Regional Models*, Seminar proceedings. London, PTRC.

Baxter, R. S. and Williams, I. N. (1978) Population forecasting and uncertainty at the national and local scale. *Progress in planning*, 9 (1). Oxford, Pergamon Press.

Benevolo, L. (1967) *The Origins of Modern Town Planning*, Trans. J. Landry. London, Routledge & Kegan Paul.

Benjamin, B. (1970) *The Population Census*. London, Heinemann.

Benjamin, B. (1974) The collection and handling of demographic data now and in the future. In H. B. Parry (ed.) *Population and its problems*. Oxford, Clarendon Press.

Bennett, R. J. and Tan, K. C. (1979) Allocation of the UK Rate Support Grant by the use of methods of optimal control. *Environment and planning A*, 11, 1011–27.

Ben-Shahar, H., Mazor, A. and Pines, D. (1969) Town planning and welfare maximisation: a methodological approach. *Regional studies*, 3, 105–13.

Berdie, D. R. and Anderson, J. F. (1974) *Questionnaires: Design and Use*. Metuchen, N.J., Scarecrow Press.

Berkshire County Council (1975) *Reading, Wokingham, Aldershot, Basingstoke: The Future of the Sub-region*. Reading, Berkshire County Council.

Bernstein, S. J. and Mellon, W. G. (eds) (1978) *Selected Readings in Quantitative Urban Analysis*. Oxford, Pergamon Press.

Berry, B. J. L. (1964) Approaches to regional analysis: a synthesis. *Annals of the Association of American Geographers*, 54, 2–11.

Berry, B. J. L. (1973) A paradigm for modern geography. In R. J. Chorley (ed.), *Directions in Geography*. London, Methuen.

Berry, B. J. L. and Baker, A. M. (1968) Geographic sampling. In B. J. L. Berry and D. Marble (eds) *Spatial Analysis*. Englewood Cliffs, N.J., Prentice-Hall.

Birmingham Inner City Partnership (1977) *Initial Policy Paper*. Birmingham, Inner City Partnership.

Black, A. W. (1978) The 1981 Census: a local authority viewpoint. *Occasional Paper* 5. Glasgow, The Planning Exchange.

Black, J. and Conroy, M. (1977) Accessibility measures and the social evaluation of urban structure. *Environment and Planning A*, 9, 1013–31.

Blake, C. and McDowall, S. (1967) A local input–output table. *Scottish Journal of Political Economy*, 14, 227–42.

Blalock, H. M. (1970) *An Introduction to Social Research*. Englewood Cliffs, N.J., Prentice-Hall.

Blalock, H. M. (1972a) *Causal Inferences in Non-experimental Research*. New York, Norton.

Blalock, H. M. (1972b) *Social Statistics*, 2nd edn. New York, McGraw-Hill.

Blalock, H. M. (1974) *Measurement in the Social Sciences*. New York, Macmillan.

Blalock, H. M. and Blalock, A. B. (eds) (1968) *Methodology in Social Research*. New York, McGraw-Hill.

Blincoe, W. (1979) Analytical models for planning housing provision: a critical assessment of current practice. *Working Paper*, 9. Department of Civic Design, Liverpool, The University.

Blowers, A. (1980) *The Limits of Power: The Politics of Local Planning Policy*. Oxford, Pergamon Press.

Boddy, M. J. (1974) Models of housing market processes and residential location: a critical review towards a methodological standpoint. In A. R. Townsend and J. G. Carney (eds), *North-East Area Study Working Paper*, 8. Department of Geography, Durham, The University.

Booth, D. J. W. and Jaffe, M. (1978) Generation and evaluation in Structure Planning. *Town Planning Review* 49 (4), 445–58.

Booth, D. J. W. and Palmer, D. J. (1976) The activity-commodity framework and its application in strategic sectoral and spatial analysis. In *Policy Analysis for Urban and Regional Planning*, Seminar proceedings. London, PTRC.

Booth, P. (1970a) Model of a town: Cambridge. *Working Paper*, 13. Cambridge, Land Use Built Form Studies.

Booth, P. (1970b) *Cambridge: The Evaluation of Urban Structure Plans*. Cambridge, Land Use Built Form Studies.

Bor, W. (1974) The Town and Country Planning Act, 1968. *Journal of the Royal Town Planning Institute*, 60 (5), 696–703.

Bourne, L. S. (1975) *Urban Systems: Strategies for Regulation*. Oxford, Clarendon Press.

Bourne, L. S. (1976) Housing supply and housing market behaviour in residential development. In D. T. Herbert and R. J. Johnston (eds), *Spatial Processes and Form*, vol. 1. London, John Wiley & Sons.

Bovaird, A. C. (1978) A framework for the monitoring and evaluation of local employment measures. *Working Paper*, 15. Joint Unit for Research on the Urban Environment (JURUE), Aston, The University.

Bovy, P. H. L. and Jansen, G. R. M. (1979) Travel times for disaggregate travel demand modelling: a discussion and new travel time model. In G. R. M. Jansen *et al.* (eds), *New Developments in Modelling Travel Demand and Urban Systems*. Farnborough, Saxon House.

Box, G. E. P. and Jenkins, G. M. (1976) *Time Series Analysis: Forecasting and Control*, revised edn. San Francisco, Holden Day.

Boyce, D. E. (1970) Towards a framework for defining and applying urban indicators in plan making. *Urban Affairs Quarterly*, 6 (2), 145–71.

Boyce, D. E., Day, N. D. and McDonald, C. (1970) Metropolitan plan making. *Monograph Series*, 4. Regional Science Research Institute, Philadelphia, University of Pennsylvania.

Boyce, D. E., Fahri, A. and McDonald, C. (1972) Specification of plan making procedures for a given planning situation. In *The Refinement of Procedures for Continuing Metropolitan Planning: A Progress Report*. Philadelphia, University of Pennsylvania.

Boynton, J. (1979) Planning policy – its formation and implementation. Paper read to Town and Country Planning Summer School, September. University of York.

Bracken, I. (1976) Estimation and cluster analysis of net migration age profiles for urban areas in England and Wales. *Regional Studies*, 10, 53–69.

Bracken, I. (1978) Simulation: methodology for urban study. *Progress in Human Geography*, 2 (1), 49–75.

Bracken, I. (1980a) *A Policy Analytic Framework for Structure Plans*. Department of Town Planning, Cardiff, UWIST.

Bracken, I. (1980b) Structure Plans: submissions and alterations. *The Planner*, 66 (5), 130–2.

Bracken, I. and Hume, D. (1979a) Problems and issues in Structure Planning: industrial South Wales. *Project Report*, 1, vol. 1. Department of Town Planning, Cardiff, UWIST.

Bracken, I. and Hume, D. (1979b) Problems and issues in Structure Planning: Mid, North and West Wales. *Project Report*, 1, vol. II. Department of Town Planning, Cardiff, UWIST.

Bracken, I. and Hume, D. (1979c) An analysis of Welsh Structure Plans. *Papers in Planning Research*, 5. Department of Town Planning, Cardiff, UWIST.

Bracken, I. and Hume, D. (1981) Key Activity Forecasting in Structure Plans: A Critique. *Papers in Planning Research*, 26. Department of Town Planning, Cardiff, UWIST.

Brady, R., Brockman, R. and Talbot, J. (1975) Issues of retail location in Structure Planning and associated modelling methodologies. In *Urban and Regional Models for Public Policy Analysis*, Seminar proceedings. London, PTRC.

Braithwaite, R. B. (1960) *Scientific Explanation*. New York, Harper & Row (1953 edn. Cambridge University Press).

Bramley, G., Stewart, M. and Underwood, J. (1979) Local economic initiatives: a review. *Town Planning Review*, 50 (2), 131–47.

Brass, W. (1974) Demographic data and prediction of national and regional population trends. In H. B. Parry (ed.), *Population and its Problems*. Oxford, Clarendon Press.

Braybrooke, D. and Lindblom, C. E. (1963) *A Strategy of Decision: Policy Evaluation as a Social Process*. New York, The Free Press.

Brazier, S. and Harris, R. J. P. (1975) Inter authority planning. *Town Planning Review*, 46 (3), 255–65.

Brech, R. (1963) *Britain 1984*. London, Darton, Longman & Todd.

Breheny, M. J. (1974) Towards measures of spatial opportunity: a technique for the partial evaluation of plans. *Progress in Planning*, 2 (2). Oxford, Pergamon Press.

Breheny, M. J. (1978) The measurement of spatial opportunity in strategic planning. *Regional Studies*, 12, 463–79.

Breheny, M. J. and Roberts, A. J. (1978) An integrated forecasting system for Structure Planning. *Town Planning Review*, 49 (3), 306–18.

Breheny, M. J. and Roberts, A. J. (1979) A forecasting methodology for strategic planning. Paper presented to the 19th European Congress of the Regional Science Association, August. London, University College.

Broadbent, T. A. (1970) An activity analysis framework for urban planning. *Working Paper*, 61. London, Centre for Environmental Studies.

Broadbent, T. A. (1975) Activity analysis of spatial allocation models. *Environment and Planning*, 5, 673–91.

Broadbent, T. A. (1977) *Planning and Profit in the Urban Economy*. London, Methuen.

Broadbent, T. A. (1979) Options for planning: a discussion document. *Policy Series*, 7. London, Centre for Environmental Studies.

Broadbent, T. A. and Jaffe, M. (1975) Published Structure Plans and urban analysis: a critique and a framework. In *Urban and Regional Models for Public Policy Analysis*, Seminar proceedings. London, PTRC.

Brodbeck, M. (ed.) (1968) *Readings in the Philosophy of the Social Sciences.* London, Macmillan.

Bruce, A. J. and Mann, H. R. (1977) The Brent Cross Shopping Centre impact study: results of the first diary study of household shopping trips. *Research Memorandum*, 522. London, Greater London Council.

Bruner, J. S. and Minturn, A. L. (1955) Perceptual identification and perceptual organization. *Journal of General Psychology*, 53, 21–8.

Bruzelius, N. (1979) *The Value of Travel Time: Theory and Measurement.* London, Croom Helm.

Buchanan, C. (1963) see Ministry of Transport (1963).

Bulmer, M. (1978) Social science research and policy-making in Britain. In M. Bulmer (ed.), *Social Policy Research.* London, Macmillan.

Bunge, M. (1979) *Causality and Modern Science.* New York, Dover.

Bunker, R. (1973) A review of AIDA and strategic choice. In *Urban Development Decisions and Finance*, Seminar proceedings. London, PTRC.

Burchell, R. W. and Sternlieb, G. (eds) (1978) *Planning Theory in the 1980's.* Centre for Urban Policy Research, New Brunswick, N.J., Rutgers University.

Burdekin, R. and Marshall, J. A. (1973) The calibration, potential development and limitations of the Forrester model. In *Urban and Regional Models*, Seminar proceedings. London, PTRC.

Burton, T. L. and Cherry, G. E. (1969) *Social Research Techniques for Planners.* London, Allen & Unwin.

Buxton, M. and Craven, E. (eds) (1976) *Demographic Change and Social Policy: The Uncertain Future.* London, Centre for Studies in Social Policy.

Cameron, G. C. and Firn, J. (1975) Towards an understanding of intra-metropolitan location and manufacturing: the Glasgow case. *Working Paper*, 12. Metropolitan Industrial Location, Inner City Employment Seminar, London, Centre for Environmental Studies.

Cameron, G. C., Firn, J., Latham, M. and MacLennan, D. (1974) The determinants of urban manufacturing location: a simple model. In E. L. Cripps (ed.), *London Papers in Regional Science.* London, Pion.

Campbell, D. T. (1957) Factors relevant to the validity of experiments in social settings. *Psychological Bulletin*, 54, 297–312.

Campbell, D. T. (1969) Reforms as experiments. *American Psychologist*, 24 (4), 409–28.

Campbell, D. T. (1972) *Methods for the experimenting society.* Department of Psychology, Evanston, Northwestern University.

Campbell, D. T. and Cook, T. D. (1976) *The Design and Conduct of Quasi-Experiments and True Experiments in Field Settings.* Chicago, Rand McNally.

Campbell, D. T. and Stanley, J. C. (1966) *Experimental and Quasi-experimental Designs for Research.* Chicago, Rand McNally.

Campbell, R. (1976) Local population projections. *Population Trends*, 5, 9–12.

Cannell, C. F., Marquis, K. and Robinson, S. (1971) Report of a tape-recorded account of interviewer–respondent reactions in three urban areas. In J. B. Lansing, S. B. Withey and A. C. Wolfe (eds), *Working Papers on Survey Research in Poverty Areas.* Survey research center, Ann Arbor, University of Michigan.

Caporaso, J. (1973) Quasi-experimental approaches to social sciences: perspectives and problems. In J. Caporaso and L. Roos (eds), *Quasi-experimental Approaches: Testing Theory and Evaluating Policy.* Evanston, Northwestern University Press.

Carlisle, E. (1972) The conceptual structure of social indicators. In A. Shonfield and S. Shaw (eds), *Social Indicators and Social Policy.* London, Heinemann.

Catanese, A. J. (1972) *Scientific Methods of Urban Analysis.* Urbana, University of Illinois Press.

Catanese, A. J., Alexander, E. R. and Sawicki, D. S. (1979) *Urban Planning: A Guide to Information Sources.* Detroit, Gale Research.

Catanese, A. J. and Steiss, W. (1970) *Systematic Planning: Theory and Application.* Lexington, Mass., D. C. Heath.

Caulfield, I. G. (1970) An alternative method of projecting the numbers and sizes of households. *Journal of the Royal Town Planning Institute,* 5 (6), 220–4.

Caulfield, I. G. and Rhodes, T. (1971) The use of an allocation model in the preparation of a Structure Plan for South Hampshire. In *Urban Growth Models,* Seminar proceedings. London, PTRC.

Cazes, B. (1972) The development of social indicators: a survey. In A. Shonfield and S. Shaw (eds), *Social Indicators and Social Policy.* London, Heinemann.

Cebula, R. J. (1974) Local government policies and migration: an analysis for SMSA's in the United States, 1965–1970. *Public Choice,* 19, 85–94. Reprinted in S. S. Nagel (ed.) (1977) *Policy Studies Review Annual,* 1, 506–14.

Central Lancashire Study (1967) *Central Lancashire: Study for a City.* London, HMSO.

Central Unit for Environment Planning, The (1971) *Severnside: A Feasibility Study.* London, HMSO.

Chadwick, G. F. (1976) *A Systems View of Planning,* 2nd edn. Oxford, Pergamon Press.

Chapin, F. S. (1965) *Urban Land Use Planning.* Urbana, University of Illinois Press.

Chapin, F. S. and Kaiser, E. J. (1979) *Urban Land Use Planning.* Urbana, University of Illinois Press.

Cherry, G. E. (1970) *Town Planning in its Social Context.* Aylesbury, Leonard Hill.

Cherry, G. E. (1974) *The Evolution of British Town Planning.* Aylesbury, Leonard Hill.

Cheshire Structure Plan (1977) Chester, County Council.

Chilton, R. and Poet, R. R. W. (1973) An entropy maximizing approach to the recovery of detailed migration patterns from aggregate census data. *Environment and Planning A,* 5, 135–46.

Chiswick, B. R. and Chiswick, S. J. (1975) *Statistics and Econometrics: A Problem-Solving Text.* Baltimore, University Park Press.

Chorafas, D. N. (1965) *Systems and Simulation.* New York, Academic Press.

Chorley, R. J. and Haggett, P. (eds) (1967) *Models in Geography.* London, Methuen.

Christ, C. F. (1966) *Economic Models and Methods.* New York, John Wiley & Sons.

Churchman, C. W. (1961) *Prediction and Optimal Decision.* Englewood Cliffs, N.J., Prentice-Hall.

Churchman, C. W. (1968) *Challenge to Reason.* New York, McGraw-Hill.

Churchman, C. W. (1969) *The Systems Approach.* New York, Delta.

Churchman, C. W., Ackoff, R. L. and Arnoff, E. L. (1957) *Introduction to Operations Research.* New York, John Wiley & Sons.

Clark, J. I. and Rhind, D. W. (1975) The relationship between the size of areal units and the characteristics of population structure. *Working Paper*, 5. Department of Geography, Durham, The University.

Cleveland County Council (1980) County Structure Plans monitoring and review. *Report*, 168. Cleveland, County Planning Department.

Cochran, W. G. (1977) *Sampling Techniques*, 3rd edn. New York, John Wiley & Sons.

Cockburn, C. (1977) *The Local State: Management of Cities and People*. London, Pluto Press.

Cockhead, P. (1978) Integrated forecasting for strategic planning and resource programming: the approach developed in the Grampian region. In *Policy Analysis for Urban and Regional Planning*, Seminar proceedings. London, PTRC.

Coelho, J. D. and Wilson, A. G. (1976) The optimum location and size of shopping centres. *Regional Studies*, 10, 413–21.

Cohon, J. L. (1978) *Multiobjective Programming and Planning*. New York, Academic Press.

Coleman, J. S. (1972) *Policy Research in the Social Sciences*. Morristown, N.J., General Learning Press.

Commission into the Third London Airport (1969) *Proposed Research Methodology*. London, HMSO.

Commission into the Third London Airport (1970) *Papers and Proceedings*. London, HMSO.

Commission into the Third London Airport (1971) *Report*. London, HMSO.

Connolly, K. (1979) *Housing: Sources of Information on Housing*. London, Department of the Environment.

Cooper, M. J. M. (1976) Government influence on industrial location. *Town Planning Review*, 47, 384–97.

Cordey-Hayes, M. and Gleave, D. (1974) Migration movements and the differential growth of city regions in England and Wales. *Report*, 33. 13th Congress of the Regional Science Association.

Coventry Structure Plan (1973) Coventry, City Council.

Coventry–Warwickshire–Solihull Sub-Regional Study (1971) *A Strategy for the Sub-region*. Coventry, City Council.

Craig, J. (1970) Estimating the age and sex structure of net migration for a sub-region: a case study – North and South Humberside 1951–1961. *Regional Studies*, 4, 333–47.

Craig, J. and Driver, A. (1972) The identification and comparison of small areas of adverse social conditions. *Journal of the Royal Statistical Society*, Series C, 21 (1), 25–35.

Crecine, J. P. (1964) TOMM – Time Oriented Metropolitan Model. *CRP Technical Bulletin*, 6. Pittsburgh, Department of City Planning.

Crecine, J. P. (1968) *A Dynamic Model of Urban Structure*, P-3803. Santa Monica, Calif., Rand Corporation.

Crecine, J. P. (1969) *Spatial Location Decisions and Urban Structure: A Time-oriented Model*. Institute of Public Policy Studies, 4. Ann Arbor, University of Michigan.

Crenson, M. A. (1971) *The Un-politics of Air Pollution: A Study of Non-decision Making in Cities*. Baltimore, Johns Hopkins University Press.

Cripps, E. L. and Foot, D. H. S. (1969) A land use model for sub-regional planning. *Regional Studies*, 3, 243–68.

Crofton, B. and Webster, J. (1974) Improving housing allocation. *The Planner*, 60 (8), 839 42.

Cross, D. T. (1972) Planning forecasting. In C. Freeman, M. Jahoda and I. Miles (eds), *Progress and Problems in Social Forecasting*. London, Social Science Research Council.

Crowther, D. (1971) Mathematical techniques as an aid to urban structure planning: a worked example. In *Urban Growth Models*, Seminar proceedings. London, PTRC.

Cullingworth, J. B. (1979a) *Town and Country Planning in Britain*, 7th edn. London, Allen & Unwin.

Cullingworth, J. B. (1979b) *Essays on Housing Policy: The British Scene*. London, Allen & Unwin.

Cullingworth, J. B. and Orr, S. C. (1969) *Regional and Urban Studies: A Social Science approach*. London, Allen & Unwin.

Dahl, R. A. (1961) *Who Governs?* New Haven, Yale University Press.

Dalkey, N. (1972) An elementary cross-impact model. *Technological Forecasting and Social Change*, 341–51.

Davidoff, P. (1968) Normative planning. In S. Anderson (ed.) *Planning for Diversity and Choice*. Cambridge, Mass., MIT Press.

Davidoff, P. and Reiner, T. A. (1962) A choice theory of planning. *Journal of the American Institute of Planners*, 28 (2), 103–15. Reprinted in A. Faludi (ed.) (1973) *A Reader in Planning Theory*. Oxford, Pergamon Press.

Davidson, K. B. (1977) Accessibility in transport/land use modelling and assessment. *Environment and planning A*, 9, 1401–16.

Davis, C. F. and Kennedy, M. D. (1970) EPS: A computer program for the evaluation of problem structure. In G. T. Moore (ed.) *Emerging Methods of Environmental Design*. Cambridge, Mass., MIT Press.

De Bono, E. (1971) *The Mechanism of Mind*. Harmondsworth, Penguin.

De Jouvenal, B. (1967) *The Art of Conjecture*. London, Weidenfeld & Nicolson.

De Jouvenal, B. (1968) Notes on social forecasting. In M. Young (ed.), *Forecasting and the Social Sciences*. London, Heinemann/SSRC.

De Kanter J. and Morrison, W. I. (1978) The Merseyside input–output study and its application to Structure Planning. In P. W. J. Batey (ed.), *Theory and Methods in Urban and Regional Analysis*. London, Pion.

Delbecq, A. L., Van de Ven, A. M. and Gustafson, D. H. (1975) *Group Techniques for Program Planning: A Guide to Nominal Group and Delphi Processes*. London, Scott Foresman & Co.

Dempster, M. A. H. and Wildavsky, A. (1979) On change: or, there is no magic size for an increment. *Political Studies*, 27 (3), 371–89.

Department of the Environment (DOE) (1969) *People and Planning: Report of the Committee on Public Participation in Planning* (Chairman: A. M. Skeffington). London, HMSO (originally published by Ministry of Housing and Local Government).

DOE (1971) *Management Networks: A Study for Structure Plans*, 2 vols. London, HMSO.

DOE (1972a) The use of evaluation matrices for Structure Planning. *Structure Plans Note*, 8/72. London, DOE.

DOE (1972b) Notes on Structure Plan evaluation. *Structure Plans Note*, 7/72. London, DOE.

DOE (1972c) An approach to Structure Plan evaluation. *Working Notes*, 82. Directorate of Planning and Regional Strategies, London, DOE.

DOE (1972d) *Development Plan Proposals: Publicity and Public Participation*, Circular 52/72. London, HMSO.

DOE (1973a) *Using Predictive Models for Structure Plans*. London, HMSO.

DOE (1973b) Decision rules in Structure Plan evaluation. *Working Notes*, 94. Directorate of Planning and Regional Strategies, London, DOE.

DOE (1974a) Evaluating the effectiveness of alternatives in Structure Planning. *Planning Techniques Paper*, 1/74. London, DOE.

DOE (1974b) *Structure Plans*, Circular 98/74. London, HMSO.

DOE (1975a) The generation of alternative strategies in Structure Planning. *Structure Plans Note*, 6/75. London, DOE.

DOE (1975b) *The Use of Indicators for Area Action – Housing Act 1974*, Area Improvement Note 10. London, HMSO.

DOE (1975c) *Renewal Strategies: Housing Act 1974*, Circular 13/75. London, HMSO.

DOE (1975d) Principles for monitoring development plans. *Structure Plans Note*, 1/75. London, DOE.

DOE (1976) Development plan evaluation and robustness: application of an analytical program and a review of measures of performance. *Research Report*, 5. Local Government Operational Research Unit, London, HMSO.

DOE (1977a) *Memorandum on Structure and Local Plans*, Circular 55/77. London, HMSO.

DOE (1977b) Monitoring for development planning. *Research Report*, 23. Institute of Operational Research, London, DOE & Department of Transport.

DOE (1978a) Ongoing review and. the need for alteration. *Structure Plans Note*, 1/78. London, DOE.

DOE (1978b) *National Dwelling and Household Survey*. London, HMSO.

DOE (1979a) *Directory of Local Authority Surveys 1978: Housing and Population*. London, HMSO.

DOE (1979b) *The Assessment of Housing Requirements*, Report by the Housing Services Advisory Group. London, HMSO.

DOE (1979c) *Memorandum on Structure and Local Plans*, Circular 4/79. London, HMSO.

Deutsch, K. (1966) *The Nerves of Government*. New York, The Free Press.

Diamond, D. (ed.) (1979) Policy forum: the uses of strategic planning. *Town Planning Review*, 1, 18–33.

Dicken, P. (1976) The multiplant business enterprise and geographical space: some issues in the study of external control and regional development. *Regional Studies*, 10, 401–12.

Dicken, P. and Lloyd, P. E. (1978) Inner metropolitan industrial change, enterprise structures and policy issues: case studies of Manchester and Merseyside. *Regional Studies*, 12, 181–98.

Directorate of Planning and Regional Strategies (1972) An approach to Structure Plan evaluation. *Working Note*, 82. London, DOE.

Directorate of Planning and Regional Strategies (1973) Decision rules in Structure Plan evaluation. *Working Note*, 94. London, DOE.

Distribution of Industry Act (1945) London, HMSO.

Doling, J. F. (1973) A two-stage model of tenure choice in the housing market. *Urban Studies*, 10, 199–211.

Doling, J. F. (1976) The family life cycle and housing choice. *Urban Studies*, 13, 55–8.

Donnison, D. V. (1972) Research for policy. *Minerva*, 10, 519–36. Reprinted in M. Bulmer (ed.) (1978) *Social Policy Reasearch*. London, Macmillan.

Donnison, D. V. (1976) The age of innocence is past: some ideas about urban research and planning. *Urban Studies*, 12, 263–72.

Drake, M. (1975) Aims, objectives and problems in Structure Plan methodology. In M. Drake *et al.* (1975) *Aspects of Structure Planning in Britain*, Research paper 20. London, Centre for Environmental Studies.

Drake, M., McLoughlin, J. B., Thompson, R. and Thornley, J. (1975) *Aspects of Structure Planning in Britain*, Research paper 20. London, Centre for Environmental Studies.

Dror, Y. (1964) Muddling through – 'science' or inertia. *Public Administration Review*, 24, 153–7.

Dror, Y. (1968) *Public Policy Making Re-examined*. New York, Chandler.

Dror, Y. (1976) Policy analysis for local government. *Local Government Studies*, 1, 33–46.

Dudley Structure Plan (1974) Dudley, Borough Council.

Dugmore, K. and Gilje, E. (1979) How useful are sample surveys for monitoring policies?. In *Policy Analysis for Urban and Regional Planning*, Seminar proceedings. London, PTRC.

Duncan, T. L. C. and Johnson, R. (1978) Research for planning: a review of research carried out by central government for Scottish regional planning authorities. *Research Paper*, 6. Glasgow, The Planning Exchange.

Dye, T. R. (1972) *Understanding Public Policy*. Englewood Cliffs, N.J., Prentice-Hall.

Earwicker, J. (1974) The future of planning. *Journal of the Royal Town Planning Institute*, 60 (4), 650–2.

East Anglia, Strategic Choice for (1974) Department of the Environment. London, HMSO.

East Sussex County Structure Plan (1975) Lewes, County Council.

Echenique, M., Crowther, D. and Lindsay, W. (1969a) A spatial model of urban stock and activity. *Regional Studies*, 3, 281–312.

Echenique, M., Crowther, D. and Lindsay, W. (1969b) Development of a model of a town. *LUBFS Working Paper*, 26. Cambridge, Land Use Built Form Studies.

Echenique, M., Crowther, D. and Lindsay, W. (1972) A structural comparison of three generations of new towns. In L. Martin and L. March (eds), *Urban Space and Structures*. Cambridge University Press.

Eddison, T. (1971) Statutory conflict. *Town and Country Planning*, 39, 343–5.

Eddison, T. (1975) *Local Government: Management and Corporate Planning*, 2nd edn. Aylesbury, Leonard Hill.

Eden, C. (1977) Modelling the influence of decision makers on the future. *Futures*, 9 (4), 272–84.

Edwards, J. (1975) Social indicators, urban deprivation and positive discrimination. *Journal of Social Policy*, 4, 275–87. Reprinted in M. Bulmer (ed.) (1978) *Social Policy Research*. London, Macmillan.

Edwards, S. L. and Gordon, I. R. (1970) The application of input–output methods to regional forecasting: the British experience. *Colston Papers*, 22, 415–30.

Elkin, S. (1974) *Politics and Land Use Planning: The London Experience*. Cambridge University Press.

Emery, F. E. (1968) Concepts, methods and anticipation. In M. Young (ed.), *Forecasting and the Social Sciences*. London, Heinemann/SSRC.

Emery, F. E. (ed.) (1969) *Systems Thinking*. Harmondsworth, Penguin.

Enzer, S. (1970) A case study using forecasting as a decision making aid. *Futures*, 2 (4), 341–62.

Etzioni, A. (1967) Mixed-scanning: A 'third' approach to decision-making. *Public Administration Review*, 28 (5), 385–92.

Etzioni, A. (1968) *The Active Society*. New York, The Free Press.

Everitt, B. (1974) *Cluster Analysis*. London, Heinemann.

Everitt, B. (1978) *Graphical Techniques for Multivariate Data*. London, Heinemann.

Eversley, D. and Cope, D. (1978) Is the census out of date?. *New Society*, 25 May.

Faludi, A. (1973) *A Reader in Planning Theory*. Oxford, Pergamon Press.

Family Expenditure Survey (1957–) Office of Population Censuses and Surveys. London, HMSO.

Feller, W. (1968) *An Introduction to Probability Theory and its Applications*. New York, John Wiley & Sons.

Firn, J. R. and Latham, H. M. (1977) *A Markov Analysis of the Clydeside Conurbation*. Department of Social and Economic Research, Glasgow, The University.

Fisher, R. A. (1973) *Statistical Methods for Research Workers*, 15th edn. New York, Hafner.

Floyd, M. (1978) Structure Plan monitoring. *Town Planning Review*, 49 (4), 476–85.

Floyd, M., Sutton, A., Friend, J. and King, L. (1977) *Monitoring for Development Plans*, Report 937R. Coventry, Institute for Operations Research.

Flynn, M., Flynn, P. and Mellor, N. (1972) Social malaise research: a study – Liverpool. *Social Trends*, 3, 42–52.

Fogarty, M. S. (1977) Predicting neighbourhood decline within a large central city: an application of discriminant analysis. *Environment and Planning A*, 9, 579–84.

Foot, D. H. S. (1973) A comparison of some land use allocation – interaction models. The Garin–Lowry model and the simultaneous regression model. In *Urban and Regional Models*, Seminar proceedings. London, PTRC.

Foot, D. H. S. (1978) Mathematical models in land use planning. In B. Goodall and A. Kirby (eds), *Resources and Planning*. Oxford, Pergamon Press.

Forrester, J. W. (1969) *Urban Dynamics*. Cambridge, Mass., MIT Press.

Freeman, C., Jahoda, M. and Miles, I. (eds) (1972) *Progress and Problems in Social Forecasting*. London, Social Science Research Council.

Friedmann, J. (1973) The public interest and community participation: towards a reconstruction of public philosophy. *Journal of the American Institute of Planners*, 39 (1), 2–7.

Friend, J. K. (1977) Dynamics of policy change. *Long Range Planning*, 10 (1), 40–7.

Friend, J. K. and Jessop, W. N. (1976) *Local Government and Strategic Choice*, 2nd edn. Oxford, Pergamon Press. Originally published (1969) London, Tavistock Publications.

Friend, J. K., Power, J. M. and Yewlett, C. J. L. (1974) *Public Planning: The Inter-corporate Dimension*. London, Tavistock Publications.

Gabor, D. (1963) *Inventing the Future*. New York, Secker & Warburg.

Gabor, D. (1969) Open ended planning. In E. Jantsch (ed.), *Perspectives of Planning*. Paris, OECD.

Galtung, J. (1969) *Theory and Methods of Social Research.* London, Allen & Unwin.

Gans, H. J. (1968) *People and Plans: Essays on Urban Problems and Solutions.* New York, Basic Books.

Gans, H. J. (1969) *Levittowners: Ways of Life and Politics in a New Suburban Community.* New York, Random House.

Gans, H. J. (1973) The public interest and community participation: a commentary. *Journal of the American Institute of Planners,* 39 (1), 3, 10–12.

Garin, R. A. (1966) A matrix formulation of the Lowry model for intra-metropolitan activity allocation. *Journal of the American Institute of Planners,* 32, 361–64.

Garner, M. (1979) Policy forum: Skeffington revisited. *Town Planning Review,* 50 (4), 412–19.

General Household Survey (GHS) (1973–) An annual inter-departmental survey sponsored by the Central Statistical Office. London, HMSO. See Social Survey Division, Office of Population Censuses and Surveys (1973).

General Information System for Planning (GISP) (1972) Joint local authority, Scottish Development Department, Department of the Environment Study Team. London, HMSO.

GIMMS (1973) An introduction to a geographic information manipulation and mapping system. (T. C. Waugh) *Inter-University/Research Councils Research and Development Notes,* 9. Edinburgh, University Regional Computing Centre.

Glaser, B. G. and Strauss, A. L. (1967) *The Discovery of Grounded Theory.* Chicago, Aldine.

Glasgow District Council (n.d.) *Glasgow: Implications of Population Changes to 1983.* Glasgow, District Council.

Glass, G. V., Willson, V. L. and Gottman, J. M. (1973) *Design and Analysis of Time Series Experiments.* Laboratory of Education Research, Boulder, University of Colorado.

Gleave, D. (1973) A simulation of the relationship between the directional components of migration. In *Urban and Regional Models,* Seminar proceedings. London, PTRC.

Gleave, D. and Cordey-Hayes, M. (1977) Migration dynamics and labour market turnover. *Progress in Planning,* 8 (1). Oxford, Pergamon Press.

Glenn, N. D. (1977) *Cohort Analysis.* London, Sage.

Gordon, P. and Ledent, J. (1980) Modelling the dynamics of a system of metropolitan areas: a demoeconomic approach. *Environment and Planning A,* 12 (2), 125–33.

Gordon, W. J. J. (1961) *Synectics: The Development of Creative Capacity.* New York, Harper & Row.

Grampian Regional Council (1976) *Analysis of Inherited Development Plans and Studies.* Department of Physical Planning, Aberdeen, Grampian Regional Council.

Grampian Regional Council (1978a) Shift and share methods of employment analysis and projection. *Research Paper,* 3. Aberdeen, Grampian Regional Council.

Grampian Regional Council (1978b) An integrated forecasting methodology for strategic planning. *Planning Research Paper,* 1. Aberdeen, Grampian Regional Council.

Grampian Regional Council (1979) Development analysis booklet, published bi-annually for each District Council Area. Department of Physical Planning, Aberdeen, Grampian Regional Council.

Grant, R. A., Thomson, B. W., Dible, J. K. and Randall, J. N. (1976) *Local Housing Needs and Strategies*. Scottish Development Department. Edinburgh, HMSO.

Gray, S. (1970) *The Electoral Register: Practical Information for Use When Drawing Samples, Both for Interview and Postal Surveys*. Government Social Survey (M151). London, HMSO.

Gray, P. G. and Gee, F. A. (1967) *Electoral Registration for Parliamentary Elections: An Enquiry Made for the Home Office*. Government Social Survey (SS391). London, HMSO.

Gray, P. G. and Gee, F. A. (1972) *A Quality Check on the 1966 Ten Per Cent Sample Census of England and Wales*. Government Social Survey (SS391). London, HMSO.

Greater Manchester Structure Plan (1979) Manchester, Metropolitan County Council.

Greenburg, C. D., Miller, J. A., Mohr, L. B. and Vladeck, B. C. (1977) Developing public theory: perspectives from empirical research. *The American Political Science Review*, 71, 1532–43.

Greenwood, M. J. (1973) Urban growth and migration: their interaction. *Environment and Planning*, 5, 91–112.

Greenwood, M. J. (1975) A simultaneous-equations model of urban growth and migration. *Journal of the American Statistical Association*, 70, 797–810.

Grey, A. (1978) The policy implications of housing forecasts. In *Policy Analysis for Urban and Regional Planning*, Seminar proceedings. London, PTRC.

Griffith, D. A. and Jones, K. G. (1980) Explorations into the relationship between spatial structure and spatial interaction. *Environment and Planning A*, 12, 187–201.

Gupta, S. K. and Rosenhead, J. (1968) Robustness in sequential decisions. *Management Science*, 15 (2), B18–B29.

Gutch, T. (1970) Planning, philosophy and logic. *Journal of the Royal Town Planning Institute*, 56 (9), 389–91.

Guy, C. M. (1976) A method of examining and evaluating the impact of major retail developments upon existing shops and their users. *Environment and Planning A*, 9, 491–504.

Guy, C. M. (1980) *Retail Location and Retail Planning in Britain*. Farnborough, Gower.

Hadley, G. (1962) *Linear Programming*. Reading, Mass., Addison-Wesley.

Haggett, P. (1967) Network models in geography. In R. J. Chorley and P. Haggett (eds), *Models in Geography*. London, Methuen.

Haggett, P., Cliff, A. D. and Frey, A. (1977) *Locational Analysis in Human Geography*, 2 vols. London, Edward Arnold.

Hakim, C. (1978) Census confidentiality, micro-data and census analysis. *Occasional Paper*, 3. Office of Population Censuses and Surveys. London, HMSO.

Hall, J., Lord, D., Marsh, C. and Ring, J. (1980) *Users Manual: Quality of Life Survey. Distribution of Responses and Questionnaire*. SSRC Survey Unit, London, Social Science Research Council.

Hall, P. (1972) Planning and the environment. In P. Townsend and N. Bosanquet (eds), *Labour and Inequality*. London, Fabian Society.

Hall, P. (1973) Urban Europe 2000: progress of a research project. *Futures*, 5, 449–56.

Hall, P. (1974) Futurology: planners, forecasts, the public and the future. *Journal of the Royal Town Planning Institute*, 60 (4), 634–5.

Hall, P. (1975) *Urban and Regional Planning*. Newton Abbot, David & Charles.

Hambleton, R. (1978) *Policy Planning and Local Government*. London, Hutchinson.

Hamilton, C. H. (1966) Effect of census errors on the measurement of net migration. *Demography*, 3, 393–415.

Hamilton, C. H. (1967) The vital statistics method of estimating net migration by age cohorts. *Demography*, 4, 464–78.

Hansen, W. G. (1959) How accessibility shapes land use. *Journal of the American Institute of Planners*, 25 (2), 73–6.

Harary, F. and Rockey, J. (1976) A city is not a semi-lattice either. *Environment and Planning A*, 8, 375–84.

Harris, B. (1968) Quantitative models of urban development: their role in metropolitan policy-making. In H. S. Perloff and L. Wingo (eds), *Issues in Urban Economics*. Baltimore, Johns Hopkins University Press.

Harris, B. (1970) Generating projects for urban research. *Environment and Planning A*, 2, 1–21.

Harris, B. (1972) A model of household location preferences. In R. Funck (ed.), *Recent Developments in Regional Science*. London, Pion.

Harris, B. (1976) Notes on the relationship between mathematical land use theory and public policy applications. In G. J. Papageorgiou (ed.), *Mathematical Land Use Theory*. Lexington, Mass., D. C. Heath.

Harris, B. (1978) The comprehensive planning of location. In R. W. Burchell and G. Sternlieb (eds), *Planning Theory in the 1980's*. Centre for Urban Policy Research, New Brunswick, N.J., Rutgers University.

Harris, B. and Wilson, A. G. (1978) Equilibrium values and dynamics of attractiveness terms in production-constrained spatial-interaction models. *Environment and Planning A*, 10 (4), 371–88.

Harris, D. F. and Taylor, F. J. (1978) The service sector: its changing role as a source of employment. *Research Series*, 25. London, Centre for Environmental Studies.

Harris, R. and Scott, D. (1974) The role of monitoring and review in planning. *Journal of the Royal Town Planning Institute*, 60 (6), 729–32.

Harvey, D. (1969) *Explanation in Geography*. London, Edward Arnold.

Harvey, D. (1971) Social processes, spatial form and the redistribution of real income in an urban system. *Regional Forecasting*. Bristol, Colston Paper.

Harvey, D. (1973) *Social Justice and the City*. London, Edward Arnold.

Hay, A. M. and Johnston, R. J. (1979) Search and the choice of shopping centre: two models of variability in destination selection. *Environment and Planning A*, 11, 791–804.

Haynes, P. A. (1974) Towards a concept of monitoring. *Town Planning Review*, 45 (1), 5–29.

Hayton, K. (1979) *An Appraisal of Forecasting Methodology and Integration in the Strathclyde Structure Plan*. Department of Planning, Glasgow, School of Art.

Heclo, H. H. (1972) Review article: Policy analysis. *British Journal of Political Science*, 2, 83–108.

Heclo, H. H. (1974) *Modern Social Policies in Britain and Sweden*. New Haven, Yale University Press.

Hedges, B. M. (1974) Surveying housing needs: An account of the 1972 Westminster Housing Survey. In *Housing*, Seminar proceedings. London, PTRC.

Helmer, O. (1977) Problems in future research: delphi and causal cross-impact analysis. *Futures*, 9 (1), 17–31.

Hensher, D. and Stopher, P. (1979) *Behavioural Travel Modelling*. London, Croom Helm.

Herbert, D. T. and Evans, D. J. (1974) Urban sub-areas as sampling frameworks for social survey. *Town Planning Review*, 45 (2), 171–82.

Herbert, D. T. and Johnston, R. J. (eds) (1976) *Spatial Processes and Form*, 2 vols. London, John Wiley & Sons.

Herbert, J. D. and Stevens, B. H. (1960) A model for the distribution of residential activity in urban areas. *Journal of Regional Science*, 2, 21–36.

Herefordshire Structure Plan (1974) Hereford, County Council.

Hertfordshire County Council (1977a) Public transport for rural communities. *Report*, 2. Transport Coordination Unit, Hertford, County Council.

Hertfordshire County Council (1977b) South West Herts: shopping impact study. A study of the potential impact of out-of-town and urban fringe shopping centres on the existing shopping and retailing structure. Hertford, County Planning Department.

Hertfordshire County Structure Plan (1976) Hertford, County Council.

Hetherington, M. F. (1973) A consideration of a household based projection model for Greater London. In *Population Projections*, Seminar proceedings. London, PTRC.

Hewings, F. J. D. (1971) Regional input–output models in the UK: some problems and prospects for the use of non-survey techniques. *Regional Studies*, 5, 11–22.

Hickling, A. (1974) *Managing Decisions: The Strategic Choice Approach*. Rugby, Mantec Publications.

Hickling, A. (1978) AIDA and the levels of choice in Structure Plans. *Town Planning Review*, 49, 459–75.

Hickling, A., Friend, J. and Luckman, J. (1979) The development plan system and investment programmes. *Report*, 2T235. Centre for Organizational and Operational Research, Coventry, Tavistock Institute for Human Relations.

Hill, M. (1968) A goals–achievement matrix for evaluating alternative plans. *Journal of the American Institute of Planners*, 34, 19–29.

Hill, M. (1972) The fallacy of 'the cost–benefit fallacy'. *Official Architecture and Planning*, 35, 103–4.

Hillman, M., Henderson, I. and Whalley, A. (1973) Personal mobility and transport policy. *PEP Broadsheet*, 542. London, Policy and Economic Planning Unit.

Hillman, M., Henderson, I. and Whalley, A. (1976) Transport realities and planning policy. *PEP Broadsheet*, 567. London, Policy and Economic Planning Unit.

Hoem, J. (1973) Levels of error in population forecasts. *Artikler*, 61. Oslo, Central Bureau of Statistics.

Hoinville, G. and Jowell, R. (eds) (1978) *Survey Research Practice*. London, Heinemann.

Hollis, J., Henderson, A. and Congdon, P. (1976) Population and household projections for London: 1976. *Research Monograph*, RM506. London, Greater London Council.

Holm, P., Snickars, F., Gustafsson, J. R. and Harsman, B. (1978) Policy-oriented housing models: some tentative applications. In P. W. J. Batey (ed.), *Theory and Method in Urban and Regional Analysis*. London, Pion.

Holman, R. and Hamilton, L. (1973/4) The British urban programme. *Policy and Politics*, 2 (2), 97–112.

Holmes, J. C. (1972) An ordinal method of evaluation. *Urban Studies*, 9, 179–91.

Holsti, O. R. (1969) *Content Analysis for the Social Sciences and Humanities*. Reading, Mass., Addison-Wesley.

Holterman, S. (1975) Census indicators of urban deprivation. *Working Note*, 6. London, DOE.

Hourihan, K. (1979a) The evaluation of urban neighbourhoods 1: perception. *Environment and Planning A*, 11, 1337–53.

Hourihan, K. (1979b) The evaluation of urban neighbourhoods 2: preference. *Environment and Planning A*, 11, 1355–66.

Housing Services Advisory Group (HSAG) (1977) *The Assessment of Housing Requirements*. London, DOE.

Housing Strategies and Investment Programmes (HIP) see Department of the Environment, Circulars 63/77 and 38/78. London, HMSO.

Hutchinson, B. G. (1974) *Principles of Urban Transport Systems Planning*. New York, McGraw Hill.

Hyman, H. H. (1975) *Interviewing in Social Research*, 7th edn. University of Chicago Press.

Hyman, G. and Gleave, D. (1977) A reasonable theory of migration. *Occasional Paper*, 2. London, Centre for Environmental Studies.

Institute for Operational Research (IOR) (1978) *Regional Report*, 962. Coventry, IOR.

Irvine, J., Miles, I. and Evans, J. (eds) (1979) *Demystifying Social Statistics*. London, Pluto Press.

Isard, W. (1969) *Methods of Regional Analysis: An Introduction to Regional Science*. Cambridge, Mass., MIT Press.

Jaffe, M. (1975) The use of potential surface analysis in Structure Plans. *Working Note*, 80. London, Centre for Environmental Studies.

Jahoda, G. (1970) *Information Storage and Retrieval Systems for Individual Researchers*. New York, John Wiley & Sons.

Jansen, G. R. M., Bovy, P. H. L., Van Est, J. P. J. M. and le Clercq, F. (eds) (1979) *New Developments in Modelling Travel Demand and Urban Systems*. Farnborough, Saxon House.

Jantsch, E. (1967) *Technological Forecasting in Perspective*. Paris, OECD.

Jantsch, E. (1969) *Perspectives of Planning*. Paris, OECD.

Jenkins, W. I. (1978) *Policy Analysis: A Political and Organisational Perspective*. London, Martin Robertson.

Johnson, J. H., Salt, J. and Wood, P. A. (1974) *Housing and Migration of Labour in England and Wales*. Lexington, Mass., Saxon House/Lexington Books.

Johnston, R. J. (1978) *Multivariate Statistical Analysis in Geography*. London, Longman.

Jones, C., Gudgonsson, S. and Lewis, J. P. (1978) A two stage model of tenure mobility. *Environment and Planning A*, 10, 81–92.

Jones, J. C. (1970) The state of the art in design methods. In G. T. Moore (ed.), *Emerging Methods in Environmental Design and Planning*. Cambridge, Mass., MIT Press.

Jowell, J. (1977) Bargaining in development control. *Journal of planning and Environment Law*, July, 414–33.

Kahn, H. and Weiner, A. J. (1967) *The Year 2000: A Framework for Speculation on the Next Thirty Three Years*. New York: Macmillan.

Kaplan, A. (1964) *The Conduct of Inquiry: Methodology for Behavioural Science*. New York, Harper & Row.

Kaufman, G. M. and Thomas, H. (eds) (1977) *Modern Decision Analysis*. Harmondsworth, Penguin.

Keeble, L. (1959) *Principles and Practice of Town and Country Planning*, 2nd edn. London, Estates Gazette.

Keeling, D. (1972) *Management in Government*. London, Allen & Unwin.

Kelly, P. (1976) Further comments on cross-impact analysis. *Futures*, 8 (4), 341–5.

Kemeny, J. G. and Snell, J. L. (1960) *Finite Markov Chains*. New York, Van Nostrand.

Kemeny, J. G. and Snell, J. L. (1972) *Mathematical Models in the Social Sciences*. Cambridge, Mass., MIT Press.

Kettle, P. and Whitbread, M. (1973) An ordinal method of evaluation: a comment. *Urban Studies*, 10, 95–9.

Keyfitz, N. (1968) *Introduction to the Mathematics of Population*. Reading, Mass., Addison-Wesley.

Kish, L. (1965) *Survey Sampling*. New York, John Wiley & Sons.

Knight, T. E. (1974) A conceptual background to the use of social indicators for the identification of areas of urban deprivation. *Economic and Statistical Note*, 21. London, DOE.

Kohout, F. J. (1974) *Statistics for Social Scientists: A Co-ordinated Learning System*. New York, John Wiley & Sons.

Koopmans, T. C. (1951) *Activity Analysis of Production and Allocation*. New Haven, Yale University Press.

Korte, H. (1978) Inter-relationships between migration, the labour market and housing need: a case study of Kreis Unna (the Ruhr). In *Policy Analysis for Urban and Regional Planning*, Seminar proceedings. London, PTRC.

Kozlowski, J. and Hughes, J. T. (1972) *Threshold Analysis*. New York, Halsted Press.

Krausz, E. and Miller, S. H. (1974) *Social Research: Social Research Design*. London, Longman.

Krueckeberg, D. A. and Silvers, A. L. (1974) *Urban Planning Analysis: Methods and Models*. New York, John Wiley & Sons.

Krumbein, W. C. (1960) The geological population as a framework for analysing numerical data in geology. *Liverpool and Manchester Geological Journal*, 2, 341–68.

Kuhn, T. S. (1962) *The Structure of Scientific Revolutions*. University of Chicago Press.

Labour Force Survey (1971–) Office of Population Censuses and Surveys, biennial. London, HMSO.

Land, K. C. and Spillerman, S. (eds) (1974) *Social Indicator Models*. New York, Russell Sage.

Langley, P. (1979) The social impact of Structure Plan policies. In *Policy Analysis for Urban and Regional Planning*, Seminar proceedings, London, PTRC.

Lassere, P. (1974) Planning through incrementalism. *Socio-economic Planning Sciences*, 8 (3), 129–34.

Lasswell, H. D. and Kaplan, A. (1950) *Power and Society: A Framework for Political Inquiry*. New Haven, Yale University Press.

Ledent, J. (1978) Regional multiplier analysis: A demometric approach. *Environment and Planning A*, 10, 537–60.

Lee, D. B. (1973) Requiem for large scale models. *Journal of the American Institute of Planners*, 39 (3), 163–78.

Lee, E. S. (1966) A theory of migration. *Demography*, 3, 47–57.

Leicestershire Structure Plan (1974) Leicester, Leicestershire County Council.

Leigh, R. (1970) The use of location quotients in urban economic base studies. *Land Economics*, 46 (2), 202–5.

Leonardi, G. (1978) Optimum facility location by accessibility maximizing. *Environment and Planning A*, 10, 1287–305.

Leonardi, G. (1979) A mathematical programme framework for the optimal location of spatially interacting activities: theory and algorithms. In M. J. Breheny (ed.), *Developments in Urban and Regional Analysis*. London, Pion.

Leontief, W. (1967) *Input-Output Analysis*. London, Oxford University Press.

Levin, P. H. (1972) On decision and decision making. *Public Administration*, 50, 19–44.

Levin, P. H. (1976) *Government and the Planning Process*. London, Allen & Unwin.

Lichfield, N. (1962) Cost-benefit analysis in urban redevelopment. *Research Report*, 20. Real Estate Research Program, Berkeley, University of California.

Lichfield, N. (1965) *Economics of Planned Development*. London, Estates Gazette.

Lichfield, N. (1969) Cost-benefit analysis in urban expansion – a case study: Peterborough. *Regional Studies*, 3, 123–55.

Lichfield, N. (1970) Evaluation methodology of urban and regional plans: a review. *Regional Studies*, 4, 151–65.

Lichfield, N., Kettle, P. and Whitbread, M. (1975) *Evaluation in the Planning Process*. Oxford, Pergamon Press.

Lindblom, C. E. (1959a) The science of 'muddling through'. *Public Administration Review*, 19, 79–99.

Lindblom, C. E. (1959b) The handling of policy norms in analysis. In M. Abramovitz (ed.), *Allocation of Economic Resources*. Stanford University Press.

Lindblom, C. E. (1965) *The Intelligence of Democracy*. New York, The Free Press.

Linstone, H. A. and Turoff, M. (eds) (1975) *The Delphi Method: Techniques and Applications*. Reading, Mass., Addison-Wesley.

Liverpool, City and County Borough of (1962) *Interim Planning Policy Statement*, 2 vols. Liverpool, City Planning Department.

Lloyd, P. E. (1977) *Manufacturing Industry in the Inner City: A Case Study of Merseyside*, Working paper series 2. School of Geography, Manchester, The University.

Lloyd, P. E. and Mason, C. M. (1978) Manufacturing industry in the inner city: a case study of Greater Manchester. *Transactions of the Institute of British Geographers*, 3 (1), 66–90.

Local Government Act (1972) London, HMSO.

London Docklands Study (1973) see Travis Morgan, R.

Los, M. (1979) Combined residential–location and transportation models. *Environment and Planning A*, 11, 1241–65.

Lothian Regional Council (1975) Introducing policy or corporate planning into local government. Report prepared by PA Consultants, 2 vols. Edinburgh, Lothian Regional Council.

Lowi, T. J. (1970) Decision making versus policy making: toward an antidote for technocracy. *Public Administration Review*, 3, 314–25.

Lowi, T. J. (1972) Four systems of policy, politics and choice. *Public Administration Review*, 4, 298–310.

Lowry, I. S. (1963) Location parameters in the Pittsburgh model. *Papers and Proceedings of the Regional Science Association*, 11, 145–65.

Lowry, I. S. (1964) *A Model of Metropolis*, RM–4035–RC. Santa Monica, Calif., Rand Corporation.

Lowry, I. S. (1966) *Migration and Metropolitan Growth: Two Analytical Models*. San Francisco, Chandler Publishing Co.

Lowry, I. S. (1968) Seven models of urban development. In G. Hemmens (ed.) *Urban Development Models*, Special report 97. Washington, D.C., Highway Research Board.

Luckman, J. (1967) An approach to the management of design. *Operations Research Quarterly*, 19, 345–58.

Lynch, K. (1972) *What Time is this Place?* Cambridge, Mass., MIT Press.

Madden, M. (1976) A population/employment/housing forecasting framework for Merseyside. In *Policy Analysis for Urban and Regional Planning*, Seminar proceedings. London, PTRC.

Madden, M. and Batey, P. W. J. (1980) Achieving consistency in demographic–economic forecasting. *Papers of the Regional Science Association*, 44, 91–106.

Makower, H. (1965) *Activity Analysis and the Theory of Economic Equilibrium*. London, Macmillan.

Malcolm, J. F. and Aitken, C. P. (1977) The impact of a superstore: Fine Fare, St. Ninian's, Stirling. *Discussion Paper*, 11, parts 1 and 2. Department of Town Planning, Glasgow, The University.

McDonald, S. T. (1977) The regional reports in Scotland: a study of change in the planning process. *Town Planning Review*, 48 (3), 215–32.

McKennell, A. C. (1974) Surveying attitude structures: a discussion of principles and procedures. *Quality and Quantity*, 7, 203–94.

McLoughlin, J. B. (1969) *Urban and Regional Planning: A Systems Approach*. London, Faber & Faber.

McLoughlin, J. B. (1973) *Control and Urban Planning*. London, Faber & Faber.

McLoughlin, J. B. (1975) Monitoring, research and intelligence in Structure Planning. In M. Drake *et al. Aspects of Structure Planning in Britain*, Research paper 20. London, Centre for Environmental Studies.

McLoughlin, J. B. and Thornley, J. (1973) Structure Planning: a preliminary testing of some research hypotheses in relation to current practice. *Working Paper*, 79. London, Centre for Environmental Studies.

McLoughlin, J. B. and Webster, J. N. (1970) Cybernetic and general-system approaches to urban and regional research: a review of the literature. *Environment and Planning A*, 2, 369–408.

MacMurray, T. (1971) Aspects of time and the study of activity patterns. *Town Planning Review*, 42 (2), 195–209.

Manheim, M. L. (1966) *Hierarchical Structure: A Model of Design and Planning Processes*, Report 7. Cambridge, Mass., MIT Press.

Manheim, M. L. (1967) Problem solving processes in planning and design (P67–3). Department of Civil Engineering, Cambridge, Mass., Massachusetts Institute of Technology.

March, L. (1976) *The Architecture of Form*. Cambridge University Press.

March, L., Echenique, M. and Dickens, P. (1971) Models of environment. *Architectural Design*, 41, 275–322.

March, L. and Steadman, P. (1971) *The Geometry of Environment*. London, Royal Institute of British Architects.

Masser, I. (1970) A test of some models for predicting inter-metropolitan movement of population in England and Wales. *University Papers*, 9. London, Centre for Environmental Studies.

Masser, I. (1972) *Analytical Models for Urban and Regional Planning*. Newton Abbott, David & Charles.

Masser, I. and Brown, P. J. B. (1974) Hierarchical aggregation procedures for interaction data. In *Urban and Regional Models*, Seminar proceedings. London, PTRC.

Massey, D. B. (1974) Models and theories in planning. In *Urban and Regional Models*, Seminar proceedings. London, PTRC.

Massey, D. B. and Cordey-Hayes, M. (1971) The use of models in Structure Planning. *Town Planning Review*, 42, 28–44.

Massey, D. B. and Meegan, R. A. (1978) Industrial restructuring versus the cities. *Urban Studies*, 15, 273–288.

Matchett, E. (1968) Control of thought in creative work. *Chartered Mechanical Engineer*, 15, 163–166.

Matthew, R., Johnson-Marshall and Partners (1967) *Central Lancashire: Study for a City*. London, HMSO.

Mazziotti, D. F. (1974) The underlying assumptions of advocacy planning: pluralism and reform. *Journal of the American Institute of Planners*, 40 (1), 38–47.

Merseyside County Council (1976) *Merseyside Industrial Monitor*. Liverpool, Merseyside County Council.

Merseyside Structure Plan (1980) Liverpool, Merseyside County Council.

Merton, R. K. (1968) *Social Theory and Social Structure: Theory of Bureaucracy*. New York, The Free Press.

Meyers, L. S. and Grossen, N. E. (1978) *Behavioural Research: Theory, Procedure and Design*. 2nd edn. San Francisco, W. H. Freeman.

Meyerson, M. and Banfield, E. C. (1955) *Politics, Planning and the Public Interest*. New York, The Free Press.

Mid Glamorgan Structure Plan (1979) Cardiff, Mid Glamorgan County Council.

Midwinter, A. F. (1978) Policy planning units in Scottish local government. *Public Administration Review*, 28, Dec., 73–90.

Miles, I. and Irvine, J. (1979) Social forecasting: predicting the future or making history? In J. Irvine, I. Miles and J. Evans (eds) *Demystifying Social Statistics*. London, Pluto Press.

Ministry of Housing and Local Government (1962) *Town Centres: Approach to Renewal*. London, HMSO.

Ministry of Housing and Local Government (1970) *Development Plans: A Manual on Form and Content*. London, HMSO.

Ministry of Transport (1963) *Traffic in Towns* (The Buchanan Report). London, HMSO.

Mitchell, R. B. (1961) The new frontier in metropolitan planning. *Journal of the American Institute of Planners*, 27 (3), 169–75.

Mobbs, T. (1975) A continuous survey of citizens in Cleveland. In *Corporate Planning Organisation and Research and Intelligence Techniques*, Seminar proceedings. London, PTRC.

Moor, N. (1973) Economic activity and employment forecasts: an assessment of their utility in planning. In *Urban and Regional Models*, Seminar proceedings. London, PTRC.

Moore, G. T. (ed.) (1970) *Emerging Methods in Environmental Design and Planning*. Cambridge, Mass.. MIT Press.

Moore, P. G. and Thomas, H. (1976) *The Anatomy of Decisions*. Harmondsworth: Penguin.

Morrison, W. I. and Smith, P. (1976) Input-output methods in urban and regional planning: a practical guide. PRAG *Technical Paper*, 6. London, Centre for Environmental Studies. Published as *Progress in Planning*, 7 (2), 1977. Oxford, Pergamon Press.

Mort, D. (1978) Population projection and employment forecasts. *Planning Exchange Forum*, 13. Glasgow, The Planning Exchange.

Mosely, M. J., Harman, R. G., Coles, O. B. and Spencer, M. B. (1976) *Rural Transport and Accessibility*. Norwich, University of East Anglia.

Moser, C. A. and Kalton, G. (1971) *Survey Methods in Social Investigation*, 2nd ed. London, Heinemann.

Murie, A. S. (1974) Eligibility constraints on the movement on households between tenures. In *Housing*, Seminar proceedings. London, PTRC.

Murie, A. S. (1976) Estimating housing need: technique or mystique? *Housing Review*, May–June, 54–8.

Myrdal, G. (1968) The necessity and difficulty of planning the future society. In W. R. Ewald (ed.), *Environment and Change*. Bloomington, Indiana University Press.

Nagel, E. (1961) *The Structure of Science*. London, Routledge & Kegán Paul.

Nagel, S. S. (1977) Basic concepts in policy studies. In S. S. Nagel (ed.), *Policy Studies Review Annual*. Beverly Hills, Sage Publications.

Nash, C. A. (1976) *Public versus Private Transport*. London, Macmillan.

National Dwelling and Household Survey (NDHS) (1978) see DOE (1978b).

National Parks Act (1949) London, HMSO.

Needham, B. (1971) Concrete problems, not abstract goals: planning as problem solving. *Journal of the Royal Town Planning Institute*, 57 (7), 317–19.

New Towns Act (1946) London, HMSO.

Newell, W. T. and Meier, R. E. (1972) Business system simulation. In H. Guetzkow (ed.), *Simulation in Social and Administrative Science*. Englewood Cliffs, N.J., Prentice-Hall.

Newton, K. (1976) *Second City Politics: Democratic Process and Decision Making in Birmingham*. Oxford University Press.

Newton, K. and Sharpe, L. J. (1977) Local outputs research: some reflections and problems. *Policy and Politics*, 5 (3), 61–82.

Nie, N. H., Hull, C. H. and Jenkins, J. G. (1975) *Statistical Package for the Social Sciences* (SPSS), 2nd edn. New York, McGraw-Hill.

Nie, N. H. (1976) *SPSS Primer*. New York, McGraw-Hill.

Nijkamp, P. (1977) *Theory and Application of Environmental Economics*. Amsterdam, North Holland.

Nijkamp, P. (1979a) *Multidimensional Spatial Data and Decision Analysis*. New York, John Wiley & Sons.

Nijkamp, P. (1979b) Gravity and entropy models: the state of the art. In G. R. M. Jansen *et al.* (eds), *New Developments in Modelling Travel Demand and Urban Systems*. Farnborough, Saxon House.

Nijkamp, P. (1980) *Environmental Policy Analysis: Operational Methods and Models*. New York, John Wiley & Sons.

Nijkamp, P. and Rietveld, P. (1979) Multilevel, multiobjective models in a multiregional system. *Research Memorandum*, 1979–3. Department of Economics, Amsterdam, The Free University.

Nijkamp, P. and Soffer, A. (1979) Soft multicriteria decision models for urban renewal plans. *Sistemi Urbani*, 2 (1), 49–64.

Niner, P. (1975) Local authority housing policy and practice. *Occasional Paper*, 31. Centre for Urban and Regional Studies, Birmingham, The University.

Niner, P. (1976) A review of approaches to estimating housing needs. *Working Paper*, 41. Centre for Urban and Regional Studies, Birmingham, The University.

Norfolk Structure Plan (1977) Norwich, Norfolk County Council.

Nottinghamshire and Derbyshire Sub-regional Study (1969) Nottinghamshire and Derbyshire sub-regional planning unit. See also Papers from the Seminar on the Progress of the Notts/Derby Sub-regional Study. *Information Paper*, 11. London, Centre for Environmental Studies.

O'Dell, A. and Parker, J. (1977) The use of census data to identify and describe housing stress. *Current Paper*, 67, Building Research Establishment. London, DOE.

O'Farrell, P. N. and Markham, J. (1975) Journey to work: A behavioural analysis. *Progress in Planning*, 3 (3). Oxford, Pergamon Press.

Ogilvy, A. A. (1979) Inter-regional migration since 1971: an appraisal of data from two sources – Labour Force Surveys and the National Health Service Central Register. *Occasional Paper*. London, Office of Population Censuses and Surveys.

Olson, M. (1969) The plan and purpose of a social report. *The Public Interest*, 15, 85–97.

Olson, M. (1970) An analytic framework for social reporting and policy analysis. *The Annals of the American Academy of Political and Social Science*, 388, 112–26.

Open University (1974) The administrative process as incrementalism: course unit D331, block H. *Approaches to the Study of Public Administration*. Milton Keynes, Open University.

Openshaw, S. (1975) An alternative approach to Structure Planning: the Structure Plan decision-making model. *Planning Outlook*, 17, 10–26.

Openshaw, S. (1977) An evaluation and critical assessment of the use of quantitative techniques in planning. *Planning Outlook*, 22 (1), 23–32.

Openshaw, S. and Whitehead, P. (1975) A decision optimizing technique for planners. *Planning Outlook*, 16, 19–33.

Openshaw, S. and Whitehead, P. (1977) Decision making in local plans: the DOT methodology and a case study. *Town Planning Review*, 48, 29–41.

Openshaw, S. and Whitehead, P. T. (1978) Structure Planning using a decision optimizing technique. *Town Planning Review*, 49 (4), 486–96.

OPCS Monitor (1980) *Dwellings – 1981 Census*, Monitor CEN 80/5, issued 15.7.80. London, Office of Population Censuses and Surveys.

Oppenheim, A. N. (1968) *Questionnaire Design and Attitude Measurement*. London, Heinemann.

Osbourne, A. F. (1957) *Applied Imagination: Principles and Procedures of Creative Problem Solving*. New York, Scribners.

Ostrom, C. W. (1978) *Time-series Analysis*. London, Sage.

Oxfordshire Structure Plan (1976) Oxford, Oxfordshire County Council.

Packer, A. H. (1975) Financing health care and education: consumer units and resource allocation. *Public Policy*, 23 (1), 39–58.

Paelinck, J. H. T. (1973) Multi-regional economic policy based on attraction analysis. In *Urban and Regional Models*, Seminar proceedings. London, PTRC.

Page, E. (1978) Why should central-local relations in Scotland be different to those in England?. *Public Administration Review*, 28, Dec., 51–72.

Pahl, R. E. (1970) *Whose City? And Other Essays on Sociology and Planning*. London, Longman.

Pahl, R. E. (1971a) Planning and the quality of urban life. *Report of Proceedings*, Town and Country Planning Summer School, London, RTPI.

Pahl, R. E. (1971b) Poverty and the urban system. In M. Chisholm and G. Manners (eds), *Spatial Policy Problems of the British Economy*. Cambridge University Press.

Pahl, R. E. (1975) *Whose City? And Further Essays on Urban Society*. Harmondsworth, Penguin.

Palmer, D. J. (1975) Planning and forecasting employment and economic development in Structure Planning. PRAG *Technical Paper*, 13 London, Centre for Environmental Studies.

Papageorgiou, G. J. (ed.) (1976) *Mathematical Land Use Theory*. Lexington, Mass., D. C. Heath.

Parry Lewis, J. (1973) Planning first and then predicting: models and forecasting in planning – 6. *Built Environment*, 2, 119–21.

Parry Lewis, J. and Bridges, M. J. (1975) Some new approaches to shopping models with particular reference to Cambridge. In *Retailing*, Seminar proceedings. London, PTRC.

Patricios, N. W. (1975) Shopping models: consumer environmental perception in spatial choice behaviour for convenience good shopping. In *Urban and Regional Models for Public Policy Analysis*, Seminar proceedings. London, PTRC.

Pavitt, K. (ed.) (1980) *Technical Innovation and British Economic Performance*. London, Macmillan.

Perraton, J. (1972) Evaluation as part of the planning process. *Working Paper*, 33. Cambridge, Land Use Built Form Studies.

Pickett, K. G. (1974) *Sources of Official Data*. London, Longman.

Pickvance, C. G. (1974) Life cycle, housing tenure, and residential mobility: a path analytic approach. *Urban Studies*, 11, 171–88.

Planning Advisory Group (PAG) (1965) *The Future of Development Plans*. London, HMSO.

Planning Bulletin on Town Centres (1962) see Ministry of Housing and Local Government (1962).

Plessis-Fraissard, M. (1976) Households: a review of definitions, trends and forecasting methods. *Working Paper*, 164. Department of Geography, Leeds, The University.

Policy for the Inner Cities (1977) *White Paper*, Cmnd. 6845. London, HMSO.

Pollitt, C., Lewis, L., Negro, J. and Patten, J. (eds) (1979) *Public Policy in Theory and Practice*. London, Hodder & Stoughton.

Polya, G. (1957) *How to Solve It*. New York, Doubleday.

Popper, K. R. (1957) *The Poverty of Historicism*. London, Routledge & Kegan Paul.

Popper, K. R. (1972) *Conjectures and Refutations: The Growth of Scientific Knowledge*, 4th edn. London, Routledge & Kegan Paul.

Porzecanski, M. de (1972) New towns: the evolution of planning criteria. *Working Paper*, 64. Cambridge, Land Use Built Form Studies.

Powys Structure Plan (1979) Llandrindod Wells, Powys County Council.

Pressat, R. (1972) *Demographic Analysis: Methods, Results and Applications*. London, Edward Arnold.

Pressat, R. (1978) *Statistical Demography*. London, Methuen.

Pressman, J. L. and Wildavsky, A. B. (1973) *Implementation: How Great Expectations in Washington are dashed in Oakland*. Berkeley, University of California Press.

Price, D. O. (1959) A mathematical model of migration suitable for simulation on an electronic computer. Paper presented to International Population Conference, Vienna.

Public Transport Plans (PTP) (from 1973) As required by art. 203, Local Government Act 1972. Amended by Transport Act 1978. London, HMSO.

Quade, E. S. (1975) *Analysis for Public Decisions*. New York, Elsevier.

Raiffa, H. (1968) *Decision Analysis: Introductory Lecture on Choices under Uncertainty*. Reading, Mass., Addison-Wesley.

Randall, J. (1973) Shift-share analysis as a guide to the employment performance of West Central Scotland. *Scottish Journal of Political Economy*, 20 (1), 1–26.

Ranney, A. (1968) The Study of Policy Content. In A. Ranney (ed.), *Political Science and Public Policy*. Chicago, Markham.

Ranney, D. C. (1969) *Planning and Politics in the Metropolis*. Columbus, Ohio, Merrill.

Rawls, J. (1971) *A Theory of Justice*. Cambridge, Mass., Harvard University Press.

Rawls, J. (1973) Distributive justice. In E. S. Phelps (ed.), *Economic Justice*. Harmondsworth, Penguin.

Reading, etc. Sub-Regional Study (1975) see Berkshire County Council.

Rees, G. and Rees, T. L. (1977) Alternatives to the census. *Town Planning Review*, 48 (2), 123–40.

Rees, P. H. (1977) The measurement of migration from census data and other sources. *Environment and planning A*, 9, 247–72.

Rees, P. H. (1979) *Migration and Settlement: 1, United Kingdom*, RR–79–3. Laxenburg, International Institute for Applied Systems Analysis.

Rees, P. H. and Wilson, A. G. (1977) *Spatial Population Analysis*. London, Edward Arnold.

Rees, T. L. (1977) The non-movers of the upper Afan: a comparison with in- and out-migrants. *Working Paper*, 2. Sociological Research Unit, Cardiff, University College.

Rees, T. L. (1978) Population and industrial decline in the South Wales coalfield. *Regional Studies*, 12, 69–77.

Regan, D. E. (1978) The pathology of British land use planning. *Local Government Studies*, 2, 3–21.

Reif, B. (1973) *Models in Urban and Regional Planning*. Aylesbury, Leonard Hill.

Reilly, W. J. (1929) Methods for the study of retail relationships. *Bulletin*, 2944. Houston, University of Texas.

Reilly, W. J. (1931) *The Law of Retail Gravitation*. New York, Pilsbury (re-issued in 1953).

Rein, M. (1976) *Social Science and Public Policy*. Harmondsworth, Penguin.

Richards, M. G. (1979) A disaggregate shopping model: some retrospective thoughts. In G. R. M. Jansen *et al.* (eds), *New Developments in Modelling Travel Demand and Urban Systems*. Farnborough, Saxon House.

Richardson, H. W. (1972) *Input–Output and Regional Economics*. London, Weidenfeld & Nicolson.

Riera, D. and Jackson, M. (1971) The design of a monitoring system for sub-regional planning. A study by Iscol Ltd, Loughborough. Nottinghamshire/ Derbyshire Monitoring and Advisory Unit.

Ripper, M. and Varaiya, P. (1974) An optimizing model of urban development. *Environment and Planning A*, 6, 149–68.

Rittel, H. W. J. and Webber, M. M. (1973) Dilemmas in a general theory of planning. *Policy Sciences*, 4 (2), 155–69.

Rivlin, A. M. (1971) *Systematic Thinking for Social Action.* Washington, D.C., Brookings Institution.

Rivlin, A. M. (1973) Social experiments: the promise and the problems. *The Brookings Bulletin*, 10, 6–9.

Rivlin, A. M. (1974) How can experiments be more useful? *American Economic Review*, 64, 346–54.

Robinson, F. (1979) Local authority economic initiatives. *Occasional Paper*, 10. London, Centre for Environmental Studies.

Robson, B. T. (1971) *Urban Analysis: A Study of City Structure with Special Reference to Sunderland.* Cambridge University Press.

Robson, B. T. (1975) *Urban Social Areas.* Oxford University Press.

Roe, P. E. (1974) An appraisal of shopping models. In *Urban and Regional Models*, Seminar proceedings. London, PTRC.

Rogers, A. (1966) Matrix methods of population analysis. *Journal of the American Institute of Planners*, 32, 40–4.

Rogers, A. (1967) A regression analysis of inter-regional migration in California. *The Review of Economics and Statistics*, 49, 262–71.

Rogers, A. (1968) *Matrix Analysis of Inter-regional Population Growth and Distribution.* Berkeley, University of California Press.

Rogers, A. (1971) *Matrix Methods in Urban and Regional Analysis.* San Francisco, Holden-Day.

Rogers, A. (1975) *Introduction to Multi-regional Mathematical Demography.* New York, John Wiley & Sons.

Rogers, A., Raquillet, R. and Castro, L. J. (1978) Model migration schedules and their applications. *Environment and Planning A*, 10, 475–502.

Rogers, P. B. and Smith, C. R. (1977) The local authority's role in economic development: The Tyne and Wear Act, 1976. *Regional Studies*, 11, 153–63.

Rondinelli, D. A. (1973) Urban planning as policy analysis: management of urban change. *Journal of the American Institute of Planners*, 39 (1), 13–22.

Roos, L. L. (1975) Quasi-experiments and environmental policy. *Policy Sciences*, 6, 249–66.

Roos, L. L. (1977) Quasi-experiments and environmental policy. In S. S. Nagel (ed.), *Policy Studies Review Annual.* Originally published in *Policy Sciences* (1975), 6, 249–66.

Roos, N. P. (1973) Evaluation, quasi-experimentation and public policy. In J. Caporaso and L. L. Roos (eds), *Quasi-experimental Approaches: Testing Theory and Evaluating Policy.* Evanston, Northwestern University Press.

Roos, N. P. (1974) Influencing the health care system: policy alternatives. *Public Policy*, 22, 139–67.

Roos, N. P. (1975) Contrasting social experimentation with retrospective evaluation: a health care perspective. *Public Policy*, 23 (2), 241–57.

Rose, E. A. (1978) Policy co-ordination and programming of employment measures by local authorities. *Working Paper*, 14. Joint unit for Research on the Urban Environment (JURUE), Aston, The University.

Rose, R. (1969) *Policy Making in Britain*. London, Macmillan.
Rose, R. (1972) The market for policy indicators. In A. Shonfield and S. Shaw (eds), *Social Indicators and Social Policy*. London, Heinemann.
Rosenhead, J., Elton, M. and Gupta, S. K. (1972) Robustness and optimality as criteria for strategic decisions. *Operations Research Quarterly*, 23, 413–31.
Roskill Commission (1971) *Report of the Commission on the Third London Airport*. London, HMSO.
Rowbotham, D. H. and Holmes, C. (1977) Ealing sample census. Paper read to the Census Research Group, County Hall, London, 15.7.77. Ealing, Town Clerks Office.
Royal Commission on Local Government in England 1966–1969 (1969) (Chairman: Lord Redcliffe-Maud) Cmnd. 4040. London, HMSO.
Ryan, A. (1970) *Philosophy of Social Sciences*. London, Macmillan.

Sackman, H. (1975) *Delphi Critique*. Lexington, Mass., Lexington Books.
Sage, A. P. (1978) *Methodology for Large Scale Systems*. New York, McGraw-Hill.
Sayer, R. A. (1976) A critique of urban modelling. *Progress in Planning*, 6 (3). Oxford, Pergamon Press.
Schatzman, L. and Strauss, A. L. (1973) *Field Research: Strategies for a Natural Society*. Englewood Cliffs, N.J., Prentice-Hall.
Schimpeler, C. C. and Grecco, W. L. (1968) Systems evaluation: an approach based on community structure and values. *Highway Research Record*, 238, 123–52.
Schinnar, A. P. (1976) A multi-dimensional accounting model for demographic and economic planning interactions. *Environment and Planning A*, 8, 455–75.
Schinnar, A. P. (1978) Invariant distributional regularities of non-basic spatial activity allocations: the Garin-Lowry model revisited. *Environment and Planning A*, 10, 327–36.
Schlager, K. (1968) The rank-based expected value method of plan evaluation. *Highway Research Record* 238, 153–57.
Schlaifer, R. (1969) *Analysis of Decisions under Uncertainty*. New York, McGraw-Hill.
Schon, D. A. (1971) *Beyond the Stable State*. London, Temple Smith.
Schuessler, K. (1971) *Analysing Social Data – A Statistical Orientation*. Boston, Houghton Mifflin.
Schultz, A. (1970) Concept and theory formation in the social sciences. In D. Emmett and A. MacIntyre (eds), *Sociological Theory and Philosophical Analysis*. London, Macmillan.
Scott, A. J. (1971) Dynamic location – allocation systems: some basic planning principles. *Environment and Planning A*, 3, 73–82.
Scott, C. (1961) Research on mail surveys. *Journal of the Royal Statistical Society*, 24, series A, 143–95.
Scottish Development Department (SDD) (1975a) Demographic analysis for planning purposes. *Advice Note*, 8, July. Edinburgh, SDD.
SDD (1975b) *Planning Advice Notes* (PAN). Edinburgh, SDD.
SDD (1979) Structure Plan monitoring: a discussion note. Report of an SDD/Regional Authorities Working Party. Edinburgh, SDD.
Self, P. (1970) Nonsense on stilts: cost–benefit analysis and the Roskill Commission. *The Political Quarterly*, 41, 249–60.
Self, P. (1975) *Econocrats and the Policy Process*. London, Macmillan.
Senior, M. L. (1974) Disaggregated residential location models, housing market

models and duality. In *Urban and Regional Models,* Seminar proceedings. London, PTRC.

Severnside: A Feasibility Study (1971) DOE and Welsh Office. London, HMSO. See Central Unit for Environment Planning.

Sharkansky, I. (ed.) (1970) *Policy Analysis in Political Science.* Chicago, Markham.

Sheldon, E. B. and Freeman, H. E. (1970) Notes on social indicators: promises and potential. *Policy Sciences,* 1 (1), 97–111.

Shepherd, I. and Newby, P. (1978) The Brent Cross regional shopping centre – characteristics and early effects. Cambridge, Retail and Planning Associates.

Shonfield, A. and Shaw, S. (eds) (1972) *Social Indicators and Social Policy.* London, Heinemann.

Siegal, J. S. and Hamilton, C. H. (1952) Some considerations in the use of the residual method of estimating net migration. *Journal of the American Statistical Association,* 47, 475–500.

Simmie, J. M. (1974) *Citizens in Conflict: A Sociology of Town Planning.* London, Hutchinson.

Simmonds, D. C. (1980) A comment on the papers from the BSRSA workshop on regional science methods in Structure Planning. *Environment and Planning A,* 12, 463–67.

Simon, H. (1957) *Models of Man.* New York, John Wiley & Sons.

Singleton, R. R. and Tyndall, W. F. (1974) *Games and Programs: Mathematics for Modelling.* San Fracisco, W. H. Freeman.

Skeffington Report, The (1969). See DOE (1969).

Smart, G. (1977) The future of development plans. *Journal of the Royal Town Planning Institute,* 63 (1), 5–7.

Smith, B. (1976) *Policy Making in British Government.* London, Martin Robertson.

Smith, D. M. (1977) *Human Geography: A Welfare Approach.* London, Edward Arnold.

Smith, P. and Morrison, W. I. (1974) *Simulating the Urban Economy: Experiments with Input–Output Analysis.* London, Pion.

Smith, P. R. (1974) The use of potential surface techniques in sub-regional planning. *Geographical Papers,* 30. Department of Geography, Reading, The University.

Smith, T. B. (1973) The policy implementation process. *Policy Sciences,* 4, 197–209.

Sneath, P. H. A. and Sokal, R. R. (1973) *Numerical Taxonomy: The Principles and Practice of Numerical Classification.* San Francisco, W. H. Freeman.

Social Survey Division, Office of Population Censuses and Surveys (OPCS) (1973) *The General Household Survey: Introductory Report.* London, HMSO.

Social Trends (1970–) Central Statistical Office, London, HMSO.

Solesbury, W. (1974) *Policy in Urban Planning.* Oxford, Pergamon Press.

Solesbury, W. (1975) Ideas about Structure Plans: past, present and future. *Town Planning Review,* 46 (3), 245–54.

Solomon, R. L. (1949) An extension of control group design. *Phychology Bulletin,* 46, 137–50.

South Hampshire Structure Plan (1974) Winchester, Hampshire County Council.

South Glamorgan Act (1975) London, HMSO.

SSRC (1980) *Users Manual: Quality of Life Survey.* See Hall *et al.* (1980).

Staffordshire Structure Plan (1974) Stafford, Staffordshire County Council.

Starkie, D. N. M. (1973) Transportation planning and public policy. *Progress in Planning,* 1 (4). Oxford, Pergamon Press.

Statistical Package for the Social Sciences (SPSS). See Nie *et al.* (1975) and Nie (1976).

Stebbing, L. S. (1970) *A Modern Elementary Logic*, 2nd edn. London, Methuen.

Steiss, A. W. (1973) Fundamental trends in the planning process model in the United States. *Planning Outlook*, 13 (2), 9–25.

Stephan, F. F. and McCarthy, P. J. (1974) *Sampling Opinions*. London, Greenwood.

Stevens, S. S. (1946) On the theory of scales of measurement. *Science*, 103, 677–80.

Stewart J. D. (1973) *Management in Local Government: A Viewpoint*. London, Charles Knight.

Stewart, J. D. (1974) *The Responsive Local Authority*. London, Charles Knight.

Stewart, J. D. and Eddison, T. (1971) Structure Planning and corporate planning. *Journal of the Royal Town Plannning Institute*, 57 (8), 367–75.

Stewart, J. D. and Greenwood, R. (1974) *Corporate Planning in English Local Government: An Analysis with Readings*. London, Charles Knight.

Stewart, J. Q. (1942) A measure of the influence of population at a distance. *Sociometry*, 5, 63–71.

Stewart, J. Q. (1947) Empirical mathematical rules concerning the distribution and equilibrium of population. *Geographical Review*, 37, 461–85.

Stewart, M. (ed.) (1972) *The City: Problems of Planning*. Harmondsworth, Penguin.

Stillwell, J. C. H. (1975a) Models of interregional migration: a review. *Working Paper*, 100. Department of Geography, Leeds, The University.

Stillwell, J. C. H. (1975b) Inter-county net migration in England and Wales. *Working Paper*, 129. Department of Geography, Leeds, The University.

Stillwell, J. C. H. (1977) Some historical tests of spatial interaction models for inter-area migration. *Working Papers*, 185, and 199 (2 vols). Department of Geography, Leeds, The University.

Stoke-on-Trent Structure Plan (1974) Stafford, Staffordshire County Council.

Stoll, R. R. (1961) *Sets, Logic, and Axiomatic Theories*. San Francisco, W. H. Freeman.

Stoner, J. A. F. (1978) *Management*. London, Prentice-Hall International.

Stouffer, S. A. (1940) Intervening opportunities: a theory relating to mobility and distance. *American Sociological Review*, 5, 845–67.

Struthers, W. A. K. and Williamson, C. B. (1979) Local economic development: integrated policy planning and implementation in Merseyside. *Town Planning Review*, 50 (2), 164–84.

Study Group on Local Authority Management Structures (1972) *The New Local Authorities: Management and Structure* (Chairman: M. A. Bains). London, HMSO.

Sudman, S. (1976) *Applied Sampling*. New York, Academic Press.

Sutton, A. (1976) The AIDA program: a user's guide. IOR *Paper*, 884. Coventry, Institute for Operational Research.

Sutton, A., Hickling, A. and Friend, J. K. (1977) The analysis of policy options in Structure Plan preparation: the strategic choice approach. IOR *Internal Paper*, 932. Coventry, Institute for Operational Research.

Swain, H. and Logan, M. (1975). Urban systems: a policy perspective. *Environment and Planning A*, 7, 743–55.

Teesside Structure Plan (1974) Middlesbrough, Teesside County Council.

Thomas, R. W. (1977) An interpretation of the journey to work on Merseyside using entropy-maximising methods. *Environment and Planning A*, 9, 817–34.

Thompson, R. (1975) Linkages between Structure Planning and other agencies. In M. Drake, et al., *Aspects of Structure Planning in Britain*, Research paper 20. London, Centre for Environmental Studies.

Town Planning etc. Act (1909) London, HMSO.

Town Planning Act (1932) London, HMSO.

Town and Country Planning Act (1943) London, HMSO.

Town and Country Planning Act (1947) London, HMSO.

Town and Country Planning Act (1971) London, HMSO.

Transport Policies and Programmes (TPP). See DOE, Circular 104/73. Amended by Transport Act 1978.

Travis Morgan, R. and Partners (1973). *Docklands: Proposals for East London*, vol. 1, main report. London, Greater London Council.

Turner, C. G. (1974) The design of an urban growth model for strategic land-use transportation studies. In *Urban and Regional Models*, Seminar proceedings. London, PTRC.

Tyne and wear Act (1976) London, HMSO.

Tyne and Wear County Council (n.d.). Tyne and Wear Structure Plan. Report of survey: background note 2. *Economy*. Newcastle, Tyne and Wear County Council.

Tyne and Wear Structure Plan (Draft) (1976) Newcastle, Tyne and Wear County Council.

Tyne and Wear Structure Plan (1979) Newcastle, Tyne and Wear County Council.

URPI (1980) *Retail Planning Methods: Bibliography B5*. Reading, Unit for Retail Planning Information Ltd.

Uslaner, E. M. (ed.) (1978) *Quantitative Methods in the Social Sciences*, Sage University Papers. Beverly Hills, Sage Publications.

Van Delft, A. and Nijkamp, P. (1977) *Multicriteria Analysis and Regional Decision Making*. The Hague, Martinus Nijhoft.

Van Est, J. (1979) The Lowry model revised to fit a Dutch region. In G. R. M. Jansen et al. (eds), *New Developments in Modelling Travel Demand and Urban Systems*. Farnborough, Saxon House.

Van Meter, D. S. and Van Horn, C. E. (1975) The policy implementation process: a conceptual framework. *Administration and Society*, 6, 445–88.

Vaupel, J. W. (1974) Muddling through analytically. In W. D. Hawley and D. Rogers (eds), *Improving the Quality of Urban Management*. Beverly Hills, Sage Publications. Reprinted in S. S. Nagel (ed.) (1977) *Policy Studies Review Annual*, 1, 44–66.

Verster, A. C. P., Van Leeuwen, I. L. and de Langen, M. (1979) The effects of the location of a peripheral self-service store. In G. R. M. Jansen et al. (eds), *New Developments in Modelling Travel Demand and Urban Systems*. Farnborough, Saxon House.

Vickers, G. (1970) *Value Systems and Social Process*. Harmondsworth, Penguin.

Vickers, G. (1974) Projections, predictions, models and policies. *Journal of the Royal Town Planning Institute*, 60 (4), 636–41.

Wagner, H. M. (1975) *Principles of Operations Research: With Applications to Mangerial Decisions*, 2nd edn. London, Prentice-Hall International.

Wakefield District Council (1979) Plans, processing and monitoring system: guidelines for development control. Wakefield, District Council.

Walker, B. (1980) Urban planning and social welfare. *Environment and Planning A*, 12, 217–25.

Warfield, J. N. (1977) *Societal Systems, Planning, Policy and Complexity*. New York, John Wiley & Sons.

Warwickshire Structure Plan (1973) Warwick, Warwickshire County Council.

Watson, C. J. (1974) Housing chains and filtering: some wider effects of the new building programme. In *Housing*, Seminar proceedings. London, PTRC.

Watson, C. J. (1976) Vacancy chains, filtering and the public sector. *Journal of the American Institute of Planners*, 40 (5), 346–53.

Waugh, T. C. (1973) 'GIMMS' – a geographic information manipulation and mapping system. *Inter-university/Research Councils Research and Development Notes*, 9. Edinburgh, University Regional Computing Centre.

Webber, M. J. (1976) The meaning of entropy maximizing models. In G. J. Papageorgiou (ed.), *Mathematical Land Use Theory*. Lexington, Mass., D. C. Heath.

Webber, M. M. (1965) The role of intelligence systems in urban systems planning. *Journal of the American Institute of Planners*, 31 (4), 289–97.

Webber, R. J. (1975) Liverpool social area study. *PRAG Technical Paper*, 14. London, Centre for Environmental Studies.

Wedgewood-Oppenheim, F. (1972) Planning under uncertainty. *Local Government Studies*, 2, April, 53–65.

Wedgewood-Oppenheim, F., Hard, D. and Cobley, B. (1975) An exploratory study in strategic monitoring. *Progress in Planning*, 5 (1). Oxford, Pergamon Press.

Weibull, J. W. (1976) An axiomatic approach to the measures of accessibility. *Regional Science and Urban Economics*, 6, 357–79.

Weiss, C. H. (1972) *Evaluation Research: Methods of Assessing Program Effectiveness*. Englewood Cliffs, Prentice-Hall.

Wenban-Smith, A. (1979) Integration of implementation, monitoring and forecasting into a single continuous process. In *Policy Analysis for Urban and Regional Planning*, Seminar proceedings. London, PTRC.

West Berkshire Structure Plan (1977) Reading, Berkshire County Council.

West Midlands Regional Study (1972) Evaluation. *Technical Appendix*, 4. Standing Conference for the West Midlands Regional Plan.

West Sussex Structure Plan (1978) Chichester, West Sussex County Council.

Wheller, B. (1975) Definitions of a dwelling. *Research Memorandum*, 453. London, Greater London Council.

White, B. (1974) Information for planning. Studies towards the collection, organisation and dissemination of information for planners. *OSTI Report*, 5198. Planning Research Unit, Department of Urban Design and Regional Planning, Edinburgh, The University. See also B. White (1974) *The Literature and Study of Urban and Regional Planning*. London, Routledge & Kegan Paul.

White Paper (1977) *Policy for the Inner City*, Cmnd. 6845. London, HMSO.

Whitehead, P. (1974) Flexibility in Structure Plans. *Planning Outlook*, 14, Spring, 31–42.

Wildavsky, A. (1964) *The Politics of the Budgetary Process*. Boston, Little, Brown.

Wildavsky, A. (1969) Rescuing policy analysis from PPBS. *Public Administration Review*, 29, 189–202. Reprinted in R. Haveman and J. Margolis (eds) (1970) *Public Expenditure and Policy Analysis*. Chicago, Markham.

Wildavsky, A. (1972) The self-evaluating organization. *Public Administration Review*, 32, 509–20.

Wildavsky, A. (1979) *Speaking Truth unto Power: The Art and Craft of Policy Analysis.* Boston, Little, Brown.

Wilkinson, M. and Howat, B. (1977) Regional reports and Structure Plans in Scotland. *Occasional Paper,* 3. Glasgow, The Planning Exchange.

Williams, W. (1971) *Social Policy Research and Analysis.* New York, Elsevier.

Williams, W. (1975) Implementation Analysis and Assessment. *Policy Analysis,* 1 (3), 531–66.

Willis, K. G. (1972a) Population studies in planning. *Planning Outlook,* 12 (1), 51–7.

Willis, K. G. (1972b) The influence of spatial structures and socio-economic factors on migration rates, *Regional Studies,* 6, 64–82.

Willis, K. G. (1972c) Geographical and labour mobility. *Papers on Migration and Mobility in Northern England,* 11. Department of Geography, Newcastle upon Tyne, The University.

Willis, K. G. (1974) *Problems in Migration Analysis.* Farnborough, Saxon House.

Wilson, A. G. (1968) Models in urban planning: a synoptic review of recent literature. *Urban Studies,* 5, 249–76.

Wilson, A. G. (1974) *Urban and Regional Models in Geography and Planning.* New York, John Wiley & Sons.

Wilson, A. G. and Kirby, M. (1975) *Mathematics for Geographers and Planners.* Oxford University Press.

Wilson, J. O. (1974) Social experimentation and public policy analysis. *Public Policy,* 22 (1), 15–38.

Wingo, L. (1961) An economic model of the utilization of urban land for residential purposes. *Papers and Proceedings of the Regional Science Association,* 7, 191–205.

Wolpert, J. (1965) Behavioural aspects of the decision to migrate. *Papers and Proceedings of the Regional Science Association,* 15, 159–69.

Wolpert, J. (1966) Migration as an adjustment to an environmental stress. *Journal of Social Issues,* 22, 92–102.

Wonnacott, R. J. and Wonnacott, T. H. (1970) *Econometrics.* New York, John Wiley & Sons.

Wright, P. H. (1978) A review of available local authority powers relevant to employment. *Working Paper,* 13. Joint Unit for Research on the Urban Environment (JURUE), Aston, The University.

Yates, F. (1960) *Sampling Methods for Censuses and Surveys.* High Wycombe, Charles Griffin & Co.

Young, M. and Willmott, P. (1957) *Family and Kinship in East London.* London, Routledge & Kegan Paul.

Zipf, G. K. (1949) *Human Behaviour and the Principle of Least-effort.* Cambridge, Mass., Addison-Wesley.

Zollschan, G. K. (1967) Working papers on the theory of institutionalization. In G. K. Zollschan and W. Hirsch (eds), *Explorations in Social Change.* Boston, Houghton Mifflin.

☐ NAME INDEX

Tyne and Wear County Council, 220, 222

Underwood, J., 320
Unit for Retail Planning Information (URPI), 320
Uslaner, E. M., 218

Van Delft, A., 95
Van de Ven, A. M., 92
Van Est, J., 220, 224
Van Horn, C. E., 248, 249
Van Leeuwen, I. K., 224
Van Meter, D. S., 248, 249
Varaiya, P., 67
Vaupel, J. W., 272, 273, 274, 275, 276, 277, 286
Verster, A. C. P., 224
Vickers, G., 84, 92, 308, 318
Vladeck, B. C., 245, 250, 257

Wagner, H. M., 286
Wakefield District Council, 101
Walker, B., 91
Warfield, J. N., 92
Warwickshire Structure Plan, 257
Watson, C. J., 223
Waugh, T. C., 133
Webber, M. J., 220
Webber, M. M., 33, 323
Webber, R. J., 133
Webster, J., 24, 313, 321
Wedgewood-Oppenheim, F., 40, 90, 316, 321
Weibull, J. W., 199
Weiner, A. J., 66
Weiss, C. H., 319
Wenban-Smith, A., 299
West Berkshire Structure Plan, 51, 62, 63, 64, 94

West Sussex Structure Plan, 35
Whalley, A., 320
Wheller, B., 172
Whitbread, M., 30, 69, 70, 72, 75, 76, 77, 88, 89, 94
White, B., 104, 133, 316
Whitehead, P., 64, 93, 94
Wildavsky, A., 89, 232, 235, 236, 242, 244, 245, 251, 257, 259, 265, 266, 293, 318
Wilkinson, M., 315
Williams, C. M., 63, 92
Williams, I. N., 213, 214, 220, 223
Williams, W., 241, 318
Williamson, C. B., 320
Willis, J., 220
Willis, K. G., 191, 192, 193, 194, 195, 196, 215, 350
Willmott, P., 215
Willson, V. L., 286
Wilson, A. G., 17, 31, 32, 33, 172, 181, 210, 212, 216, 218, 224
Wilson, J. O., 277
Wingo, L., 212
Wolpert, J., 192, 215
Wolverhampton Structure Plan, 51
Wonnocott, R. J., 172, 215, 350
Wonnocott, T. H., 172, 215, 350
Wood, P. A., 223
Worcestershire Structure Plan, 51
Wright, P. H., 320

Yates, F., 217
Yewlett, C. J. L., 92, 319
Young, M., 215

Zipf, G. K., 199, 215
Zollschan, G. K., 255

□ SUBJECT INDEX